CURRENT DISCOURSE ON EDUCATION IN DEVELOPING NATIONS:
ESSAYS IN HONOR OF B. ROBERT TABACHNICK AND ROBERT KOEHL

CURRENT DISCOURSE ON EDUCATION IN DEVELOPING NATIONS:
ESSAYS IN HONOR OF B. ROBERT TABACHNICK AND ROBERT KOEHL

MICHAEL AFOLAYAN
DIDACUS JULES
AND
DALLAS BROWNE
EDITORS

Nova Science Publishers, Inc.
New York

Copyright © 2006 by Nova Science Publishers, Inc.

All rights reserved. No part of this book may be reproduced, stored in a retrieval system or transmitted in any form or by any means: electronic, electrostatic, magnetic, tape, mechanical photocopying, recording or otherwise without the written permission of the Publisher.

For permission to use material from this book please contact us:
Telephone 631-231-7269; Fax 631-231-8175
Web Site: http://www.novapublishers.com

NOTICE TO THE READER
The Publisher has taken reasonable care in the preparation of this book, but makes no expressed or implied warranty of any kind and assumes no responsibility for any errors or omissions. No liability is assumed for incidental or consequential damages in connection with or arising out of information contained in this book. The Publisher shall not be liable for any special, consequential, or exemplary damages resulting, in whole or in part, from the readers' use of, or reliance upon, this material.

This publication is designed to provide accurate and authoritative information with regard to the subject matter covered herein. It is sold with the clear understanding that the Publisher is not engaged in rendering legal or any other professional services. If legal or any other expert assistance is required, the services of a competent person should be sought. FROM A DECLARATION OF PARTICIPANTS JOINTLY ADOPTED BY A COMMITTEE OF THE AMERICAN BAR ASSOCIATION AND A COMMITTEE OF PUBLISHERS.

LIBRARY OF CONGRESS CATALOGING-IN-PUBLICATION DATA
Current discourse on education in developing nations : essays in honor of B. Robert Tabachnick and Robert Koehl / Michael Afolayan, Didacus Jules, and Dallas Browne, editors.
    p. cm.
Includes index.
ISBN 1-59454-774-2
1. Education--Social aspects--Developing countries. 2. Comparative education--Developing countries. I. Tabachnick, B. Robert. II. Koehl, Robert Lewis, 1922- III. Afoláyan, Michael Oládèjo. IV. Jules, Didacus. V. Browne, Dallas.
LC2605.C87   2006
370.9172'4--dc22   2005028865

Published by Nova Science Publishers, Inc. ❖ New York

Contents

Foreword		ix
	Gloria Ladson-Billings	
Introduction:	Just for The Bobs!	xiii
	Michael O. Afoláyan, Didacus Jules and Dallas Brown	
PART I:	**DISCOURSE ON COLONIAL, POSTCOLONIAL, AND NEOCOLONIAL IMPACTS ON EDUCATION**	1
Chapter 1	English Rustic in Black Skin: Postcolonial Education, Cultural Hybridity and Racial Identity in the New Century *Cameron McCarthy*	3
Chapter 2	Power and Educational Development: Small States and the Labors of Sisyphus *Didacus Jules*	17
Chapter 3	Tai Solarin: The "Benjamin Franklin" of Nigeria *Michael O. Afoláyan*	31
Chapter 4	The Global Politics of Educational Language Policy in Tanzania *Frances Vavrus*	41
Chapter 5	Colonial Heritage and the Dimensions of Kenyan Education: The Case of Kikamba Schools *Chang'aa Mweti*	51
PART II:	**DISCOURSE ON GENDER AND EDUCATION**	63
Chapter 6	The "Bottom Power" Concept: The Philosophy of the Female Bargaining Strategy in Nigeria and its Implications for Schooling *Arit Oku-Egbas*	65
Chapter 7	African Women and Politics: A Case Study of Chief (Mrs.) Margaret Ekpo of Nigeria *Felix K. Ekechi*	97

Chapter 8	Women's Higher Education in Nigeria: A Shift in Cultural Paradigm *Mabel O. N. Enwemnwa*	**121**
Chapter 9	Journey As Metaphor: The Personal Story of an African Woman in Education *Precious O. Afoláyan*	**131**
PART III:	**CRITICAL CHALLENGES TO DEVELOPMENT, RESEARCH, AND TRAINING**	**141**
Chapter 10	Action Research and Teacher Education in the U.S. and Namibia *Ken Zeichner*	**143**
Chapter 11	Capacity Building Effort and Brain Drain in Nigerian Universities *Bankolé Oni*	**161**
Chapter 12	Dealing with the Ghost of the Colonial Past: Science Education in Nigeria *Toye J. Ekunsanmi*	**177**
Chapter 13	School Reforms in Post-Independence Ghana: Trends and Issues in Special Education *Anthony M. Denkyirah*	**193**
PART IV:	**LESSONS FROM THE INDUSTRIALIZED WORLD**	**205**
Chapter 14	Hey Dude! It's not the Computer: Technologies, Curriculum and Governing the Self *Thomas S. Popkewitz*	**207**
Chapter 15	Fordham and Ogbu meet Miss Ruby: Acting White versus Academic Success *Marguerite W. Parks*	**223**
Chapter 16	Taking American Students for a Cultural Plunge into Japan and Avoiding the Tourist Experience & Returning to Japan: Initial Cultural Challenges *Scott Johnston*	**237**
PART V:	**TRIBUTES TO THE BOBS – INTELLECTUAL, PERSONAL AND REAL**	**257**
Chapter 17	Teaching and Raising the Tabachnicks *David Tabachnick*	**259**
Chapter 18	Robert L. Koehl: Our Father *Stefan Koehl, Jeremy Koehl, Sarah Koehl and Mabel O. N. Enwemnwa*	**267**

Chapter 19	Teaching Educational Development and Curriculum Planning in the 21st Century: Discursive Ruptures in the Conversations About Planning for Modern Citizenship Through Public Education *Marianne Bloch*	**271**
Chapter 20	Children's Books about Africa and the Africana Book Award *Patricia Kuntz*	**289**
Chapter 21	What is it that You Want to Do? The Inquiry Pedagogy – A Tribute to Bob Tabachnick *Zachary Cooper*	**301**

Remembrances — **303**
  Dianne Bowcock

About the Contributors — **305**

Index — **311**

Foreword

Gloria Ladson-Billings
University of Wisconsin-Madison

For many years I have worked with pre-service teachers to help challenge their knowledge and perceptions about the African continent. One of the activities I do ask them to list all of the countries of Europe they can in 10 minutes. Typically, my students—young, bright, and well educated—list at least 20 European countries. After they list the countries I create a graph demonstrating the class' knowledge of European countries. That graph always slopes upward with no one unable to list at least 10 countries and many clustered at the high end of the graph.

Next I ask the students to list all of the African countries they can in 10 minutes. Quickly I sense their frustration and dismay over not being "competent" at a school-type task. At the end of the 10 minutes many students have written less than 15 countries out of the over 50 found on the continent. The graph I construct from their responses slopes in the opposite direction of the first one. When we look at the two graphs I ask the students to explain the discrepant visuals. "We were never taught anything about Africa," is the most common explanation the students offer. "Why?" I ask, "Isn't it important?" Students look nervously down toward their desks. They really can't explain their ignorance and they can't explain why they are embarrassed by it.

Comparative studies receive relatively little attention in U.S. education. Comparative work done by people who are either international scholars or have spent extensive (and intensive) periods of time in international contexts rarely shows up on course syllabi or reading lists in most U.S. education courses. However, this volume is comprised of scholars at various phases of their careers—early, mid, and late—who have deep investments in issues of international and global education. U.S. students do not know very much about the countries of Africa because these countries cannot be understood outside of the history and foreign policies that implicate the United States. The same thing might be said of Latin America, the Caribbean, and increasingly Asia. The only way that broader and more complex perspectives of the post-colonial world can emerge are in the presence of post-colonial voices. Globalization, for better or worse, is a part of our post-modern, postcolonial condition. Unless we do systematic study of the way global forces impact material realities and our symbol systems we cannot make sense of our world and our place in it. The responsibility for the study of the global, transnational, trans-cultural, and/or comparative does not reside merely on those we see as "other." However, their perspectives cannot be marginalized in the discourse. This collection contains a superb mixture of voices and perspectives from around the world. But, it also contains a wonderful homage to two scholars, B. Robert Tabachnick and Robert Koehl whose work represent the leading edge of comparative education.

Although I have been asked to write a foreword I actually feel as if I am getting an opportunity to write a tribute. This volume celebrates both the men and the works that are B. Robert Tabachnick and Robert Koehl. Bob (Tabachnick), as most people know him is a very special scholar and gentleman. Like many of the contributors, I got to know him through his work before I met him. As a graduate student at Stanford University I had a chance to read his work in social studies education. Unlike many social studies educators in the U.S. Tabachnick took an international perspective. He raised questions about perspectives and world view that were not often asked in social studies education during this time.

Fortunately, my association with Bob went deeper and further than merely reading his scholarship. In 1991 I became Bob's colleague at the University of Wisconsin-Madison and I learned firsthand what a wonderful person he was. My first office in the Department of Curriculum and Instruction was situated between Bob Tabachnick's and Thomas Popkewitz. On the surface we were an odd grouping—the Africanist, the womanist, and the postmodernist. However, I remember those early years as amazingly collegial and deeply satisfying. Bob was an excellent adviser and mentor not only to his students but also to me as a junior scholar. His office was a haven for international students, especially those from Africa. Bob's many years in Africa gave him important insights into the students' perspective and he encouraged them in ways that few people in our department could.

But, Bob was not only a good adviser and mentor he also was a superb scholar. He love to work on collaborative projects as his work with people like Millard Clemmens, Ken Zeichner, Tom Popkewitz, Mary Louise Gomez, and Marianne Bloch attested to that collaboration. One of the things that Bob was especially skilled at was seamlessly weaving together scholarship and teaching. His work on reflective teaching was deeply entwined with projects with pre-service teachers who were trying to understand the nature of their own practice.

A special memory I have of Bob was during the Department of Curriculum and Instruction's preparation for his retirement. Tom Popkewitz organized a symposium that featured his former students and a number of his colleagues. I had the responsibility of putting together a memory book. I got photographs and statements from a variety of people who knew and worked with Bob. However, my favorite set of photos and statements came from his older brother. He sent some pictures of Bob as a little boy and his accompanying statement said something like, "Dear Bob, Congratulations on your retirement. Although I don't know exactly what you do, you must do it well because so many people have had nice things to say about you. My most significant memory of you came when one day at the beach I hit you and you started to cry. When mom asked you what was wrong you said, 'nothing.' From that day on I knew you were a great guy and a special brother." His statement, though not at all related to Bob Tabachnick the professional man, was a wonderful exemplar of Bob Tabachnick the human being—self-effacing, self sufficient, and intensely loyal.

Many of the contributors to this volume owe their early career development to Bob Tabachnick. He provided them with intellectual support and a psychic safe-haven in the United States. Their passion for their teacher/mentor is palpable and genuine.

My association with Bob Koehl is less well established. I knew he was a scholar in comparative education and that his departmental home was in Educational Policy Studies at the University of Wisconsin-Madison. My experience of him was mostly second hand—through his students. One of the patterns that became quite evident to me was how often international students included both "Bobs" on their committees. Both men were deeply invested in international/comparative education and both supported international students fully.

This volume includes scholars writing from and about many parts of the world—the U.S. Kenya, Tanzania, Nigeria, Ghana, the Caribbean, Japan, Namibia—as well as friends and family members who share deeply personal and heartfelt remembrances of both men. Both Bob Tabachnick and Bob Koehl have secured their intellectual legacies not through this volume alone but rather through the depth of the relationships they have cultivated over the years.

INTRODUCTION: JUST FOR THE BOBS!

Michael O. Afoláyan, Didacus Jules and Dallas Brown

Southern Illinois University Edwardsville
Permanent Secretary, Ministry of Education, Culture, Youth and Sports, St. Lucia, West Indies
Southern Illinois University Edwardsville

The anomalous tendency in today's academia is for individuals to feel important and fortunate because of the prestige of the institutions to which they are affiliated. To the contrary, it should be the other way round; institutions should be, or should feel being, important and fortunate only by virtue of the quality of people in them. We can say this about the University of Wisconsin-Madison, an institution that was fortunate enough to keep within the four walls of its Big Ten citadel two outstanding individuals who gave more than seven decades of combined meritorious services to the university. These two gentlemen are Bob Tabachnick and Bob Koehl. From the essays and tributes in this volume, we see that "passion," "humanitarianism," and "scholarship" are three words that constantly ring the bell at the mention of these two names among their former students, colleagues, and even family members. To be able to salute them with this *schriftfesten* is a honor for all those who have been involved in the project, and to pull this great team of wonderful friends, colleagues, and relatives who share the emotional as well as intellectual connection with the Bobs is a laudable accomplishment. As we see in all the chapters of this book the themes articulated are those that both Bob Tabachnick and Bob Koehl espoused and took seriously in all their years of intellectual as well as social functions.

The book is divided into five parts. The first part focuses on critical discourses on colonialism and its impact on education in developing countries. The opening chapter, Cameron McCarthy's essay, is written against the backdrop of deepening xenophobia and ethnic absolutism a form of "racial cruelty" that has come to dominate human relations between individuals and groups world wide in the new millennium. McCarthy argues here that these tendencies towards ethnic absolutism and ethnic essentialism have their counterparts in schooling where debates over identity and the curriculum in the educational field have been clouded by ethnic particularism and dogmatism with enormous consequences for contemporary school youth and their teachers. As an alternative frame of reference,

Cameron McCarthy attempts to theorize his autobiographical journey from his inauguration in postcolonial education in the British Caribbean and his ultimate displacement to the academy in the United States. McCarthy writes about race relationships in education from the viewpoint of radical instabilities that inform our understanding of identity and subjectivity. He uses the term "radical instability" to underline the expiration of old forms of knowledge about race centered on unreflexive, quantitative, behavioral and fixed strands in social science and education. In doing so, he seeks to offer new understandings of race relationships, which are always contextualized and immersed in forms of experience that exceed the more orthodox academic cannon and mainstream curriculum organization, experience, and interpretation. In chapter two, Didacus Jules examines the interplay of power in the dynamics of international collaboration in education and how universities and the multilaterals exercise hegemony on the discourse of educational development internationally. Speaking from direct experience in negotiating the agenda of small states at an international level, it exposes the inherent contradictions of this unequal balance of power and ways in which the language of international collaboration is contradicted by the hegemonic interests of the donor community and more powerful states. In the context of the tribute to Tabachnick and Koehl, it posits the role of institutional and individual subjectivity in shaping the developmental paradigms of the multilaterals and argues for a more aggressive exposition of the contradictions in the discourse as a way of asserting the right of developing countries to shape their destinies through their education systems and not allow it to be dictated by the financial-intellectual complex. Michael Afoláyan's apolemic essay in chapter three presents the case of a passionate proponent of education for self-reliance in Nigeria. The man, Tai Solarin, whose vision of education is admirable across the African continent, is little known to the Western world. This essay introduces the person Tai Solarin to the discourse of education in developing nations. Through the words of one of Solarin's admirers, Femi Osofisan, and those of Solarin himself, the essay presents a bird's view of Solarin's social and intellectual worldviews. In her own chapter, Frances Favrus explores the concept of an *international language* from the perspective of international, national, and local policy actors involved in the debate over the medium of instruction in secondary schools in the United Republic of Tanzania. It focuses on the reasons why secondary-school age youth support the current policy of using English, rather than Swahili, even though they acknowledge its failure on pedagogical grounds. Finally, the author contends that the views of youth cannot be understood without examining how the belief that one knows English, whether proficient or not, constitutes a central feature of the educated, cosmopolitan person in Tanzania today. Concluding the first part of the book, Chang'aa Mweti sheds some light to our knowledge of how colonial heritage affected storytelling in an African traditional society, the Akamba community of Kenya. The essay briefly touches on the historical and cultural overview of this unique community. Mweti notes certain factors that eroded Akamba storytelling in formal settings, and further discusses the impacts of colonialism, and the influence of the MAUMAU movement. He also explains other factors that have salient roles and consequences in formal and informal education in the Akamba community. These factors include foreign religions, especially Christianity, neocolonialism, and the level of teacher training. He concludes by explaining how cultural filters do construct the people's worldview.

The second section focuses on the discourse on gender and education. The section opens with an essay on the "bottom power" concept in Nigeria education where Arit Oku-Egbas presents the historical formation and commonplace usage of the bottom power concept in contemporary social context of educational practices in Nigeria. With a strong voice of dissent, Oku-Egbas uses a postmodernist and deconstructivist approach, to argue that this concept is an extension and expression of gender inequity and social misnormal that have crept into the frameworks of schools at all levels of Nigerian education. Next in the second part is Felix Ekechi's essay which first pays tribute to Professor Koehl, as a teacher, scholar, and humanist. Ekechi then carefully examines the sociopolitical legacy of Chief (Mrs.) Margaret Ekpo of Nigeria, noting that, by her breaking the artificial barriers erected against women's political participation, this quintessential feminist of the 20th and 21st centuries, opened wide the door of politics to Nigerian women. It is no wonder that women could gratefully say to Mrs. Ekpo, "You came...and you gave us articulation." The essay closes with expressions of love by Nigerians for the illustrious educator, nationalist, patriot, and zealous promoter of women's rights. In Mabel Enwemnwa's chapter, the author argues that the effects of colonialism, the peripheral position of women in "Third World" or developing countries, as well as cultural beliefs around the education and access to higher education of women, do vary globally. The implications of the Cultural Reproduction theory that women have forged their own meaning systems in response to the societal position that they are made to assume, are also beginning to change. This shift in cultural trends and attitudes is beginning to positively impact upon African women's access to higher education programs, as well as to their participation in national economic and technological development. In the study that informed this article, Enwemnwa observes that though there are still some limitations in their way, there is increased awareness among Nigerian women about higher educational opportunities and benefits. There also appears to be increased and demonstrable determination on their part to avail themselves of existing opportunities in educational as well as political arenas. Enwemnwa notes that the change in attitudes has resulted in more women getting into various programs in technology and sciences where women were not traditionally represented. However, families' socio-economic status and government policy implementation processes were also examined and found to be pertinent factors in the paradigm shift in women's participation. This essay shows that although women still trail men in opportunities, a lot has been done policy-wise to narrow the gap, thus bringing more women to the fore-front in very sensitive and strategic positions in the society. In her "Journey as metaphor," Precious Afolayan concludes the second section of the book by examining her life experience as an African woman who came to the United States primarily to support her husband, a role often accepted as norm in the Nigerian society. Precious traces her travel experience across the continental U.S.A. over a period of more than two decades; and uses this construct as a metaphor for the long and windy road it has taken the African woman to attain a status beyond the stereotypical societal expectation. She also credits Bob Tabachnick's earlier encouragement as a significant part of her decision to complete her graduate education whereby helping her to seal an aspect of her cumbersome cultural and intellectual journey.

 Critical challenges to development, research and training is the main thrust of the third section of this book. It opens with Ken Zechner's essay which discusses the use of action research as a tool for teacher development in preservice teacher education programs at the University of Wisconsin-Madison and in the post-independence national educational reform in the southern African country of Namibia. The discussion illuminates some of the possibilities that action research offers for helping teachers to become more central players in educational reform. It also focuses on some of the problems that can arise from incorporating action research into teacher education. Bankole Oni explains in his own chapter that the role of the university in capacity building in Africa cannot be underestimated. This author argues that right from colonial times universities in Africa and especially Nigeria have built the needed capacity for the management of institutions and the economy. According to him, unfortunately this is no longer the case today. The capacity building potentials of Nigerian universities as in most African universities have become unsustainable due to the nature and dynamics of the political and economic environment of these institutions. The implication of this is that the hope of African development in the new century is grave. This is because without the ability to build capacity, sustain the process and ensure the effective utilization of what has been built, nations like Nigeria and indeed in all of Africa and developing nations, may not be able to achieve the desired integration into the global system in the new century. In the chapter that follows, Toye Ekunsanmi brings his readers back to the corridor history, arguing that like other ancient civilizations, the peoples that now make up Nigeria maintained their traditional science and technology long before they were colonized. According to him, the adoption of "Western Science" by Nigerians has not taken into consideration the possible obstacles which a new learning system could bring. Non-implementation of government policies, poor economy and its associated low morale, plus chronic lack of direction have contributed to make science unpopular among Nigerian students. Ekunsanmi further notes that most Nigerian scientists have been labeled as mere theorists, and the society has lost confidence in them. Obviously, the necessary environment, infrastructure needed to drive a viable path to self-dependence in science and technology are lacking. Only a culturally directed, community-oriented science curriculum directed toward learning by doing, and takes into account the cultural backgrounds of teachers and learners could bring Nigeria back to its path of greatness in science and overall development. Government needs to take positive actions on policy execution, adequate funding and training of science teachers. The patronage of locally manufactured goods should be a priority in order encourage indigenous technology and redeem the country from eternal dependence on foreign technology. Oke examines critical issues facing quality higher education in Nigeria. With the experience of running Ladoke Akintola University, one of the newer universities devoted to technology in Nigeria by one of the authors, and many years of research on Nigerian universities by the other, these authors note some of the hidden and not-so-hidden factors that affect the running of universities in developing nations of the world, especially in sub-Saharan Africa which Nigeria exemplifies. Financial and political influences are some of those critical factors that make and/or break the organization and running a technical university in a purely consumer based, non-industrialized economy. Curriculum development, student activism, workers' union and many more are some other factors that the authors discuss. In concluding this section, Anthony Denkyirah provides a unique perspective on special education in Ghana where although educational services for individuals with disabilities only started in the mid-1950s, five decades later, remarkable strides have been made in special education. The author notes, however, that in spite of the progress being made, it is lamenting that ironically, services are still delivered pretty much the same way as they were delivered in the 1950s. Individuals served include those who are officially classified as deaf or hard-of-hearing, visually impaired or blind as well as those who are classified as mentally retarded. The special, segregated, residential system remains the main service-delivery model. Lack of resources and non-existence of a national policy on disability to guide stakeholders in special education are major drawbacks. The future is bright for special education because of the government's commitment to using information technology and distance education structures for the training of teachers and parents.

The fourth section of this book focuses on lessons to learn from developed (industrialized) nations of the world. This section opens with Tom Popkewitz's deconstructivist essay, "Hey dude! It's not computer: Technologies, curriculum, and governing self." Here, the reader quickly sees that Tom Popkewitz's interest in technologies has less to do with machines or "hardware," but more to do with the assemblage of practices that function to inculcate virtuous habits and the self discipline that enables one to feel empowered, given voice, and self-actualized with the proper education. This notion of technology is examined in an on-line curriculum and two research practices in contemporary school reforms. Design is a word that appears across the sites and provides a thread to think about the principles of action and participation. The problem of design is told as giving voices, agency and empowerment to those selected. Yet he argues that this is far from what is going on. Design is a technology of the self that administers the freedom of the individual and is thus an effect of power. Popekewitz's chapter is immediately followed by that of Marguerite Parks. Parks brings us to a closer view of the educational culture and the academic success of African American students. She presents these as serious issues of social and intellectual relevance in today's American society. She points out, however, that when we look at individual teachers who uphold high expectations of their students, both academically and morally, children of color in today's schools can achieve academic success. This chapter looks at one such teacher; one amazing woman who for 64 years told her students that "academic success" was just academic success; it was not "acting white." Mrs. Ruby Middleton Forsythe taught in a one-room all-black school at Pawleys Island, South Carolina. This essay centers on one possible reason for the extraordinary success of the students of Holy Cross-Faith Memorial School and their teacher "Miss Ruby." Two articles fused into one on Japan by Scott Johnston involve an educator's effort to step out of his comfort zone and cross cultural and national boundaries. In the first part of the chapter, Johnston examines how students from a small liberal arts college in the U.S. make sense of a 3-week stay in Japan. The similarities, not differences, between the students and their host families, are highlighted. In the second part, Johnston examines the cultural challenges he faced when he now returned to Japan for a permanent stay. Since he had lived in Japan earlier, Johnston was not unaware of what to expect; however, this did not eliminate problems of adjusting to living and working in Japan again as an educator. Though these feelings of discomfort soon dissipated with time, this article reminds us that experienced international teachers/researchers face cultural challenges even when returning to a familiar country.

The final section of this book specifically pays tribute to the two Bobs. One way to bring to life Bob Tabachnick's approach to education is to tell the story of his involvement in one's education. This is exactly what his son, David Tabachnick, did in this opening chapter of this section. He notes that Bob had always fostered creative engagement of students, and he, his son, had also been in the receiving end of this extraordinarily altruistic pedagogy of Bob, the father. David further notes that Bob Tabachnick is suspicious of educational planning in developing countries that comes from a distance. Thus, Bob often sits with people and asks them what they think they need, want, and how they think they can accomplish them. Bob tries to get people's perspective, reducing theories to practical ideas that make consensus possible. This, indeed, is the story of Bob Tabachnick as told by David Tabachnick. In a heart-felt tribute to their own father, Stefany, Jeremy and Sarah Koehl give a précis of their lives the man that brought them to live. Theirs is an extraction of Robert L. Koehl, the man who raised them. They note how they have shared this father with his students who they quickly recognized as also important parts of his life. They summed up their father's philosophy of life in what he taught them about what their perspective should be when it comes to their service to humanity. "Altruism is not enough," Koehl would tell his children; "the road to hell is paved with ill-informed, good intentions." They hope that the legacy of their father's scholarship and idealism continue through them, their own children, and their father's former students and colleagues. Their testimony is quickly followed by that of Mabel Enwemnwa who narrates her encounter and dealing with the man she found to be her benefactor, and intellectual father. Marianne Bloch, a colleague and friend of the two Bobs provides a tribute as well as critical perspective on the enduring pedagogy and legacies of Tabachnick and Koehl. For many years, Bloch drew from the insatiable and profound knowledge of the two respected colleagues while she team-taught the popular graduate class in educational development and curriculum planning, a class that she continues to teach solo after the two men retired. Bloch carefully examines products of empirical as well as action research that continue to inform and provide her the adequate pedagogical tools for guiding the talented and well-informed graduate students, mostly international students, in the course. Patty Kuntz's chapter on children's books about Africa includes a tribute to both Bob Tabachnick and Bob Koehl, both of who were instrumental in Kuntz's co-founding of the national book review committee that examines top children's books about Africa and the annual Africana Book Award. In this chapter, Kuntz gives a historical overview of the University of Wisconsin-Madison's African Studies Outreach Center which she directed for many years. This chapter also examines some critical issues concerning picture books on Africa. Kuntz chronicles African children books that have been identified and determined over the years as superior published works. Following Kuntz's chapter, Zachary Cooper talks briefly of his encounter with, and perspective of Bob Tabachnick. He found Tabachnick to be a man of letters whose power of mentoring lies in his ability to encourage and instill free and inquisitive mind in his mentees. Cooper shares his experience working with Bob Tabachnick and how this experience has influenced his own perspective on life. Last but not the least is the verbatim rendition of two e-mail messages from Dianne Bowcock. Dianne played a major role in finding some old students of the two Bobs at the outset of this book project. Unfortunately, before the project would take off, Dianne passed away. We thought her respect for the Bobs as well as enthusiasm and encouragement for the project are worth noting. May Dianne's soul rest in peace!

With this Schriftfesten, we greet, honor and uphold the legacies of our friends, colleagues, professors, mentors, intellectuals and humanitarians, B. Robert Tabachnick and Robert Koehl. We wish them many more years of productive lives as they are surrounded by people they love and as they enjoy the retirements they so much deserve.

PART I:
DISCOURSE ON COLONIAL, POSTCOLONIAL, AND NEOCOLONIAL IMPACTS ON EDUCATION

Chapter 1

ENGLISH RUSTIC IN BLACK SKIN: POSTCOLONIAL EDUCATION, CULTURAL HYBRIDITY AND RACIAL IDENTITY IN THE NEW CENTURY

Cameron McCarthy
University of Illinois, Urbana-Champaign

> Take him and cut him out in little stars,
> And he will make the face of heav'n so fine
> That all the world will be in love with Night
> And pay no worship to the garish sun...
> (William Shakespeare, *Romeo and Juliet*, Act II, Sc.ii)
>
> -----
>
> The mind of man is capable of anything--because everything is in it, all the past as well as all the future. (Joseph Conrad, *Heart of Darkness and Other Tales,* 1992, p.186)
>
> ----
>
> Ah! The whole diaspora shakes in my skin. (Anthony Kellman, "Isle Man," 1993, p. 15)

INTRODUCTION

Within the past few years, I have come to the growing recognition that my writing about race and identity has been a form of postcolonial therapy, an exercise in opening up and pasting over contradictions of knowledge, place, context, and belonging. Writing for me, as I imagine it is for all intellectuals pursuing these topics, is as much a tortuous act of concealment and reinscription as it is one of transcending disclosure. Consider the vast sea of sociological ink now being spilled on the topics of class, or race, or identity. Consider the boatloads of chapter afloat on these subjects. Can we really argue that this ever-expanding volume of writing has led us to other than a very partial, adumbrated understanding of the operation of these dynamics? Can any of us really claim that we have come to a final or definitive understanding of racial logics or the operation of identity formation?

Here, at the beginning of the twenty-first century--the great information age, the age of hypermodernization that classical social scientists and their disciples had told us would usher in the withering away of encrusted and sedimented atavism--we are faced in human societies with the unleashing of ever more virulent forms of particularism and localism operating in politics and popular culture. As a disturbing instance, nationalism and xenophobia in Europe--in the former Yugoslavia, in Germany and France--rip at the heart of the great icons of civilization in the West; a civilization against which everything in the third world and everything within the underclasses of the metropole are counterposed. In the Middle East and on the continents of Africa, Asia and South America, the politics of identity have been fought out in bloody skirmishes and long nights of horror such as those of Israel versus the Palestinians, Hutus and the Tutsis of Rwanda and Somalia, the heartless ethnic cleansing of the African population in Sudan, and the excesses of proto-fascist regimes in Indonesia and in Guatemala --just to mention a few examples of spectacularly gruesome forms of racial/ethnic cruelty. And, in giving this litany of racial horror, I must note that we now live after the purgatorial fires descended on New York and the Pentagon on 9/11 with the transformed circumstances of the world's major power, the US, conducting wars in Afghanistan and Iraq, motivated by retributive politics and instinctive xenophobic fears.

As an academic who has over the last decade sometimes pontificated on matters of race and identity, I must admit a sense of bewilderment at the endless stream of racial cruelty that resides in the hearts of human beings in our relations with each other across the globe. Contemplating race relations in this country, I am both enraged and dismayed by the virulence of the hostilities and resentments unleashed in America against its disenfranchised Latino/a and African American inner-city poor. At the same time, I am revolted by suburban excesses and the salivatory prosecution of suburban will in the politics of both liberal and conservative politicians and policy intellectuals. In these matters the contemporary observer on race and identity simply walks in the footsteps laid down in the sands of time. It was, after all, the great colonial novelist Joseph Conrad (1992) who, in *Heart of Darkness*, proffered his own disorientation on identity questions through the narrating persona of Marlow. Reflecting on the exorbitant atrocities perpetrated by imperialism in Africa, Marlow uses a nostrum to effectively distance himself from Europe's project of subjugation of the native: "The mind of man is capable of anything--because everything is in it, all the past as well as all the future" (1992, p. 186). As a writer, Conrad, too, was implicated. He was a product of Europe, a seafarer, whose characters like himself, pursued their imperial fantasies and desires onto the bodies of the native even as they tormented themselves about the "evil in the hearts of men." Like Conrad every writer has his demons. And, "Like a jig shakes the loom/Like a web is spun the pattern/All of us are involved/All of us are consumed" (Carter, 1979, p. 44). Is it the demons in our hearts that we write to exorcise? As it was with Conrad's fiction, is, perhaps, the ultimate purpose of our writing the great disavowal of our implication in life's history? In racial matters, is the postcolonial intellectual, indeed, washed in the blood of the lamb?

Perhaps every postcolonial writer is a descendant of the forces that produced Conrad's phosphorescent naturalism, Conrad's blind spots and his all-consuming evasion of the role of the bourgeois self in the trauma of the native. On this matter "truth will not (be) out." In the bright gleam of the realist fiction of the novelist, the anthropologist, the social scientist, the historian, the educator hides the entrails of the imperialist lie. The author's claim to the vantage point beyond passion, beyond complicity and collusion is not to be trusted. The author writing on race and identity conceals as much as he discloses. The intellectual observer, it would turn out, would have his stake in the apprehension and containment of the native. He, too, would have his own dreaming map of possession and rambunctious ownership. As Wilson Harris (1960) suggests in *The Palace of the Peacock*, "Donne, too, was my brother" (p. 42). The colonizer would inhabit the body of the colonized. The colonial text would freeze and fix the native in the stillness of eternity. The colonizing text of the anthropologist ethnographer would close and bind the frame of the village. The urban sociologist would "tell it like it is" about underclass fecundity and degeneracy. For years and years, the student of history, of anthropology, of sociology, of education would read and perform these texts of ethnicity, of self and other. And then one day, the bright, motivated student, too, would arrive at the place of her/his calling, would become an anthropologist, a sociologist and a writer of fictions about others. The intellectual had finally reproduced himself. The newborn academic, the living Narcissus, would deploy his gaze on the world with the fervor of a brand new Baby Bell.

The postcolonial intellectual, the child of the Native and the King, always disavowed his own participation in this hypocrisy of completeness and the hierarchy of the global racial order. He, too, maintained his innocence. Dressed in the hand-me-downs of Prospero, he declared his blamelessness before the world and before his peers in the American academy. But truth be told, in the matter of racial identity formation the postcolonial intellectual also is a creature of paradox: he has, for instance, an enormous appetite for the imperial symbolic, fine garments, literature and haute cuisine while ceaselessly denouncing imperialism's excesses at home and abroad. I am a child of that paradox: the product of the exorbitant British presence in the Caribbean and the African slave who would be put out into the fields to work, and chained and bridled at the door. I am, too, part of that peculiar progeny of British imperialism whom Sidney Greenfield (1968) would call "English rustics in black skin."

In this essay, I attempt to write about race from the perspective of the radical instability with respect to race-based forms of knowing and identification. I write from the point of view of the perishability of the sociological understanding of the race question. It is written to seek out racial knowledge in other places than the controlled study or the omniscient intent to organize the field of race relations theory, or the ethnographic excursion into the colonized life world of the other. It seeks out new understandings in new places: in the realms of popular culture, in the realms of literature, in the realms of the imagination, in the realms of the filmic fantasy, and in the quiet agonism of postcolonial self-exploration and self-understanding. I speak for all those lost souls, who like Derek Walcott, are "divided to the vein," and who--may God grant us the courage--find solace only in the exploration (1986, p. 18). This is the enigma of arrival of the postcolonial intellectual. In the matter of her/his investigation of the subject of conflicted racial identity formation, the postcolonial soul can know no peace.

USES OF CULTURE

I begin this essay, then, with this confession: that all along, my writing on race in the United States has been informed by an attempt to straddle, frantically to stabilize, the conflicted biography of being born and educated in the periphery, Barbados, and coming into academic practice as an immigrant intellectual operating in the imperial center, the United States. My understanding of race, my foregrounding of its instabilities, its "nonsynchrony," as I called it in earlier work (McCarthy, 1988), is more than a little propelled by my own autobiographical elopement or displacement from the third world to the imperial center, home of "the Great Satan." I live everyday, like Ishmael in Herman Melville's *Moby Dick* (1851), in danger of being swallowed up and consumed in the churning belly of the Whale. I proceed, then, with the deepest sense that there is a complexity to the story of race that writing merely adumbrates, never fully discloses. This is the paradox of all postcolonial intellectual writing on the varied forms of life and the differentiated cultural and economic realities of the metropole and the periphery alike. While I will not continue this essay in the confessional mode, it must be understood that everything that follows herein is in fact informed by the postcolonial predicament: the reality of, perhaps, permanent exile or banishment from any singular or fixed community and the attendant lost of full understanding of one's racial self. The imperial inheritance is finally a bag of gold, a bag of bones (Morrison, 1977).

THE ENGLISH BOOK

There is a scene in the cultural writings of English colonialism which repeats so insistently after the early nineteenth century--and, through that repetition, so triumphantly *inaugurates* a literature of empire--that I am bound to repeat it once more. It is the scenario, played out in the wild and wordless wastes of colonial India, Africa, the Caribbean, of the sudden, fortuitous discovery of the English book. (Bhabha, 1994, p. 102)

One of the limitations in current postcolonial theory and methodology regarding the analysis of racial identity and center-periphery relations--and indeed this is true of other critical minority discourses such as Afrocentrism and multiculturalism--is the failure of proponents to account for the conditions of production of their own intellectual work and their contradictory interests and affiliations. As Ali Behdad (1993) has pointed out, postcolonial theorists often present the analysis of center-periphery relations within a zero-sum framework in which all agency, power, and moral responsibility emanate and flow from the center. The postcolonial theorist therefore appoints her/himself as a stand-in or proxy for the oppressed third world; a third world of the imaginary--a third world that is unstratified, uniformly underdeveloped--and one in which the social field has been completely leveled by the mechanisms of exploitation and cultural domination. Even more critically--in the work of some writers such as Molefi Asante (1993, 2000), Martin Carnoy (1974, 1993), Philip Altbach (1987), Philip Altbach and Hassan (1997), and Michael Parenti (1993, 1995)--the imperial text, the text of colonial education, the text of Euroamerican canonical literature, tends to deliver reproductive [neo]colonial effects, seemingly untouched by indigenous practices or movements. Within these frameworks the dwellers of postcolonial societies are, too often, hypothetical subjects, model addressees of colonizing discourses. Absent are the voices, cultural practices, and meaning of style of concrete, historical postcolonial and indigenous minority subjects. Even more disturbing is the methodological tendency to abrogate the whole field of accommodations, negotiations, and trestles of association, affiliation, feeling that link dominant and dominated political and cultural entities both locally and globally.

In this essay, I take a different view of the dynamics of culture and race. I point to interconnections and continuities between prima facie racially and ethnically antagonistic groups (for example, the continuities of theme and form between Anglo-colonial novelists like Joseph Conrad and Afro-diasporic and anti-colonial writers such as Chinua Achebe or George Lamming). I also call attention to the contradictions within atavistically declared "pure" racial or ethnic communities (for instance, radical class tensions within the black communities of South Africa or the United States and the class hierarchies within the third world). One never fully knows with terms such as "race," "identity," or "culture." To study race, identity or culture and to intervene in their fields of effects one must be prepared to live with extraordinary complexity and variability.

The texts and performativity of these constructs are always subject to aberrant decodings, aberrant meanings, and the dynamic play of histories and contexts. This is not to deny the often virulent force of racial dynamics, racial inequality, and racism. But, it is to announce and acknowledge the broad, tangled and knotted human engagements and productivities that attend the racial encounter between different individuals and groups. It is to reference the subtle play of desire and the commingling of cultural and symbolic forms in the registers of commodified and uncommodified practices of group expression, group history, even, group ancestry. It is to recognize that racial/ethnic heritage of any particular group always exceeds the memory and purposive grasp of its purported or self-declared bearers.

THREE VIGNETTES

Permit me to relate three brief vignettes that illustrate the dynamic encounter between racially dominant and subaltern cultural forms in which processes of rearticulation constantly subvert the putative stability of center-periphery ethnic relations. The first story is autobiographical, foregrounding of my encounter with hegemonic English and American literature as an undergraduate student at the Cave Hill campus of the University of the West Indies in Barbados in the late 70s; the second story highlights an example of the unexpected association between canonical literature and the rise of radical vernacular poetry writing in the Caribbean; and the third story is one told by Manthia Diawara of the subversive impact of African American popular music in 60s French Africa and the way it functions as an alternative cultural capital. These three stories illustrate the instability of racial meanings and challenge any narrow-minded construct of culture as ethnocentric property. They also foreground the radical multiplier effects that cultural forms release in everyday human encounters across the divides of nation, locality, and race.

STORY I: ANGLO-AMERICAN CULTURE WAR

One of the contradictions of cultural production in the third world, even in the postcolonial era, is the multiplicity of surreptitious, and not so surreptitious, lines of connection that link the postcolony to the metropole. The postcolony is not ever simply an original entity unto itself shorn of the imprint and trace of the metropole. It is in many ways an impure copy full of the warp and woof of empire--an alloy of many racial, cultural and economic metals, so to speak. Formal and informal cultural life in education and society reveal these connections in the everyday existence of the postcolonial subject. I can speak of these matters of cultural hybridity first hand. Growing up as a child in Barbados in the '60s and the '70s, one existed in a constant state of negotiation between the cultural form of England and that of the emergent post-independence island. Education was a particularly poignant site of the transaction of the competing needs, desires and interests of the metropole and the indigene. Curriculum content, school ritual, and the formal history of the school system pointed to England. Every single important examination was either set or marked in the metropole. For instance, my high school "Advanced Level" examinations were the matriculation exams for the University of Cambridge. Examinations in Barbados were truly external and "objective"--we were the subject-objects of British cultural suzerainty.

As a youth my social fate was in the hands of the markers of the General Certificate of Education of the Cambridge Examination Board. Passes or failures in these exams, which one sat at the end of high school, had material social meaning in Barbados. This arrangement continued into university, where again the University of the West Indies followed a practice of requiring all end-of-year examinations to be vetted by outside examiners mainly from England, but occasionally from the United States and elsewhere. Often these outside "monitors," as they were called, demonstrated their eminence by giving lectures to students when they were visiting. On one such occasion, the outside examiner for my "American Fiction" course came to give a lecture on Ernest Hemingway's novels. Here was one of the incredibly ironic, but normally unremarked, moments of the postcolonial situation in Barbados: an American authority on a "great" American fiction writer giving a presentation to the Caribbean students of an American fiction class normally taught by an "eminent" Englishman. There we were, caught in the crossfires of the postpartum Anglo-American war over culture. In the University of the West Indies Program in English Studies, all the American writers, ancient or modern, black or white, were stuck in the American Literature course and separated out from a course called "The Moderns." The latter course of study was reserved for the great British writers, which included one luminous American transplant to England: T.S. Eliot. The "eminent American scholar" gave his lecture on the greatness of Hemingway's fiction. The Barbadian students didn't buy it and the technical flaws of Hemingway's novels were insistently raised. The eminent American scholar floundered on questions that focused on the massively flawed love scene between Jordan and Maria in *For Whom the Bell Tolls* in which the narrator utters those incredible words: "And the earth moved from under her feet." The eminent American scholar was a bit flustered. The eminent English scholar looked gleeful. A great victory was won that day for Great Britain by the educated troops of "Little England." Remarkably, I got a call a few days after this Anglo-American skirmish from the gleeful English lecturer congratulating me for my critical challenges to the "orthodoxy" of the American: "He" (The eminent American lecturer) did not appreciate what "we" were doing down "here." There I was, the child of empire, clumsily serving as the vessel of Englishness and hopelessly thrown into the field of what seemed to me interminable Anglo-American cultural hostilities.

Power as exercised in culture takes devious routes. American writers of great prominence in the American school curriculum and in the academy regarded as Eurocentric and canonical here in the U.S.--in the hands of British imperialist scholars operating overseas in the theater of the empire's Atlantic rim--had suffered a canonical declassification and a technical demotion. Whitman was "potentially a great poet" but lacked "disciplined attention to technique and form"; Eugene O'Neil was "one of the few noteworthy American playwrights"; T.S. Eliot "had given up America for England." Black Americans like Richard Wright, James Baldwin and Ralph Ellison were emergent writers of the "protest novel" or the "jazz novel."

And, American women writers? Well, besides Emily Dickinson, no American woman of letters was mentioned at all. In Barbados we stood in culture not as property owners but as interpreted texts, actors in the shadow of power on the world stage, and pretenders to middle-class status in the postcolony.

Imposed canonical literature, what I call the "imperial symbolic," was and is the cultural capital central to the politics of class formation in postcolonial settings like Barbados. In a matter-of-fact way, imperial cultural form plays a critical role in the elaboration of indigenous aesthetic and social hierarchies and cultural distinctions.

STORY II: T.S. ELIOT AND THE RISE OF THE POSTCOLONIAL VERNACULAR

But metropolitan canonical cultural form can also serve radical purposes and can be subjected to aberrant decoding and rearticulated within new horizons of association and feeling and new fields of possibility. Edward Kamau Brathwaite (1984) tells a different story of the imperial symbolic than the one I told above. His story is one about the felicitous impact of the poetry of the canonical high modernist writer, T.S Eliot, on the rise of vernacular poetry in the Caribbean. Again, the moment here is one of hybridity; the medium and conduit of this improbable connection is one of the most powerful modernist carriers of hegemonic and counter-hegemonic cultural form and wish fulfillment--the phonograph record:

> For those who really made the breakthrough, it was Eliot's actual voice--or rather his recorded voice, property of the British Council--reading "Preludes," "The love song of J. Alfred Prufrock," *The Waste Land* and the *Four Quartets*--not the texts --which turned us on. In that dry deadpan delivery, the riddims of St Louis (though we didn't know the source then) were stark and clear for those of us who at the same time were listening to the dislocations of Bird, Dizzy and Klook. And it is interesting that on the whole, the Establishment couldn't stand Eliot's voice--far less jazz! Eliot himself, in the sleeve note to *Four Quartets*...says: "What a recording of a poem by its author can and should preserve, is the way that poem sounded to the author when he had finished it. The disposition of the lines on the page, and the punctuation (which includes the *absence of* punctuation marks...) can never give an exact notation of the author's metric. The chief value of the author's record...is a guide to the *rhythms*." (Brathwaite, 1984, pp. 30-31).

The vernacular translations of Eliot's poetry transacted through the powerful medium of the phonograph record connected the canonical with the everyday and spilled over into the dream of autonomy for Caribbean letters. Here, in one striking movement, Brathwaite gives credence to Raymond Williams's thesis in *Culture and Society* (1958) of the semiautonomous role of culture, its essentially communicative, translatory function across the Manichean divide of centers and peripheries. The culture of the third world is therefore the polysemic text of contestatory identities. It is also brimful of the flotsam and detritus of the metropolitan culture industry. Like seasoned bricoleurs, emergent Caribbean writers fished Eliot from a sea of historical ruins and breathed new life into the literary landscape and map of twentieth century Caribbean cultural form and meaning of style. This was, in the language of Derek Walcott (1993), a "felicitous moment" of hybridity!

STORY III: AFROKITSCH

The play of cultural hybridity in lived and commodified culture not only is produced in the context of third world encounters with Eurocentric cultural form. It is also released in the encounters between the delegitimated cultural forms of marginalized groups such as African American working classes and their third world counterparts in the periphery. Manthia Diawara (1992) tells the story of the powerful impact of African American RandB and Soul in late '60s Africa. In this case, the return of diasporic energies from Black America to the African continent unsettles the hegemonic grip of French high culture in the West African neo-colony of Mali. In this context, working-class African American cultural form becomes French African "cultural capital." New centers are created in the world and old ones undermined. According to Diawara:

> In 1965, Radio Mali advertised a concert by Junior Wells and his All-Star-Band at the Omnisport in Bamako. The ads promised the Chicago group would electrify the audience with tunes from such stars as Otis Redding, Wilson Pickett, and James Brown. I was very excited because I had records by Junior Walker, and to me, at the time, with my limited English, Junior Wells and Junior Walker were one and the same. (That still happens to me, by the way.) It was a little disappointing that we couldn't have James Brown in person. I had heard that Anglophone countries like Ghana, Liberia, and Nigeria were luckier. They could see James Brown on television, and they even had concerts with Tyrone Davis, Aretha Franklin, and Wilson Pickett. Sure enough, the concert was electrifying. Junior Wells and his All-Star Band played "My Girl," "I've Been Loving You Too Long," "It's A Man's World," "There Was a Time," "I Can't Stand Myself," "Papa's Got a Brand New Bag," "Respect," "Midnight Hour," and, of course, "Say It Loud (I'm Black and I'm Proud)." During the break, some of us were allowed to talk with the musicians and to ask for autographs. The translator for us was a white guy from the United States Information Services. I remember distinguishing myself by going past the translator and asking one of the musicians the following question: "What is your name?" His eyes lit up, and he told me his name and asked me for mine. I said, "My name is Manthia, but my friends call me J.B." .... I got the nickname J.B. from my James Brown records. The next day the news traveled all over Bamako that I spoke English like an American. This was tremendous in a Francophone country where one acquired subjecthood through recourse to *Francite* (thinking through French grammar and logic). Our master thinker was Jean-Paul Sartre. We were also living in awe, a form of silence, thinking that to be Francophone subjects, we had to master Francite like Leopold Senghor, who spoke French better than French people. Considered as one who spoke English like Americans and who had a fluent conversation with star musicians, I was acquiring a new type of subjecthood that put me perhaps above my comrades who knew by heart their *Les Chemins de la Liberte* by Sartre. I was on the cutting edge--the front line of the revolution. You see, for me, then, and for many of my friends, to be liberated was to be exposed to more RandB songs and to be *au courant* of the latest exploits of Muhammad Ali, George Jackson, Angela Davis, Malcolm X, and Martin Luther King, Jr. These were becoming an alternative cultural capital for African youth--imparting to us new structures of feeling and enabling us to subvert the hegemony of *Francite*. (Diawara, 1992, p. 287-288)

Here again, the performativity of culture exceeds its origins. Black America meets West Africa through the circulatory force of the culture industry: of records, videos and music concerts of the stars. There is nothing pure about being black or African. There is nothing original: all is intertextuality, rearticulation, translation. There is no transcendent core: all is epidermis. All is movement in the Black Atlantic (Gilroy, 1993). The sound and fury of race signifies everything and nothing.

THE MOVEMENT OF CULTURE

Of course these processes of hybridity are not exclusively articulated in the periphery. Contemporary developments in the new century reveal a return of the subaltern gaze onto "the eye of power itself" (Bhabha, 1994). Huge dually disorganizing and integrative energies are exerted from the periphery to the center. This is particularly articulated in the movement of masses of third world people to the metropolitan center bringing new tropes of affiliation and cultural affirmation as well as the new sources of tension and contradiction along the lines of race, class, gender, nation, sexuality, and religion. The metropolises of first world societies now struggle to absorb these subaltern subjectivities. State policy and political economies in Europe, the United States, Australia and Canada now desperately wrestle with the radical challenges and opulent possibilities that the energetic peoples relocated from Africa, Asia, the Caribbean, Latin America and the Middle East present to their new found homes. In The Tourist (1989), Dean MacCannell tracks the new energies of globalization that strike at the heart of old imperial powers, transforming them from within:

> Twenty-five years ago the dominant activity shaping world culture was the movement of institutional capital and tourists to the remote regions, and the preparations of the periphery for their arrival.... Today, the dominant force--if not numerically, at least in terms of its potential to re-shape culture--is the movement of refugees, "boat people," agricultural laborers, displaced peasants, and others from the periphery to centers of power and affluence. Entire villages of Hmong peasants and hunters recently from the highlands of Laos, have been relocated and now live in apartment complexes in Madison, Wisconsin. Refugees from El Salvador work in Manhattan, repackaging cosmetics, removing perfume from Christmas gift boxes, rewrapping it in Valentine gift boxes. Legal and illegal "aliens" weed the agricultural fields of California. The rapid implosion of the "third world" into the first constitutes a reversal and transformation of the structure of tourism. (MacCanell, 1989, pp. xvii)

This tide of mass movement has striking and provocative effects in the realm of culture and literature. It has led, for example, to a virtual transformation of the canons of literature in the center itself. According to Pico Iyer (1993), a new multiperspectival, heterogeneous cultural force is overwhelming and reshaping canonical cultural forms in England and elsewhere:

> The Empire has struck back, as Britain's former colonies have begun to capture the very heart of English literature, while transforming the language with bright colours and strange cadences and foreign eyes. As Vikram Seth, a leading Indian novelist whose books have been set in Tibet and San Francisco, says, "The English language has been taken over, or taken to heart, or taken to tongue, by people whose original language historically it was not.".... The centers of this new frontierless writing are the growing capitals of multicultural life, such as London, Toronto, and to a lesser extent New York, but the form is rising up wherever cultures jangle. (p. 68)

Iyer's observation leads us away from the eruptions of simple-minded nationalisms and the calcified identity politics that rule the political imaginations of our time. For after all, "no race has a monopoly on beauty, on intelligence, on strength/and there is a place for all at the rendezvous of victory" (Aime Cesaire, quoted in Said, 1993, p. 310).

Ultimately, then, who can claim ownership of culture or ethnicity as a final property? The transactions of culture in the modern world forcefully undermine the claim to cultural exceptionalism. Radically underlying the material reality of forces at the center of global capitalism--forces such as colonial domination and racial oppression--are the cultural settlements of what Raymond Williams (1961) calls "The Long Revolution." In the Long Revolution, culture is the alchemy of opposites, the alchemy of classes and races, the point and site of radical hybridity. Culture is also the site of the radical disintegration of biologically derived unities of race, ethnicity, or nation. Culture's polysemic movement constantly challenges the modality of conqueror-conquered or oppressor-oppressed as it undermines, reassembles, and reconfigures long-held traditions, affiliations and meanings of style into whole new "forms of life." Williams describes this movement of culture in socio-environmental and ecological terms:

> The conquerors may change with the conquered, and even in extreme cases become indistinguishable from them. More usually, a continually varied balance will result. Of the Norman conquest of England, for example, it is impossible to say that it did not change English society, but equally the eventual result was a very complex change, as can be seen most clearly in the history of the language, which emerged neither as Norman French nor as Old English, but as a new language deeply affected by both. (1961, pp. 137-138)

CONCLUSION

Drawing on Williams's insight, and the insights provided by the vignettes of hybridity presented above, I have tried to talk in this essay about race through the prism of culture. In so doing, I am trying to promote a rethinking of constructs such as race, identity, and cultural heritage. I argue that the experiences and practices that these concepts seek to summarize are far more dynamic than the ways in which we normally conceptualize them in educational and social science research. I suspect that the dynamism and heterogeneity of the myriad everyday human encounters that produce and reproduce cultures and identities are thwarted in education because even the most radical research continues to be overburdened and weighed down by the legacy of behavioral social science and psychology. Against the latter, much is still measured in the educational field. By contrast, it is in literature, in painting, and in popular culture and popular music that the dynamism and complexity of identity, community, and so forth are restored and foregrounded.

Of course, the position I am taking runs up against the current politics of racial identity formation, specifically in the areas of multiculturalism, education, and the politics of curriculum reform. Here, racial understandings underlying the discourses of some multiculturalists and their Eurocentric opponents mark out indelible lines of separation between the culture, literature, and traditions of the West and the culture and traditions of the third world. These highly ideologically charged understandings of identity treat culture as a distinctive form of property that is indisputably owned or possessed by one or another racial group. This is, indeed, one of the symptoms of the racially corrosive heart of human kind that I alluded to earlier.

In the vignettes foregrounded in this essay, I refuse this Manichean model of racial identity formation. I challenge the glib opposition of the West to the non-West and the curricular project of content addition that now guides the thinking of many of the proponents of identity politics and multicultural reformist frameworks. I have sought instead to foreground specific examples of the complexity and variability of identity formation within the domains of personal autobiography, dominant and subaltern popular culture, and postcolonial literary aesthetics, as well as the so-called canonical traditions of the West. I believe that these sites of popular culture and literary production constitute spaces for the exploration of difference, for interrogating the cultural silence over race and identity in education and society, and for opening up a wide ranging conversation over curriculum reform in the context of the radically diversifying communities we now serve in the university and in the schools. Throughout this essay, then, I have adopted a cultural studies approach to the topic of racial identity formation by foregrounding historical variability, shifting social contexts and environments, and the inevitable trestles of association between the canon and the quotidian, the empire and the postcolony, and suburban and inner-city "realities."

As I have noted at the beginning of this essay, I speak, then, with at least two voices. The first is as an intellectual whose formative and perhaps most decisive education occurred in a third world country, the postcolony of Barbados. I am, for better or worse, a child of empire--an "English rustic in black skin." My other voice is that of an Afro-Caribbean immigrant intellectual displaced to the putative center of the industrial world. I now live in the belly of the beast, a supplicant to a neurotic Uncle Sam. In pursuing this theme of hybridity and duality, I have partially disclosed the agonistic war that wages within the hearts and minds of postcolonial souls, like my self, who inhabit the firmament of the American academy. For whom does the postcolonial intellectual speak? Where is his constituency? Where is his theoretical and political warrant? Where is his intellectual and cultural home? I pursue these themes of incompleteness, duality and discontinuity concerning race, culture and identity, to ward off the costly politics of ethnic and cultural dogmatism and absolutism and the shortedsighted programs of Eurocentrism and ethnocentrism that now threaten to eviscerate the educational imagination. I argue against the current tendencies to oppose the Western culture against the cultures of the non-West, the first world against the third world, and so forth. I want to argue with Edward Said (1993) that any single overmastering or ruling identity at the core of the curriculum--whether it be African or Asian or European or Latin American--is in fact a confinement. Such a closed cultural or intellectual system consolidates a kind of illiteracy about one's racial others that is impractical and dangerous in a society in which the demographics of ethnic diversity have outstripped the meaningfulness of a curriculum founded on nineteenth-century principles of ethnic homogenization and the neutralization of difference. Furthermore, as Aime Cesaire has argued "No one group has a monopoly on intelligence or beauty." I therefore argue for curriculum reform in the area of race relations that is founded on the principle of the heterogeneous basis of all knowledge and the need to find the subtle but abiding links that connect groups across the particularity of ethnic affiliation and geographical and cultural origins and location.

REFERENCES

Altbach, P. (1987). *The Knowledge Context.* New York: SUNY.

Altbach, P. and Hassan, S.M. (1997). *The Muse of Modernity: Essays on Culture as Development in Africa.* Chicago: Africa World Press.

Apple, M. (1993). *Official Knowledge.* New York: Routledge.

Asante, M. (2000). *The Painful Demise of Eurocentrism.* Chicago: Africa World Press.

Asante, M. (1993). *Malcolm X as Cultural Hero and Other Essays.* Trenton, New Jersey: Africa World Press.

Behdad, A. (1993). Traveling to teach: Postcolonial critics in the American academy. In C. McCarthy and W. Crichlow (Ed), *Race, Identity and Representation in Education* (pp. 40-49). New York: Routledge.

Bhabha, H. (1994). *The Location of Culture.* New York: Routledge.

Brathwaite, E.K. (1984). *History of the Voice.* London: New Beacon.

Carnoy, M. (1974). *Education as Cultural Imperialism.* London: Longman.

Carnoy, M. (1993). *The New Global Economy in the Information Age.* State College, Pennsylvania: Penn State University Press.

Carter, M. (1979). You are involved. *Poems of Resistance* (p. 44). Guyana Printers Limited.

Conrad, J. (1992). *Heart of Darkness and Other Tales.* New York: Oxford University Press.

Diawara, M. (1992). Afrokitsch. In G. Dent (Ed). *Black Popular Culture* (pp. 285-291). Seattle: Bay Press.

Ellsworth, E. (1989). Why doesn't this feel empowering? Working through the Repressivemyths of critical pedagogy. *Harvard Educational Review, 59*(3): 297-324.

Garrett, L. (1994). *The Coming Plague.* New York: Farrar, Strauss and Giroux.

Gilkes, M. (1975). *Wilson Harris and the Caribbean Novel.* London: Heinemann.

Gilroy, P. (1993). The *Black Atlantic: Modernity and Double Consciousness.* Cambridge, Massachusetts: Harvard.

Giroux, H. (1994). *Disturbing Pleasures.* New York: P Routledge.

Grant, L. (1984). Black females' "place" in desegregated classrooms. *Sociology of Education.57,* 98-111.

Grant, L. (1985). *Uneasy Alliances: Black males, Teachers, and Peers in Desegregated Classrooms.* Unpublished manuscript, Southern Illinois University.

Greenfield, S. (1968) *English Rustics in Black Skin.* New Haven, CT: College University Press.

Hall, S. (1992). Cultural studies and its legacies. In L. Grossberg, C. Nelson, P. Treichler (eds.), *Cultural Studies* (pp. 277-294). New York: Routledge.

Harris, W. (1960) *Palace of the Peacock.* London: Faber.

Herrnstein, R. and Murray, C. (1994). *The Bell Curve.* New York: Free Press.

Iyer, P. (1993 February). The empire writes back, *Time* (pp. 68-73).

James, C.L.R. (1978). *Mariners, Renegades and Castaways: The Story of Herman Melville and the World We Live in.* Detroit: Bewick/ed.

James, C.L.R. (1993). *American Civilization.* Cambridge, Massachusetts: Blackwell.

Kellman, A. (1991 Spring). Isle man. *Graham House Review* (14), p. 15.

Nkomo, M. (1984). *Student Culture and Activism in Black South African Universities.* Connecticut: Greenwood.

Omi, M. and Winant, H. (1993). On the theoretical concept of race. In MacCannell, D. (1989). *The Tourist: A Theory of the Leisure Class.* New York: Schocken.

McCarthy, C. (1988). Reconsidering liberal and radical perspectives on racial inequality in schooling: Making the case for nonsynchrony. *Harvard Educational Review 58*(2), pp. 265-279.

McCarthy and Crichlow (eds.), *Race, Identity and Representation in Education* (pp. 3-10). New York: Routledge.

Melville, H. (1851). *Moby Dick: Or the White Whale.* New York: Harper.

Morrison, T. (1977). *Song of Solomon.* New York: Signet.

Nietzsche, F. (1967). *On the Genealogy of Morals.* W. Kaufman, trans. New York: Vintage.

Omi, M. and Winant, H. (1993). *Racial Formation in the United States.* New York: Routledge.

Parenti, M. (1993). *Inventing Reality.* New York: St. Martin's Press.

Parenti, M. (1995). *Against Empire.* San Francisco: City Lights Books.

Preston, R. (1994). *The Hot Zone.* New York: Random House.

Said, E. (1993) The politics of knowledge. In C. McCarthy and W Crichlow (eds.), *Race, Identity and Representation in Education* (pp. 306-314). New York: Routledge. In New York: Routledge.

Spring, J. (1991). *American Education: An Introduction to Social and Political Aspects.* Boston: Beacon Press.

Walcott, D. (1986). A far cry from Africa. *Collected Poems:1948-1984* (p. 18). New York:Noonday.

Walcott, D. (1993). *The Antilles: Fragments of Epic Memory.* New York: Farrar, Straus and Giroux.

Williams, R. (1958). *Culture and Society.* London: Chatto and Windus.

Williams, R. (1961). *The Long Revolution.* London: Penguin.

Wright, E. (1978). *Class, Crisis and the State.* London: New Left Review.

Chapter 2

POWER AND EDUCATIONAL DEVELOPMENT: SMALL STATES AND THE LABORS OF SISYPHUS

Didacus Jules
Permanent Secretary for Education & Human Resource Development St. Lucia

INTRODUCTION

Robert Tabachnick and Robert Koehl are two intellectuals who embody special attributes and a facilitative disposition to Third World educational development. Both of them have been university professors whose pedagogy has been empowering to their students. Both of them at different times have served as consultants and advisors to various multilateral agencies in the sphere of education. This biographical dialectic enabled them to utilize their teaching and research experience in advising developing countries on their educational development and that field experience in turn considerably infused their approach to teaching and learning. By virtue of reputation and disposition, their courses gained popularity particularly among international students who felt comfortable with their pedagogy. As I will argue in this paper, there is an intellectual conceit that often resides within the halls of academia that assumes the posture of infallible prescription and which is based on the unequal relations of power in the nexus between knowledge broker and arbiter of financial allocation (whether grant or loan). Bilateral and multilateral agencies acting in concert with universities wield considerable power in determining which paradigm gains currency at any given moment. I will argue that the rhetoric of the multilaterals is not often matched by their practice and that small states in particular have a difficult time negotiating their particular agenda especially where these may differ from the prescriptions established by the financial intellectual complex.

At the heart of this issue is the question of power. In education, there is a long lineage on the exposition of power as a dynamic in development. It has long been recognized that underlying the dynamic of education are the relations of power which exert formative governance on the nature of the educational interaction, the structures through which education is delivered, the content that is considered appropriate, relevant and necessary and the quality and extent of the resources allocated to the educational project. The study of power in education and in the cultural sphere has found its most articulate and current expression in the works of persons like Apple (the structural dynamics of power in education) Chomsky (the politics of power) Freire (the role of power in creating ideological perspective in education) etc.

UNIVERSITIES AND MULTILATERAL AGENCIES – ESTABLISHING THE PARADIGMS OF INTERNATIONAL DEVELOPMENT

Universities and research institutes play a special and indispensable role in the financial intellectual complex. As centers for higher learning and knowledge production, universities are often utilized/contracted by multilaterals to undertake specific research on their behalf. There is a revolving door between the university and the bilaterals and more so, the multilaterals. Many noted academics and educators have also played leading roles in the formulation of new paradigms and the construction of what is accepted by the multilaterals as the current thinking on education. Eminent academicians like Carnoy, Sachs, and Psacharopoulos have decisively fashioned the debate on various challenges in education and, in so doing, have helped to define global agenda that in turn exert pressure on local systems to conform.

It is by virtue to their access to and command of intellectual as well as material (financial) resources that the multilateral institutions are able to define a global hegemony in the sphere of education. It is the ideas and constructs that are developed and promoted by donor (grant or loan) financing that become the "cutting edge" in education reform agenda worldwide particularly in developing countries. For many of the world's poorest nations, donor financing is what makes education for the marginalized possible and it is precisely that reality that gives the multilaterals the power of dictation to developing countries. Karns and Mingst (1992) have argued that multilateral agencies "make a difference in international interactions because they are utilized by and have influence on even the most powerful states" (p.1). They have further noted that "patterns of IGO [international governmental organizations] instrumentality and influence need not be constant but changes in such patterns will shape the evolution of both organizations and the regimes in which they might be embedded" (p.2). This work is important to the understanding of the ways in which Western hegemony is exercised through multilateral institutions and come to inflect the development agenda of the state in developing countries. Indeed as a result of the increasing engagement of these multilaterals with civic action groups and non-governmental organizations (principally through the instrumentality of donor funding) this influence has now extended beyond the sphere of the state to the incorporation of civil society.

At the level of the state, multilateral instrumentality and influence are central to the construction of hegemonic paradigms in international education that in turn set the pace and standard for national reforms by virtue of the conditionalities that are established and the simple selection of what can or cannot be funded (despite the contextual rationality of the request). It takes an exceptionally strong political will at the national level to establish an educational agenda that does not converge with or replicate the dominant paradigm and an even greater strength to say no to funding that would result in a deviation from the national agenda. Moreover because of the hegemony exerted by the multilaterals, conformity to international prescriptions can serve as a powerful symbolic statement of a regimes' modernizing intent. This has been admitted by UNESCO itself, as the following lengthy quotation attests:

> ICOs [international cooperation organizations] are virtually by definition based in rich countries that provide the funds for international cooperation, are staffed by well educated professionals who have access to the most advanced knowledge about education and how to improve it, and in some cases conduct leading-edge research themselves. There is thus a prevailing attitude that 'donor knows best'. This results in pressures for countries to adopt policies and practices sometimes directly drawn from policies and practices in more developed countries that are not well-adapted to the local conditions in recipient countries, or else reflect the fad of the moment or are simply wrong. At various times in the long history of international cooperation in education, ICOs have advocated: vocational education (sometimes a European "dual education" model), comprehensive education, and incorporation of education components into "integrated rural development" projects. At one point there was an extreme emphasis on "basic education" (however important this clearly is) to the exclusion of all other investments in education, even though education systems are integrated wholes and improving the flow of well-prepared students through the basic levels naturally results in increased demand for more and better provision of education at higher levels. In each of these cases the ICO community has done an about face concerning these policies, after urging recipient countries to adopt them." (UNESCO 2004)

Small states are particularly vulnerable to donor dictation as there is often an arrogance of size associated with the prescriptions offered. As a result of the work done by the Commonwealth, there has at least been some sensitization of the bilateral and multilateral agencies on the vulnerabilities and peculiarities of small size. As we shall see later in this chapter, the concept of vulnerability (which is so real to educational planners and policy makers of small states) can be conveniently ignored.

Beyond the power wielded by the donor agencies has been the tendency to oversimplify lessons of research particularly when the conclusions add more legitimacy to the prevailing paradigm. King, Palmer and Hayman (2004) have shown how multilateral agencies have sometimes simplified the lessons of research and that by ignoring the contextual assumptions on which best practice learning is based, the prescriptions become weak and their outcomes dubious. The above cited authors gave the example of the research finding (Lockheed, Jamison and Lau 1980) on farmer education and productivity that was translated into a whole series of policy documents with the exclusion of the critical contextual caveat. Lockheed, Jamison and Lau 1980 contended that four years of education have a beneficial impact on agricultural productivity; they asserted that education makes a difference to farm productivity of about 10% in a *modernizing environment*. Subsequent citations of this research oversimplified it to state that four years of basic education makes a difference to even *traditional* agricultural practice. The contextual caveat of education making a difference in a *modernizing environment* was totally distorted somewhere in the translation from research finding to policy prescription. It would make for even more interesting research to investigate the cases in which these findings were utilized as policy prescription and to discover what the consequence of this distortion was to developing countries.

It goes without saying that not in all cases has the advice of international consultants and donor agencies been detrimental to developing countries. There are two fundamental determinants to this. The first is *institutional subjectivity* – the extent to which the culture of a donor agency is open to real dialogue with recipients, the extent to which the agency is listening to local analyses and solutions. In the development community, there is a very active lexicon of development in which concepts (invariably emerging from democratic and grassroots struggles) are eventually appropriated and assume a more desiccated, technocratic meaning. Thus it has come to pass that notions such as "popular participation," emanating from the struggles of democratic educators like Freire and Apple, whose original meaning referenced vital engagement and empowerment by a vibrant constituency has now been appropriated, sanitized and commoditized into the notion of "stakeholders." Notwithstanding this, one can detect a progressive erosion of old barriers and resistant paradigms under the increasing demand for accountability by civil society.

Institutional subjectivity must also be situated in its broader political context – the agenda of bilateral agencies are intrinsically bound (notwithstanding whatever operational autonomy that they enjoy) to the foreign and aid policies of their governments. Aid has historically been tied in this way and even with the emergence of the so-called "Third Way" regimes and their much publicized de-linking of their aid agencies, some things never change. The forms and characteristics of the conditionality might change but conditionalities will always exist. Aid will always be tied to some conditionality or another - if not market conditionalities, then political conditionalities. And not all conditionalities are negative – to insist on proper public financial accountability, democratic openness and involvement of key constituencies is laudable but what has always been the problem with conditionality is the imposition of the donor's "self-image" and the absence of respect for diversity and difference.

The other determinant is the issue *of individual subjectivity.* In other words the ideological (in its broadest sense) and attitudinal disposition of the individual consultant and the ways in which this subjectivity interpolates his/her approach to the assignment. Good consultants are able to bring considerable experience and add real value to the efforts being undertaken within a national space. They are able to, as the first order of business, to listen carefully and digest what the aims and aspirations of the intended reforms are and then to bring the refracted perspective of other best practices, and the lessons of successful as well as failed efforts to illuminate the challenge faced by the implementing country.

That is where the impetus for this book originated: Tabachnick and Koehl were teachers who demonstrated the capacity to learn from their students. They offered the only courses available at the time within the educational policy department of the University of Wisconsin–Madison on international education. For students of the Third World coming to Madison, this was a magnet and an empowering space that enabled us to focus on concerns affecting our education systems. With students from the Caribbean, Africa, Asia, the Middle East, Europe and the Americas, the pedagogy of "the Bobs" made it possible for us to share experiences, research common problems and debate contentious issues. They brought an empathy that was respectful of cultural idiosyncrasies and accommodating of difference. Their most eloquent statement of faith in the regenerative capacity of third world people was their agreement to "sponsor" a course that a group of students from developing countries wanted to design, and offer as a self-run colloquium on "Issues and Challenges to Education Reform in the Third World." From within this group later emerged a Vice Chancellor of the University of Zimbabwe and World Bank Associate (Peter Dzvimbo); a Nigerian professor of Southern Illinois University Edwardsville (Michael O. Afoláyan); a world class writer, theorist, and endowed professor at the University of Illinois, Urbana-Champaigne (Cameron

McCarthy); and a Permanent Secretary for Education in the Government of St. Lucia and World Bank consultant (Didacus Jules). It proved to be one of the most dynamic and exciting courses in education policy and every participant became a tutor responsible for presenting his or her assigned part of "the curriculum."

Much of the outcome of these engagements depends heavily on the disposition of the experts involved; the world view and ideological outlook of the consultant in relation to developing countries is critical. A consultant who sees the Third World as "the heart of darkness" and hole of poverty and underdevelopment will bring to the assignment a posture of infallibility in the paradigms proposed by the multilaterals. One with a truly empathetic ear will seek to achieve a more profound understanding of the situation of the country and ensure that the solutions proposed – while consistent with international best practice – are best fitted to the peculiarities of place and context.

SMALL STATES AND THE CHALLENGES OF EDUCATIONAL DEVELOPMENT

Small states have had a particularly difficult time in the international arena negotiating their education reform agenda. The smaller states of the Caribbean (the grouping known as the Organization of Eastern Caribbean States) have for the past 10 years been undertaking a comprehensive education reform mainly supported by CIDA grant funds (Canadian bilateral) and more recently with supplementary (loan) support from the World Bank. This reform – the OECS Education Reform Strategy - seeks to both harmonize and modernize their national education systems and has been defined through the cooperative endeavor of the national ministries of education contributing their best expertise to this regional initiative. The regional reform agenda constituted an ideal framework within which national authorities could elaborate national education sector development plans. In the context of this approach, donor agencies could provide umbrella support to common elements while still providing bi-lateral assistance to individual states.

The multilaterals have become increasingly impatient in their dealing with small states because to them, the constraints of size do not justify the administrative and other costs of dealing individually with small states. Even in the case of the regional reform agenda described earlier and notwithstanding the obvious advantages in such an approach, the multilaterals found it difficult in practice to change their own aid management practices to properly support the initiative. The tendency towards what I call "projectization" of reform is inherent to the hegemonic role of the donor agencies. Projects are finite, measurable, more subject to control than systemic reforms and therefore more amenable to the imposition of conditionalities through which the underlying political agenda of the sponsoring state can be realized. Even while CIDA embraced the OECS Education Reform Strategy, the strategy still had to be reduced to project status – the Eastern Caribbean Education Reform Program (ECERP) - to be palatable to the agency and to ensure that Canadian grant funds were separately accountable. Every agency expressing an interest in supporting the initiative sought to carve its own niche in what ideally ought to have been a basket of resources from which the OECS countries could draw in conformity to the strategy.

In the implementation of the reform strategy, experience quickly confirmed that the challenges of education reform are inseparable from the wider context of public sector reform. In developing countries and in small states in particular, education reform must inevitably converge with health initiatives (HIV-AIDS education, health and sanitation promotion etc.), with the struggle for improved governance (local government structures and their articulation with school boards, citizenship education, constitutional rights, rights of women and children), with cultural identity issues (preservation and promotion of indigenous cultures and languages), with the economy (skills training and job creation, economic empowerment etc). Even when the education reform agenda incorporates the Ministry of Education as a central site for change, there is a glass ceiling beyond which the reforms are impeded since ministries of education need to interface with other key public service entities such as ministries of finance, and constitutional authorities such as teaching service and public service commissions.

Multilateral agencies tend not to be interested in fundamental reforms of the institutional administrative apparatus, relying instead on project implementation units that are often established as "oases of progress and privilege" within ministries of education and isolated from the day to day operational inelegance of the public service:

> Another is the tendency of international cooperation organizations (ICOs) to use project implementation units to manage their projects rather than work through the permanent education structure (UNESCO 2004)

As a result of this approach donors can often successfully complete their discrete projects but fail to impact on the overall administration and management of the institutions that are effectively responsible for the sector impacted by the project. Ultimately (and beyond the life of the project and the horizon of the donor) this may serve to unravel whatever gains might have been recorded by the project as there is no strategic sustainability with the system or the sector to guarantee this. UNESCO in a very tangential manner arrived at this conclusion:

> The large multilateral banks operating in the region, which account for a very large portion of total financial flows, are development organizations but are also financial institutions. As such their task is to lend money, and that imperative tends to produce "pressure to lend." Even such laudable (financial) aims as maintaining a positive net flow of resources from the banks to their borrowers result in a preference for lending operations that are large, readily-prepared and efficient to process. This frequently influences the size of their projects, the mode of implementation (using project implementation units), their reluctance to engage in small-scale and participatory activities, and other biases…

> Project-based funding does not tend to strengthen countries' permanent capacities to manage their own sector improvement activities, develop their own skilled and experienced staff or integrate project-related activities into the regular operation of education sector ministries (UNESCO 2004).

Although the lexicon of the development community has increasingly incorporated the notion of partnerships – this means as many different things as there are donor agencies. There is no universal understanding of what partnership entails although one would assume that to be meaningful any notion of partnership ought to involve an equitable power relation.

Unfortunately history has shown that mutuality is only expressed in the context of equal strength and, in international affairs, it is not a moral assertion but a détente between poles of equal strength.

GLOBAL AGENDA AND LOCAL BETRAYALS

I want to discuss the concrete experience of one small island state – St. Lucia – in its effort to articulate a comprehensive education sector development plan and to explore the ways in which the aspirations of small states are so easily frustrated and treated inconsequentially by multilaterals. The experience is situated in the wider context of the rhetorical flourish that characterized the EFA 2000 Conference and the assertions made that no country with a clear plan would suffer for want of the necessary resources.

THE EFA AGENDA, THE WORLD BANK AND SMALL STATES

No process of educational development has been as broadly subscribed to as the Education for All Initiative. Starting with Jomtien, local and international civil society and the NGO community rallied around the dream of a world of educational opportunity as was never done before. Indeed small island states and certainly the Caribbean undertook the most extensive preparatory work that had ever been done in the lead up to an international event.

At Jomtien, one of the main issues pushed by the Caribbean region was an argument for the broadening of the definition of "basic education." Given the inequities and disparities that existed on a global scale, the preference among the multilaterals was to focus on literacy and education up to primary level. The view of the Caribbean on this was that, notwithstanding this deficit, it was anachronistic at the dawn of the 21st Century to set the benchmark so low. Defining basic education at this level and making it a global focus could disadvantage those developing countries that had already met these targets and were seeking to build on these accomplishments. We will return to this issue to show how these definitional postures translate into operational guidelines for the multilaterals that effectively disadvantage small states.

While on the one hand the international community is awakening to the alarming educational gaps and deficits that exist within and between regions and countries, this awareness is not matched by the resources needed to adequately address the issue. Aid commitments to education fall far short of what is required to achieve the dramatic transformations that the global visions call for:

> The context is that the overall volume of bilateral aid commitment has dropped in absolute terms during the 1990s (although the high level at the beginning of the 1990s is partly due to exceptional commitments at the time of the Gulf War). Aid Commitments to education as a proportion of overall aid have remained steady at around 15%. For those countries providing disbursements data, proportions of overall aid to education have increased over the decade. For multilaterals, aid to education has varied throughout the decade, although overall, it tends to remain less than 10%. The total absolute volume of bilateral aid commitment to education has remained roughly the same throughout the decade. Multilateral commitments to education

rose from $1000m in 1990, to nearly $2000m in 1994, falling back to $1,300m in 1998. (Bentall, Peart, Carr-Hill and Cox 2001)

The emergence of international NGOs has provided a focal point for civil movements to play a more decisive role in global compacts on education and to inflect the policy prescriptions of the multilaterals (and bilaterals). Civic movements involving teacher organizations, parents, community activists have been able to construct local agenda demanding equity and access for marginalized groups and with the ubiquitous rise of the Internet, they have been able to develop global coalitions and a global presence. At the World Conference on Education in Dakar, the Global Campaign for Education (GCE) "mobilized public opinion on the need to hold governments accountable for the promises they made at the first, 1990, education summit in Jomtien, Thailand" (Hynd 2000). Following on recommendations presented by Oxfam International, it lobbied multilaterals and governments to ensure the provision of an extra $8 Billion annually over the next ten years to achieve the goals of education for all. The GCE proposed a comprehensive package of measures that included increased aid (increasing the proportion of aid from the current 2% to 8%); debt relief and private capital support. The call for clear resource provision allied with firm political will was central to the Global Action Plan and has been the persistent failure of the Dakar framework. There is an apparent lack of consensus at the international level with respect to mobilizing resources for education. According to the EFA Global Monitoring Report 2002, while 28 countries had been identified by UNESCO as being at the greatest risk of not achieving the EFA goals, only 6 of then are on the FTI list of 18 drawn up by the World Bank.

In this regard, the international NGOs shared common cause with the world's poorest and most vulnerable countries including small states. Indeed despite unequivocal statements in Dakar by the President of the World Bank that no country with a well conceptualized education sector plan would suffer for want of resources to realize the objectives of the Dakar framework, the outcome of the World Forum yielded no such support. The divide between the readiness of developing countries to make EFA a reality and the anemic commitment of the developed countries on the resourcing and timeline questions could not have been wider.

Coincidental to the process leading up to the EFA Initiative, St. Lucia had undertaken its own process aimed at developing a comprehensive and integrated education sector development plan. This initiative was consistent with the assertion by King, Palmer and Hayman (2004) that "Ministries of Education and Skills Development [in developing countries] *need to plan for holistic systems of education* which integrate secondary education, technical and vocational education, and tertiary education into a coherent entity." Often countries prepare plans to meet donor requirements. St. Lucia's view was preparing separate plans to meet different purposes can become dysfunctional. The process utilized in this experience was a highly participatory one which involved the establishment of expert panels for each sub-sector, review of existing studies of all kinds, the amalgamation of all existing commitments and protocols, and zonal meetings throughout the entire country with teachers, parents and community members to discuss the draft plan. The final plan was brought to a national consultation with all stakeholder organizations and its statistical indicators were incorporated into the Ministry's annual statistical reporting format so that progress on implementation could be measured publicly. It was estimated that more than 15,000 persons (almost 10% of the national population) were actively involved in the preparation of the plan

(A fuller discussion of this process will be presented in the forthcoming article Albertin, M. and Jules, D. "Stakeholder Involvement in the Education Sector Development Plan in St. Lucia"). The formulation of the sector plan constituted one critical element in St. Lucia's Basic Education Reform Project with the World Bank and the process utilized was deemed to have been an international best practice by the Bank team associated with the project.

Given the positive assessment of the Plan process and outcome and the fact that this process did take into account the Jomtien conclusions and all other commitments and protocols, an argument was presented by the Government of St. Lucia to the multilaterals a) expressing an absolute political will to the implementation of the plan, b) offering the St. Lucia effort as a potential early win for the fast track initiative that was under consideration by the multilaterals in the lead-up to Dakar. The thinking was that so little had been achieved after Jomtien that it was necessary that Dakar not be another grand rhetorical flourish and one way of ensuring this was for the international community to commit unequivocally to at least a few countries whose successes could prove that the goals of education for all were attainable. The recommendation made by St. Lucia was that the fast track initiative comprise a representative grouping of countries including one or two most populous countries whose educational deficits were large, and small states with the potential to holistically remodel their education systems to show case how EFA could dynamize development. The St. Lucian policy makers were convinced that small size could be turned to advantage as it would be possible – with the necessary support – to model the reforms in an integrated manner and at comparatively less cost than was necessary for larger countries.

A donor consultation was convened to discuss the possibilities of grant and other support and to fashion a holistic response by the donor community to the plan's implementation. Like the Dakar conference the conclusions of this effort proved more rhetorical than concrete. The World Bank indicated its willingness to finance the component related to the achievement of universal secondary education which was a vital highlight of the plan. Based on this undertaking, the Ministry again undertook a comprehensive process of consultation and more detailed planning. Universal secondary education was treated not simply as the expansion of opportunity at that level, but equally importantly, the reform and improvement of the quality of education provided. The detailed planning involved the following initiatives:

- The establishment of a *Council on Secondary Education* comprising District Education Officers and Principals of all secondary schools to serve as an overall project advisory and governing body for the attainment of universal secondary education;
- The definition of *new standards* for secondary education – curricula standards (involving core curricula, articulation with practical application of knowledge in every subject field); infrastructural standards (involving new minimum specifications for construction of secondary schools and attention to disability access, disaster proofing etc); resource standards (establishing and guaranteeing new minimum resource requirements for schools);
- *Upgrading of existing schools* in accordance with the new standards;
- *Construction of new schools* to ensure that the demographic/geographic deficits were addressed;

- *Reinforcing the articulation of secondary education* with other educational sectors (both backward and forward linkages with primary education, with tertiary education and with economic and social opportunity). This also involved reform of assessment modes for entry into secondary level as well as continuous assessment throughout the secondary education phase.

The project that emerged from that process called for an investment of approximately US$50 million - an amount that would have made it possible for all of the necessary changes to be made. Following a lengthy preparatory process, the World Bank finally indicated that it was only prepared to provide US$12 million of the funds required – leaving a significant resource gap of over US$35 million to be found! To rescale a tightly integrated project of $50+ million into a US$15 million envelope with the Bank insisting that integration be preserved was a frustrating and futile exercise. This project is still in the implementation phase but has experienced many problems, many of which could be traced to the inadequacy of the resources provided and the dictation of what should be preserved within an emaciated pie. A simple statistic was the fact that the design work done by the architects, utilizing the new infrastructural standards, have estimated the cost of construction of a new secondary school to be approximately US$6.5 million – the implication of this is that 87% of the scaled down project funds would have to be channeled to construction of the two new secondary schools alone, leaving 13% to cover teacher training and upgrading, curriculum reform, repair, refurbishment and re-equipping of existing secondary schools and so much more!

Despite all of its technocratic sophistication, the World Bank's prescriptive power leveraged by its financial clout pays scant regard to the local wisdom of planners in the field unless their solutions find endorsement in the conclusions of their externally imported consultants. And so it is that a vision with so much promise and such extensive stakeholder "buy-in" (to use the Bank's own language) can conclude as a shadow of its potential.

TEACHER RECRUITMENT - FROM SOUTH TO NORTH: INDIVIDUAL OPPORTUNITY VS. NATIONAL CATASTROPHE

An important conclusion permeating this chapter is the lesson that, notwithstanding the rhetoric of the multilaterals and the international donor community, at the operational and implementation level educational development is stymied by the dynamics of unequal power. Innovation, creativity and imaginative financial/resource management in developing countries mean little unless they find "sponsorship" by consultants or staff within the donor community. As the knowledge management paradigm gains currency, a necessary battle that must be fought by developing countries (and small states in particular) is the same classical struggle over "whose knowledge is of most worth?" The differential of power within the international arena gives to the multilaterals that power of definition and selection to determine whose knowledge is worth incorporation into best practice and the new common sense.

Another contradiction that has been kept hidden in the development aid discourse has been the power and the pull exercised by developed countries to meet their labor shortages to the detriment of developing countries. A highly illustrative example is the recent effort by the small Commonwealth states to stem the hemorrhaging of teachers to the United Kingdom and the United States. The dynamic of that effort for those who were intimately involved exposed the contradictions between the prescriptions of aid and development support and the practice and pursuit of national self-interest. I was a member of the Working Group established by the Commonwealth Ministers to develop a Protocol on Teacher Recruitment and Migration and was one of the delegates negotiating the interests of small states in this matter.

For many years, an important component of bilateral aid in education has focused on teacher training and development and the discourse on this has punctuated the necessity of teacher development and professionalism to building regenerative capacity in education. It is part of the accepted wisdom in educational planning that teacher capacity is an inescapable requirement for educational improvement and for changing educational outcomes. One would expect that given the conventionality of this perspective, the countries that have "so generously" supported teacher training and development would consider it an undermining of their best efforts for developing countries to allow the widespread "brain drain"/migration of teachers.

As several of the Education Ministers of small states pointed out at the 15th Commonwealth Meeting of Ministers of Education in Edinburgh (October 2003), the active and aggressive recruitment of teachers to work in developed countries posed a serious threat to the sustainability of the educational endeavor in these countries. The Minister of Education of Jamaica Hon. Maxine Henry-Wilson revealed that about 700 Jamaican teachers were recruited in one year alone by Britain and the United States leaving Jamaican schools severely understaffed. What was even more disturbing is that some of these teachers were recruited in the middle of the academic year and were simply uprooted from the system, making it more difficult for the education system to accommodate itself to that hemorrhaging. The impact of this recruitment drive on the Commonwealth as a whole has been significant – a BBC Report disclosed: 5,564 teachers from elsewhere in the Commonwealth were given permits to work in England. South Africa was the largest single source, losing 1,492, followed by Jamaica (523) and Zimbabwe (268).

When one considers that Africa will need approximately five million extra teachers if the continent is to achieve universal primary education by 2015 (the worldwide target date set by the United Nations), the insensitivity of the British establishment in facilitating this recruitment effort – which is nothing less than a brain drain of capacity as well as skills – becomes apparent. In the negotiations leading to the Commonwealth Protocol, the British delegation strenuously resisted every effort of the affected countries to impose a strict regulatory regime arguing that the British Government could exercise no control over the recruitment agencies. They further resisted any suggestion that it would then be left to the affected countries to prevent the operation of recruitment agencies within their national jurisdictions. This was countered by the argument that should a Third World country seek to recruit the best nuclear minds from the British establishment, there is no doubt that the British Government would find every means to prevent this exodus on the grounds of national security! When one factors into the equation, the debilitating impact of the HIV-AIDS pandemic on the teaching profession in many African countries, the scale of teacher recruitment in further depleting the best and most qualified is even more disturbing. A genuine commitment by Britain and other developed countries to the goals of EFA would necessitate not only an undertaking to manage this migration of teachers but equally importantly ensure adequate compensation and support to the education systems thus affected. Embedded in the discourse and narrative of the Protocol negotiations was a surprising disregard for notions of national sovereignty and even for accepted developmental considerations. For example, the small states argued that because the drain of teachers represented such a loss of capacity in the context of their size, their education systems would be set back by many years and the vulnerability of small states would be further increased. The British delegation rejected the notion of vulnerability as "emotional language" even though vulnerability is an academically accepted concept that has been thoroughly explicated by Commonwealth scholars in relation to the location of small states in the global nexus.

The statement subsequently made by the British Minister for Higher Education Hon. Alan Johnson that the Protocol "will prevent the exploitation of the scarce human resource of poor countries" was little more than a rhetorical face-saving device in the face of the stiff opposition of his delegation to every concession in the Protocol.

The fact that developing countries had to put up such a strenuous fight to safeguard their educational future in an association as consensual as the Commonwealth and under a British administration that has claimed to be more committed to international justice and fairness than any other, shows clearly that the pursuit of self-interest remains paramount in the conduct of international relations and that it is the dynamics of power rather than the rhetorical paradigms that determine the direction and outcome of global initiatives.

CONCLUSIONS

Through the dynamics of two issues affecting small states, I have sought to show how power remains a determining factor in the formulation of educational policy at the international level and that the multilateral agencies serve principally to reinforce the hegemony of the powerful. The agenda of education reform and the definition of the knowledge that now constitutes the accepted common sense and best practice are substantially shaped by these forces thus making it difficult for developing countries and in particular small states to make real progress. Much of what happens under the umbrella of international cooperation is heavily symbolic and governing regimes in developing countries are sometimes left with little option but to subscribe to the prescriptions offered if they are to be assured of financial and other assistance. In some instances, this subscription by the governments of the poor is used by ruling elites to do what Fuller describes as "signal their modernizing intent" without substantially re-shaping education to the cause of national empowerment.

Universities and multilateral agencies of the North evolved their own mechanisms of mutuality to further this agenda and it is in this context that the work of academics committed to education as a tool of the emancipation and empowerment of peoples can find greater appreciation.

REFERENCES

Apple, M. (1985) *Education and Power*. Ark Paperbacks: Boston.

CARICOM Press Release "Ministers of Education Make Plans for More Effective Programs."*http://www.caricom.org/pressreleases/pres81_04.htm*

Freire, P. (1985) *The Politics of Education*. Bergin and Garvey: Massachusetts.

Karns, M. and Mingst, K. (1992) *The United States and Multilateral Institutions: Patterns of Changing Instrumentality and Influence*. Routledge: London

Bentall, Peart, Carr-Hill and Cox (2001) *Thematic Studies: Funding Agency Contributions to Education For All.* UNESCO: Paris

McMeekin, R. W. (2004) "Management of International Cooperation in Education In the Countries of Latin America and the Caribbean" in *Education Management in Latin America and the Caribbean: Are We on the Right Track*. OREALC/UNESCO: Santiago

http://news.bbc.co.uk/2/hi/uk_news/education/3620962.stm - Tougher 'teacher poaching' rules – BBC Report of Thursday, 2 September, 2004

http://news.bbc.co.uk/2/hi/uk_news/education/3620962.stm - Tougher 'teacher poaching'

http://uk.news.yahoo.com/040902/325/f1t1x.html - Reuters

http://uk.news.yahoo.com/040902/325/f1t1x.html - Reuters Report "Commonwealth ponders teacher 'brain drain'" *Thursday September 2, 06:32 PM*

http://uk.news.yahoo.com/040902/325/f1t1x.html - Reuters Report Commonwealth ponders teacher "brain drain" *Thursday September 2, 06:32 PM*

Report "Commonwealth ponders teacher 'brain drain'" Thursday September 2, 06:32 PM *rules – BBC Report of* Thursday, 2 September, 2004

Hynds, B. (2000) Education for All. Will It Ever Happen? A Report by Bill Hynd (OXFAM, -Canada), Representing CCIC at the Dakar Forum (June 2000).

King, K. Palmer, R. and Hayman, R. (2004). *Bridging Research and Policy on Education, Training and Their Enabling Environments*. University of Edinburgh www.devstud.org.uk/conference/workshops/2.6/DSA%20Education%20Panel%20Word.doc

UNESCO (2002) Report – *High Level Group on Education For All, Abuja*, Nigeria 19-20 Nov 2002.

Chapter 3

TAI SOLARIN:
THE "BENJAMIN FRANKLIN" OF NIGERIA

Michael O. Afoláyan
Southern Illinois University Edwardsville
With an essay by Tai Solarin

INTRODUCTION

The goal in this chapter is to introduce, in just a few words, one of the least celebrated, yet, among the great heroes of education, in the 20th Century; a man who left a legacy that remains unparalleled by virtue of his mobilization of youths and education of the masses all across Africa. His name is Tai Solarin (I refer to him here as TS). I have used the metaphor "Benjamin Franklin" to describe TS because of what I found to be incredible similarities, with a few exceptions, in the lives of these two great heroes of educational and social history. Take for example, predating the independence of the United States, Benjamin Franklin was born in 1706 in the Massachusetts harbor town of Boston. Franklin was a publisher, an educator, a philosopher, an inventor, a political activist, a statesman, and a "just do it" pragmatist. More than anyone of his time, Franklin published numerous educational essays and books. Chief among his publications were the *Pennsylvania Gazette*, and *Poor Richard: An Almanack*. He founded and funded the first circulating library in the world, and just eleven years later, he founded the famous Ivy League institution, the University of Pennsylvania, Philadelphia. Tai Solarin, on the other hand, was one of the most objective and constructive critic of the colonial and postcolonial governments of Nigeria. He was an avid writer, founder and builder of a school that remains even in the minds of his critics, the model and vestige of education for self-reliance in all developing nations of the modern world. The school he founded on January 27, 1956 is Mayflower School in Ikenne, a city half an hour from the Lagos harbor, and where he was born and raised. Tai Solarin died in 1994 at the age of 72. A few notable differences between Benjamin Franklin and Tai Solarin are that in life and death, the former was appreciated by his country, while the latter in life and even in death, still struggles to find his rightful place of honor in the history of his people.[1] In the words of Sheila Solarin, the widow of TS, "it is hard to tell whether or not Nigeria appreciated Solarin's legacy, but Nigerians sure do." Franklin was one of the richest men to live during his own time. TS was not. In what follows, Tai Solarin's life and legacies are presented in a nutshell.

A REVIEW OF HIS EARLY LIFE

TS' Biographers

A few individuals have written about the early years of TS. One of my favorite works on him is an edited book *Education for Greatness: Selected Speeches of Dr. Tai Solarin* done by a young accountant who never studied under Solarin, but admired him, Prince Sulaiman Dave Bola-Babs. Bola-Babs has dedicated a significant part of his young life organizing non-profit organizations for advancing the humanitarian and educational courses of TS. His 265-page book displays some 48 pictures of TS in action, and was foreworded by the Nigerian educator and former education minister, Babs Fafunwa. This same author single-handedly founded and funded *http://wealthandwisdomconsult.com/tai_solarin.html*, a major website in honor of Tai Solarin.

Recounting his own experience with TS is Dr. Wale Omole, a dentist, wrote three books on Tai Solarin. Each book point to the fact that it was through TS' mentorship and encouragement this renown dentist developed his ambition to be a dental surgeon. Omole recalled how his friends called him by the nickname "Doctor." One day, TS asked why this was his nickname, to which he replied because he wanted to be a doctor. This childhood ambition that TS saw in Omole prompted the former to encourage him, planting in him the seed of e medical profession. No wonder why Omole became a dentist.

Another great admirer of Solarin is Dr. Bamidele Babalola, an ex-May and practicing physician in Barbados, West Indies. His book, *Oga Tasere*, is simply a celebration of TS' indefatigable leadership, vision, and care. The book's dedication sums up Babalola's sentiment: "This work is dedicated to the loving memory of TAI, my dearly beloved principal, a great mentor, an exemplar *par excellence*, a most dependable friend and an indefatigable teacher; to Sheila for being so motherly, affectionate and such a dedicated teacher; to Corin and Tunde, the second generation, for being so tolerant and understanding in sharing their great parents with the rest of us.

Writing about TS, Richard Carrier (1995) notes that a major part of this unique man's accomplishments was his passion for functional literacy and civil responsibility. For instance, he notes that Solarin wrote consistently for the *Daily Times* since 1958 and the *Nigerian Tribune* since 1967, and contributed to numerous other papers in Nigeria like *The Guardian*. Solarin was credited as "the only known Nigerian columnist to have a continuously running column lasting over twenty years, and he routinely wrote well over thirty articles a year." Even Tai proudly said that there were people in Nigeria who eagerly read his column for ten

---

[1] As of the time the final version of this book is heading for the press, Mrs.Sheila Solarin is being conferred with the Membership of the Federal Republic of Nigeria (MFR), a high honor conferred only on civilians of notable contribution, courtesy of the Federal Government of Nigeria.

straight years or even more. Besides his writing several books, Carrier notes that Dr. Solarin often joined in public talks and symposia at schools and colleges all throughout Nigeria.

TS' Life of Challenges

As a columnist, Solarin was a relentless critic of Nigerian military rule, as well as of corruption in the government and religious organizations. This stance constantly got him in trouble. Tai Solarin was marked for assassination in 1966 by the corrupt civilian government left in place by the British in 1960, but his life was saved by the January 15 military coup. He was often jailed for his public remarks, the worst being in Jos in 1984. Lasting seventeen months, Jos was one of the longest detention experience of his life, all for simply suggesting that the military should surrender rule to the public within six months. He was detained regularly again by the government in 1990 for similar upsetting remarks.

As noted, Tai Solarin was born in Ikenne, Ogun State, Nigeria, in 1924. He grew up under the British colonial administration of Nigeria. As a Nigerian citizen, a de facto British (and Commonwealth) citizen, TS served as an Air force pilot under the British flag during WWII. It was there that he met a young female British naval officer, Sheila, and they became very close friends, and were later married. TS Returned to Nigeria in 1951 with his wife, Sheila, and became a teacher at Molusi College, a comprehensive secondary school in Ijebu-Igbo. He was soon disenchanted with the conservative and anti-progressive stances of Molusi as well as those of many schools, all of which were under British or mission administrations. He quickly resigned from the school, and with no money at hand, started a private school in 1956. He called the name of the school, Mayflower. The name was taken in reflection over the history of the American Pilgrims who left England for the New World because of their quest for freedom. Indeed, on one of the first walls to be built by the students of Mayflower remains the painting of the Pilgrims' merchant vessel, The Mayflower. Students were free with this head teacher who ate in the same dinning room and with the same kind of bowls with the students. Oga Tai (meaning Master Tai) was his *nom de guerre* at school. Mayflower School started with only 60 students in 1956. Today, the school is constantly running anywhere between 6000 and 7000 students.

THE UNIQUENESS OF MAYFLOWER: THE CURRICULUM

The vision of Tai Solarin was to provide education for self-reliance in Africa's most populous country, Nigeria. Unlike mission and government schools, religion was neither imposed nor opposed at Mayflower. School was a boarding house built by students. Students built the classrooms or studied under the trees; they also built the dorms in which they lived. If they wanted to worship according to their faiths, they had the approval Oga Tai except that they had to build their religious centers on campus. Students of Mayflower planted, harvested and processed the food they ate. They raised the cattle, fisheries, piggeries, andpoultry for their consumption. Nothing produced by students was for sale. For many decades since its inception and up until now, Mayflower has remained *nuli secondus* in Nigeria whenever it comes to the provision of quality education and life-sustaining curricula. The students' academic achievements are noticeable. In addition, Mayflower is the only school consistently with multiple ethnic group attendees. It is also the only school with staff and students of multiple nationalities across Africa. The graduates of Mayflower are found all over the world and in all walks of life

EDUCATION AND LIBRATION

For nearly four decades, the late Dr. Solarin and his wife, Sheila, persistently fought for free and compulsory education (from first grade through high school) for all Nigerian children. As earlier noted, TS was disenchanted with the conservative and exploitative tendencies of mission and colonial schools. He felt that these schools only prepared children of the few "fortunate" members of the society for colonial and mission services. Besides, the schools provided education with strings attached to them. For instance, the curricula and modes of operation were designed in a way that the learners were so ill-equipped that they were neither mentally liberated nor socially empowered to cope with basic social living. In spite of its humble beginning with 60 students in 1956, by summer of 2004, Mayflower had grown to several thousand 7000 students, and has become a K-12 institution that includes elementary, junior high and senior high schools.

TS found the history of the American Pilgrims of 1620 fascinating, and so he constructed his vision around the model of its history. He believed that the Pilgrim's history evoked images of escaping persecution for a new life of freedom. Thus, he named the new school "Mayflower." It was to be a school for all children," Tai said, "discriminating against none." Tai Solarin believed, like great minds in the caliber of Paulo Freire, and John Dewey that the goal of education is to liberate the mind and empower the learner. Today, Mayflower is so much in demand that the waiting list is inexhaustible. Mrs. Sheila Solarin, Tai's wife since 1951, still lives on campus where her husband lived and died.

ENCOUNTERING THE SAGE

Quite unlike many of Solarin's biographers, I never attended Mayflower School, and neither did I ever have a direct, face-to-face meeting with the late sage. However, our paths have crossed on a few instances. Indeed, it has always been as if I knew TS very closely. First, as a child growing up in the 1960s, I heard so much of his non-conformist radical but benevolent deeds. I was captivated by, read and heard of his defiant stances against the powers-that-be which made the imported alcoholic beverages a status symbol which only the high and mighty of the land could drink. The same colonial and later the neo-colonial authorities banned the native brewed *ogogoro*, which was of equal or superior potency, demonizing it as contraband. Indeed, if Ogogoro was found with any citizen, it was ground for prosecution, persecution and incarceration. In fact, the English name given to *ogogoro* was *Illicit Gin*. The story of his courage in challenging the status quo left an indelible memory in my mind, even as a child.

My second encounter with TS was through an interesting personal experience. I once sent money order by registered mail to a cousin of mine who was living in the same Western State of Nigeria in the amount of about Forty Naira (approximately $3.00). The money was never delivered. TS was then the Public Complaint Commissioner for the Western State, my state of residence as of the time of the incident. I sent him a letter of complaint to which he personally replied, assuring me that although postal services were a function of the Federal Government, being a federal government agency, however, his office would do whatever it could to work together with the Nigerian Postal Services to investigate the issue. The postal system in Nigeria was so inefficient at that time that anyone would laugh at such promise - Anyone who did not know TS, that is. At that time, a person who wanted something important to be delivered across the country was smart enough to send somebody who would catch the bus, the train, or whatever means of transportation was available and deliver the article by hand so as to be sure it got to its destination. For someone to complain about a lost mail was like suing the driver's union because somebody sounded the horn too loudly on a street in Lagos, and still expect his case to be heard by the court authorities. Yes, the investigation lasted more than one year, and yes, I lost count of the number of my visits to the "MOD Investigation Unit" of the central post office in Ibadan; but yes, too, I got a duplicate money order and was proud to say that my resiliency coupled with the listening ears of TS to a common citizen that I was, paid off.

Again, while in high school, I read so many of TS' journalistic articles, many of which have long been in public domains. Two of our English teachers, Mr. Oguntona, and Mrs. Olayeni, would make us read them for comprehension. My favorite of his essays was the one titled, "May Your Road be Rough," a New Year "prayer," the full content of which I will share at the end of this chapter. Though I cannot remember the context in which the article was written, nor the original publication in which he wrote it, I remember vividly that the prayers that were offered in that article left everyone of us in class thinking. In that New Year "prayer," TS did not pray for wealth or fortune for his readers; he prayed for their "roads to be rough in the New Year." For, according to him, without challenges, there would be no need to make efforts, and without efforts, there would be no victories. In a reward-oriented, benevolence-seeking Yoruba cultural milieu in which we grew up, it was an enigmatic and paradoxical to read an article that actually prayed for difficult times. Three decades after the event, many of us who sat in the same classroom reading the same essay reminiscent on the positive effect that the TS philosophy as articulated in that essay has had on us.

Finally, as a graduate student at Yale University in New Haven, CT, in the early 1980s, my academic advisor, Ivan Dihoff, called me into his office one early Friday morning and told me we had to do something urgently as he just heard on the news that Tai Solarin had been jailed by the government of Nigeria. He asked if I would join in drafting, and signing a letter of complaint to *Amnesty International* so as to call the Nigerian government to order. My first reaction was one of apprehension. I told Ivan bluntly, that I was a Christian and would not want to risk exposing myself and my Nigerian family members to the much feared Nigerian State Secret Services (SSS) by protesting the imprisonment of a sworn atheist. It was then that Ivan told me of how much TS did in changing his life as a young American who went to Nigeria in the 1960s. He also reminded me of the revolutionary contributions of TS to the education of the common people. At that point I, myself, started to reflect on my earlier encounters with the man. I realized that indeed this was not the man who should be sitting behind the iron bars while the social state of the nation continued to be in disrepair. I realized that it was indeed most, if not all, of those who threw him in jail actually deserved to be behind the bars – they were cheaters of the nation, while TS was the teacher. And a few years down the road, getting to meet American friends like Dr. Timothy Madigan, Dr. Mary Dillard and many more who had so much respect for Solarin's social criticism, educational vision, and humanist endeavors rejuvenated my interest in TS and his educational philosophy.

THE MAKING OF THE HERO

First, Tai Solarin was a common man in uncommon circumstances, doing uncommon deeds in unusual times. Below, I quote at length, the testimony of Femi Osofisan, the renowned Nigerian playwright and professor of theater, who on July 2004, at the First Tai Solarin Memorial Lecture in Lagos, Nigeria, gave a picture of the humanistic effort of Solarin. He told of the story of TS' complete disenchantment with the show of helplessness on the part of the Nigerian government and the entire populace which would not respond to a simple task of treating the dead with dignity and reverence. His response to this situation earned him the scornful nickname of *gbokugboku*, that is, the carrier of the dead, to which I earlier alluded. The people's attitude defied normalcy and civility, and Osofisan captures the main thrust of the story in his lecture:

> For, although "*Gbokugboku*" does translate indeed as "the carrier of corpses", it is only disturbing when taken in its literal sense. But as we shall see, however, it has a metaphorical dimension, a connotation more profound than that surface meaning, in which it assumes positive significance. . . .
>
> The nickname was invented deliberately to deride the man. It was meant to mock him and discourage him from one of the civic duties that Tai had chosen to perform, against the prevailing common tide. For Tai Solarin was never one to see a corpse on the road and simply pass by, as the rest of us would do. That was how the name came about.
> At that time, just as nowadays, one of the recurrent scandals in our nation was the sight of dead bodies dumped regularly on the highway, and which would remain there for weeks unclaimed, till they rotted away. Invariably these bodies would carry various signs of deliberate mutilation—with perhaps the head, or a limb, or the private organs, shaved off.
> But it was not just this gruesome sight, as unsettling as it was, that was the scandal; nor even the shocking contemplation that some of our countrymen could be so desperate and so ruthless as to assault their fellow men in this crude and barbarous manner.
> The real scandal, as far as Tai saw it, was in the way we reacted, we who saw these corpses. Of course, our first reaction would be the expected shock and revulsion. We would exclaim and shake our head and click our tongue with the appropriate hisses and cries of alarm. But almost immediately afterwards, we would turn our eyes aside, and hurry away, probably muttering prayers and invoking the blood of Jesus!
> But that's all we would do. None of us would take any step about having the corpse removed, not to talk of giving it an appropriate decent burial. The body would therefore lie there untouched, and begin slowly to bloat and decompose before our very eyes. Day after day we would pass by and watch this gory drama, shaking our heads at the spectacle of a once-human body disintegrating slowly, its flesh gradually drying and peeling off the bones, till the rest of the carcass was cleaned off by weather and vermin. Or sometimes, particularly in the busy streets of the large towns, it is vehicles that would run over the corpses, scatter them into fragments on the tar, and carry the bits away, plastered to the tyres.

After the first day, as we continued to pass by in our helplessness, we would gradually lose our shock and outrage, and reconcile ourselves to the view. The dead body would become just debris on the road, just another abandoned piece of refuse.

And in the course of time, petty traders or food vendors would be seen calmly erecting their counters and carrying on their trade with bubbling enthusiasm right next to some decomposing human corpse! And even churches, or mosques, would be conducting their services enthusiastically, with some corpse rotting away just outside one of the windows!

That was the picture in Tai Solarin's time; and it is still, very sadly, the same scenario today. Mysteriously mutilated corpses are still being dumped on our highways. They lie there and decompose there, while we walk by and turn our eyes somewhere else.

But—No! Tai said one day. No humane society should be allowed to continue to treat its citizens this way. Death should not be an excuse for the ill-treatment of the dead, even if we were uncertain about the corpse's identity! We could not continue to neglect the obligation of decency we owe one another as human beings, whether dead or alive.

So, whenever he saw another body on the road, Solarin would interrupt his journey, go and purchase a coffin, seek some helping hands, and carry the corpse to the nearest police station in protest. Again and again he did this, dragging journalists along, trying to goad the police into action, and with the power of public embarrassment get them to do their duty.

It was a singularly compassionate, and courageous, undertaking. Solarin was teaching us a necessary lesson, to the rest of us, that there is a solidarity between all human beings which no circumstances should erase. (pp. 8-11).

Apparently, Solarin was a visionary, a revolutionary, and a dreamer. To paraphrase the lines of George Bernard Shaw, even when other people may see things as they are and ask why they are so, TS often saw things as he would like them to be and asked why they were not so. He then moved on and did them. His were never the proverbial dreams of a dog, which live and die in the belly of the dog. When he thought of great ideas, he moved on to implement them. Equally so was the fact that Tai never perceived himself as an intellectual juggernaut or an expert. He simply saw himself as a realist and an amateur, building the ark of knowledge, rather than erecting a titanic full of dupes and "Made in Nigeria" con artists. This was a good virtue for him; after all, the old cliché still holds that "experts built the Titanic and it sank but an amateur built the Ark and it floated." Solarin challenged the human mind to dare to try. In his preface to *No witches, no angels: My credo*, Solarin writes:

> The idea . . . is to get the Nigerian youth, the African youngster, to develop a spine; to dare to think. To dare to ask questions. To dare to do, and fail; for it is from failure (that) we pick up courage to do and succeed. . . . I owe my success in all considerations to my refusal to accept time-honoured precepts. I don't do things one way because somebody else did them that way. I always want to do them some other way if only to prove they could also be done that other way. The result has been bounteous harvests. . . .(p.v)

It is no wonder why we see the legacy of Tai Solarin linger many years after his death. The hope is that many more generations will uphold the legacy. In traveling in Nigeria, United States, the Caribbean and England, and interviewing graduates of Mayflower school who partly or wholly spent their high school years under the tutelage of Solarin, functional literacy, self-reliance, resiliency, dissent and a non-conformist pose were some of the recurrent characteristics that I found in all of them.

Finally, I believe that understanding Solarin requires a deeper understanding of his perspectives on life. It is clear that a lack of this understanding was the bone of contention between him and many of his detractors, especially, the Nigerian government and its agencies. I would like end this chapter by providing one of Solarin's most enduring but interesting essays on life, which I had alluded to. This essay provides TS perspective on life in a nutshell. It is titled, "May Your Road Be Rough!"[2]

MAY YOUR ROAD BE ROUGH

I am not cursing you; I am wishing you what I wish myself every year. I therefore repeat, may you have a hard time this year; may there be plenty of troubles for you this year! If you are not so sure what you should say back, why not just say, 'Same to you'? I ask for no more.

Our successes are conditioned by the amount of risk we are ready to take. Quite recently, I visited a local farmer about three miles from where I live. He could not have been more than fifty-five. He still suffered, he said, from the physical energy he displayed as a farmer in his younger days. Around his hut were two pepper bushes. There were two cocoyams growing round him. There were snail shells, which had given him meat. There must have been more around the banana trees I saw. He hardly ever went to town to buy things. He was self-sufficient. The car or the bus, the television or the telephones, the newspaper, Vietnam or Red China were nothing to him. He had no ambitions whatsoever, he told me. I am not so sure if you are already envious of him. But were we all to revert to such a life, we would be practically driven back to cave-dwelling.

On the other hand, try to put yourself in the position of the Russian or the American astronaut. Any moment from now the count, 3, 2, 1, is going to go, and you are going to be shot into the atmosphere and soon you will be whirling round our Earth at the speed of six miles per second. If you get so fired into the atmosphere and you forget what to do to ensure return to Earth, one of the things that might happen to you is that you could become forever a satellite, going round the Earth until you die of starvation and even then your dead body would continue the gyration!

When, therefore, you are being dressed up and padded to be shot into the sky, you know only too well that you are going on the roughest road man has ever trodden. The Americans and Russians who have gone were armed with the great belief that they would come back. But I cannot believe that they did not have some slightly foreboding contingency of the non-return. It is their courage for going in spite of the apprehensions that makes the world hail them so loudly today.

The big fish is never caught in shallow waters. You have to go into the open sea for it. The biggest businessmen make decisions with lightening speed and carry them out with equal celerity. They do not dare delay of dally. Time would pass them if they did. The biggest successes are preceded by the greatest heart-burnings. You should read the stories of bomber pilots of World War II. The Russian pilot, the German pilot, the American pilot or the British pilot suffered exactly the same physical and mental tension the night before a raid on enemy territory. There were no alternative routes for those who most genuinely believed in victory for their side.

---

[2] My gratitude goes to Madam Sheila Solarin who granted me the permission to publish this essay in its entirety.

You cannot make omelettes without breaking eggs; throughout the world there is no paean without pain. Jawaharlal Nehru has put it so well. I am paraphrasing him. He wants to meet his troubles in a frontal attack. He wants to see himself tossed into the aperture between the two horns of the bull. Being there, he determines he is going to win and, therefore, such a fight requires all of his faculties.

When my sisters and I were young and we slept on our small mats round our mother, she always woke up at 6 a.m. for morning prayers. She always said prayers on our behalf but always ended with something like this: 'May we not enter into any dangers or get into any difficulties this day.' It took me almost thirty years to dislodge the cankerworm in our mother's sentiments. I found, by hard experience, that all that is noble and laudable was to be achieved only through difficulties and trials and tears and dangers. There are no other roads.

If I was born into a royal family and should one day become a constitutional king, I am inclined to think that I should go crazy. How could I, from day to day, go on smiling and nodding approval at somebody else's successes for an entire lifetime?

When Edward the Eighth (now Duke of Windsor) was a young, sprightly Prince of Wales, he went to Canada and shook so many hands that his right arm nearly got pulled out of its socket! It went into a sling and he shook hands thenceforth with his left hand! It would appear he was trying his utmost to make a serious job out of downright sinecurism. Life, if it is going to be abundant, must have plenty of hills and vales. It must have plenty of sunshine and rough weather. It must be rich in obfuscation and perspicacity. It must be packed with days of danger and apprehension. When I walk into the dry but certainly cool morning air of every January 1st, I wish myself plenty of tears and of laughter; plenty of happiness and unhappiness, plenty of failures and successes, plenty of abuse and praise. It is impossible to win ultimately without a rich measure of intermixture in such a menu. Life would be worthless without the lot. We do not achieve much in this country because we are all so scared of taking risk. We all went the smooth and well-paved roads. While the reason the Americans and others succeeded so well is that they took such great risks.

If, therefore, you are about, in this New Year, to win any target you set for yourself, please accept my prayers and your elixir- May your road be rough! (TAI SOLARIN, January 1, 1964).

The life of Solarin is better summarized in the carefully selected phrases of Omofolabo Ajayi-Soyinka, a graduate of Mayflower School who was sent to Mayflower specifically because of the wisdom of TS and unique curricula of Mayflower. "As a father to his two children, Solarin was strict and devoted; as a husband to his only wife of more than four decades, he was attentive; as an educator, Tai Solarin was thorough and passionate; as a disciplinarian, he was total and complete; as a disciplined person, he was uncompromising; and as a mentor, he was influential." His is the story of an unsung hero whose praises will continue to be heard for many generations to come from the mouth of many men and women who were fortunate enough to learn under his feet.

REFERENCES

Adenubi, A. (ed.). 1985. *Timeless Tai: A collection of the writings of T. Solarin*. Lagos: F and A, 1985.

Afolayan, M. O. 2003. Apes, Obey! The historical enigma of discord between higher education and the military in Nigeria. In Oyebade, A. *The foundations of Nigeria: Essays in honor of Toyin Falola*. Trenton, NJ: Africa World Press. 247-267.

Babalola, B. 2004. *Oga Tasere*. St. Michael, Barbados: Africana Ventures.

Bakare, A. 2000. *Sheila: A lady of courage*. Lagos: GM Communications.

Bola-Babs, S. 2001. *Education for greatness: Selected speeches of Dr. Tai Solarin*. Lagos, Nigeria: Spirosensual Wealth & Wisdom Limited.

Fajemilua, Bayo. *Tai Solarin: The man and his rebellion*. Akure, Nigeria :Flocel Publishers, 2001. xvii, 293 p.

Mamora, Y. 1997. *Alaaye oku: Akojopo ote lara awon apileko Dokita Tai Solarin*. Ikeja:John West Publications.

Mayflower School. 1976. *Mayflower School: 20th Anniversary celebration*. Ikenne.

Mayflower School. ND. *Merry Mayflower – A booklet of school hymns*. Ikenne

Okanlawon, A.B., Fasanmi, O. T. (Eds). 2000. *Tai Solarin: The making of a humanist*. Ijebu-Ode: Admass Publishing.

Omole, W. 1985. *Tai Solarin's adventure: A practised philosophy*. Ibadan: AR-RauphCommercial Press.

Omole, W. 1994. *Tai Solarin's foot-print On the sand of time*. Mushin: Inland Printing and Publishers.

Solarin, T. 1991. *The halo around the year 2000 AD*. Ikenne.

Solarin, T. 1994. *Not God's Injunction*. Ikeja: John West Publishing.

Solarin, T. 1994. *No witches, no angels: My credo*. Ikeja: John West Publishing.

Chapter 4

THE GLOBAL POLITICS OF EDUCATIONAL LANGUAGE POLICY IN TANZANIA

Frances Vavrus
Teachers College, Columbia University
New York, USA

Outgoing African Union (AU) chairman Joaquim Chissano of Mozambique on Tuesday made history by partly using Kiswahili to address the continental body's third annual summit in Addis Ababa...Chissano, who also retires from the Mozambican presidency later this year, read more than two thirds of his report and farewell speech in Kiswahili, thus becoming a pioneer in the utilization of an African language during a continental summit... 'The working languages of the Union and all its institutions, if possible, include African languages, as well as Arabic, English, French and Portuguese,' reads article 25 of the AU Act.
-Pan African News Agency, July 7, 2004

Swahili is not an international language. It's a language that is spoken a lot in East Africa . . . but it's only known here in East Africa. And it's not everyone in these countries who knows Swahili well. There are differences in the Swahili of Kenya, Uganda, Burundi, and Zaire [Democratic Republic of Congo]. If we use Swahili, we will be like an island.
-Tanzanian Form 4 graduate, 2001

INTRODUCTION

During the past few months, there has been an increasing recognition of Swahili as an international language. In June, Microsoft announced that it would translate its Office software into Swahili ("Microsoft", 2004); in July, the African Union decided to make Swahili one of its official languages, with the outgoing president of the Union, Mozambique's President Chissano, giving his farewell address in Swahili ("Swahili baffles", 2004); and in September, at a meeting of the East African Community, its Council of Ministers requested the governments of Kenya and Uganda to set up national Swahili councils similar to the one in Tanzania, and they called for the establishment of an East African Community Kiswahili Council ("East African", 2004).

Despite these moves, key ministers within the Tanzanian government rely on the argument that Swahili is not sufficiently international to justify using it as the medium of instruction at the post-primary levels (Komba, 2003). For more than four decades, the government of Tanzania has struggled with its educational language policy and with the role of Swahili in cultivating a national identity. Throughout the *ujamaa* era of the late 1960s and 1970s, the government of President Nyerere made declarations about its intention to use Swahili at all grade levels to promote its principal goal of building national unity; nevertheless, English remained the medium of instruction at the secondary and tertiary levels throughout this period. By the early 1980s, with *ujamaa* in abeyance, any moves to change the language policy were all but abandoned (Rugemalira et al., 1990). The 1982 Presidential Commission on Education, for example, stated clearly that "English will be the medium of education at post primary levels where the teaching of Kiswahili as a subject will also be strengthened" (Ministry of Education, 1984, p. 21). The most recent official statement on the matter, the 1995 *Education and Training Policy*, reconfirmed the use of English on the grounds that it was essential for improving the teaching of science and technology that would ultimately make Tanzania a more globally competitive country (MOEC, 1995). Little mention of national unity through educational language policy is made in this document or in the 1997 Culture Policy [*Sera ya Utamaduni*]. Moreover, the Minister of Education and Culture refutes studies by a number of Tanzanian and foreign educational researchers showing that secondary school students do not know English sufficiently well to learn science, or other subjects, through this medium (Brock-Utne, 2004). Thus, one finds a situation where the actions of Joaquim Chissano and Bill Gates suggest an increasingly international role for Swahili while key Tanzanian ministers promote policies that reserve this role for English.

This chapter does not set out to the question of what the educational language policy in Tanzania ought to be; instead, it explores debates over international languages and, in particular, arguments for the continued use of English as the medium of instruction at the secondary level as articulated by the people most affected by this policy: Tanzanian secondary school students. In the pages that follow, I will consider how support for the current policy among secondary-school age youth represents their complex identities as cosmopolitan, educated persons. In particular, I want to explore the reasons why students who acknowledge the failure of this policy on educational grounds, i.e., they admit to limited comprehension of certain subjects in secondary school because they didn't understand the medium of instruction, would, nevertheless, strongly embrace the policy as essential for the internationalization of their lives and of the country as a whole.

In this chapter, I utilize Bonny Norton's definition of identity to analyze young people's views about educational language policy. Norton writes, "I use the term *identity* to refer to how people understand their relationship to the world, how that relationship is constructed across time and space, and how people understand their possibilities for the future" (1997, p. 410). Central to Norton's definition is the idea that identity is dynamic and that it derives largely from an imagined view of one's future place in the world. I also draw upon Arjun Appadurai's work on cosmopolitanism and the imagination to orient the study toward the social rather than the psychological to understand shared sentiments about language policy. Appadurai makes a distinction between fantasies—a private, temporary longing—and imagination, which he sees as a collective, future-oriented vision (1996). In the case of Tanzanian secondary school students, I contend that their support of the current educational language policy cannot be understood without exploring their sense of themselves as educated and as cosmopolitan, meaning, in this case, being members of an international community where English, not Swahili, is the medium. I now turn to consider briefly some of the changes in education policy and economic orientation during the past several decades that have shaped young Tanzanians' sense of self in the world before moving into a discussion of the study itself.

HISTORICAL OVERVIEW

The use of Swahili in the education system was closely tied to the 1967 policy of *Education for Self-Reliance* (ESR) that was part of the country's socialist development program—*ujamaa*—promoted by Tanzania's first president, Julius Nyerere. It was explicitly opposed to the Western model of modernization that privileged urban development, free markets, and production for export as one finds in the country's economic policies today. Instead, the primary goal of *ujamaa* was rural development because it was acknowledged that the vast majority of the population lived outside the urban centers and made their living through agricultural production. The education policy of ESR was intended to complement this comprehensive rural development strategy by emphasizing primary schooling for the masses—using Swahili as the medium of instruction—rather than secondary and tertiary education for the elite. However, Nyerere's strong nationalist ideals did not bring about the anticipated change in the use of English to teach school subjects at the secondary and tertiary levels even though the justification for English has shifted dramatically: during the *ujamaa* era, the argument for deferring the change in policy was that Swahili was not yet ready to serve as the medium beyond primary school because additional corpus planning was required; in contrast, the current justifications for retaining the policy address competitiveness in the global marketplace and costs associated with creating Swahili materials (Brock-Utne, 2004; Komba, 2003).

FIELDWORK ON MOUNT KILIMANJARO

The Kilimanjaro Region is considered by many to be in the vanguard of education and engagement with international actors and institutions. This region ranks second in the nation in terms of the number of students who complete primary school (MOEC, 1999), and, for a region making up only 5% of the country's population, it has a disproportionate share of its public secondary schools (9%) and private secondary schools (21%) (MOEC, 1996). One reason for these figures is that formal education has been a feature of social life for more than 100 years, when Chagga chiefs on the mountain vied with each other for missionaries who would set up schools, churches, and dispensaries in their communities (Bennett, 1964; Rogers, 1972). With the introduction of coffee as a cash crop in the late 19th century, many Chagga households had money to invest in the building of roads and clinics. It was education, however, that received the bulk of these new funds: "By far the most important cash investment the Chagga made in the new ways was in paying school fees for their children. The demands for education on Kilimanjaro grew from early mission times and a generation later became unremitting" (Moore, 1986, p. 129). The economic and educational advantages for people in Kilimanjaro because of their engagement with the coffee trade have given the Chagga the reputation of "East Africa's 'moderns'" (Setel, 1995, p. 3). Although this characterization glosses over the great variability in the degree to which Chagga families have participated in and benefited from the sale of coffee, it does highlight the particular relationship among education, identity, and international affairs in this region (Howard and Millard, 1997).

The education situation in Kilimanjaro today has been greatly affected by the precipitous global drop in the export price of coffee. Over the past eight years, the price farmers receive for their crop has fallen by 50% (Oxfam, 2001), while fees at private secondary schools—the majority of the secondary schools in Kilimanjaro—have more than doubled (Vavrus, 2001). Not only has the drop in coffee prices affected parents' ability to pay for schooling, but the structural adjustment policies implemented since the mid 1980s have led to a concomitant increase in the cost of fertilizer and pesticides needed for profitable coffee production. In short, many families are finding it more difficult to send their children to secondary school, but this has neither diminished their desire, nor their children's desire, to do so.

This observation about the desire for secondary schooling is based on six periods of intermittent fieldwork between 1996 and 2004 in Old Moshi, a community of approximately 20,000 people living on the slopes of Mount Kilimanjaro (Vavrus, 2003). I include debates over language policy in the longitudinal ethnographic study I am conducting because I believe they highlight changes in young people's orientation from the nation as the broader context for their cosmopolitanism to a global "imagined community" of youth who converse in English and traverse national boundaries with relative ease (c.f. Anderson, 1983).

This chapter focuses on one small slice of this project, namely, four focus group discussions held in 2001 with some of the secondary school students whom I taught in 1996 during a year of participant observation at a co-educational boarding school in Old Moshi.[1] In 1996, the students had completed a questionnaire and had written essays about what they thought they would do after graduation and, in particular, what they wanted to be doing in the year 2000. In 2000, I had the opportunity to return to Tanzania; I sent a questionnaire to 225 of my former students, and 125 of them responded.[1] All of them volunteered to participate in focus group discussions in 2001, but I invited only the 82 currently living in the Kilimanjaro Region. Thus, although the student body of the boarding school consisted of young people from across Tanzania, the focus group discussions included a disproportionate number of Chagga youth whose views may not be representative of youth throughout the country.

The desire to continue in school past Form 4 or to find employment in the non-agricultural sectors of the economy was common to almost all of the 282 students who completed the questionnaire and essay task in 1996, when they were still in secondary school. However, the follow-up questionnaire in 2000 revealed that less than half of these young men and women were employed or in school. Moreover, over 40% of the young women but less than 15% of the men reported living at their parents' homes with no employment (Vavrus, 2001). This situation of completing secondary school but finding few employment or post-secondary educational opportunities may explain why only 13% of the respondents said they were more satisfied with their lives now than they were four years ago. Although these young people were fortunate in having been able to complete lower secondary school—an opportunity afforded to less than 15% of the population—this educational experience neither satisfied their educational goals nor has yet created opportunities for steady employment for most of them (National Bureau of Statistics and Macro International, 2000).

The focus groups in the summer of 2001 provided an opportunity to discuss in greater depth both the positive and negative events described in the essays. Even though most of these former students were unemployed, almost all of them insisted that they had gotten one very important employment-related benefit from attending secondary school that they would not have gotten at a technical school: they had "learned English". There was only one young woman who said, in hindsight, that she would have preferred a tailoring school rather than a secondary school because she would have found employment more easily. She felt that she had no marketable skills, and this included knowing English, but no one else in the four focus groups expressed a similar opinion. In contrast, these young women and men insisted that learning English was an invaluable part of their school experience. Each group admitted that they were not using English very much right now—except for those who were still in school—and none of them opted to conduct the focus group discussion in English, preferring, instead, to talk solely in Swahili. Nevertheless, they believed their knowledge of English would help connect them to the world beyond Tanzania because English, they noted repeatedly, is an "international language". The following comments (in Swahili except where italicized) illustrate these sentiments:

- "Another advantage of knowing English is that if you get a friend from another country you can communicate with them" (focus group #1—young woman).
- "If you go to another country, you will discover that the language used to communicate with others is English" (focus group #3—young man).
- "If you know English, you can use it for communication with people other than Tanzanians" (focus group #3—young man).
- "Swahili is not an *international language*. It's a language that is spoken a lot in East Africa . . . but it's only known here in East Africa. And it's not everyone in these countries who knows Swahili well. There are differences in the Swahili of Kenya, Uganda, Burundi, and Zaire [Democratic Republic of Congo]. If we use Swahili, we will be like an island" (focus group #4—young man).

The focus group discussions became quite animated at times, especially when I challenged one group on the idea that English is critical for international communication in Africa. Two of the participants responded strongly by saying that Tanzanians need to learn the language to communicate with other Africans and not just with Europeans and Americans. One young man admitted that it is the colonial legacy of English that makes some people oppose its use, and he explained that there is growing opposition to the use of English among some groups of students and faculty at the University of Dar es Salaam. However, he was very concerned about the consequences for communication in Africa if Tanzanians do not know English:

> Last year, during the Uhuru [Freedom] Torch celebration, there were a lot of foreigners there along with [Tanzanian] university students. You know, many university students are poor in English because there is no one there like Mr. [one of the English teachers at their secondary school] to make the students speak in English because they are *free* there. They are fearful to speak in English, but this is sad. There were students there from other countries like Kenya

and South Africa who were surprised that our university students don't know English well. There are Form 6 students who know English better than they [university students] do.

A young woman in the same focus group then added her pragmatic assessment of the situation by saying, "Because Africa depends on Europe, both of these languages [English and Swahili] are important for a person to know." She added that the status associated with knowing English is not because it is the language of the United States but because it is an international language: "When Africans see someone speaking in English, they are very impressed and they respect them. Yes, even if they are not well educated but only know this language, they are respected." For her, and for many others, English cannot be separated from the notion of an educated person, who, at present, gains much of their respect from being a member of an international, English-speaking community.

The focus group discussions revealed the complexity of the educational language policy as students acknowledged their frequent difficulties in understanding the content of lessons conducted in English. Nevertheless, they remained committed to maintaining English as the medium of instruction at the secondary level or to expanding its use to the primary and pre-primary levels. Some people mentioned a recent study showing that Tanzanian students do poorly on their national exams because of their low proficiency in English. My review of government data supports this claim: The most recent statistical profile from the Ministry of Education and Culture shows a continuation of the pattern in which 70-79% of the students taking the national Form 4 examination receive a Division 4 (lowest division) or fail completely (MOEC, 1999). The reason for these disappointing results, according to the Executive Secretary of the National Swahili Council in Tanzania, is "students' low level of understanding of the English language resulting from the weak foundations of the subject in primary schools" (Raphael, 2001, p. 1).

These former students were well aware of the barrier to learning that English poses at the secondary level, but their solution was to intensify the use of English rather than abandon it. Thus, my proposal to use Swahili as the medium of instruction throughout the education system while teaching English as a subject was roundly rejected. These young people were unconvinced by my example of German students who are taught in German but know English well even though they study it only as a subject. The difference, according to one Form 6 graduate, has its roots in the economic conditions in Tanzania that make it difficult to get the books and facilities necessary to do a good job of teaching English as a subject:

> It's fine [to study English as a subject only] in countries . . . like Germany and other European countries, but their foundation from the beginning of their studies is good. They write their books in their own language from the beginning, and English is taught as a subject. The books we have are in English, but the language we use for everything is Swahili. For others in Tanzania, for example, they use their *mother tongue language* although they also know Swahili. So if we could do this [bilingual teaching] from the beginning, there wouldn't be a problem. The problem here is a result of our poverty. Where will we get the money to change these books, to change computers (laughter)? This is where our problem lies. Of course, it is good to be taught in a language you know. You will understand well and succeed in your studies.

At the time, I took this young man's argument about the cost of producing bilingual or monolingual Swahili materials at face value. However, it became more intriguing after spending six weeks in Tanzania during the summer of 2004 visiting the same schools in which I had worked in 1996, 2000, and 2001: While listening to the radio one morning in July, I heard a discussion of the educational language policy that made the same argument as the student's about the prohibitive cost of switching from English to Swahili as the medium of instruction at the secondary level. Why, I asked myself, is the government so concerned about the cost of making textbooks in Swahili when it has done a poor job of getting textbooks—English or otherwise—into Tanzanian schools in the first place? The schools I visited rarely had class sets of books, except for the English language readers donated by the British Council's English Language Teaching Support Project. If there aren't many textbooks in the schools at present, as other scholars have noted (Samoff, 1999), then the argument about the high cost of materials production belies a more fundamental reason for opposing the use of Swahili as the medium of instruction. It appears that opposition has more to do with the ways students' and policy makers' situate themselves and their country in an international community than with the prices associated with textbooks or teacher training. This is an issue that warrants further exploration with these students in the coming years, especially if Swahili does become a working language of the African Union and of the global Microsoft network.

CONCLUSIONS

In conclusion, I have attempted to show that young people's reasons for supporting English as the medium of instruction at the secondary level are inextricably linked to their identity as educated members of an international community united by its use of English. Government officials may share these sentiments and believe sincerely that the goal of promoting international communication through English takes precedence over the reality that many Tanzanian students do not adequately understand the language to use it as the medium of instruction. By examining the arguments about educational language policy made by secondary school graduates, I have attempted to shift the focus of research on educational language policy from what ought to be done from the perspective of researchers (cf. Philipson, 1992; Skutnabb-Kangas, 2000, 2004) to what should be done from the perspective of those most affected by the policy. As sociolinguist Alastair Pennycook contends, "A more plausible way forward is through a critical engagement with people's wishes, desires, and histories, that is, a way of thinking that pushes one constantly to question rather than to pontificate" (1998, p. 343). Pontificating is what professors are wont to do, but it is also vital to engage with people's desires to make sense of apparent contradictions between sound pedagogy and sound policy.

REFERENCES

Anderson, B. (1983). *Imagined communities*. London and New York: Verso.
Appadurai, A. (1996). *Modernity at large: Cultural dimensions of globalization*. Minneapolis and London: University of Minnesota Press.
Bennett, N. (1964). The British on Kilimanjaro: 1884-1892. *Tanganyika Notes and Records*, 63, 229-244.

Brock-Utne, B. (2004). *'But English is the language of science and technology'—The language of instruction in Africa—with a special look at Tanzania* [Online]. Available at http://www.netreed.uio.no/articles/Papers_final/brock_utne.pdf

Brock-Utne, B. (2002). *Language, democracy and education in Africa.* Uppsala: Nordiska Afrikainstitutet.

Brock-Utne, B. (2000). *Whose language for all? The recolonialization of the African mind.* New York and London: Falmer Press.

East African Officers Want Kiswahili Councils (14 September 2004). Africa News [Online]. Available at http://web.lexis-nexis.com/universe/doclist?_m=3bda7869ca62252ed8e34b1a26a5e676andwchp=dGLbVzb-zSkVband_md5=d5f75120c65e0e3793700296d7a4c6c6.

Howard, M. T., and Millard, A. V. (1997). *Hunger and shame: Poverty and child malnutrition on Mount Kilimanjaro.* New York and London: Routledge.

Komba, S. (8 July 2003). Change to Kiswahili in schools pre-mature. *The African* (unpaged).

Microsoft to launch in Kiswahili. (17 June 2004). BBC News World Service [Online]. Available at http://news.bbc.co.uk/2/hi/africa/3816717.stm

Ministry of Education (1984). *Educational system in Tanzania towards the year 2000.* Dar es Salaam: Ministry of Education.

Ministry of Education and Culture [MOEC] (1999). *Basic education statistics in education 1994-1998.* Dar es Salaam: Ministry of Education and Culture.

Ministry of Education and Culture [MOEC]. (1997). *Sera ya Utamaduni* [Culture policy]. Dar es Salaam: Ministry of Education and Culture.

Ministry of Education and Culture [MOEC]. (1996). *Basic education statistics in Tanzania (BEST) 1994 regional data.* Dar es Salaam: Ministry of Education and Culture.

Ministry of Education and Culture [MOEC]. (1995). *Education and training policy.* Dar es Salaam: Ministry of Education and Culture.

Moore, S. F. (1986). *Social facts and fabrications: "Customary" law on Kilimanjaro, 1880-1980.* Cambridge, UK and New York: Cambridge University Press.

Norton, B. (1997). Language, identity, and the ownership of English. *TESOL Quarterly, 31*(3), 409-429.

Oxfam. (2001). *Bitter coffee: How the poor are paying for the slump in coffee prices.* [Online]. Available: http://www.oxfam.org.uk/policy/papers/coffee.htm. [2001, June 27]

Pan African News Agency (7 July 2004). *Mozambique's Chissano addresses summit in Kiswahili* [Online]. Available at http://web.lexis-nexis.com/universe/document?_m=d169edc652a500537f78e9a6a05a9118and_docnum=5andwchp=dGLbVzb-zSkVband_md5=bcb40a9f1517a40ca059aac91dcd65dd

Pennycook, A.(1998). *English and the discourses of colonialism.* London: Routledge.

Philipson, R. (1992). *Linguistic imperialism.* Oxford: Oxford University Press.

Raphael, L. (2001). *Language teaching in tatters-BAKITA.* Sunday Observer [Online]. Available at: http://www.ippmedia.com/observer/2001/07/08/observer7.asp.

Rogers, S. G. (1972). *The search for political focus on Kilimanjaro: A history of Chagga politics, 1916-1952, with special reference to the cooperative movement and indirect rule.* Unpublished doctoral dissertation, University of Dar es Salaam.

Rugemalira, J. M., Rubagumya, C. M., Kapinga, M. K., Lwaitama, A. F., and Tetlow, J. G. (1990). Reflections on recent developments in language policy in Tanzania. In C. M.

Rubagumya (Ed.), *Language in education in Tanzania* (pp. 25-35). Clevedon, England: Multilingual Matters.

Samoff, J. (1999). *No teacher guide, no textbooks, no chairs: Contending with crisis in African education.* Paper presented at the 43rd Annual Meeting of the African Studies Association, November 11-14.

Setel, P. (1995). *Bo'n town life: Youth, AIDS, and the changing character of adulthood in Kilimanjaro, Tanzania.* Unpublished doctoral dissertation, Boston University.

Skutnabb-Kangas, T. (30 September 2004). *The one common feature in multilingual schooling: Politics and emotions rule while research results are invisibilised.* Paper presented at the International Symposium on Imagining Multilingual Schools, Teachers College-Columbia University.

Skutnabb-Kangas, T. (2000). *Linguistic genocide in education—or worldwide diversity and human rights?* Mahwah, NJ: Lawrence Erlbaum.

Swahili baffles African leaders. (6 July 2004). BBC News World Edition [Online]. Available at http://news.bbc.co.uk/2/hi/africa/3871315.stm

Vavrus, F. (2003). *Desire and decline: Schooling amid crisis in Tanzania.* New York: Peter Lang.

Vavrus, F. (2001). *"Running away from temptation": School fees and sexual risk in an era of AIDS.* Paper presented at the Comparative and International Education Society, March 14-17, Washington, D.C.

In: Current Discourse on Education in Developing Nations
Editors: M. Afolayan, D. Jules et al. pp. 51-62
ISBN 1-59454-774-2
© 2006 Nova Science Publishers, Inc.

Chapter 5

COLONIAL HERITAGE AND THE DIMENSIONS OF KENYAN EDUCATION: THE CASE OF KIKAMBA SCHOOLS

Chang'aa Mweti
University of Minnesota, Duluth

INTRODUCTION

This chapter will try to shed some light into how colonial heritage affected storytelling within the Akamba community of Kenya. It will also touch on historical as well as cultural overviews of the Akamba community. It looks at the various factors that eroded Akamba storytelling in the formal setting, including colonialism, the MAUMAU movement, informal education and so on. Finally, the essay will conclude by defining how our cultural filters construct our world view.

WHERE IN THE WORLD IS UKAMBA!

In what follows, I will provide a broad overview of the Akamba people of Kitui District, East of Kenya. In this culture, one person is often referred to as "Mukamba" while two or more are called "Akamba." Sometimes "Kamba," is used as the plural form, but this is usually an evidence of a lack of proficiency in the use of the language and of the knowledge of the culture. In reality, the Akamba people speak "Kikamba" as their language, while "Ukamba" is their land. This may be interchangeably used with "Ukambani." Kenya is a major country in East Africa with a long history of connectivity to the outside world. Indeed, it was to my amazement when I got to the United States and asked an American student at my new university whether or not he knew Kenya. The student looked at me and said, "Is that a new kind of soap? I was shocked at the ignorance so blatantly expressed. In geographical terms, Kenya covers approximately twenty five thousand square miles, which is about a quarter the size of Britain, or twice the size of Holland (Mbiti, 1983). The country is divided into provinces. They are: Eastern, North Eastern, Western, Central, Rift Valley, Coast, Nyanza and Nairobi provinces. Each province is divided into "districts" and each district is divided into "divisions," and each division is divided into "locations." Each location is divided into "sub-locations," and each sub-location is divided into "villages." Ukamba land lies in the Eastern Province of Kenya. It stretches southwards from the equator, towards the Kenya-Tanzania border, and westwards from near the shores of the Indian Ocean towards the Kenya hinterland. During the colonial administration, Ukamba was divided into two districts. The first was Machakos district on the west, and the second one was Kitui on the east. This chapter mainly concentrates on the Akamba of Kitui, where I come from. However, as recently as 1993, Ukamba was further divided into four districts, thus Machakos was split into Machakos and Makueni districts, while Kitui became Kitui and Mwingi districts. The size of the land has not increased, but the population has, and to make it easier for the Neo-colonial administrative purposes, the Kenyan government has created more districts, not only in Ukamba land but also in other parts of the country.

AKAMBA STORYTELLING AND ITS ERODING FACTORS

In Akamba formal schooling, storytelling is practiced only in the lower grades 1-3. As students move up in grade levels, storytelling diminishes and almost vanishes by the time they complete the twelfth grade equivalent. Having been a teacher myself in Kitui district, I believe several factors contribute to this trend, among which are: Storytelling is not a part of the primary (elementary) school curriculum; storytelling is not tested in Kenya Certificate of Primary Education (K.C.P.E); Kikamba language is discouraged in schools, and pupils are not comfortable telling their stories in English; when used at all, storytelling is formalized, metamorphosing into different names e.g. (composition, passage, essay). It thus often escapes the immediate experience of the child's life; well-known local storytellers are not invited to come to schools to tell stories, supposedly because they do not speak English, and therefore are not considered "educated;" and all of the above have taken place due to colonial legacy, a historical phenomenon which I will further discuss later in the chapter.

COLONIALISM: GENESIS AND METHODS

The colonizing of Africa started more than a hundred years ago, when the capitalist powers of Europe sat in Berlin in 1884 and divided up the entire continent of Africa into colonies. The three major powers involved were Britain, France and Germany. The British, which colonized Kenya, applied indirect rule as their method of administration. This was a system whereby the Queen/King of England ruled through a governor, provincial officer, district officer, chief and assistant chief in Kenya. In this way, the African chiefs and their assistants were used as "puppets" by the colonial regime. There were two types of colonization: "standard colonization" and the "settler colonization." Standard colonization meant a number of Europeans were sent to administer a colony for a period of time without the intention of staying for good. It was easier for these colonizers to leave when the Africans demanded their freedom. On the other hand, settler colonization meant the opposite. More

Europeans were sent to settle in the colonies for good. It was particularly in these areas where bitter and bloody battles were fought seeking independence from the colonizers. Such countries included: Kenya, Algeria, (Rhodesia) the present Zimbabwe, and (Nyasaland) the present Malawi. The fight was tense because the crucial factor was land. The African attitude towards land was different from that of the Europeans who held the notion that land was a commodity for sale. On the contrary, Africans did not view land that way. For them, land belonged to all people. It was the link between the living, the dead and posterity. This was because Africans communicated with their ancestors through land, offering sacrifices of food or drink, poured down, and so on. The concept of "unoccupied land" as wasteland was alien to Africans.

The Maumau

In Kenya, there was a strong movement which resisted the European domination. It was known as the MAUMAU, which was an acronym in Kiswahili language for Mzungu (European); Aende (Go); Ulaya (Europe); Mwafrika (African); Apate (Get); Uhuru (Freedom). This movement started in 1952 and gained ground until 1955. Many Kenyans as well as Britons died in the struggle. The physical presence of the colonizers which had started in the 1880s ended in the 1960s. Ghana, formerly called (Gold Coast), was the first Black African country to attain independence in 1957, under the late president Kwame Nkrumah. By 1960, 21 countries had attained independence. By December 1966, there were 32 independent African countries. In fact, in less than ten years, 90% of Africa's population had attained political independence.

Colonial Impact

The impact of colonialism was great. Mazrui (1986) contends that colonialism and Christianity brought a different moral order, whereby important Western and Christian ethical factors entered the domains of African systems of life. This conflict or friction was felt when intruders asked questions like whether it was right for a man to have more than one wife, or whether sexuality outside marriage was sinful, and many other questions. The West was using its cultural lenses to look at the African culture. Tarr (1994) takes this notion of colonialism as it pertains to misconceptions, and warns that "cultural filters inhibit clear perception" (p.62). These were major moral dilemmas for Africa implying a permanent change as a result of colonialism and Christianization, which prompts Mazrui (1986) to ask, "How then could their impact be anything but an epic drama?" (p.14). I would like to point out that Islam did not create as much friction as Christianity did among Africans. First, Islam did not penetrate deep inland, and second, Islam religion shared some common grounds with the African traditional beliefs, for example, marrying more than one wife, and honoring the traditional African dances, practices which Christianity denounced. Mazrui's argument is that it is unfair to use one's cultural lenses to measure the standards of another culture. As the Kikamba proverb cleverly puts it, "you can not see the picture, while you are in the frame."

From the perspective of certain Neo-Marxist critics and theorists, most of what is happening in Africa today is as a result of colonial legacy. Of course, this assumption carries both constructive and negative ramifications, the latter being the case most of the time. For example, the European model of education was introduced in Africa and clashed with the informal education of Africans. Colonialism imposed its control of the social production of wealth through military conquest and subsequent political dictatorship. The celebrated African creative writer and literary theorist Ngugi (1986) asserts

> ...but the colonialists most area of domination was the mental universe of the colonized, the control through culture of how people perceived themselves and their relation to the world. (p.16)

I consider this statement to be true simply owing to the colonial legacy present in educational institutions. There is the tendency for the African child to begin looking at himself/herself from the "outside." The alienation became even more reinforced in the teaching of history, geography, music and of course "storytelling", where the subliminal assumption was and still remains that the bourgeois Europe was always the center of universe. To situate this picture more succinctly, it is like we have two situations - the coming of European model of education which does not provide "our" storytelling, and the existing traditional model of informal education which thrives in storytelling model. Therefore, these two models (European and African) get mingled together, and in search of being "western" Fuller (1991), the African storytelling model becomes marginalized.

However, storytelling finds its way into the more advanced grades through the works of writers like Ngugi wa Thiong'o of Kenya, Chinua Achebe from Nigeria and Camara Laye from Guinea. The European model works against traditional ways. For example, every minute of the day is planned and more structured, but Africans are not used to learning that way in their informal setting. Hence, this becomes a period of confusion as schooling becomes less traditional and more formal.

INFORMAL EDUCATION AND THE AKAMBA COMMUNITY

The idea of informal education had been established in many African societies, including the Akamba people, even before the coming of the Europeans. In public discussions and meetings, wisdom was acquired and spread freely and equally to all members of one community. This knowledge, much of which had been assembled practically through one's experiences, was then passed from one generation to another by word of mouth. Some scholars would call this "informal" education because it was not "institutionalized." Kenyatta (1966) noted that informal education begins at the time of birth and ends with death.

For the Akamba people, this education was functional because the curriculum was relevant to the needs of the society. For example, Akamba education was family and community centered because the family and community were fully interdependent. Parents and community members knew the contents of the education that was handed down to the young people. Parents and community members were the 'teachers and exemplars' to follow, hence the education represented social and cultural continuity for the Akamba society.

COLONIAL EDUCATION AND CHRISTIANITY

With the coming of western education to the Akamba people, much of Akamba traditional or informal education was destroyed and learning was institutionalized and professionalized, and the mainstream of thought was concentrated on the child's education. Since education was aimed at children and adolescents, parents sent their children to school in great numbers. Parents sacrificed a lot in order to have their children acquire knowledge which missionaries and the colonial administration described as enabling them to earn more. However, the irony was that knowledge gained at this time was for mere literacy and a foreign way of life. Colonial education was designed to make the African a faithful subject to the colonizer. What the colonizer wanted was an educated labor force to help develop the colony's economy and provide chiefs and assistant chiefs capable of participation in "indirect rule" applied by the British. The missionaries, for their part, wanted the Africans to be able to read the Bible for easier conversion to Christianity. Thus, initially the education provided was related to reading the Bible, and preparation for baptism.

Those who were being converted into a new faith started looking at themselves from the eyes of "outsiders." Tar (1994) explains of a situation whereby an African student of his was going for his theological studies in America and was advised by his church thus, "Go to America and learn to preach like the white man preaches...do not come back here telling stories like untrained tribal preachers and Pentecostals do" (p.13). This is an apparent misconceptualization of the purpose of western education that made many Africans to believe that their traditions and storytelling were primitive, and that the white man never used stories in preaching. Not that the Europeans did not value storytelling, but I think their acts of storytelling were based on the European model. Moreover, their stories had no frame of reference which was vivid to the Africans because storytelling carries the unique features that characterize the society where it is narrated. Unfortunately, this ideology, or perception still remains among some Africans.

Ngugi (1993) in his recent book, *Moving the Center,* stresses the same notion from a different angle. He explains that under colonial rule, native cultures were repressed while through the school system other imported traditions were encouraged. Using his own personal experience as an example, he writes " For instance, in the school that I went to, Scottish country dances were allowed even as the so- called tribal dances were banned" (p.88). The colonial and Christian interventions were interwoven. For example, the Christian intervention into peoples' cultures is explained by revealing the adage heard all over Africa again and again, when Mendelsohn (1962) asserts,

> The missionary came to us and said, we want to teach you to pray! So the missionary told us to close our eyes. We closed our eyes and learned to pray. When we opened our eyes, there was a Bible in our hands, but our land was gone (p.21)

I may apply this cliché to the near annihilation of storytelling of the Ahamba people by saying that when the Akamba people opened their eyes, there was a Bible in their hands but their storytelling tradition was gone. In other words, the problems of educational mobilization could not be separated from the problems of adjustments to a new faith and its values. Therefore, it is clear that western education was aimed at converting the Mukamba to a new culture and a new faith, and those who came to it had to renounce certain aspects of the

Akamba culture and belief systems. The setting of education was changed. The individual no longer learned from the family and community, and the western educated individual was cut off from the family and community, as the education was acquired outside the home. Parents did not know what their children were learning. This western education was part of the change in the enlargement of social scale and this enlargement was not part of continuity, but a process of change. As a result, in learning the new, the old had to be challenged, discarded, or completely modified. For example, initiation rites were regarded as pagan, satanic and primitive and the school was completely separated from the family. Traditional storytelling was deemed primitive and thus useless. Old people were no longer viewed as source of wisdom. The western educated person was converted into a new faith that taught the individual that he/she had a soul rather than one that was connected across time and people to ancestors and future generations. Further, education also was viewed as a private individual possession. In a nutshell, the western capitalism had set in, and it became crystal clear that indeed all that the imperial powers attempted through schooling was to train the colonized for the roles that suited the colonizers.

POSTCOLONIAL PHASE

The move by African countries to attain independence was very swift, starting with Ghana in 1957. Kenya attained her independence from Britain in 1963, and Jomo Kenyatta became the first president. So, a post-colonial era was entered and Kenya expanded national systems of education to the fullest financial capacity. There was economic need to train manpower to take over vacant positions formerly held by foreigners. This was a process of Africanization in the sense that positions formerly held by foreigners were going to be taken by Africans themselves. Initially though, the Africans in Kenya did not accept easily western education (due to its demands as explained during the colonial era), and it took some time before they changed this attitude towards education. Why did Kenyans finally accept western education? A major factor in this move was the conviction that the monopoly of high positions in the modern urban sector held by the Europeans and Asians during the colonial era was due to the type and quality of the education they had received. So, Kenyans felt that if they themselves were to exercise real power in their country after independence, they had to acquire an education similar to that of the Europeans.

Therefore, the British educational pattern was confidently copied in Kenya after independence. By the same token, the British curriculum was duplicated and in this context, this type of curriculum lacked relevance and imagination for the Kenyan people it was meant for, and indeed the Akamba people as I will explain later. It is at this era where as a student and a teacher, my personal experience will aid me a lot. Dewey (1964) stresses how important it is for the curriculum to be relevant to the child's experience. To this end, he writes,

> The child is taken out of his familiar physical environment, hardly more than a square mile or so in area, into the wide world -yes and even to the bounds of the solar system. His little span of personal memory and tradition is overlaid with long centuries of history of all people (p.340)

At this point I feel the need to bring in the notion of "culturally relevant pedagogy" as a vital tool in teaching and learning. Ladson-Billings (1994) treats this notion with great expertise and explains the approaches applied by some successful teachers of African-American children. When the teaching does not build upon the child's cultural understanding of the world around him/her, the teaching is bound to fail. Ladson-Billings writes,

> By building bridges or scaffolding that meets students where they are (intellectually and functionally), culturally relevant teaching helps them to be where they need to be to participate fully and meaningfully in the construction of knowledge. In contrast, assimilationist teaching assumes that the students come to class with certain skills and suggests that it is impossible to teach those who are not at a certain skill level (p. 96)

This underscores my contention about the British curriculum which could only expose Akamba children into cultures for which they had no frame of reference, in the words of Paulo Freire, they cannot name their world! For example, the Akamba children were exposed to alien concepts heavily clothed in British patterns and traditions. The child's environment and his/her cultural frame of reference were not considered. Children read primers depicting the British country side, English animals, trees and seasons. For example, if an Akamba child reads a sentence like: "Jim and Sue were making a snow man under a birch tree while a bear trotted by" s/he has no idea what a birch tree or a bear look like, neither would the child know what snow is. Kamuti (1992) gives a more vivid and personal example as a Kamba student himself, under these circumstances, when he says:

> One American teacher told us that on every Christmas Eve night, Santa Claus flies in his sled drawn by eight reindeer and goes down the chimney of every house delivering gifts in colorful boxes tied with ribbons to give to good children. We had no idea what he was talking about (p.132).

The kind of stories read by the Akamba children was so detached from their environment that learning was difficult. The storytelling was baptized and referred to "composition, writing of passages, essay writing and dictation." In other words, the African storytelling was deemed primitive...just as the people themselves. School examinations were still imported from Europe and set by people who were removed from the immediate child's environment. Another crucial issue was that of teaching methods which were repetitive and laborious. In fact, an authoritarian and impersonal attitude characterized the social contact between teacher and pupil as I am about to explain in my discussion about teacher and student relationship.

TEACHER-STUDENT RELATIONSHIP

As a carryover from colonialism, African teachers did not connect with their students' feelings. Some humiliated their students physically and psychologically. Like the colonial masters, teachers made sure that their presence was felt by their students. Growing up I can still recall during my primary schooling in the late sixties, teachers called us all kinds of names. If you did not understand an alien concept, the teacher would call us names like: monkey, donkey or cow. The kind of questions they had for us were not guided to help us use our creativity or imagination. If a teacher asked a question, in most cases there was only one answer which was based on the teachers' train of thought. This brings to memory a personal experience. One day, a teacher came to our third grade class and said, "If I give you two cats today, and three cats tomorrow, how many cats of yours will you have altogether?" We raised our hands, and he chose me to respond. "Six", I said. The whole class was shaking with suppressed chuckle as he approached to hit me since according to him and the class, I had not responded correctly. However, I explained that my father had given me another cat at home; and if he, the teacher, gave me his five cats, added to the one I already had, I would end up with six cats of my own!

NEO-COLONIAL PHASE: LANGUAGE MATTER

Next I turn to language issue and show how our Kikamba language also was suppressed by the school system. The students were made to feel ashamed of their own mother-tongue, and this affected the state of storytelling. Language is a very sensitive issue, and has raised heated debates in many cultures. In the United States, like in many societies of the world, it is even a political topic of discussion. For example, some of the former conservative presidential candidates like Pat Buchanan had argued for the need to make English the official and sole language of the U.S. Questions like which will be the official or national language of any given society are entertained all the time in many societies. Views that language can be divisive or unifying can be considered myths according to Ayo Bamgbose, the Nigerian scholar who argues:

> There are five major myths about language in Africa, namely: many languages divide, one language unites, imported language is neutral, imported language is more efficient and finally African languages are inadequate (Lecture, UW-Madison, March 6, 1995).

I argue that language issue affects storytelling in education among the Akamba community. Nobody can talk about language issues and escape the mention of both colonialism and Christianity which are the pillars of ideologically loaded concepts such as racism, prejudice, imperialism, capitalism. To this end, Ngugi (1986) writes: "The choice of language and the use to which language is put is central to a people's definition of themselves in relation to their natural and social environment, indeed in relation to the entire universe" (p.4). Every major European language such as English, French, German or Portuguese, etc used in any African country, was not the choice of the Africans themselves, but the language was imposed on them by the colonial powers. As I have mentioned before, the Akamba storytelling was told in the evening around the fireside in the Kikamba language. Children listened to the struggles against nature and other animals, all of which reflected real struggles in the human world. Cooperation as the ultimate good in the community was a constant theme. Our storytellers made the stories come alive through the use of words and images and the inflection of voices. We therefore learned to value words for their meanings and nuances. So Kikamba for us was not a mere string of words but had suggestive powers well beyond its immediate and lexical meanings.

When the Akamba child went to school, this harmony was broken as the language of his/her education was no longer the language of his culture. Our Kikamba language was deemed inferior to English. It was only in lower grades that vernacular was taught, and as a student moved to upper grades, his/her language was suppressed. One of the most humiliating experiences was to be caught speaking Kikamba in the vicinity of the school. The child was severely punished by way of corporal punishment, which ranged from three to six strokes of cane on the buttocks! Or, the culprit was made to carry a metal around the neck with inscriptions such as "I am a donkey, or I am a cow, or I am stupid". In short, we were made to be ashamed of our own language and our creativity and imagination were curtailed. When I became a teacher in the mid-seventies, I fell into the same brainwashing, and insisted that Kikamba should not be spoken in the school compound! That is why I would never buy the argument that the colonial impact was shallow. The physical presence of the colonial administrators was brief, but the effects or impact of their domination last to this day, in some ways, however subtle it may be. We were made to read stories from other cultures and our own stories were marginalized. How in the world could the Akamba storytelling survive in the formal setting under these conditions?

On the other hand, English was encouraged and those who excelled in it were highly rewarded. As one would imagine, the education system in Kenya, or in Africa in general, has had the structure of a pyramid: thus a broad primary base, a narrowing secondary middle, and even narrower University apex. Parents also reinforced the learning of English because they thought the more their children acted like Europeans, the more opportunities they would have. (Mutava, 1981) So, the fate of "storytelling" in education among the Akamba people was not only the language aspect per se, but the entire change of attitude towards our culture. The attitude was negative because people had internalized claims that they were inferior, and that their language and culture were inferior, as everything dealing with tradition was deemed primitive and backward. Children stopped communicating with their parents because they were now not sharing the same mental world and this has adverse cultural effects.

Young people stopped respecting their culture. When I taught at Kiangwa Primary School, in my village of birth, I organized groups of pupils, boys and girls and composed folksongs. We sang these songs on special occasions or just for enjoyment. The songs were themselves like interesting stories that the community understood and appreciated very much because they touched their lives. Some of my colleagues disrespected my methodology wondering how an "educated person" could lower himself and sing like the traditional women who were not educated! Teachers were not alone in this view, because some members of the community, while not rebuking me, asserted that I could have become a "witch doctor" if I had never gone to the Western school.

I am not arguing that the learning of English should not have taken place. I am advocating the "respect" for the child's mother-tongue, Kikamba, which should aid the learning of any other foreign language, without making children feel ashamed of Kikamba. I think any language policy, whether internal or external, would be damaging if it denies a child the opportunity of using his/her mother-tongue as a starting point in understanding the world. It is like swimming upstream. Teaching in the mother tongue provides vital link between the home, the community, the local environment and the school. The importance of a mother tongue is explained by Okech and Hawes (1986) when they say this:

> In order to investigate the most appropriate language policy for the efficient primary education of Yoruba children in Nigeria, the University of Ife, in association with the ministry of education, set up the Ife Six Year Project. The project confirmed what common sense

would have probably have suggested, namely, that children enquire, enjoy and participate when they are learning in a medium they understand (Yoruba) and are far more passive when they are struggling with the medium of a foreign language (English) (p.100).

CULTURALLY RELEVANT AND IRRELEVANT PEDAGOGY: KENYA VS U.S.A

We understand the world around us through our cultural lenses. It becomes difficult when we find ourselves exposed to different cultural frameworks as I am about to explain. For example, I came to the United States in 1986, and lacking proper guidance I registered for a course in political science at UW-Whitewater, Wisconsin. I did not know anything about the culture of the United States, let alone its politics. Our professor used terms like liberal, conservative, far left, far right, moderate democrat/republican.... terms which were alien to me, and which had no frame of reference in my upbringing. I had no idea what he was talking about. I barely got a "C" grade in that course. I would like to explore this concept of culturally relevant pedagogy from a different perspective. I have already discussed how difficult it was for us African children to learn alien concepts from a European perspective. Now, would the "West" experience the same frustration if the teaching offered to them was outside their frame of reference? In order to answer this question, I will use my personal teaching experience both in Kenya, and in the U.S, using "storytelling" as my teaching methodology, and the aspect of relevance or irrelevance will be depicted in the process.

I started teaching in the mid-seventies, and after teaching at Kivyuni, Wingemi, and Ikutha primary schools, I was finally transferred to Kiangwa Primary school, in my village. I taught the highest grade which was seventh. Either from the respect for my culture, or some other inner motives, I felt that our students needed to read something they could relate to. Between 1974 and 1976, I wrote seven stories, but I will use just one of the seven stories to illustrate my point. There were no typewriters in our school, and no duplicating machine either. I used my hand to write over forty copies throughout the night in order to have each of my pupils have his/her copy of my story as I wrote the questions on the blackboard the next day.

In almost every story question, my seventh graders scored very highly, and they were interested in the stories. They could relate to some of the themes in my stories. When I talked about lizards getting into my house as I slept, they had seen many lizards in their homes as well. When I mentioned in my story about my garden helper missing, not only did they understand, they knew him by his name. I was talking of a world they knew because we shared the same experience. They were only struggling with the aspect of the analytical and grammatical parts which were good exercise for their brains as I helped them out in the grammatical challenges. My "storytelling" to them was culturally relevant.

In one of his recent books, *Moving the Centre: The Struggle for Cultural Freedoms*, Ngugi wa Thiong'o (1993) treats this same notion under the title "Freeing Culture from Eurocentrism." He explains about his own schooling at Makerere University in Uganda, where they read the writings of British Isles from the time of Chaucer, Spencer and Shakespeare up to the twentieth century of T.S. Elliot, James Joyce and Wilfred Owen. He writes:

It was actually at Makerere University College, but outside the formal structure that I first encountered the new literatures from Africa and Caribbean. I can still recall the excitement of reading the world from a center other than Europe...Even titles like Peter Abraham's "Tell Freedom" seemed to speak of a world that I knew and a hope that I shared (p.4).

I brought all my original stories to the United States and in the fall of 1988, UW-Whitewater, sent me to Parker High School in Janesville, Wisconsin, to start student teaching. My areas were English and Theater, dealing with seniors in High School. I chose the shortest and simplest of all my seven stories and gave it to the school secretary to type it for me. Parker High School students did not score as high as my seventh graders in Kiangwa Primary School had scored many years back. The highest score was 18 out of 20, i.e. 90%, and the least score was 5 out of 20, i.e. 25% for the scores. The students were unhappy, and they lost interest in re-reading the story for our corrections. I could see frustration on their faces. Some even said that the story was "stupid" and did not make sense to them. There is no better example for me than this, to explain how culturally irrelevant pedagogy can impede the learning of an individual be it a child or an adult.

Let us look at my story more closely. It is loaded with my cultural baggage most of which was alien to these white middle class high school students. For example, the "beauty and behavior" assertion, in connection with marriage in my second paragraph had no cultural frame of reference to them. Marriage by "customary law" third paragraph was an alien concept too. In my fourth paragraph, the notion of somebody's wife entertaining the entire family, husband's friends, relatives and parents might have been an insult to the female students at Parker High School! Marriage in the Akamba society is a union between two families/relatives, while in the west; it is a union between two individuals.

Finally, the style of questioning was itself different. Now, I was asking the "West" to look at the world not from their center, but from a different center. As a result, they concluded that the story was "stupid," a term that culturally shocked me; for in my 13 years of teaching experience in Kitui, Kenya, I had never heard a student term his/her teacher's work "stupid." These stories are powerful tools in demonstrating the notion of culturally relevant/irrelevant teaching/learning.

SCHOLARLY VISION

I believe that there is no culture superior to another one, and that we understand the world around us through our cultural lenses. There is no serious lack of knowledge about Africa at this time and age, but what I believe is lacking is reliable quality in the knowledge that is available. Anyone who is seeking knowledge may be overwhelmed by what has already been gathered and stored away in a variety of sources and a variety of languages. However, much of this knowledge ranges from indifferent scholarship through rumors, to deliberate falsehood. Of course there are some enlightening studies as well.

There is no defensible reason I think, for promoting research and writing on Africa unless such endeavor is to lead to a genuine understanding of Africa. About two decades or so, of intensive and extensive research and writing have done much towards eradicating some of the worst myths and stereotypes about the image of Africa. In fact, in some areas, scholarship has shifted from total denigration to uncritical praise. It is my hope that the truth should be found somewhere in the middle, where Africa is neither beast nor super human, not devil nor archangel, just human and at home in the universe, generally making a mess of some of life's preoccupations but doing remarkably well at others.

The emergence of folklore as a recognized respectable academic discipline in America has coincided not only with the growth of African Studies here in the US, but also with the growth of "healthier attitudes" among African and African American scholars towards their own cultural traditions. Up until recent times, under the misdirection of Colonial and Christian-based educational programs, few scholars of African descent would consider the oral traditions of their people worth the attention of scholarly research. They had been brainwashed. Ironically though, many of them were at the same time condemning almost every foreign work on African culture. Ngugi wa Thiong'o of Kenya is among the pioneers who have led African scholars to "decolonize" their minds.

REFERENCES

Achebe, C. (1959). *Things Fall Apart.* New York, N.Y. 10036. Fawcett World Library.

Dewey, J. (1964). *On Education: Selected Writings.* London, The University of Chicago Press, Ltd.

Kamuti, K. (1992). *We The PanAfrikans: Essays on The Global Black Experience.* New York, New York.

Mazrui, A. (1986). *The Africans: A Triple Heritage.* Canada: Little, Brown and Company Ltd.

Mbiti, John S. (1969). *African Religions and Philosophy.* Nairobi, Kenya: University Press.

Mbiti, John S (1991). *Introduction to African Religion.* Nigeria, Heinemann International Literature and Textbooks.

Mendelsohn, J. (1962). *God, Allah and Juju Religion in Africa Today.* New York: Thomas Nelson and Sons.

Ngugi wa Thiong'o. (1986) *Decolonizing the Mind: The Politics of Language in African Literature.* Nairobi, Kenya: Heinemann, Kenya.

Ngugi wa Thiong'o. (1993). *Moving the Centre: The Struggle for Cultural Freedoms.* London:James Currey Ltd.

Okeech, Jack Green, and Hawes, Hugh. (1986). *Readings in Curriculum Development in Primary Schools.* Nairobi, Kenya: Kenyatta University Faculty of Education.

Tarr, D. Double Image: (1994). *Biblical insights from African parables*: Mahwah, New Jersey: Paulist Press.

Part II: Discourse on Gender and Education

Chapter 6

THE "BOTTOM POWER" CONCEPT: THE PHILOSOPHY OF THE FEMALE BARGAINING STRATEGY IN NIGERIA AND ITS IMPLICATIONS FOR SCHOOLING

Arit Oku-Egbas
Africa Regional Sexuality Resource Centre, Lagos, Nigeria

INTRODUCTION

"Bottom power" is a Nigerian coinage which embodies the concept and widely accepted belief that the female body is an invaluable asset and a source of power for the possessor, enabling her to have a certain degree of manipulative/bargaining power vis-à-vis those who may desire access to her body. (Emphasis appears to be placed on the general genital area though in the Nigerian context bottom refers largely to the backside and the flare of the hips; that which is visible to the eye. The size of the bottom appears to be important aesthetically; the more the backside swells, the wider the hips, the better. The ideal of this kind of anatomy is what is commonly called 'ikebe super'--where ikebe refers to the size and rotundity of a woman's backside and super has the usual meaning of very good or very delightful. Large breast (or bustline) is also important in as far as it contributes to what is generally called figure 8). But the breast does not feature much in the bottom power discourses perhaps because of its association with maternity.

Thus, in the context of the educational institutions, which is the focus of the research in this chapter, the assumption is that bottom power can become a substitute for brain power in gaining the female subject the fruits of education, among other benefits, crucial to her success and survival. This concept, in a sense, is not far removed from that which views the female body as a commodity in the economic sense, which can be exchanged for cash. This has developed into a phenomenon that has ramifications for even post-secondary education in Nigeria.

The point that needs to be made at the outset is that this conceptualization of bottom power is part and parcel of the socialization processes of Nigerians such that both men and women hardly question the nature of the transaction it embodies--why a woman/girl in an educational institution should be coerced into, or find herself in a situation whereby she has to contemplate, even if remotely, the sexual servicing of her teacher in order to obtain a good grade in school. Though shrouded in a hazy phrase, bottom power refers to a woman's ability to strategize, plan aforehand and negotiate the exchange of sexual intercourse for a good grade, a house, a job etc. In other words, the female, well aware that her body is labeled an "asset", in the sense that it is desired by the opposite sex, consciously uses the so-called "asset" to the best advantage whenever the opportunity arises.

Because of the lightness with which it is treated, its acceptability and the manner in which it is propagated, this conceptualization of bottom power very effectively conceals the fact that in more cases than not, it is no more nor less than a synonym for sexual harassment, most especially for the female participant who is under the influence, control and jurisdiction of her teacher.

At this point, it is perhaps necessary to emphasize that in order to better demonstrate the complexity of this phenomenon, the chapter will deal with the subject of bottom power on two levels. On one level, the chapter will show how Nigerian men and women are socialised to view and internalise the concept, and at another level, which is the main objective of the chapter, the reader will be made to see bottom power for what it really is, through the use of Critical Discourse Analysis. In a sense, the task here is a redefinition of an old concept.

Within the Nigerian context, therefore, the assumption is usually that a female student has exercised her powers of seduction--bottom power -- when the female student and her male teacher enter into this kind of sexual transaction. In which case, the female is viewed as the active agent, the one with the power, who sets an agenda for herself, initiates a sexual bargaining process with her body as sole bargaining chip; the aim of which is to obtain good grades, or some other advantages.

What this mind-set completely neglects or conceals is the fact that in many cases it is actually the male teacher who initiates the bargaining process but, in some instances, may leave it open to the student to make up her mind. However, given the power relations between teacher and student, more so in the Nigerian context, this carries an implied threat. The student is bound to be worried, and even scared. The fear that sanctions might be imposed may influence her final decision. So some teachers may actually make advances which appear non-threatening on the surface but rely on the students' "suppositions of the implied threat to support their demands" (Robson, 1993: 110). This, by its very nature, already constitutes sexual harassment, where sexual harassment is defined as "an asymmetrical power relationship in which the person with power tries to introduce sexual issues into the relationship" (Tyler and Boxer, 1996: 110).

The extreme, perhaps, is the scenario whereby the teacher, who certainly wields more power than the student, threatens her with sanctions - failure usually should the student not comply with his demands. There are of course cases where the female student actually initiates the sexual bargaining except that contrary to bottom power discourses, she cannot exercise sanctions in any form, and technically therefore, she has no power over her teacher. Should he choose to ignore her overture, she has no way of enforcing her demands. In which case, one can safely assume that, should the teacher be agreeable, he was not forced or coerced into it.

Given this background, it is easy to understand how sexual harassment of women by men has become entrenched within the system and permeated all sectors of society: the classroom, office, hospital, and so on. Indeed, according to a newspaper report, "Faces of Sexual Assaults on Women" (*Nigerian Tribune*, Tuesday 25 April 1995): "It (sexual harassment) may be between the boss in a workplace and his subordinate, between lecturers and students and most often medical personnels [sic] and patients. "Yet, because bottom power as it is conceptualised tends to distort the reality of the existing power relations between females and males, especially in the classroom and workplace contexts, sexual harassment is hardly viewed as such when it does occur. The females are in the circumstances held as largely responsible for and guilty of inviting whatever they get by way of harassment of this nature. This is largely a result of the bottom power they are assumed to possess and to wield to their personal gain and advantage.

As much as possible, however, to facilitate greater analysis and deconstruction of the concept of bottom power, and to allow for the fact that in certain cases female students do make use of the so-called bottom power, sexual harassment is minimally employed in this chapter and replaced by the term "sexual bargaining". The term is, however, used while recognizing the fact that the student is bargaining from a more vulnerable position; a position of less power. Unlike the teacher, the student's power is very limited. She possesses a body which her teacher desires and society eroticizes; to that extent, she can consider her body an asset. But that same body can be abused, especially within the student-teacher relationship. Hence, in a sense, the female student may be said to possess some degree of power but within a highly disempowering context.

Some may argue that cases may exist where both teacher and student enter into a sexual relationship on an equal and reciprocal basis. If, for the sake of argument, one accepts that this is a possibility and that both parties are able to ensure that their personal relationship has absolutely no influence on their business relationship, it would still appear quite suspect to on-lookers. This is perhaps why such student-teacher or employer-employee relationships are discouraged.

All put together, one is wont to agree with Robson (1993) that "there is some degree of ambiguity in many of the non-violent acts that are usually considered as sexual harassment". Requests for dates, for instance, "must be placed in context" before a verdict of sexual harassment is attributed to them. But, as she further notes, there are also clear-cut and unambiguous forms of sexual harassment "such as the explicit bargaining for sexual favors in return for academic or workplace rewards" (p. 110 emphasis added), which is what bottom power embodies.

THE PROBLEM

Like other sexuality-related topics, the concept of bottom power has not been much debated in formal or official circles in Nigeria. If addressed at all, it is largely in informal discourse where the issue is trivialized and jokes made about it. Women are constantly the butt of sexist, crude jokes revolving around bottom power in public transportation, on the streets, in bars and even in informal discourses within otherwise official circles such as offices and schools. This contrasts quite sharply with the silence more or less, in formal discourses, which are those which qualify for documentation. But with celebrated American cases like that of Anita Hill, in addition to the work of the several women's organisations (especially those associated with the higher institutions of learning), the topic of sexual harassment is becoming recognised as an important issue and is discussed much more openly, even in the press. (In October 1991, Hill, a professor of law in the United States brought allegations of sexual abuse, allegedly having occurred in the 1980s, against Clarence Thomas who was a presidential nominee to the Supreme Court. Though Thomas' appointment was eventually confirmed, for some, there remains a doubt as to who spoke the truth. What made the case even more memorable to Nigerians and others on the African continent was the fact that both accuser and accused were African-Americans. While for some Americans, she had done no more than wash the races' dirty linen in public, for others, "she had struck the most powerful blow yet, after two decades of feminist struggle, against sexual harassment of women in the workplace" (McKay, 1992:272). "The Anita Hill effect" as it has been described, brought on something akin to a "genderquake" in that "the balance of power as it relates to gender changed possibly for good. The 'story' of sexual harassment and how men and women saw it differently shook the country..." (Wolf, 1993: p.5)

It was only in 1989 that the National Council on Education set up a committee to look into the issue of sexual harassment in the more formal environment of the school system. But even in newspapers and policy documents, the dominant discourses tend to reiterate the bottom power mind-set, thus effectively placing the blame and responsibility on the female participants. As such, vulnerability of women in situations of sexual harassment within the school system for instance, is concealed or downplayed. When handled in this manner, the tendency is that the seriousness of the problem is greatly diminished. It is not seriously tackled and thus continues to occur unabated.

It follows from this that no effective legislation or policy is put in place to handle these problems relating to sexual harassment when they do arise in schools and neither are the girls equipped to cope with the awkward situations they may find themselves in as a result of this. These sexuality-related problems become a matter of greater concern when viewed in the light of the prevalent HIV/AIDS pandemic, other STDs and unwanted pregnancies.

At the same time, it is generally acknowledged that education is the key to empowerment of the African girl-child and provides the knowledge, skills and self-confidence necessary to participate in development processes. The Framework for Action to Implement the World Declaration on Basic Education for all stresses the need to remove every obstacle that hinders the active participation of women and further states that:

> Priority action should include educational programs for women and girls designed to eliminate the social and cultural barriers that have discouraged or even excluded them from the benefits of regular education programs and to promote equal opportunities in all aspects of their lives. (*The World's Women: Trends and Statistics*, 1995: 89)

OBJECTIVE OF THIS CHAPTER

The main objective of this chapter is to show that despite profuse references to women's (bottom) power and the wiliness they are purported to have derived from Eve, the first Woman, bottom power as it operates within the school system is at best an ambiguous asset. The reference to Eve, derived from the Biblical account in Genesis of the first created woman who persuaded her husband Adam to eat of the forbidden fruit, is a recurring theme in newspaper reports on sexual harassment. Elsewhere it has been pointed out that polemics against women are as old as history itself and were common for example during the late Middle Ages in Europe. "Generally speaking, the arguments were based on old misogynist themes; woman is cursed by the sin of Eve, crooked because made from a rib, bestial by nature, greedy and crafty" (Gallagher, 1981:ll). In the final analysis many female students, be they active instigators or merely coerced into the process, are still quite vulnerable in the bargaining that occurs. The emphasis here therefore is on the impact of sexuality on the empowering process of education of the female within the context of bottom power. Some of the major issues addressed in this study include, the conditions (or factors) that enable the bottom power phenomenon (and discourses) to flourish within the education system in Nigeria; structures that serve to propagate, perpetuate, and legitimize the bottom power syndrome while simultaneously trivializing its correspondent sexual harassment for women; the dynamics of the bottom power bargaining process within the classroom environment; the extent to which this process is disempowering to the female students; and how bottom power, as it is conceptualized, problematizes (or fails to problematize) the question of desire and pleasure as against the reality of risks, dangers of female sexuality.

METHODOLOGY

The empirical data for this research is culled largely from my personal experience as a Nigerian woman who was at first in the education system as a student, and later as a teacher. As aptly noted by Harding: "Knowledge is supposed to be based on experience..." (Harding, 1987 in Candiru, 1992:12). This is supported by documented evidence wherever available, especially media texts (newspaper articles). While my theoretical framework will be informed by a feminist critical viewpoint, my analytical framework will be based to a large extent on discourse analysis; to be more precise, Critical Discourse Analysis (CDA).

One major challenge in undertaking a project like this is to overcome the taboo surrounding the subject of sex/sexuality in formal discourse while at the same time propelling informal discourse into the academic sphere and lending it the same authenticity and power that is usually attributed to empirical research carried out in the positivist tradition. This is while bearing in mind that the larger proportion of social knowledge and human experience in general, cannot be measured in the laboratory complete with matching control experiments. The phenomenon of bottom power falls into this category. The reality is that the knowledge, experience and viewpoint of women take second place to that of men usually, are less valued and, hence, hardly qualify for documentation. This is why a feminist critical viewpoint, a woman-centered approach which documents a woman's view of bottom power is important in order to better understand the peculiar problem and the needs arising thereof.

"Feminist standpoint epistemology argues for a feminist research not only located in, but proceeding from the grounded analysis of women's material realities" (Candiru, 1992:12). This is one of many feminist researchers giving voice to the great need within academics to critique the polemics of patriarchy that conceives of exclusive and exhaustive divisions.., between a dominant or false and a subversive or true discourse. What is useful for us is the suggestion to be read out of Foucault's work that we "analyze the historically and discursively specific ways in which woman has figured as a constitutive absence" (Martin, 1992:285

emphasis added). The feminist standpoint lends legitimacy to women's voices, allowing women to also fill the position of knowers in academic discourse.

Macdonell puts it in another way, noting that epistemology on which the science of knowledge is based "seeks to provide a guarantee that some forms of discourse (but not others) by following the approved mode will give 'valid' knowledge" (1986:60). We owe a lot to Foucault in this regard because, as Macdonell aptly puts it, Foucault's work "covertly dismantles the trap." Foucault gave researchers a chance and the freedom to enquire from angles other than prescribed ones.

Meanwhile, Critical Discourse Analysis, the main tool of analysis in this chapter, focuses on the role of discourse in the (re)production of dominance. Where dominance is defined as the "exercise of social power by elites, institutions or groups that results in social inequality including political, cultural, class, ethnic, racial and gender inequality" (van Dijk, 1993:248-249). CDA assumes a political agenda in that the ultimate aim is to achieve change through critical understanding of social problems. In addition, it provides the analytical tools for examining the relation between society, discourse and social cognition. Social cognition is a key issue here because it deals with what has been termed 'mind management' allowing us "to link dominance and discourse" and "explain the production as well as the influence of dominant text and talk" (van Dijk, 1993:257). This is achieved by highlighting the relationship between text, talk, social cognition, power, society and culture.

POWER, DISCOURSE, AND THE CONSTRUCTION OF REALITY

It is only fair to ask in this section that whose reality is being constructed here? Is it the Woman's Body? Whose power is contested, and whose is wielded?). The emphasis here is on examining some of the structures which serve to create, propagate, perpetuate, legitimate and reproduce dominant ideology even when the ideology is so entrenched, that it tends to distort reality. The key concepts to be tackled include power, discourse and the role of discourse in the "(re)production and challenge of dominance" (van Dijk, 1993:249) within the basic structure of patriarchy, seen from the perspective of feminism. The role feminism plays here is to provide one with an alternative lens with which to view society and its associated discourses, and to show that there is (an)/are alternative form(s) of reality. Parpart and Marchand (1995) have noted that human subjects understand and experience life within a discursive and material context. This context, particularly the language/discourse that "explains" the concrete experiences of daily life, influences and shapes the way individuals interpret reality (p. 3). It is important to note that alternative media (for example feminist publications) produce alternative discourses, which counter the discourses of the dominant media. But usually, the alternative media are limited by several factors including lack of political clout, limited financial resources and technical infrastructure for propagating their own views. Hence, the dominant discourses tend to hold sway over alternative voices.

The important thing to note, therefore, is that members of a society tend to construct/interpret reality based on prevalent discourses, among other influences, which usually mirror the dominant ideology-- the beliefs, thoughts and ideas of those with social power in that society. Social power, van Dijk notes, is based on privileged access to socially valued resources, such as wealth, income, position, status, force, group membership, education or knowledge (1993: 254).

In patriarchal societies (a term applicable to societies in both the North and South), these resources are controlled by men, or overwhelmingly in their hands, and form the backbone of male power in these societies. In patriarchal societies, it is the men who have special access to and control of discourse,' they are the ones who have most to say in every sphere of human existence and interaction: in the education system, religion, the courts of law, in government, in decision-making, culture and in the mass media. The media are particularly important because they are playing an ever expanding, crucial and influential ideological role as socializing agent, as well as in the molding of public opinion. Ideologically, media are seen as the "contemporary mediators of hegemony" in concert with other Ideological State Apparatuses (a term coined by Althusser) which include institutions such as religion, education, politics, the law and culture (van Zoonen, 1994: 34).

Recognizing the extent of the power and influence the media (dominant media especially have in controlling discourse and the public mind,[8] it is not surprising that, like other crucial social resources, "newspapers in Africa [and doubtless in most parts of the world] are written by men, for men about the affairs of men..." (Longwe and Clark, 1992 in Gallagher and Quindoza, 1995: 17) Part of the role of dominant discourse, such as that propagated by male-dominated media such as newspapers, is to maintain the discourse-power relations in society. "There is no doubt," as Gallagher (1981) has noted, "that cultural images reflect and promote the values of the powerful" (p. 11). Dominant discourse achieves or maintains this status quo through various strategies which may include concealment of dominance, and control of social knowledge. Concealment of dominance operates in several ways. For instance what happens in the case of bottom power is that the discourses tend to distort the true picture of the power relations between a female student and her male teacher, such that the feeling people have is that the student is the one with power and in control. The other 'concealment strategy' is the manner in which the dominant discourses on bottom power tend to trivialize the issue, restricting it to the sphere of informal discourse and thus effectively concealing its broad effects on women.

According to Villarreal, the very thoughts of those in subordinate positions are said to be shaped by the ideology of a dominant class, which determines their wants and prevents them from thwarting the control exercised by those in command. (1994: 202) Van Dijk, one of the major proponents of Critical Discourse Analysis, explains this further when he says that power involves control "by (members of) one group over (those of) other groups" and this is usually achieved through "action" and "cognition" whereby "a powerful group may limit the freedom of action of others but also influence their minds." The crucial point, as he further explains, is that 'modern' and often more effective power is mostly cognitive, and enacted by persuasion, dissimulation or manipulation among other strategic ways to change the mind of others in one's own interest. It is at this crucial point where discourse and critical discourse analysis come in: No doubt, managing the mind of others is essentially a function of text and talk. (1993: 254)

But it is equally crucial that the reader understands the concept of mind management as it relates to text and talk, and hence, discourse. It serves to explain how that in some instances, dominance appears to be co- or jointly produced with the collaboration of the dominated. In other words, mind management can be so thorough or so effective that at some point, the dominated internalise, "accept dominance and act in the interest of the powerful out of their own freewill. This is where the term "hegemony" is applicable (van Dijk, 1993: 255).

It is, however, simplistic to imagine that where power is concerned, it is one actor wielding all the power to the disadvantage of a victim who is forced to succumb. In reality, we are speaking of complicated processes where the struggles are rarely between one actor who tries to carry out his or her will and others who are victims. Multiple negotiations are taking place... (Viltarreal, 1994: 204)

Even the actor with less power, less control over social resources, less control over discourse, is involved in the negotiations and bargaining to gain some degree of advantage in any form in which this kind of advantage can be got. Discourse, as earlier cited, "is the site where meanings are contested and power relations determined". In other words, discourse itself is not static. There is room for negotiations, room for alternative discourses to germinate even if the power behind the dominant discourse is so great that it casts doubts on, suppresses and strives to silence what otherwise might emerge as counter-hegemonic discourses, which can "challenge the power of hegemonic knowledge and offer alternative explanations of reality" (Foucault 1972; 1979; 1980; in Parpart and Marchand, 1995).

Given this background, there arises an urgent need to dismantle or deconstruct language/discourse in a given society in order to understand and analyze the way meaning is layered brick-by-brick to construct a given and accepted reality in that society. Then, and only then, can the researcher begin to see, as Foucault has aptly noted, that the so-called "truth" in that society is simply "a partial, localised version of 'reality' transformed into a fixed form in the process of history" (Parpart and Marchand, 1995: 2).

DECONSTRUCTING BOTTOM POWER DISCOURSES

In order to understand how meaning and reality are constructed within the context of bottom power, there is a need to explain the recurrence of Christian and Biblical images. To do this, one must take a backward gaze -- into history. Nigeria came under the influence of Christianity, first and foremost, through the freed slaves who were resettled in Sierra Leone from about 1792. Malaria made life intolerable for the early European missionaries and explorers so they depended more on the African converts who could better withstand the lethal (at least to Europeans) malaria fever. With time, efforts were made to overcome the hostile climatic conditions. Soon, churches (mainly Anglican and Methodist) and schools were set up in Abeokuta from about 1846, and later in Lagos. The Presbyterians also built churches and schools in Calabar and the Cross River regions. (Parrinder, 1969).

Of course, these initial efforts were later supported by colonial administrators who represented the economic and political interests of the British when they arrived later in the Nineteenth Century. However, what is modern day Nigeria came into being in 1914, when the two British protectorates of Northern and Southern Nigeria were merged, marking the official beginning of British colonial rule. Colonial rule came to an end with Nigeria's independence on October 1, 1960. Today, English is still the official language and remains the language of instruction in the schools, government ministries, law courts etc. The important thing to note, however, is the intimate link between the first formal schools and the Church. Education, in the sense that we know it today, was first introduced by the early missionaries in the missionary schools, initially run by the Europeans, and later by Nigerians, trained by the same missionary establishments (or affiliated institutions abroad).

This is not negating the fact that Islam has a strong influence in Africa. According to Parrinder (1969), "The Christian mission in Africa, apart from Nubia and Ethiopia, was cut off by Islam from the seventh century and was hardly renewed for eight hundred years" (p. 120). Nigeria also has a strong Muslim presence, being the most populous nation in Black Africa. In spite of these figures, formal education is more intimately associated with Christianity and the Church, than Islamic education which is more restricted and tends to concentrate on teaching the Koran and Arabic language. Yet it is formal education that grooms the civil servants, judges, journalists etc. who are the opinion makers and more likely to contribute to media output. In any case, whether Christian or Muslim doctrine, there is a point of confluence-- the belief that the woman's place is in the home as wife, childbearer, carer and homemaker. In fact, Judeo-Christian images and stories in the Bible, which are regular features of the bottom power discourses, tend to be constructed/formulated along the lines of binary opposites such as: good/evil, man/woman, weak/strong etc. These binary oppositions also feature in the bottom power discourses, especially in newspaper articles. When deployed within the context of bottom power, they are very effective in that they not only provide rich, vivid and familiar imagery but they tend to support and lend credence to the bottom power mind frame and discourses. Invariably, this serves to neutralize dissident voices.

THE SOCIO-CULTURAL CONTEXT OF BOTTOM POWER

"In recent times, discussions, arguments and counter-arguments on sexual harassments in the nation's tertiary institutions have reached a crescendo... Probably, more worrisome is the fact that the problem is not limited to tertiary institutions alone but the post primary schools as well" (Omosebi, *Nigerian Tribune,* Tuesday 24 October 1995). In fact, the problem is so pervasive that as the chapter will show, students in the primary institutions are also affected. Hence, when I speak of female students, the group includes students in the primary (ages 5-13), post primary (11-17) and tertiary institutions (ages 15 and above). As the age groupings indicate, age is not the important factor in determining the grade (class) of a student as it is in England for instance. Other factors include financial resources of students and their intellectual (at least in principle) abilities. It is not uncommon that a student is withdrawn from school pending the time when resources will be more available. When such a student returns to school, S/he will undoubtedly have younger classmates. Sometimes, a brilliant student can get double promotion. In other words, (s)he would skip a class and would be younger than other class members. So, in dealing with sexual harassment, I refer to female students in educational institutions generally. I do not share the opinion held by some Nigerians that being an older female justifies, or makes harassment by a male teacher more bearable.

It is widely accepted that education contributes to economic growth. As Tilak (1989) puts it, economic development is achieved, through its ability to increase the productivity of the population or the labour force in particular, which leads to *increase in individuals' earnings.* (p. 11 - Emphasis added)

Perhaps no one has imbibed Tilak's assumption better than the Nigerian parent. Education is valued very highly in Nigeria and most parents do all in their power to see that their children acquire as much of it as they are able to afford, since it is perceived as the main weapon against downward socio-economic mobility in a society in which affluence is revered and openly displayed, sometimes to obscene levels. For many poor families, the assumption is that educating the eldest child (son in particular) ensures that he will be able to pay the school fees for the younger siblings in due course. This is an old-age insurance scheme for the parents where welfare structures do not exist.

In discussing the education of female children, one must bear in mind the fact that even today, the education of female children in Nigeria takes second place. In the African setting as a whole, little attempt is made to hide the fact that men are considered more valuable than women in almost all aspects of life. As Agheyisi (1985) has noted,

> Traditionally, Nigerian society has carved out the women's place to be in the home, regarding her as an "object to be seen and admired (and used) -but not heard. Consequently, her job is childbearing and rearing...Most Nigerian parents' attitudes to (higher) education is biased against their female children. They are often readier to make financial sacrifices for their sons' than for their daughters' educational pursuits. (pp. 149 and 150)

Of course, this construction of reality along essentialist lines together with the discourses that sustain it, shields the fact that increasingly, Nigerian women, educated or not, take active part in economic activities outside the domain of the household. This is in addition to the productive and reproductive duties they have always done within the household. Today, Nigerian women are, perhaps, even more committed to providing for parents and younger siblings than Nigerian men. In fact this is not just a recently discernible trend. Denzer (1992) has observed that unlike the "ideal British wife" who did not work outside the home, "Yoruba women did not expect their husbands to provide the full support of their households." The reality in fact was that "in times of economic crisis such as the depression of the'1930s, women's incomes often saved families from severe hardship" (p. 117).

These socially constructed values surrounding femaleness inform the attitudes of girls towards education as well as the way male teachers view female students. Although the trend is changing, if somewhat slowly, the women (certainly much fewer than men) who have had access to education are still overly concentrated in what are considered as more-female disciplines or professions such as the clerical and service industries as well as in the arts, education and medical faculties of higher institutions of learning (Agheyisi, 1987). The reason for this can be traced back to the early missionaries, the mission schools, and the conception of education along essentialist lines, whereby girls were seen to require education basically to enable them fulfill socially dictated roles. Denzer (1992) observes that though girls in colonial Yorubaland, for example, received training in the early mission schools side-by-side with the boys, they however received vocational instruction considered appropriate to their sex. The girls were taught domestic science while boys "learned agriculture and the industrial skills and techniques necessary for the new jobs created in the colonial economy" (Denzer, 1992: 117-118).

Firstly, the socio-cultural and historical factors so far highlighted serve to socialise both girls and their male teachers into the mind-frame that girls are intellectually less capable than boys. Secondly, these assumptions provide the leeway for the kind of sexual bargaining explored in this chapter. All the ingredients to support the assumptions are there and are instilled into both men and women from childhood through social institutions, such as culture, tradition, religion, the family, the media and language, and reinforced by the schools.

The situation is further exacerbated by poverty, which is exemplified by the effects of structural adjustment programmes, which began in the 1980s. Certainly, should resources become scarce, the first to be removed from school are the girls. According to Rose (1995) presenting evidence from case studies, adjustment policies have an effect on the demand for education through the imposition of user charges and increases in other costs of schooling, such as costs of transport and learning aids, because of the differences in parental perceptions of opportunity and direct costs of boys' and girls' education, it has been observed that daughters are often withdrawn from school before sons in times of economic hardship. (p. 132)

Thus, for a girl-student fortunate to be in school, the generally held view, sustained by the bottom power discourses, is that sexual bargaining with teachers presents an option worth pursuing in order for the girl to be able to remain in school when faced with failure and/or repetition of a year. Earlier, attention was drawn to the fact that human beings understand, experience life and operate within a discursive and material context. This material and discursive context within which the human subject grows and is familiar with is informed by the dominant ideologies which are usually patriarchal in nature. This assertion is borne out by the fact that when female students face the threat of failure, for instance, some girls do resort to bargaining with their bodies. In the same way, a teacher who finds a student physically attractive may threaten her with failure, just so that he may have his way with her.

The extent to which socialisation rules the lives of individuals is further borne out by the fact that, sometimes, girls from reasonably comfortable backgrounds, with no obvious financial constraints, also resort to, or succumb to sexual bargaining. This is largely because bottom power discourses conceal the vulnerability of the female as student, and the gravity and consequences of the transaction involved. This is achieved by keeping the discourse essentially on the informal level, trivializing the practice and imbuing it with a false sense of ease and play, in which the male is depicted as being at a disadvantage, the loser, the one conquered. By and large, the girls who decide to employ this strategy feel they have a bargain: getting what they want almost for nothing, so to speak. But the situation is even more complicated than this.

In order to understand better the complex factors contributing to the said socialization processes and pervasive bottom power mind-set, one needs to examine more fully the Nigeria situation and the bottom power phenomenon. It is important to acknowledge that, important though education is in Nigeria, funds for acquiring it are not always easily available. Education is not free at any level although it was much better funded prior to the advent of structural adjustment. Attempts were made in the past in some parts of the country to make primary education free; but such attempts did not succeed for very long. The oil boom period of the 70s was a period of plenty for those in state-funded schools. And even in tertiary institutions, fees and meals were so heavily subsidized that the privileged few who could gain admission to university studied almost for free. But according to statistics, in the 1979/80 academic session (immediately prior to the SAPped 80s) when the female population was documented to be highest, "for every female undergraduate, there were about six male undergraduates!" (Agheyisi, 1987:151). The statistic speaks for itself; even in times of plenty, females were still highly disadvantaged.

However, from that period of plenty, Nigeria was catapulted into a period when many students (even those from previously middle and lower-middle class homes) could not be assured of three meals and some could not pay for accommodation. The situation paved the way to various kinds of bargaining, initiated by male staff and at other times by the female students. For example, Robson (1993) reports that following the report of a sexual harassment committee in 1990, female students in Ahmadu Bello University "started complaining about sexual harassment from both lecturers and administrative staff especially those entrusted with allocation of hostel rooms to female students" (p. 113).

Under the stringent circumstances, some of the students learnt to depend on a single meal a day, while others scrounged and scraped to put together a single meal. Nevertheless, there is always a general feeling, expressed especially by the male students, that the situation can never be as bad for female students as it is for the males. The female students, it is' said, could always resort to using their bodies to get whatever they want. The point is that female students who choose to, or who under pressure are coerced into sexual bargaining in exchange for good grades or other advantages are not always the poorest students. Actually in this regard, some girls were very strategic. Having come to terms with the fact that they had to seek alternative source(s) of income, they chose to associate with one boyfriend economically buoyant enough to supply their needs rather than going with several men. While some female students may see the commoditization of their bodies as an escape path, there have been many others who have resisted and found other options.

"Sex" is not a subject that Nigerian parents discuss with the children. When parents struggle to pay school fees and find pocket money, they make it abundantly clear that they expect value for their money in the form of acceptable educational outcomes. Few, if any, girls can go home and discuss problems of sexuality with their parents. And, by and large, those female students who are confronted with sexual bargaining cannot even discuss the issue with their parents. They conceal the fact from their parents by whatever means they can invent. This of course gives unscrupulous male teachers the chance to go to extreme lengths to have their demands met, with no fear of repercussions.

This is coupled with the fact that in the African setting, the teacher figure is one that the community at large (parents, children and leaders) respect and reverence. In some parts of Nigeria, girls are still expected to kneel when greeting their teachers. Nigerian culture for instance encourages children, and especially girls, to be obedient and respectful of older people generally. A child must speak to an adult only when spoken to and disagreeing with an adult is almost tantamount to disrespecting the adult. In fact a younger person is not expected to make eye contact with an older person when addressing the elder. Many a time, even in the lecture rooms of tertiary institutions, a student may choose to keep her/his opinions to her/himself rather than be seen to openly disagree with the lecturer.

In a scenario like this, it is unlikely that a female student would be able to stand up to a teacher who demands sexual favours, even if it disgusts her. Much less can she resist the teacher if he threatens her. Neither is she likely to tell her parents, especially if she is from a poor home in the villages or rural areas where resources and schools are not easily available. Even in big cities like Lagos where the middle class, more affluent, pampered students can be found, broaching a sex-related problem with a parent can still present a problem, though it is common among this social class, for a parent to protest over a teacher whipping a child. In some instances, depending on how influential the parent is, a teacher may be fired, or corporal punishment prohibited in the school, based on such a complaint. The point being made here is that the tabooing of sex as a subject of discussion is a great disadvantage to girls faced with sexual harassment. It leaves them with very little scope for protest or action, irrespective of social class.

In fact, in some instances, parents have been accused of indirectly encouraging, or at least turning a blind eye to this type of bargaining between their daughters and male teachers. A girl returns home complaining (but perhaps in guarded language) that a male teacher "disturbs" her or touches her unnecessarily. Some parents may take the offensive stance and ask why, for instance, the teacher picked her in particular out of the fifteen or more female students in her class. The implication is that the girl may have done something to arouse his interest and the most likely area of scrutiny would be the wardrobe of the girl.

Some other parent's response may be to scold the girl or warn her to face her studies "squarely," while reminding her of the sacrifices being made on her behalf and the percentage of the family's hard-earned income going into financing her studies. These responses, of course, mirror the bottom power mind-set and discourses where the woman is largely to blame even for the sexual misdemeanour of the male. Responses like these effectively serve to stop the girl from making any further complaints. She must seek a way to solve 'her' problem.

At this point, it is important to take a brief look at a period in the history of Nigeria when bottom power discourses were at their record high and became more or less acceptable in Nigerian phraseology. The 1970s is considered the oil boom years of Nigeria marked by an oil and oil products exportation euphoria during which Nigeria swung from being a self sufficient economy with a vibrant agricultural export sector (cocoa, palm products, rubber) to importing "food, stock fish, custom made wines and cars, frozen meat and chicken..." (Ihonvbere, 1994: 21), and the then popular American Uncle Ben's brand of rice. But the so-called oil boom years came to an end when the price of oil took the downward plunge at about 1979. This, and the cumulative effect of years of mismanagement of the economy, ushered in the structural adjustment era and its accompanying hardships in the mid-80s. To make matters worse, the Second Republic, which was Nigerians second attempt at a democratically elected civilian government, under President Shehu Shagari was described as "a major disaster that set the country back by over five decades," characterized by "political irresponsibility and intolerance, corruption, mismanagement, waste and the privatization of public office." (Ihonvbere, 1994: 118). This propelled the economy towards total collapse and marked a turning point in the history of Nigeria. There emerged types of "patron-client" relations whereby various factions sought to grab their share of what had become popularly known as the "national cake" through a "patron" occupying a "lucrative" position (Ihonvbere and Shaw, 1988). The result of this was that public funds were diverted to private hands. The elites took to looting the public purse while organising "wild all-night parties as prostitution, drug pushing and foreign currency speculation became lucrative business." (Ihonvbere, 1994: 21)

Bottom power discourses flourished simultaneously. The women who allegedly spent the men's money took the greater share of the blame; they were apparently more evil than the male elites and rulers who misused their privileged position as public office holders. And in the scheme of things, every female who was successful by Nigerian standards (i.e. owned a car, a house or was gorgeously dressed) was seen as using bottom power. The bottom power discourses of this period provided the basic framework which subsequent discourses built upon.

WICKED DAUGHTERS OF EVE, WEAK SONS OF ADAM: DISCOURSE ON SEXUAL HARASSMENT IN THE NIGERIAN PRINT MEDIA

"Men accused of committing sexual harassment should answer in like manner, 'the women whom God created that walked about naked make them to commit the crime'", is the advise given by Okebabs in the *Daily Sketch* (December, 1995) in a parody of the scene in the Garden of Eden where Adam makes excuses to God, -blaming Eve, for his apparent failure to abstain from eating of the forbidden fruit. Says Gallagher (1981), "The mass media's role is primarily to reinforce definitions and identities set in a framework constructed for and by men" (p. 30). The sample of articles from the Nigerian press, which address the question of sexual harassment bear testimony to this assertion. The following quotation, like the earlier one, carries most of the recurring elements of the bottom power discourses, including the scathing criticism of the way women dress.

In Nigeria when people talk of bottom power it is assumed this is the power exclusively of women - their sexual endowment to have their way and to exercise power over men. Hence, I disagree with Diane Elson's (1991) assertion with regard to bottom power in the West African context when she says: "Wives of wealthy and well-connected husbands can acquire resources easily and exercise what is expressively known as 'bottom power', and is a derivative of their husband's power" (p. 19). The discourses on bottom power are by their very nature derogatory and hence never associated with the sacredness of an institution like marriage. In fact, bottom power is a power vested in women, not men. It's as though women's bodies tend to cast a spell on men: bewitch them, so to speak. A married woman is never seen to be exercising bottom power if she can acquire lucrative contracts by virtue of her being married, unless she acquires them through another man who is not her husband. At worst she may be said to be using 'long leg' or just plain lucky. But if an unmarried woman acquires the same benefits through a male friend, this would be labeled bottom power because the assumption is that she got it by commoditising her body. The pity is that the label of bottom power would be plastered on her even if she did qualify for the contract.

"Women in the exercise of their bottom power would wear provocative dresses to interviews, to face tender boards [sic] and get whatever they want because of the weakness of the male." (Olutokun, *Daily Times* June 24, 1994:11). The motif of wicked females wielding their power to the detriment of weak males who fall prey to their potent sexual magic is a very visible one in many newspaper opinion articles which dwell on the topic of sexual harassment. It is also apparent that this is a discursive devise which tends to conceal the vulnerability of women in many of these situations. It also conceals the lust of the men who sometimes misuse their positions as authority figures: teachers, employers, to coerce women into sexual relationships. The discourses distort the reality of the power relations of men versus women in these situations.

In fact it is quite clear that the question, "Who is really harassing who? Is it the teacher harassing the student or the other way round," posed by a writer in another article, is merely a rhetorical question rather than a genuine quest for answers and solutions to the pressing problem of sexual harassment. For soon after posing the question, the said writer continues thus,

> ...by the time an average Nigerian (female) student leaves the secondary school, she has outgrown the school two times over. It is on record that some of these secondary school students are mothers... Added to this is the fact that these so called endangered species has [sic] perfected the art of calling the shots from behind so much so that it is now the teachers who are in trouble. (Omosebi, Nigerian Tribune 24 October, 1995. Emphasis added).

It is always the men, the teachers who are in trouble. The discourses imply that the women have no problems at all, and virtually ask to be sexually harassed. It follows that women, therefore, do not need protection by the law. This assumption appears to be lodged in the minds of those who attempt to devise or implement policies meant to deal with the problem. From the above excerpt, it's as though being a mother or being a female of a more mature age means one must be more amenable to harassment or renders sexual harassment less of a crime.

What seems equally obvious, even from the Biblical images which are generously deployed with regard to the sexual matters discussed, is the fact that the sexual bargaining is regarded a sin in which women are assigned the role of the devil. In this way, men are seen to be manipulated by forces beyond their control--evil as against the men's alleged human weakness. This biblical imagery is very effective in that it is one which most Nigerians, even children, can easily relate to. In essence, absolving men of blame means they can carry on this assault without any guilt feelings. It is the women who feel guilty or uneasy. They carry the burden of guilt for the society for dressing in "revealing and suggestive dresses that make men go crazy, hungry and thirsty for them," as one writer puts it. Yet, the situation is such that women have no control of.

Okebabs, in a previously cited article which carries the heading, "Women Should be More Cautious," professes to having "misplaced his condemnation" in the past by laying the blame for sexual harassment on the males. The author continues thus:

> The point that has to be made clear to those fighting against sexual harassment is that men only react to the invitation from females who walk about near naked and display their bodies to be seen (emphasis added).

Statements like this keep the bottom power discourses and mind-set alive, thus effectively serving to stem any reaction from women. Given the power that prevalent discourses have in propagating the ideology of a dominant group, in this case men, a student propositioned by her teacher will undoubtedly hesitate to report the matter. Instead, she would search herself to discover what she had done to attract this male attention. This is, perhaps, one of the very reactions these discourses aim to achieve.

In essence therefore, while carrying out the discourse analysis of media reports, it is important to account for what actually occurs when sex (i.e. bottom power) is spoken about, to discover who does the speaking, the positions and viewpoints from which they speak, the institutions which prompt people to speak about it and which store distribute the things that are said... (Foucault, 1978). In other words, one is interested in knowing what makes this discourse possible and what its social functions are. In addition, there is a need to explore how these discourses play a major role in struggles for power taking place within society (Brookes, 1995).

Who does the speaking? Whether the speaker is male or female, the point is that it is overwhelmingly a male perspective that is being heard and held as the norm. Apart from the fact that the percentage of men who contribute to newspaper editorial/opinion pages far outnumber the women, the fact is that socialisation processes are so thorough that it is the dominant male view that is often heard, imbibed and reiterated. Such views are not always propagated in an obvious or pedagogic manner, says van Dijk. Rather, they are "reproduced by subtle, routine, everyday forms of text and talk that appear 'natural' and 'quite acceptable'"

This is obviously the case with the bottom power discourses which tend to echo each other.

> Parents nowadays, instead of frowning, smile on their half clothed daughters...Have you ever beheld the spectacle of shame...She goes to the lecture room fully clothed with more than three quarter of bare [sic] revealing sumptuous and volumptuous [sic] breasts and her body hugging bodice as transparent as a coming rain. (Falade, *Nigerian Tribune, 24* October, 1995)

This article purportedly places the blame for sexual harassment on the society, especially parents who turn a blind eye to their 'scantily clothed female offsprings.' But once again, the blame is placed on the females and their powers of seduction and the males are absolved of responsibility for whatever happens. As Fatade concludes: "I have nothing but pity for the poor teacher for the untold pains and tortures he suffers from the gory pictures presented by these daughters of Eve."

Clearly, the articles so far highlighted, and the conceptualisation of the bottom power practice, fail to problematize the concept of sexual pleasure and its effect on the desiring subject which can offer one explanation as to why bottom power or sexual bargaining as a practice is sustained in spite of the interdiction on sex and emphasis on a kind of sexual austerity (morality?) which society (pre)tends to adhere to.

In spite of the apparent emphasis on Christian values--the institution of marriage, virginity, chastity, abstinence until marriage and thereafter, allegiance to one spouse, the Christian model of 'mutual conjugal fidelity' is one that is lost on the Nigerian society. These are usually binding on the woman only as society does not frown as much when men fornicate before and after marriage, or when they acquire more than one wife.

The onus is on the woman to ensure that she is faithful to her spouse. Yet, the scriptures abound with passages admonishing the Christian pilgrim (more usually addressed to the man) to be cautious, vigilant in avoiding sexual immorality and sins of the flesh. In many ways, Christianity lauds the quality of self-restraint, with the onus weighing heavily on the man because "the husband is the head of the wife, even as Christ is the head of the Church..."(Ephesians 5:23).

If therefore, bottom power discourses arise from, or are grounded in what may be considered Christian morality (as the language seems to suggest), then the contradictions are obvious. In other words, the bottom power discourses tend to ignore the Christian doctrines where they would seem to curtail or restrain men's sexual activities, while emphasizing those aspects which serve to control women's sexuality. The question that naturally arises from this is: Given these apparent contradictions, what are the social functions of the bottom power discourses? What are they meant to achieve?

Certainly, the undue emphasis on the way females dress seems to suggest that one of the functions of the bottom power discourses may be a desire (either conscious or subconscious) to exercise some degree of control over women. Women who dress in a manner which tends to ignore, defy or disregard traditional/culture-based dress codes, are seen as too independent, defiant, out-of-control or a threat in a society where women and their sexuality are supposed to be under the control of fathers or husbands or even brothers. University students (and secondary school students) are certainly notorious for striving for sophistication, and for dressing in the most daring, Western-style clothes which may not be acceptable to men in the society. Sometimes, this mode of dressing tends to breed fear in the men. I once witnessed a situation on the streets of Kampala whereby a woman who wore a mini skirt was chased by a mob of men (which continued to swell in number), wielding sticks and all manner of weapons who wanted to teach her a lesson for daring to 'expose' herself. Luckily, a man who whisked her off in his car rescued her. But this kind of reaction is common. A Nigerian girl dressed in this manner will do well to avoid the motor parks where if she is not physically assaulted, will be greeted with shouts of "ashewo" --Yoruba for prostitute.

The following observation about secondary school girls, made by one of the earlier cited writers is worth a comment if only because of the sheer absurdity of it:

> Even at the secondary school level, the male teacher is at the mercy of his female pupils. As young as they are, they taunt him with their wiggling duck walk and rest their hands on his desk to reveal their young rounded dangling mammalian glands to the aging man who must have grown tired of his wife's dried up sagging sacks. If he now lifts a hand--they will shout sexual harassment (Falade, *Nigerian Tribune,* 24 October, 1995)

One wonders if the writer bears a grudge against the young female students for having "young rounded mammalian glands." It is difficult to see where the girls are to blame even though the writer goes to absurd levels in an attempt to absolve the man from responsibility for what occurs during sexual bargaining in the classroom. He, in fact employs language which is obscene or to say the least, offensive, especially to women and contradicts the austere Christian airs of the bottom power discourses. Of course, in the male scheme of things, women's views/sensibilities do not matter.

The above excerpt is a good example of the way in which societal discourses are tailored to control and influence the lives of women and their sexuality. In the case of the said teacher, age does not affect him; older men need (extramarital) sex more. And so he remains forever young and is allowed to go after underage girls in the pretext that they ask for it and he is, in fact, powerless to resist these very 'powerful' young girls. Meanwhile, his wife, who is probably much younger than him, has "dried up sagging sacks." In other words she has no more use. She has done her part-- borne the man's children and suckled them. In fact, she must pity her husband and accommodate and entertain his lustful, embarrassing adventures; and so must his young female students. In essence, we must all feel nothing but pity for the poor, beleaguered fellow "who must have grown tired" of his wife's dried up body and yet has to put up with the "young, rounded, dangling mammalian glands" of the she-devils he has as students!

But in the attempt to keep men above blame, what the bottom power discourses have done is reduce the men to the status of weaklings, mere puppets or babies, incapable of controlling their sexual urges. As the following section will further show, the form of the discourse serves not only to mask but also to distort the dynamics of power, as it operates within the context of bottom power sexual bargaining in the classroom.

POLITY VERSUS REALITY OF CLASSROOM BARGAINING

Until perhaps quite recently, the concept of bottom power and the sexual bargaining that surrounds it were hardly ever associated with sexual harassment as defined in the West. Bottom power, as well as other rude, sexist words such as 'ikebe' (See footnote 1) are common expressions that many Nigerian women grow up to accept and live with. Great anger and resentment can - and do - well up inside a woman who passes by a group of men and is greeted by a chorus of 'ikebe super' or bottom power, accompanied by snide and knowing grins. She will be particularly hurt when she gets this standard treatment even from a group of children, barely ten years old. But even with all the anger, she will not be able to put a name to the situation because she will have no means of fighting back or prosecuting her verbal assailants. Most women suffer the assault but would be described as 'abnormal' if they 'overreact' to what is generally considered as 'normal' practice.

However, the practice is trivialized to the extent that it remains virtually in the realm of informal discourse. The conspiracy of silence in formal discourse is so successful that the actual sufferers are forced to keep their agonies to themselves for fear of being ridiculed or seen as having invited the unwarranted attack. It was only in 1989 that the National Council on Education first set up a committee to look into the issue in the more formal environment of the school system. This was the result of what was described as "Repeated incidents and reports of sexual harassment in schools" (Mahmoud, 1992 in Robson, 1993:11). It is, however, interesting to note that just as in the newspaper reports, the question of the dress mode of females crops up once again in one of the major recommendations submitted by the education committee. The recommendation reads: "Girls should be discouraged from cheapening their womanhood by dressing in an indecent or seductive way." Thus, the blame is officially placed at the door of the female student. She must first ensure that she has not violated the dress code(s) of those who constitute the particular sexual harassment committee to which she reports the incident.

Altogether, seven major recommendations were submitted by the committee. They are:

1. Girls in institutions of learning should henceforth not be drafted to entertain, or serve dignitaries, at ceremonies, or public functions, or meetings. 2. A sexual harassment committee should be set up at State level to handle all reported cases of sexual harassment in institutions and take appropriate action about them. Membership of the committee should include: (a) two senior members of staff of the institution concerned; (b) a retired female principal, or teacher; (c) two religious leaders from the surrounding community; (d) two senior student representatives (male/female; (e) one representative of the National Council of Women's Societies; (f) one representative of the Federation of Muslim Women's Association of Nigeria; and (g) one legal practitioner. 3. A sexual harassment complaints bureau should be set up at the local government level to lyase with the state sexual harassment committee in the handling of all reported cases of sexual harassment in educational institutions. 4. The marking system in the institution should be arranged in such a way that no one teacher shall enjoy the monopoly of grading a candidate's script. 5. Girls should be discouraged from cheapening their womanhood by dressing in an indecent or seductive way. 6. Senior boys should be prevented from harassing their fellow female students. Any senior boy found guilty of harassment should be disciplined. 7. Guidance counsellors should be enjoined to give girls in institutions appropriate counselling.

It is perhaps necessary that further research be carried out in future to ascertain the extent to which some of the recommendations have been followed in the institutions of higher learning. The fourth recommendation, for instance, appears to be quite a useful one. The suggestion is that the grading of students should be arranged such that "no one teacher shall enjoy the monopoly of grading a candidate's script." This has far reaching advantages especially if it is made the tradition in the school rather than the exception when a case of sexual harassment is brought before the committee. The latter is the more usual scenario. But in the latter situation, the double grading of the script of the student in question does not completely guarantee the eradication of victimisation. Experience has shown that there is a great deal of solidarity amongst most males especially when it comes to the question of sexual harassment or sexual matters generally. As a male colleague once said, with reference to the very insensitive manner in which a male judge handled a case of defilement of a female minor, "we [referring to the men] are all interested parties." I agree with this view. When it comes to sexual matters (especially when the female concerned is neither a wife, a daughter, nor sister), men tend to support each other and make light of the issue.

Hence, the tendency is that even if a first marker down-graded a student, the second marker is unlikely to show-up his colleague, especially if they are both male and have had the chance to discuss the matter. Perhaps the solution would be to seek out a neutral second grader, who is neither familiar with the student nor the accused lecturer. Of course this would be both time-consuming and expensive even though it might turn out to be more effective. Nigerian universities are currently highly cash-strapped and at the time of writing this research chapter, most of them have been closed for months because of a tussle between the university staff who are demanding higher pay, and the government. Given the problems, financial and otherwise, the institutions are facing, it seems unlikely that the university authorities would seek to implement the fourth recommendation, which would mean extra work for the already disgruntled staff. Generally, the tradition in Nigerian universities is for one lecturer to teach, set the questions as well as grade the scripts, or at least the answers to questions s/he has set.

While recommendation #4 appears very reasonable, recommendations #2 and #3 are quite impracticable and very difficult to implement. Firstly, the suggestion is that sexual harassment committees be set up at two levels--at local government and state level, "to handle all reported cases of sexual harassment in institutions and take appropriate action about them." Already, one can foresee that if handled in this very high official and grand manner, there is the likelihood that one will inevitably encounter the hurdles or obstacles inherent in government bureaucracy.

It gets even worse because it is further suggested that the membership of the committee should include two senior members of staff of the institution concerned; a retired female principal, or teacher; two religious leaders from the surrounding community; two senior student representatives (male/female); one representative of the National Council of Women's Societies; one representative of the Federation of Muslim Women's Association of Nigeria; and one legal practitioner.

Anyone remotely familiar with the Nigerian situation will be well aware that it would be extremely difficult or well nigh impossible to get all these personalities together to form a quorum to hear at state level, all cases of sexual harassment from the different institutions of higher learning. If all the parties involved are to be willing to carry out this task diligently, it will mean that the financial rewards (sitting allowance, food allowance, transport, accommodation, out-of-station allowance, etc.) must be worth their while. It is difficult to envisage a situation whereby, the ministry of education in each of the thirty-six states of Nigeria would be willing to set aside such a lump sum of money, especially within the context of structural adjustment, for this project. This is more so in light of the attitude of society in these matters. Furthermore, it is difficult to imagine that such a group representing several viewpoints and with varying affiliations, both religious and secular, would easily come to an agreement over any one issue.

In addition, and perhaps more importantly, hardly any female student would be willing to report a case of sexual harassment if it would mean that it becomes a matter to be heard at state level. It would only expose such a student to more ridicule, perhaps press coverage and greater public scrutiny and disgrace. The case of Ahmadu Bello University (A.B.U), cited by Robson (1993: 113), would serve as a good example here. Apparently, in 1990, after the report of a sexual harassment committee had been released, students made bold to report cases of sexual harassment from lecturers and administrative staff. In response to this,

> A committee was established to formally receive and act on complaints but one of the most widely accused officials was made the secretary of the committee, thus making it impossible for most women to report cases of harassment to the committee...

All in all, looking at the seven main recommendations, there is no direct reference to the sexual bargaining in the classroom or the situation whereby a male lecturer propositions a female student. Yet this is the trickier scenario. Instead, recommendation 6 reads: "Senior boys should be prevented from harassing their fellow female students. Any senior boy found guilty of harassment should be disciplined" It is important that this situation be avoided, but equally important is that teachers be prevented from harassing their female students. Given the predominance of the bottom power mind-set, one can well imagine the kind of advice guidance counselors (recommendation #7) are likely to give female students - "Behave yourself, dress properly." In the actual fact, the male teachers who pressure their female students may require counseling even more.

Defending the Nigerian Government's decision to make the report and recommendations available to the various educational institutions, leaving it open to them to use the material as they deemed fit, the Minister of Education said:

> We try not to interfere. We say, there in the report. This is what we have found; it is left to each institution to take the report. Recommendations are made as to how to approach the issue. You use the recommendations in any way that is suitable to you, but please do something. (*Newswatch*, February 24 in Robson, 1993:112)

The dangers inherent in such an open-ended and amorphous policy statement must be obvious to anyone who is even remotely familiar with the difficulties women face when they attempt to establish a case of sexual harassment. But such statements help to further emphasize the point that in Nigeria, sexual harassment is trivialised and informalised, for a purpose. This trivialisation, and the informality associated with it is so ingrained into societal structures that it is reproduced even when attempts are made to propel the concept into the formal sphere where legislation can take effect.

The Education Minister went on to say:

> Whether it is real or imaginary, you know there is always a girl who is not doing well, she could fabricate a story and say because somebody made advances and say she did not give in [sic] do well who use this example of the amorous lecturer to pass her exams.

There are obviously some words omitted in this quotation but it has been reproduced exactly as it appeared because the general meaning is clear and very significant coming from the Minister of Education. It is a prime example of how society (men especially) views the issue of sexual harassment. In spite of the attitude of policy makers and those in authority, mostly male, efforts are still being made by women's groups like Women In Nigeria (WIN) and others, especially in higher institutions of learning to produce alternative discourses on sexual harassment which counter the dominant, hegemonic discourses. Conferences and seminars are being organized, research carried out, and questionnaires deployed in an attempt to document the view of women, hitherto drowned by the bottom power discourses.

For example, at Ahmadu Bello University in Zaria, "a lot of students and workers" as reported by Robson (1993: 112-113) "complained of sexual harassment" during an all-female seminar conducted after a case of rape on the campus. Although, the participants were unwilling to present their complaints in a formal manner because they were afraid of repercussions [sic] at two levels. Firstly, ridicule and suspicion they could encounter from the community and secondly, possible punitive measures from the accused persons who were mostly their lecturers or their superiors, the mere fact that women are now meeting and discussing these issues, is a major achievement in itself. Also on the list of successes is the case in 1992 where a student in a Nigerian university won a case in court in which she accused her lecturer of "failing her deliberately because she had refused his sexual advances" (Newsletter of African Association of Political Science, No. 16, September, 1994).

The volume entitled *Breaking the Silence: Women Against Violence,* edited by Robson which is the main reference material of this chapter, is testimony to the efforts of concerned women in Nigeria. The document is a result of the tenth annual Women in Nigeria conference with the theme "Women and Violence" which took place in Zaria from 8-10 April, 1992. The successes gained by individual women and women's groups in the effort to curb sexual injustices, even if limited, are worth highlighting, because, what has been happening in the classrooms, and is still largely the case, is the scenario whereby a male teacher propositions a female student but does not see himself as committing a crime. He is well protected by societal attitudes, structures and the dominant patriarchal and hegemonic discourses. It once was a common joke in university circles that because the teaching profession is so poorly remunerated, sleeping with female students is one of the few "fringe benefits" of the teaching staff. consequently, the male teacher has no fear of repercussions because the student is unlikely to report the case; and even if she does, there is no likelihood she will win against her instructor.

Given the situation, the girl, if offended by her teacher's sexual overtures, will generally keep her grievances to herself. Indeed, she must do everything she can, not to hurt the teacher's feelings since society places the blame on women. Again, she must try not to hurt the teacher's feelings so as not to put her whole career at stake. If she wants to rebuff the teacher's advances, however, she must do it with the utmost care so as not to jeopardize her grades or even earn an outright failure. On the other hand, she may resign herself to her 'fate' as a woman and take the prescribed 'easy' way out. Yet, the easy way out is never easy because of the inequality in power relations. It is unlikely that she will think of reporting the case, for reasons already noted. One needs only take a look at the press reports, the policy recommendations so far highlighted, and the prevalent discourses about bottom power and female students. It is unlikely that she will get sympathy from any quarter, not even from the wider community or her parents, unless she is fortunate to be in the vicinity of women's groups who take active interest in this kind of problem and who are ready and willing to support her. But even then, this would only mark the beginning of the thorny road to having her case heard on an official level.

When a male teacher demands sexual favours in exchange for a pass mark, the student may not be the dullest in her class. She may be the most physically attractive or appealing to the male teacher. "The sexual harassers are of various types," writes Awe,

> There are those lecturers who are rather saintly, so to say. They are only interested in one of their female students, and no more. A student so picked by any of the lecturers will continue to fail until she sees the light. (*Nigerian Tribune*, 24 October, 1995)

Sometimes, long before the teacher makes his advances known to the subject of his attention, the entire class is already well aware of the teacher's feelings. For in some cases, the teacher picks on the female student, openly overburdening her with questions or making her undertake numerous designated tasks in the classroom. If she is constantly thus embarrassed before her colleagues, she may begin to perform poorly, depending on her age and experience, degree of exposure, and the classroom atmosphere. Her male colleagues almost invariably tease her to distraction, making her life unbearable. She may confide her worries and fears to her female colleagues and close friends; but she will hardly ever report her problems to the authorities and least of all to her parents, since there are no laid-down procedures to protect her interests. According to the research carried out in Ahmadu Bello University in Zaria, the general picture was that "young and unmarried women suffer more sexual harassment than older and married women. In addition, students experience more than women workers" (Robson, 1933:113). A Nigerian student has this to say:

> When I first arrived at the university, one teacher kept giving me poor marks, and would always then ask me to come to his office "unless I wanted to fail" When I told friends, their comment was "You know what he wants. What are you going to do?" I did not pass. (*Newsletter*, AAPS, No.16, September 1994: 5)

Many students like the one above, rather than succumb to sex or report the case, accept failure and repeat a class. They have felt that even if they reported the case nothing would come of it, or worse still, they might be ridiculed for it. In essence, many students have felt that it might be easier to accept any grade than go through the regrading procedure, reckoning that reporting the matter carried far greater risk. The general opinion has been that the regrader may be bound to empathize with the colleague rather than the student who might end up marked for greater victimization for daring to accuse a member of staff.

The reality is that policies and legislation tend to see sexual harassment only in terms of victimization as regards grades. Yet, technically, sexual harassment as it is legally defined includes, as Tyler and Boxer (1996) found,

Not only the notion that it is unacceptable to make submission to sexual advances a condition of advancement or employment but also the notion of the unacceptability of a hostile or offensive working environment created by unwanted sexual advances, request for sexual favours and verbal or physical conduct of a sexual nature. (p110)

Sometimes, however, the male teacher succeeds in completely hiding his designs on a female student until an appropriate time, when he can be alone with the girl. He may have cause at some point to ask her to stay behind after the normal classroom activities for one reason or another. In the smaller towns and in the villages where students may be expected to carry out some domestic chores for the teachers, even in the teachers' homes, there is a great deal of opportunity for the teacher's personal and private interaction with a female student.

When such an opportunity presents itself, the male teacher is likely to declare that he 'loves' the female student and would like to 'take her out'. But where that fails to work, some teachers may give up their effort while others may make some new veiled threats. Occasionally, there are some who, from the start, make it clear to the female student that there is much at stake for her if she refuses his advances. This category of lecturers is described in one of the press reports as, randy lecturers, who insist on Biblically "knowing" their female students...who tie the success of their female students to how much [sic] sexual favors they get... (Awe, *Nigerian Tribune,* 24 October, 1995).

Yet, there are instances in which the female student may herself send out amorous signals to the male teacher and may make the first move. A former student at the University of Calabar is quoted as citing the "increasingly younger" age of teachers as a problem for a girl at the age where she is "turning into a woman" (Newsletter of AAPS, No.16, September 1994: 5). The point that must be reiterated here is that a female student cannot coerce or force her male lecturer into a sexual relationship because she has no means of exercising sanctions.

Emerging from this discussion is the fact that the classroom bargaining process is often quite complicated and is one of unequal exchange because of the unequal power relations between the teacher and the student. Even so, the student is not always and everywhere the victim, since she may exercise her own agency, her so-called bottom power, although ultimately, it is she who is restricted by virtue of her position as the less powerful in the bargaining process. But worse still, she has no say in the final outcome of the bargaining process. She has no protection should she opt to get out of the bargaining which, in any case, may have been initiated without her consent. Should she, however, decide to play along in a bid to maximize her returns or profits, she has no way of ensuring that she will get the bargain she has 'paid' for. She is entirely at the mercy of the male teacher.

But even if the female student does succeed in achieving the desired result through sleeping with her teacher, the bottom power she has exercised is disempowering in as far as she can hardly be expected to acquire the skills or expertise necessary to hold her own in the competitive job markets of today. Hence, though she may have undergone several years of education and acquired a certificate, she has not achieved much in terms of increasing her capabilities. Yet, this is one of the ways in which formal education is meant to empower recipients to contribute to socioeconomic progress. Put in another way, for a developing country like Nigeria, huge losses are incurred in terms of much needed manpower and the huge financial investment put into education in the face of acute economic depression.

As such, there remains a huge limiting factor even in cases where the classroom bargaining is initiated by the female student herself perhaps in an attempt to seek an 'easier' route to achieving her educational goals or as a result of coming to terms with a real or perceived intellectual weakness in herself.

DESIRE, PLEASURE, AND THE DANGER OF THE FEMALE STUDENT-MALE TEACHER POST BARGAINING SEXUAL RELATIONSHIP

In Nigeria, the topic of sex and sexuality education is still considered a taboo subject to teenagers both at home and in school[1]. In spite of these hang-ups, when young girls ignorant about sex do get pregnant, most have to drop out of school permanently. Making a case for sex education -in Nigeria, Adesemewo observes that a pregnant teenage girl "is extremely lucky if she is able to resume her education after delivery. In Nigeria, the poverty level is already very high, so unplanned parenthood can only worsen the terrible economic situation..." (Adesemewo, 1987:67). The irony of this is that the person responsible for the pregnancy is usually unaffected even if he is a student or teacher in the same school!

An unwanted pregnancy is just one of the problems that might arise when the bottom power bargaining is pursued to its ultimate conclusion. Ilumoka (1992) has noted that the availability of information and contraception to inhabitants of rural areas, the illiterate and young people under the age of 18 years is still restricted. It is perhaps in order to note here that in fact, attaining 18 years of age does not automatically guarantee access to available contraceptives. Though the trend may be changing nowadays, generally the community would frown on the idea of a young unmarried girl taking it upon herself to seek to use contraceptives because it would be seen as an obvious sign of waywardness. This stigmatization acts to limit the confidence of girls who otherwise would have sought counseling on and the use of contraceptives. This brings into sharp relief the bind in which young girls find themselves in that societal norms to which they are expected to conform do not always tally with the reality that the young girls experience in their day-to-day interaction with the opposite sex within the same society. In essence, 'wayward' girls, the rebels, survive better while the 'good girls' may end up undergoing a series of abortions, or dropping out of school.

Unwanted pregnancies and how to deal with them thus remain a problem in Nigerian society and probably will for a long time to come. (p. 87). As Ilumoka (1992) has further noted, the situation is made worse by the criminalization of abortion such that it is only legally allowed for the preservation of the mother's life. The situation is such that one guilty of the offence is liable to imprisonment for up to fourteen years. What this means in real terms is that, because of the risk involved, abortion fees are high and they tend to be performed by the "least experienced doctors in the least equipped clinics" (p. 91). And it is to be expected that very young girls who have no money and must keep their pregnancies a secret from their parents and guardians, form the larger percentage of those who resort to "untrained 'backstreet' abortionists, friends or self-help." (p. 91)

---

[1] More recently some level of progress has been made by some States such as Lagos State - the first State in Nigeria to introduce comprehensive sexuality education into the school curriculum in the 2001/2002 academic session. A national sexuality education curriculum for upper primary, junior secondary, senior secondary and tertiary institutions was approved in 2001

As devastating as an unwanted pregnancy might be to a young female student within the Nigerian context, it is nowhere near the danger inherent in contacting the deadly HIV virus, which has become a major threat to young people in the sub-Saharan African region. According to Mirembe, quoting UNICEF and a Panos (July 1996) report titled "AIDS and Young People," AIDS is foremost a disease of the young... Young women particularly in developing countries are at great risk...Young people are at risk partly because of their behavior and partly through the attitudes, expectations and limitations of the societies in which they grow up...The most fundamental risk facing young people stems from simple ignorance of the dangers of sex... (from the editorial of *The Crusader* n.d.)

But AIDS/HIV is not the only danger. STDs generally are on the increase worldwide and are proving more and more resistant to available antibiotics. According to a report published in 1995, "Each year, about 330 million new cases of STDs occur, of which 90% are in developing countries." (*Facing the Challenges of HIV, AIDS, STDs: A Gender-Based response,* p. 6) In the light of practices like bottom power bargaining, it is little wonder that, as the same report further notes, higher proportions of young women than young men acquire HIV infection through sex because they are exposed to the virus at an earlier age. Thus, Female vulnerability has become increasingly clear in Africa and Asia" (p. 5). Given this very gloomy picture, how does a teenage girl, inexperienced in sexual matters, and who has perhaps been coerced into a sexual encounter, cope with these dangers?

A 1995 survey carried out in Calabar, south eastern Nigeria, (see The survey carried out by Girls' Power Initiative which appears in *Reproductive Health Matters, No.* 6 of November 1995, p. 169), young girls ages 11-17 attending the International Women's Day celebration were asked to write down "questions that had been bothering them, but that they had been afraid to ask." As is customary with that age group, many of the questions centered on reproductive health issues. Some of the questions posed by the girls go a long way to emphasize the point that huge, and often dangerous, gaps exist in the knowledge that young, and perhaps, physically mature girls possess about reproductive health matters. Some of the questions included:

"What happens when girls have sex at an early age?" "...how do we get pregnant?" "If I am pregnant and I don't tell my mother, what will happen?" "How can we have sex without being pregnant?" And so on.

The irony is that these questions were asked by young girls who live within the very context that sustains the bottom power discourses. Are we to believe that these same teenagers (who going by their ages are either in secondary school or the first/second year of university) form part of a group of wanton temptresses who flaunt their bottom power in the face of older, mature males and cause them to succumb? Are these the same female students described in the press reports and other bottom power discourses?

What is even more frightening is that the bottom power discourses, even in policy documents, completely neglect or fail to address the issue of the dangers of sex in the present era. Emphasis is placed overwhelmingly on the evil it embodies as a sinful act and on the misdemeanor of the participants, most especially the female participant. Neither is the element of pleasure adequately problematized. The bottom power discourses tend to also over-emphasize the transactional component of it. In other words, the females are perceived as taking part basically on the level of a business transaction, using their bodies to advantage to get what they want knowing that the men are easy prey. This of course is not the true picture of things. In reality, the men are not weak; they are in complete control of the situation.

For a girl coerced into this arrangement, it is a time of emotional torment. Her reputation as a woman, which the same society dictates must be pure, may be at stake. Yet, society will not also condone failure. Should she fail, she would have shattered the dreams of her family; the dream of having a daughter who is a medical doctor or engineer, for instance. Her failure would further support societal claims that 'girls never make it; their place is in the home'. The nagging question is: if undisturbed by the lustful attentions of her teacher, would the girl not succeed?

Some of the girls eventually capitulate under pressure, acquiescing to sexual intercourse, knowing fully well that is what the teacher desires. They really have no choice but to comply, seeing that the power relations are such that the student is in a disadvantaged position. If she refuses, she is doomed, if she accepts, then she joins the ranks of the 'prostitutes in the higher institutions of learning.' After all, most female graduates whether intelligent, hardworking or not, already carry that label. The girl rationalizes that if she is discrete and careful, no one else needs to know. She concludes that sex is quite a small price to pay for a pass mark or good grade since there is no visible sign on the body to show for the 'little indiscretion.' Of course, viewed in the light of unwanted pregnancies, STDs and HIV/AIDS, this assumption is not wholly valid. The degree to which patriarchal dictates control the lives of women is the point to be noted here. The men make the rules and they are in the position of authority. The women have no choice but to conform, if they must gain some respite. An illustrative example is the case of Vivian, a student in the first year of secondary school. She says of one of her male teachers: "He always insists on caning us (i.e. girls) on our buttocks. The more we wiggle our bums, the lesser caning we get. So, we know how to escape getting more lashes of cane from him" (Sunday Tribune, 12 November, 1995, p. 10). For the men, it is obvious that the sexual bargaining is initiated or accepted mainly for the sexual gratification they hope to derive from it, and not because they are weak, and the women evil, as the discourses tend to imply. While the female student's bargaining chip is her body, for the male teacher, his bargaining power as noted elsewhere rests in the "score sheets which are the life-line to good grades and graduations [sic] for their female as well as male students." (*Sunday Tribune,* 12 November, 1995). However, the secrecy and hastiness with which these 'illicit' sexual encounters are carried out are such that the participants may not give much thought to the question of safer sex.

A common scenario is one whereby a teacher initiates the bargaining process, piling the pressure on a female student who may be initially hesitant, undecided, even scared. During the process of persuasion or coercion (sometimes accompanied by threats), the teacher's lust/emotions tend to build up, sometimes really going out of proportion and obvious in his day-to-day interaction with the student. His lust is apparently fuelled by the resistance/rejection from the student. Occasionally, the more the female student resists, the greater the teacher's determination to have his way with her. In a sense, the girl faces a no-win situation given that she has to deal with this teacher on a daily basis. He is completely in control and he has the power to decide her fate. At the time when the student may reach her turning point, either as result of the pressure from the teacher or a lot of soul searching and consultation with female peers, they (both student and teacher) may be unprepared for a sexual encounter; both in terms of contraception and safety from disease. But the teacher would not want to waste any time for fear that she may change her mind.

The next problem to overcome would be that of an appropriate venue since more likely than not, the teacher would be a married man and cannot take his 'date' home. Neither can they retreat to the hostel. In the circumstances, the teacher normally decides to take the 'date' to a small, back alley hotel where they are both unlikely to run into mutual acquaintances. A lot of these can be found in the cities and towns in Nigeria. Apparently, the male teachers who indulge in these sexual affairs have regular, cheap ones where they take their 'dates.' Actually, these joints do not qualify as hotels. They are usually in the form of seedy, rest houses or drinking places with a few rooms attached for those who may require them.

In the awkward situation that ensues, the girl is probably shy and in strange and not very comfortable surroundings where she is alone with her teacher who is perhaps fondling her. She is tense and can hardly look him in the eye; how then can she demand that he use a condom? She wants to get it over and done with as soon as possible, perhaps so does he. In the scenario, foreplay is practically non-existent and this increases the risk of HIV/AIDS transmission for the girl who may be hurt and bruised in the process. But she cannot protest or caution her teacher, her superior. This brings to the fore, once again, the question of the unequal power dynamics. Even outside the classroom and in the 'bedroom,' the female student is still at a disadvantage. She has no way of enforcing anything. After an encounter such as this, one can only imagine what the relations between the student and teacher will be, back in the classroom.

The catch is that the teacher may have enjoyed the one encounter so much that the student is doomed to such performances if she is to pass any course by that teacher. In other words, whether she is intellectually capable or not, she will not have much of a choice. The teacher may even spread the word to his close male colleague(s)! By this stage, if the girl feels adequately threatened and would like to take action based even on the shaky legislation available, she would be scared out of her wits. She would reckon that she has no moral obligation to do so given that she has actually slept with the teacher already. She would be forced to endure and keep her mouth shut. The nightmare of having to sleep her way through school, even if against her will, must leave a lasting mark on the girl, her self-esteem and self-worth. In which case, for her, education has only served to disempower, rather than empower her. The point that must be reiterated in concluding this section of the chapter is that these sexual relationships between female students and their male teachers are fraught with dangers not only for the girls, even though they are more vulnerable, but for their teachers as well. Yet these dangers are completely ignored in the discourses about bottom power whether in formal policy documents or in newspaper reports.

CONCLUSION

This chapter has critically explored the Nigerian concept of bottom power as it impacts on females and female sexuality within the education system. And the conclusion reached is that bottom power as it is understood and practiced disempowers, rather than empowers women, because it increases their vulnerability to abuse and disease, among other disadvantages. In the light of these, it becomes crucial that the practice of bottom power within the education system be discouraged as much as possible. It was, in fact, a recognition of the magnitude of the problem that led to previous attempts to address the issue--for example the task force set up by the Ministry of Education which came up with the recommendations discussed earlier in this chapter. What is clear, however, is that the bottom power problem is a very tricky one to deal with because of the thoroughness and pervasiveness of the bottom power socialization processes.

Hence, strategies evolved or solutions to the problem have to be transformative in nature. To begin with, it is important to work towards bringing the discourse into the open, especially in the educational institutions. In addition, efforts have to be made to release the discourse from the realm of jokes into the more formal realm where it can be treated with the seriousness that the situation calls for. This chapter is an additional effort to the effort of women's groups which have tried to bring sexual harassment into focus through organizing seminars, workshops and symposia on the topic, and documenting their findings. However, one aspect which has hitherto been overlooked and which this chapter has dealt with is how the prevalent bottom power mind-set serves to conceal as well as promote the sexual harassment of females in Nigerian.

But it is also obvious that merely introducing the topic into the formal realm is not enough. It must be followed by well thought-out policies which adequately recognize and address the intricacies, peculiarities and problems arising from the bottom power mind-set within the Nigerian system. Existing policies, like the one highlighted in this chapter, are themselves influenced and informed by the bottom power mind-set and this renders legislation ineffective and impracticable within the existing structures. Therefore, in addressing the issue of sexual harassment of females within the education system in Nigeria, the bottom power mind-set as a major contributing factor, must be given due attention.

In effect, the overall aim of policies should be to make the problem of bottom power more broadly recognized and punished. In this regard, students ought to be well appraised of the problems once they register in schools. Disciplinary measures ought to be made known to both staff and students and enforced to serve as deterrent. This is to ensure accountability. One major reason why disciplinary measures, devised in previous policies, have tended to be ineffective has been because visible perpetrators of the bottom power ideology have been made members or even heads of disciplinary committees. In this way, ideology and personnel reinforce each other. One of the ways to break this vicious cycle is to allow students to decide or choose those to constitute disciplinary committees. Generally, students are quite knowledgeable about teachers and members of the community who have the discipline, character and moral standing to become members of such committees. It is also important that cases be heard within individual schools and not at state or national level, firstly, to avoid bureaucratic bottlenecks and secondly, to make it easier for affected girls to report cases.

One of the strategies for making bottom power more visible is to include concerned groups within society, especially parents and women's groups, in deliberations to seek solutions to the problem, and as members of disciplinary bodies. This will also make it easier for girls to turn to parents and others in the community for support when faced with sexual harassment.

In addition, questionnaires which address the issue of sexual harassment can also play an important role in checking the bottom power problem. These can be issued out to students periodically, while ensuring that the students who fill them remain well protected and anonymous. This is while recognizing that such questionnaires are likely to be opposed by a majority of the Nigerian teaching staff. Nigerian culture does not usually permit a situation whereby a junior or subordinate appraises the performance of the elder or superior. The elder or superior is always assumed to be wiser and, therefore, always right. But this is precisely why the practice of bottom power, though harmful, has gone on unhindered for so long.

As earlier stated, in order for solutions to be effective, they must aim at transforming or changing some of the structures as they exist today. There is, indeed, the need for change, as this chapter has shown. The far reaching and negative impact of the bottom power practice calls for immediate and more effective action to discourage and eventually put a stop to this practice within the Nigerian education system.

NB: This chapter was originally written in partial fulfillment of my Master of Literature degree at the Institute of Social Studies, The Hague, The Netherlands In 1996. I would like to acknowledge the contributions of my supervisors, Renee Pittin and Loes Keysers.

REFERENCE

Adesemowo, P.O. (1987) "Adolescence Sexuality: The Need for Sex Education in Nigeria" in E. Lambo (ed.) *The Nigerian Journal of Economic and Social Studies* vol.29, (1), 61-75.

Agheyisi, R.U. (1985) "The Labour Market Implications of the Access of Women to Higher Education" in *Women in Nigeria Today*, Zed Books, London.

Antrobus, P. (1989) "The Empowerment of Women" in R.S. Gallin et al. (eds.) *The Women and International Development Annual, vol. 1,* Westview Press, Boulder, San Francisco, and London, pp. 189-207.

Birke, L. (1992) "Transforming Biology" in H. Cowley and S. Himmelweit (eds.) *Knowing Women: Feminisms and Knowledge,* Polity Press in Association with the Open University, Cambridge and Oxford. pp. 66-77.

Brookes, H.J. (1995) "Suit, tie and a touch of juju--the ideological construction of Africa: a critical discourse analysis of news on Africa in the British press" in *Discourse and Society,* vol.6 No.4, Sage, (London, Thousand Oaks and New Delhi) pp. 461-494

Butler, M. and Paiseley, W. 1980 *Women and the Mass Media*, Human Science, New York. Candiru, E.S. (1992) "Toward an Alternative Framework for Fertility Analysis: A Contextual Study of Patriarchal Power and Women's Marital Fertility Among the Lugbara, Uganda" (Research Chapter, ISS, The Hague).

Curran, J. and Gurevitch M. (eds.) 1991 *Mass Media and Society,* Edward Arnold, London.

Denzer, L. (1992) "Domestic Science Training in Colonial Yorubaland, Nigeria" in K.T. Hanson (ed.) *African Encounters with Domesticity,* Rutgers University Press, New Brunswick, New Jersey, pp. 116-139. Elson, D. (1991) "Male Bias in the Development Process" in D. Elson (ed.) *Male Bias in the Development Process,* Manchester University Press, Manchester.

Facing the C hallenges of HIV, AIDS, STDs: *Response* (1995), KIT, SAFAIDS and WHO. A Gender Based

Foucault, M. (1978) *The History of Sexuality Introduction.* Vintage Books, New York.

Foucault, M. (1984) *The Use of Pleasure* (Volume 2 of The History of Sexuality) Pantheon Books, New York.

Gallagher, M. (1981) *Unequal Opportunities: The Case of Women in the Media,* UNESCO Press. Houston, M. and Kramarae, C. (1991) "Speaking from Silence: Methods of Silencing and Resistance" in *Discourse and Society,* Sage, London, vol.2(2), pp. 223-342.

Ihonvbere, J.O. and Shaw, T.M. (1988) *Towards a Political Economy of Nigeria,* Avebury, Aldershot.

Ihonvbere, J.O. (1994) *Nigeria: The Politics of Adjustment and Democracy,* Transaction Publishers, New Brunswick and London.

Ilumoka, A.O. (1992) "Reproductive Rights: A Critical Appraisal of the Law Relating to Abortion" in M. N. Kisekka (ed.) *Women's Health Issues in Nigeria,* Tamaza, Zaria.

Johnson, H. (1992) "Women's Empowerment and Public Action: Experiences from Latin America" in M. Wuyts et al., (eds.) *Development Policy and Public Action*, Oxford University Press in Association with Open University, pp. 147-172.

Keller, L. S. (1992) "Discovery and Doing: Science and Technology, An Introduction" in *Inventing Women: Science, Technology and Gender,* Polity Press in Association with Open University, Cambridge and Oxford, pp. 12-32.

McKay, N.Y. (1992) "Remembering Anita Hill and Clarence Thomas: What Really Happened When one Woman Spoke Out" in Toni Morrison (ed.) *Race-inq, Justice, En-gendering Power: Essays on Anita Hill, Clarence Thomas, and the Construction of Social Reality,* Pantheon Books, New York, pp. 269-289.

Parrinder, G. (1969) *Africa's Three Religions:* Sheldon Press, London.

Parpart, J. and M. Marchand 1995) "Exploding the Canon: An Introduction/Conclusion" in J. Parpart and M. Marchand (eds.) *Feminism, Postmodernism, Development,* Routledge, London,pp. 1-22.

Robson, E. (ed.) 1993 *Breaking the Violence: Violence, Women in Nigeria, Kano.* Women Against Violence.

Rose, P. (1995) "Female Education and Adjustment Programs' A Crosscountry Statistical Analysis" in *World Development,* vol.23. No. 11, pp. 1931-1949.

Schneider, B.E. and M. Gould (1987) "Female Sexuality: Looking Back into the Future" in B.B.Hess and M.M. Ferree (eds.) *Analysinq Gender: A Handbook of Social Science Research,* Sage, Newbury Park.

Sorenson J. "Mass Media and Discourse on Famine" in *Discourse and Society,* Sage, London,vol.2(2), pp. 223-242.

Stacey, J. (1993) "Untangling Feminist Theory" in D. Richardson and V. Robertson (Eds.)*Introducing Women's Studies: Feminist Theory and Practice,* Macmillan, London, pp. 49-74.

The World's Women 1995- Trends and Statistics, United Nations, New York.

Thorne, B. et al (eds.) 1983 *Language, Gender and Society,* Newbury House, Massachusetts.

Tilak, J.B.G. (1989) *Education and Its Relation to Economic Growth, Poverty, and Income Distribution: Past Evidence and Further Analysis,* World Bank, Washington (Research Chapter No. 3).

Tyler, A. and D. Boxer (1996) "Sexual Harassment? Cross-Cultural/Cross-Linguistic Perspectives" in *Discourse and Society,* vol.7 No.1, Thousand Oaks, London, pp. 107-133.

van Dijk, T.A. (n.d.) "Analysing Racism Through Discourse Analysis- Some Methodological Reflections" in John H. Stanfiels II, Rutledge M. Dennis (eds*.) Race and Ethnicity in Research Methods,* Newbury Park, C.A. pp. 92-134.

van Dijk, A.T. (1993) "Principles of Critical Discourse Analysis" in *Discourse and Society,* Sage, London, vol.4(2), pp. 249-283.
van Zoonen, L. (1994) *Feminist Media Studies,* Sage, London.
Villareal, M. (1994) "Wielding and Yielding: Matters of Theory and Method" in "Wielding and Yielding: Power, Subordination and Gender Identity in the Context of a Mexican Development Project, (Ph.D thesis, University of Wageningen).
Wolf, N. (1993) *Fire With Fire,* Charge and Windus, London

Chapter 7

AFRICAN WOMEN AND POLITICS: A CASE STUDY OF CHIEF (MRS.) MARGARET EKPO OF NIGERIA

Felix K. Ekechi
Professor Emeritus, Kent State University
Ohio, USA

PRESCRIPT

Let me begin this essay with a caveat: First, I would like to use this opportunity to congratulate the two professors Robert Tabachnick and Robert L. Koehl, who are being honored with this festschriften the-occasion- of their retirement from the University of Wisconsin-Madison. My special tribute goes to Professor Koehl, my former teacher and doctoral director. I want him to know that I still think highly of him, as a teacher-scholar, a humanist, and above all (I hope he will agree), a dear friend. As I said of him elsewhere, he received me with open arms when I arrived in Madison, and he also treated me with respect, which endures. In the dark days of the Nigeria-Biafra War (1967-70), Koehl was a bundle of solace to me, a comforter, a sympathizer, and an active supporter of our Biafran cause. Thus, as President Nelson Mandela of South Africa once said of friends in need: "They must never be forgotten!" Therefore Professor Koehl, you will never be forgotten.

My association with Professor Koehl began in 1965, when I started my Ph. D. program in the History Department of the University of Wisconsin-Madison, with a special focus on African Studies. I was his Project/Research Assistant for the first two years of my study, during which time we accumulated volumes of bibliographical material on various aspects of Nigerian/African colonial history and culture. Professor Koehl at this time was a new comer to the field of African historical studies, having hitherto been a well-established specialist in German history. His two major publications, *RKFDP: German Resettlement and Population Policy 1939-1945* (1957), and *The Black Corps: The Structure and Power Struggles of the Nazi SS (1983)* attest to his reputation in German history. As he himself explained, his formal entry into Nigerian/African area studies began with "a research trip to Nigeria in *1966* supported in part by the Midwest Universities Consortium." (See: Footnote to essay "The

Uses of the University: Past and Present in Nigerian Educational Culture," in *Comparative Education Review (XV, 2 (1971): 116-131)*

What seems to have enthroned Professor Koehl as a scholar/specialist in Nigerian/African colonial history were his three seminal and critical articles dealing with British colonial policy on Nigerian cum African education. I would even venture to say that these essays catapulted him to the mainstream of African historical studies. The first was actually a book review entitled "Transplanting British Universities to Africa and India"(Journal *of Higher Education (XXXIX,* No. 1, *1968:50-54),* in which Koehl sharply criticized British advocacy for "adapted" (i. e. inferior) colonial education for Africans, which emphasized vocational education. As he correctly pointed out, Africans resisted any education system that left them as "inferiors" vis-a-vis the wider world. Thus,

> From the very beginnings of the mission schools, Africans demanded noting but the best. If that best was Greek and higher mathematics, then the students and the faculty too could not be put off with more "practical" education. Education that fits men only to be inferiors, however well "adapted" to the needs of the moment (if they can be agreed upon), soon becomes debased into a mere tool of class tyranny. (p. 51)

Then followed the two-part essays in *Comparative Education Review (Vol. XV,* Nos. 2 & 3 (1971), namely, "The Uses of the University: Past and Present in Nigerian Educational Culture." In the first part Koehl masterfully assailed British/European notions of African societies and cultures as being static rather than dynamic, as well as their arrogance of the "civilizing mission". He writes, inter alia:

> Among the crimes committed against Africans the myth of an unchanging indigenous culture which white men either destroyed or 'preserved' still functions as an interpretive device, downgrading Africans' autonomy in coping with European incursions. Similarly, the foolish notion that Nigerians 'borrowed' their educational culture wholesale from their [British] conquerors, who somehow 'transferred institutions' like weed-seeds in the ballast, still persists."(Vol. XV, Part 1:116)

It was against this backdrop that he forcefully argued that, contrary to received opinion, Nigerians did not embrace British education culture wholesale, which was after all deeply rooted in the (British) "dominant groups' values and expectations." (Vol. 15, Part 2: 367). Rather, Nigerian universities operated on the basis of national interest and aspirations, and thus upheld the ideals of the generations of West African Western educated elite ("the gammas and deltas") who sought to combine "practical education for life and service with a democratizing and *indigenous* humane curriculum." (Ibid.: 370; see also Vol. XV: 125-128) Consequently, "In spite of their vicissitudes, Nigerian universities have proved to be much tougher than the fragile 'imports' pictured by some writers. Their survival is related to their functionality, and to their relationship to Nigerian educational culture." (p. 377) Koehl's central point was that Nigerians did not embrace the British colonial education system "wholesale", but rather, selected aspects of the education system to serve their own ends.

Until his retirement, Professor Koehl and Professor Tabachnick offered graduate seminars on Nigerian colonial education, as part of the College of Education's comparative education program. I had thus originally intended to focus attention on the tyranny of colonial education in Africa as a befitting tribute to Professor Koehl, but circumstances beyond my control interposed. Nevertheless, I hope the sketchy commentary on him as a humanist, an erudite scholar, and a truly African/Nigerian enthusiast suffices. As the Igbo say, half a glass/cup is better than an empty one.

Let me then turn to the major theme of this chapter: An examination/exploration of the political and social legacy of Chief (Mrs.) Margaret Ekpo. It might be useful to begin with this portrait of the legendary feminist and frontline female Nigerian nationalist, which appeared in the *Nigerian Chronicle* in 1995:

> Whereas [most Nigerian] ...political giants... and patriots have faded into oblivion in their own life times, [Mrs. Ekpo's] never-ending social relevance to the cause of feminism and women's emancipation, has immortalised her as a heroine, a nationalist, and a zealous promoter of women's rights. *(Nigerian Chronicle,* 14 March 1995)

The above epigraph accurately captures Mrs. Ekpo's essence and sociopolitical significance. Now ninety (90) years of age (2004), frail, and "nearly blind," she must be seen as being truly an indomitable nationalist and patriot as well as "the quintessential feminist of the twentieth century." Born in Creek Town, Calabar on July 27, 1914, the same year that "British Nigeria" was born, (NOTE: Modern Nigeria was created by the British Government in 1914, when the two separate administrative units-Northern and Southern Provinces-were amalgamated.) Emerging in the era of decolonization, Margaret Ekpo "joined hands with those eminent Nigerians to fight for the independence of this nation." *(A Political Biography* (1995), p. 52) First and foremost, she was educated in mission schools, and began her life career as a trained schoolteacher in the Presbyterian Mission. Margaret Ekpo (nee Obiasulor, an Igbo man) was later married to one Dr. John U. Ekpo, also from Creek Town, Calabar. The couple later settled at Aba, a vibrant Igbo trading city in Eastern Nigeria, where the Efik doctor worked as an Assistant Medical Officer at the Aba General Hospital. It was thus at Aba that Mrs. Ekpo's political consciousness and career began, and Aba also remained the base of her sociopolitical operation until 1966, when her political career came to an end following the military coup d'etat that toppled the Nigerian First Republic in that year.

To begin with, Mrs. Margaret Ekpo appeared on the Nigerian political scene in the 1940s, when she dabbled into politics under the umbrella of the National Council of Nigeria and the Cameroons (NCNC), the foremost nationalist political party in colonial Nigeria. She rose quickly in political circles, essentially because of her feminist and political activism. Her name thus became synonymous with nationalist and feminist politics. Margaret Ekpo was of course the foremost feminist and female political activist from Eastern Nigeria, whose entry into politics certainly helped to redefine and/or deconstruct the popular, but misleading, image of the" typical" African woman. A large amount of rubbish has been written about African women being politically aloof and thus consigned to "home and hearth". (Cf. Ekechi, "Perceiving Women as Catalysts," *Africa Today. Vol.* 43, 3 (1996: 235. Wiper, 1989: 300) But, as this study demonstrates, Mrs. Ekpo's *political* activism destroyed all this nonsense. In essence, her foray into active politics illuminates our understanding of African woman's political participation in modern politics, despite the fact that social and political conventions combined to undermine women's political roles in modem times. Worldwide, women's voices of protest seem to suggest that women, in contrast to men, have remained out of the political realm for a long time. (Cf. Rose U. Mezu 1994, Somyamoorthy and Renjini 2000; Chowdhury et al. 1999, Ogundipe 1994.) In Africa, to be sure, European colonialism coupled with social and political inequalities between men and women certainly contributed to women's unequal participation in politics. In essence, cultural and institutional constraints, as African feminists have agonized, have conspired to politically marginalize women. Thus lamenting the denial of human rights to women, attorney Susan Onyeche remarked: "The birth of a female was a thing of misery to every home [in traditional Igbo society, and no doubt elsewhere]. The position of women in the scheme of things was therefore not desirable. Nobody could talk of the [political] Rights of women because there was none." *(Transition,* 2003: 206) The Nigerian feminist Bilkisu Yusuf put it even more poignantly: the social and political institutions "fashioned and developed" by men were basically constructed "with an almost complete neglect of the role of their womenfolk." (Ibid.) But whatever the case, as Margaret Ekpo's case illustrates, women ultimately scaled the ramparts. It should however be emphasized that African women, and particularly Nigerian women, have traditionally played critical roles in politics. As an African woman has proudly asserted, "I've been a man, " implying she had played political/social roles like men. (For illustrations see: Nina Mba, *Nigerian Women Mobilized* (1982); Felix K. Ekechi, "Perceiving African Women as Catalysts (1996), also "Women and the Democratization Process in Africa (2003); P. K. Uchendu, *The Role of Nigerian Women in Politics: Past and Present* (1993).

THE STORMING OF THE BARRICADES OF POWER

By the 1940s, as already noted, Mrs. Margaret Ekpo literally and symbolically "stormed the barricades" of male-dominated politics and society. Essentially, she seems to have had the courage and temerity to "pry open" the citadel of men's political power; or, as Rose Mezu describes it, she must have shed "the complexes of the years of [women's] denigration and self-abasement." (Mezu, 1995:77) By her own account, Mrs. Ekpo joined the NCNC at a time when it was virtually a male-dominated political party. In that case, her foray into party-politics is historic, and a manifestation of her principle of gender equality. After all, said Mrs. Ekpo defiantly, "I feel, primarily, that I am a human being created by God," and so, "It doesn't make a difference whether I am a woman or not. I feel that what a man can do, I can also do...." (Interview 1993, in *Biography, p.* 52) Among other things, her entry into party politics heralded a new era: it marked the beginning of the bursting open of the seemingly all-male "political club," as Mrs. Ekpo jokingly described the early years of the NCNC. Equally significant, she dabbled into politics when that profession/career was considered men's exclusive preserve, therefore unusual for women to venture into (politics). Thus, Mrs. Ekpo still remains a historical legend, and, indeed, a social phenomenon.

But perhaps more remarkable is the fact that, Margaret Ekpo was the first female appointed to serve in the Nigerian Eastern House of Chiefs at Enugu (1953). A year later, she was also nominated as a special member of the Eastern House of Assembly, again the first woman to be so honored.

By her own admission, Margaret Ekpo loved the NCNC. Thus presumably her loyalty to the NCNC, as well as her commitment to the nationalist and feminist causes, won her a place/position of honor and respect that resulted in her selection as the sole female member of the NCNC delegation to the Nigerian Constitutional Conference in London, in 1953. While there, she captured the imagination of many, including the news media. This glowing portrait of this legendary Nigerian feminist, which appeared in the widely read West Africa magazine (22 August 1953: 773), certainly reflects Mrs. Ekpo's social and political significance:

> When the Nigerian representatives landed in London for the Constitutional Conference they stepped from the plane, for the most part arrayed in a variety of national dress. The gold and the blues mingled bravely with the white and the green... [It was spectacular]. Yet when Mrs. Ekpo emerged, it was not her dress, attractive though that might be, that held the attention so much as Mrs. Ekpo herself. Here was no unsophisticated, painfully shy, easily embarrassed example of [African] womanhood; no cumbersome, slow-moving, slow-thinking market mammy, but an up-to-date woman, used to the world and its ways, a woman of affairs, capable, adroit, skilled at planning campaigns for causes she adopts. And who can doubt that in Eastern Nigeria her main occupation is the cause of women.

Similar words of praise and recognition came from the British feminist Dr. Edith Summerskill, formerly Minister of National Insurance. Of Mrs. Ekpo she wrote: "While the newspapers devoted space to the procedural and administrative aspects of the new constitution, they failed to highlight a matter of great interest to more than half of the population of our respective countries, the women.... Mrs. Ekpo is with the [Nigerian] delegates representing the National Council of Nigeria and the Cameroons...." In addition to being a politician, Dr. Summerskill concluded, Mrs. Ekpo is a teacher, and "has successfully combined [her] work with marriage." (Quoted in the *Nigerian Chronicle, 14* March 1995, p. 7)

In 1961, Mrs. Ekpo was *elected* in a landslide to the Eastern House of Assembly at Enugu, again as one of the few female elected politicians throughout Nigeria Her victory, according to her biographers, was particularly significant and epoch making.

> She moved from being the woman who took a particularly keen interest in the proceedings of the Eastern House of Chiefs to a member sitting in the House of Assembly and contributing directly to debates. [Moreover, her] victory spelt a new lease of hope for democracy in Nigeria. Besides beating men to the seat, her victory was remarkable in the sense that she contested the elections outside her original homeland [Calabar].... Coming from Creek Town in present Cross River State, she won election in Aba. It was a demonstration of her overwhelming popularity and an indication of the confidence reposed in her that she performed better than the five Igbo men who contested the elections against her. (Women in Nigeria, *Margaret Ekpo: A Political Biography,* 1996, p. 36)

Equally remarkable is the fact that Mrs. Ekpo's entry into active politics *opened the door of politics to other women.* Herein lies her ever-enduring legacy in Nigerian social and political history. Her contribution to women's political participation has thus earned her the reputation of being a pioneer, a trailblazer, and a catalyst.

As to be expected, Chief (Mrs.) Margaret Ekpo became virtually "the voice of women of Eastern Nigeria," in the sense that she proved to be the most vocal and eloquent promoter of women's causes and/or rights, not only in the Eastern House of Assembly but also beyond. "As part of her self-initiated schedule, Margaret took visits to her constituency... in order to feel the pulse in terms of their desires and expectations.... She aggregated the demands of her constituents and brought them to the House and where necessary to the Minister whose portfolio was directly in charge of the issues on the ground." (Political Biography, p. 36) Thus her political agitation for progress, and commitment to the cause of feminism earned her the sobriquet "the lioness of the East."

"I Defended the Cause of Women"

The above quotation derives from my interview with Mrs. Ekpo (September 29, 2000), in which she forcefully asserted that she indeed "fiercely defended the rights of women," a claim that seems clearly attested by her crusading campaigns against women's exploitation and her relentless advocacy for women's social and political empowerment. In her autobiography, Mrs. Ekpo reveals that she had had a longstanding political dream, that is, to "climb to the top and then try and bring along some women to that exalted position." And she added: "I read a lot about [female] role models like Florence Nightingale, Mrs. Ransome-Kuti, Mrs. [T.] Ogunlesi [both of Nigeria], Mrs. Gandhi and others." Evidently aspired by these eminent female leaders, Mrs. Ekpo seemed resolved to emulate them. As she confessed, "I believed that I'll be a great woman one day," just like these women. (Political *Biography, p. 52*) Needless to say that her dream was realized, inasmuch as Margaret Ekpo eventually rose to political prominence and successfully brought women into the political fold To this day, she is still widely acclaimed as "the great champion of women's causes," exemplified in her fervent advocacy for women's overall empowerment.

Commitment to the cause of feminism can possibly be traced back to Margaret Ekpo's activities during her years as a schoolteacher. For example, she reportedly opened a vocational school for girls, namely, the Windsor Sewing Institute, in Calabar, of which not much is still known. But like most technical schools of its genre, the Institute served as a center for the training of women and young girls in sewing, cookery, laundry and other skills that enabled women to enhance their standard of living. Thus the Windsor Institute must have played a significant role in the provision of rudimentary education for women, as well as to the promotion and advancement of their socioeconomic welfare.

As Mrs. Ekpo herself affirms, commitment to women's education seems to have been deeply rooted in her basic social ideology, that is, gender equality. "I have always believed in gender equality," meaning equal rights and opportunities for all. (Interview 1999) Thus the education of women must be said to have formed part and parcel of her feminist ideology/agenda. After all, as she has persuasively argued, "Without education you cannot do anything. You cannot raise your head above others." Therefore, "education first, [and] then all other things will be added unto you." *(Political Biography, p. 51)* In pursuance of this education philosophy, or education for a better life, Mrs. Ekpo herself attended the Rathmine School of Domestic Economics in Dublin, Ireland in 1946 from whence she obtained a diploma in Domestic Economics. Parenthetically, while in Ireland, she gained a first hand knowledge of Irish women, and the experiences informed her book, *European Women as I See Them,* copies of which apparently no longer exist. (Interview, 1999) Though preoccupied with politics, Mrs. Ekpo nonetheless continued to express interest in women's vocational education, as reflected in the attendance of international conferences on women's education, such as the World Women's International Domestic Federation Conference, held in Moscow, Russia in 1963. She is said to have also operated a sewing and hairdressing business at Aba.

GENDER TRANSMORGRIFICATION OF NIGERIAN POLITICS

Without question, it was Mrs. Ekpo's feminist-oriented *political* activism that by and large catapulted her into national prominence. Perhaps more importantly, her entry into politics significantly altered/changed the demography of political participation, inasmuch as she succeed in bringing other women into the political arena. With the possible exception of Mrs. Funmilayo Ransome-Kuti, the incomparable Yoruba feminist and political activist, no Nigerian woman appears to have been as vocal, and as relentless, in the fight for the cause of women as Chief (Mrs.) Ekpo was. Mrs. Ramsome-Kuti (1900-1978) was a Yoruba radical feminist from Abeokuta, whose feminist ideology also centered on gender equality. As she often reminded women: "[we] were created with blood and flesh [just] like men." Therefore, "we [should jettison the feeling of] inferiority to men, [which] we inherited from our mothers...." (Johnson-Odim and Mba, For *Women and the Nation, p. 102)* In effect, women should have the courage to assert their human and political rights. To this end, Mrs. Kuti founded numerous women's organizations, such as the Abeokuta Women's Union (AWU), the Nigerian Women's Union (NWU), and the Federation of Nigerian Women's Societies (FNWS). These associations by and large not only promoted feminist solidarity, but they also advanced women's sociopolitical liberation and empowerment. Put differently, these organizations ensured that women's voices were heard in both the social and political spheres. For example, under Mrs. Kuti's leadership, Abeokuta women revolted in 1948, against the imposition of city tax on them. Their confrontation with the Alake (king) of Abeokuta resulted in the abrogation of the tax law on women as well as in the self-exile of the traditional ruler. This celebrated tax revolt thus signified women's collective power, and/or ability to bring about sociopolitical change. (For details see Johnson-Odim and Mba.) Similarly at Aba, Margaret Ekpo founded the Aba Market Women's Association (AMWA) in 1945. As analyzed below, this association proved to be an effective instrument for the social mobilization and political radicalization of women in Aba. As Mrs. Ekpo herself explained, it was the formation of the AMWA that enabled her to henceforth "talk politics" to the women, who hitherto had apparently remained politically uninvolved. At any rate, the AMWA became the visible symbol of gender/feminist solidarity and the fulcrum of Margaret Ekpo's social and political activism and power.

According to Mrs. Ekpo, it was the scarcity of salt (in the aftermath of the Second World War) that provided the stimulus for the formation of the AMWA. Simply stated, she devised an uncanny strategy to mobilize, and politically radicalize, Aba women by exploiting the salt situation. This is how she explained her maneuvers, described as "the politics of the table salt":

> At first it was not an easy job to gain the support of the women, but at this point in time, the Second World War had just ended, and an essential commodity such as salt was very difficult to get. So I used that opportunity to go round the shops, and got control of the salt and told the women that if they refused to come forward and register their names in the Aba Market Women's Association, salt would not be sold to them. (Ibid., pp. 10-11; Political Biography, p. 10-12)

Essentially, because 'there were nowhere else to buy salt in Aba," and because "the food they prepared had become increasingly tasteless without salt," women felt constrained to come. Moreover, their exasperated husbands, who reportedly had grown tired of eating meals without salt, pleadingly "asked their wives to go [and look] for [salt], even if in caves." Determined however to achieve her sociopolitical ends, Mrs. Ekpo reportedly refused initially to sell the salt to the women. Rather, she "rolled out her 'manifesto' " thus: "I am only too willing to give you all the salt you require, but only if you became members of the Aba Market Women's Association." While the more outgoing women complied forthwith, the seemingly culturally and politically conservative ones reportedly went back home to first seek their husband's approval. But it seemed to be a foregone conclusion: "the continuous preparation of food without salt and its attendant drab taste forced these men into allowing their wives to join others in the new association." The AMWA had thus begun. Political radicalization followed social mobilization, as clearly reflected in Mrs. Ekpo's powerful political message to the women:

> Do you realise that we shall join hands with our men and liberate our country from the shackles of colonialism? Do you know you have the power to drive these colonial masters out? Do you know that your sons can become District Officers just like the white men you see around? Do you realise that [those] European quarters, European hospitals, European cemetery can all be yours? They can all be yours if you want it; and that is if you fight for your independence. *(Political Biography, pp. 11-12.* Also *Nigerian Chronicle, 14* March *1995, p. 7)*

Cynics might question whether Margaret Ekpo, in fact, retailed the salt at inflated prices, just as the Alake (king) of Abeokuta did under almost similar circumstances. (Cf. Johnson-Odim and Mba, p. 86) But no matter: the politics of the table salt had proven to be a masterful strategy for the mobilization and radicalization of women in Aba. As it turned out, the Aba Market Women's Association, and other equally powerful women's organizations, to which we shall return, proved in subsequent years, to be potent forces in local and regional politics.

By all accounts, the radicalization process at Aba received a new lease on life with the advent of Mrs. Ransome-Kuti to the scene in *1949.* She had been invited to Aba by Mrs. Ekpo presumably to help her further energize Aba women as well as to inculcate in them a higher degree of feminist and political consciousness. Mrs. Ransome-Kuti, as sources reveal, did not disappoint her host. Her speeches and admonitions are said to have embodied aspects of her familiar feminist ideology of social and political equality. Specifically, she is said to have stressed to Aba women the importance of feminist solidarity, as well as the critical importance of increased political involvement, especially in matters that relate directly to the advancement of women's human and political rights. As she often warned, "we have to join hands together" to fight for women's rights, and particularly political empowerment. Mrs. Kurt's entreaties apparently injected a new dynamism to Margaret Ekpo's campaign for women's political empowerment, as she informed her mentor later. Meanwhile, in appreciation, Mrs. Ekpo presented Mrs. Knit an honorarium of unknown amount, in the name of the Aba Market Women's Association. But she refused the offer, on the grounds that, women leaders "must place themselves on the same level as the poorest women." (Johnson-Odim and Mba, p. 100) At any rate, relations between the two indomitable feminists remained close and cordial, exemplified in their collective response to the shooting of coal miners at Enugu, in November 1949, to which we now turn.

THE COAL MINERS' DEBACLE AND NIGERIAN RESPONSES

On 18 November 1949, twenty-one coal miners were fatally shot by the British colonial police at Enugu, and fifty-one others were seriously wounded.'[8] According to government official reports, the shooting was the result of a "sit down" or "go-slow" strike organized by the miners, who protested the non-payment of wage demands. The miners had demanded "just twelve pence over the former basic wage rate of 1/6d per diem." But the Colliery Corporation, under the managing director Mr. R. Bracegirdle, refused to accede to the demands, "until the output of coal is increased sufficiently to meet the men's demands." The result was the "sit down" strike that ultimately led to the shooting. Acting under the mistaken impression that the Railway Corporation had detained their husbands, wives of the miners thereupon stormed the Colliery office, and reportedly broke windows with stones, and uprooted plants from the Colliery Manager's garden. *(West African Pilot,* 18 and 21 November 1949) Peace apparently returned temporarily when "Police eventually dispersed the crowds without having to make arrests," even though a few of the women reportedly sustained injuries.

But whereas the colonial administration typically condemned the women's behavior, and insisted that they acted out of blind hysteria, Nigerian nationalists, on the other hand, extolled the women's protest. "Let it be borne in mind that the [so-called] `hysterical' women are of the same breed as the amazons of Aba who [in 1929] staged those riots that shook the bedrock of a nation. Far from being hysterical or neurotic, they knew what was happening and decided to conquer, regardless of consequences." Therefore, the blamed for the crisis was placed squarely on the shoulders of the colonial officials. Indeed, Nigerian nationalists vigorously challenged the administration's claims or propaganda that the miners were out to ruin government enterprises in the country by engaging in strike action.

> Let us hear no more about the thousands of pounds being daily lost. Let us not be wooed into hard-hearted conclusion that the hewers are black guards to make demands that would mean running the mines at a loss.... We the people cannot help but indict officialdom for pursuing a policy that forces hard working men to drastic steps and their suffering women folk to revolt. (West African Pilot, 21 Nov. 1949)

At any event, the British colonial administration laid the blame for the eventual tragedy (massacre) on the miners, insisting that they (miners) had planted "dangerous explosives" in the Iva Valley mines. The official explanation, therefore, was that, Government simply reacted to the miners' "dangerous" schemes:

> The police were [accordingly] detailed to carry out ... precautionary operation. About noon on Friday the evacuation of dangerous explosives from the Iva Valley and Obwetti mines commenced. Three lifts were made without interference, but in continuing the evacuation at Iva Valley mine the police were surrounded by a large number of miners, armed with crowbars, picks, machetes and spears, who rushed the police and attempted to disarm them and obtain possession of the explosive store. [At that point, the police fired at the miners], so as to ensure public safety. The result was the death of "eighteen men and thirty-one wounded. " (West *African* Pilot, 21November 1949. "Police Fire Enugu Strikers...."

Occurring in the heat of the nationalist movement, the shooting of the coal miners at the Iva Valley Colliery, in Enugu, could not but galvanize Nigerians to retaliatory action. Shocked and outraged, Nigerians expressed their frustration against British colonialism in the storm of protests and violence that followed the "intolerable" tragedy. Labor union leaders, for instance, were predictably incensed over the Enugu massacre, and consequently mobilized their rank and file for concerted action. "The cold-blooded massacre of about forty [sic] of our kith and kin at Enugu... is a challenge to the country as a whole and to labour in particular. If any occasion has called for concerted action and the jettisoning of sectional interests and sympathy, the present one does." (Ibid. 24 Nov. 1849) Accordingly, demonstrations erupted in virtually all the major cities in southern Nigeria, including Lagos, Enugu, Port Harcourt, Onitsha, Owerri, and Aba. The massive demonstration at the Yaba Stadium, in Lagos, was said to have symbolized the unity of Nigerians against British barbarism. In the words of the Federal Treasurer of the Nigerian Youth Movement, Bode Thomas, "The shooting has united the east and west as never before." (Ibid. 24 Nov. 1949) Press reports of events in Lagos indicated that the passion for revenge was extremely high. According to the papers, "secret instructions" were given to the Igbos in Lagos "to bring cutlasses to the meeting at the Yaba Stadium." Bloodshed was however averted, because the local leaders "warned all those with cutlasses not to use them yet." But, as Bode Thomas predicted, "There will be further disorders. We cannot keep the people calm after what happened to the miners." *(West Africa, 3* Dec. 1949, p. 1145)

While in London, the two NCNC leaders Zik and Mallam Sa'ad Zungur, also joined in the fray. In their messages of condolence to Nigerian compatriots, they sharply chastised the British administration for the wanton massacre of Nigerians at Enugu, which, as they say, "smacks of barbarism of an inexcusable type." Zik's personal telegram reads as follows:

> Shocked to learn of shooting of our people. Accept our sympathy. We cannot justify shooting of workers. This is a challenge to the whole nation. West Africans in Britain were stunned on reading the sad news in the newspapers. They are mobilising public opinion against this shocking incident.... World awake to reaction in Nigeria *(West African Pilot, 23* Nov. 1949, also 26 and 29 Nov. 1949)

International outrage against the Enugu incident was widespread, as reflected in the demonstrations in such cities like London, Berlin, Moscow, and Kingston, Jamaica to name but a few. In his public address at Trafalgar Square, London on 4 December 1949, Zik predictably escalated the rhetoric of decolonization:

> The people of Nigeria cannot continue to accept as their destiny the denial of their human rights.... Let us reinforce our rank and file in the fight for freedom. ... Be of good cheer my compatriots. The struggle for African
> freedom may be long and gloomy, but behind the cloud of suffering and disappointment loom the rays of hope and success on the distant horizon. (Robert O. Collins, 1971, p. 221)

Nigerians' reactions to the shooting of the coal miners were almost immediate, and at times violent. First, there were urgent calls by members of the Zikist Movement to put the perpetrators of the atrocity on trial. To this end, the Igbo State Union, the largest pan-Igbo organization in colonial Nigeria, took the initiative in setting up a commission of inquiry. Nationalist leaders, too, as well as the Nigerian colonial administration appointed a National

Emergency Committee of inquiry. On the whole, calls for a public show of solidarity reverberated throughout Southern Nigeria. Hence, demonstrations took place in cities like Aba, Calabar, Enugu, Onitsha, Owerri, and Port Harcourt, most of them violent. The West Africa magazine, for instance, reported of the events in Owerri and Port Harcourt respectively, as follows:

> Following the shooting at Enugu on November 18 [1949] an ugly situation developed in Eastern Nigeria. On November 22 it was reported that one European had been killed at Owerri.... Serious rioting and looting also occurred at Port Harcourt on November 25. Police sustained casualties in baton charges and fired thirteen rounds. One rioter was killed.... A two-day general strike was declared in the town for November 26-27. Loading and unloading of ships was stopped and all business ceased. Europeans only moved about with police escorts and howling mobs smashed shop windows, looted stores and even threw telephones into the streets.... All European women and children were evacuated to the Government Rest House and guarded. (West Africa, 3 Dec. 1949, p. 1145)

Missionaries' accounts also shed some light on the Port Harcourt incident. According to the Church Missionary Society (CMS) missionary, Mrs. Francis, shops were looted, including that of a local businesswoman, who confronted the looters with remarkable tenacity and courage. (Francis to Baring Gould, 1 Dec. 1949, CMS Archives: AF35/49G3/G4) In addition to the alleged looting, Port Harcourt residents were enjoined to observe Friday, Saturday, and Sunday as days of mourning. "No one was to go to work on Friday and Saturday, and no churches were to be open on Sunday." Missionaries' reaction to the Sunday proclamation was predictable, and immediate. Again to quote Mrs. Francis:

> The [CMS] pastors and leaders of all the Christian Denominations met at the [CMS] Bookshop to discuss what they should do. They decided to get a notice, if possible, into all papers and on the air that evening: to the effect that people needed the help of God more and no less in these circumstances [.] [And] that the churches would be open as usual on Sunday, and [that] all Christians were called upon to attend [church services] and pray for the guidance of God. The notice was broadcast, and all the Papers, even the new ones, published it on Saturday morning, at the request of the African Christian leaders.... [Consequently,] churches were crowded on Sunday. (Ibid.)

Also writing from Onitsha, where the members of the Zikist Movement had declared 26th November a day of mourning, the CMS Archbishop C. J. Patterson explained the impact of the Enugu tragedy on Onitsha to the authorities in London:

> We have been having our troubles and excitement as you may have heard. There was a tragedy of twenty-odd lives lost when Police opened fire at Enugu in a Colliery demonstration.... It should have been contained as an industrial dispute but the politicians have jumped in with inflammatory oratory and some young men on the look out for loot have thrown a few stones & [have caused] some damage.... [Here] at Onitsha four shots were fired, no one was killed & the loot was one of [a] bottle of whisky, all told. It is not yet quite settled. Our Nationalists will [declare] "National Days of Mourning" which no one has the courage to ignore.... The Churches have got up a Relief Fund for the Bereaved (thanks to the Christian Council.... [Throughout] the Diocese a call to worship and witness on Christmas

Day... has been sent out under the signature of the Four Bishops (2 Black and 2 White). I believe we will have a good Christmas! (Patterson to Rev. H. D. Hooper, 15Dec. 1949, CMS: AF35/49 G3/G5).

All told, the Enugu debacle sent shock waves throughout Eastern Nigeria. (For recent studies on the subject see: Akpala 1965; Iweriebor 1996; Brown 2002)

MARGARET EKPO AND THE ABA RIOTS

Riots and looting characterized the Aba women's response to the Enugu crisis. To be sure, the Enugu tragedy had inevitably plunged Aba women into predictable militancy reminiscent of the Women's War or the Aba women's revolt of 1929 against British Indirect Rule system. Under Mrs. Ekpo's leadership, a mass demonstration of both the AMWA and the newly formed Eastern branch of the Nigerian Women's Union (NWU), of which she was the president, was held at Aba on 23 November 1949 against the British massacre of Nigerian coal miners. Mrs. Ekpo and two other male politicians, Jaja Wachukwu and S. O. Mazi reportedly addressed the crowd at the rally. But Mrs. Ekpo and Jaja Wachukwu were said to have particularly warned against violence. Yet violence erupted, allegedly because of Mrs. Ekpo's "mob oratory." According to official reports, Mrs. Ekpo had unreservedly condemned the shooting of the miners, and even intimated that had any Nigerian woman been among those killed at Enugu, the town "would have known no peace" at all. In short, Nigerian "women would have launched a counteroffensive aimed at achieving the same results as the colonial masters had [inflicted] against the coal miners." (Political Biography, p. 15) It is therefore possible that Mrs. Ekpo's incendiary speech might have ignited Aba women's angry passions.

Thus, despite appeals for calm, Aba women reportedly went into a rampage against British establishments, as "yelling and fighting mad crowds looted [company] stores... including that of Messrs. G. B. Ollivant, [and they also] attacked Government offices and brought businesses to a standstill." The damage estimated at over L8, 000, (Nwaguru, 1973, p. 159) quite predictably brought forth government response. First, European women and children were evacuated from Aba to Umuahia (a nearby city). Second, the police opened fire at the unarmed demonstrators, even though, as the Acting Resident acknowledged, Mrs. Ekpo and Jaja Wachukwu had pleaded for a peaceful resolution of the crisis. In his words:

> Mrs. Ekpo came up. She and Wachukwu begged me-[acting] like persons possessed ... not to use the police but to give them time [to settle the matter]. After 10-15 minutes they [the women] began to retreat at the behest of Mrs. Ekpo.... Wachukwu and Mrs. Ekpo [then] unloaded a car full of recovered loot, again saying that the looting was criminal and not part of their plan. (Mba, *Nigerian Women Mobilized, p. 171)*

Nevertheless, Margaret Ekpo and Jaja Wachukwu were held responsible for the Aba riots. In particular, Mrs. Ekpo's militancy, or "mob oratory", is said to have actually galvanized the rioters into a violent action. Consequently, she was placed under house arrest, and ordered to report hourly to the police. Her home was also thoroughly searched, ostensibly to recover possible "illegal" materials in her possession. But even though no incriminating evidence was found, the colonial administration still considered her a political risk, i. e. a threat to peace; hence the attempt to have her deported from Aba. Happily, Aba women's collective intervention, as expressed in street protests, foiled the proposition. *(Political Biography, p. 16)*

THE WOMEN'S MARCH TO ENUGU

There then followed the momentous women's march to Enugu. Of course when provoked and mobilized, Nigerian/African women have collectively responded to challenges. (Cf. Mba, 1982, Wiper, 1989) In tat case, the women's march to Enugu in December 1949 represented a clear evidence of feminist solidarity, on the one hand, and, on the other hand, an expression of Nigerian women's collective outrage and militancy over the Enugu debacle. Mobilized under the joint leadership of Mrs. Margaret Ekpo and Mrs. Ransome-Kuti, women delegates from the Aba and Abeokuta branches of the Nigerian Women's Union (NWU) respectively converged at Enugn on 17 December 1949 for the primary purpose of dramatizing their outrage against the shooting of the miners. First and foremost, the delegates reportedly visited the wives of the miners, as well as the wounded miners, who were being treated at the Enugu General Hospital. This was followed by a public rally at which both Mrs. Ekpo and Mrs. Kuti reportedly spoke critically of British overrule that resulted to the massacre of the coal miners. Still in a show of feminist solidarity, the delegates gave approval to the Enugu Women Association's earlier demonstration. Additionally, Mrs. Ekpo and Mrs. Kuti are said to have strongly encouraged the leaders of the Enugu Women's Association to intensify their commitment to feminist causes, and to forcefully "place before the government the strong feelings of the association about the education of women." (Mba, pp. 172-73) Presumably impressed by the visit of the NWU delegates, the Enugu Women's Association reportedly changed its name to the Nigerian Women's Union, Enugu Branch. In gratitude, too, the association's leader thanked Mrs. Kuti for her inspiring admonitions. "Before [your visit], women at Enugu had no right to probe into the affairs of their country. [But now you have] educated us." (Ibid.) In a sense, Mrs. Kuti had pointed to them how to look at politics from a feminist perspective.

Mrs. Ekpo, too, seemed profoundly affected (energized) by Mrs. Kati's eloquence, political rhetoric, and radical feminism. As she gratefully wrote to her,

> I cannot explain to you what new spirit you have poured into me. I am now 100 times stronger than before. I have printed our [NWU] constitution into English, Efik and I[Abo. I want to surprise the women [in Aba] on the 14^{ls} January [1950] to tell them of the wonderful inspiration I have derived from you. (Ibid. p. 270)

MARGARET EKPO AND POLITICAL ACTIVISM

Margaret Ekpo's political activism, as already noted, began about 1945, when she joined the NCNC. But by 1953, she had come of age politically, having been appointed to the Eastern House of Chiefs (EHC) in that year (some sources say 1954) as the first and only female politician to serve in that august body. Even though her tenure in the EHC was short-lived (1953-1958), yet "Margaret [had] made history as the first female member of the House of Chiefs." (Political *Biography, p.* 18) A year later (1954), she was once again nominated to serve as a special member in the Eastern House of Assembly (EHA), where she remained until 1966. In 1961, as noted earlier, Mrs. Ekpo was elected on her own right to the House, where she distinguished herself as an eloquent speaker, a political strategist, and a fighter par excellence in the cause of feminism and national liberation. By all accounts, the Eastern House of Assembly offered Mrs. Ekpo a political platform to forcefully articulate the special interests and concerns of women, and thus deservedly emerged as the "lioness of the East." As she claims, "I was the voice of the women of Eastern Nigeria," insofar as "I defended the rights of women everywhere." Of course, Margaret Ekpo's political and feminist voice was not the only female voice in the Eastern House of Assembly from 1961. On the contrary, she joined hands with Mrs. Janet Mokelu from Onitsha, and Madam Ekpo Young from Calabar to forcefully articulate women's special interests in and out of the EHA. But the feisty Mrs. Margaret Ekpo remained unrivaled in the cause of feminism in Eastern Nigeria and beyond. Margaret Ekpo, as feminist scholars have recently affirmed, was certainly "far more articulate than her women counterparts in the [Eastern and] Western House of Assembly, and was [particularly] eloquent in making demands on behalf of women." (Mba, 269) In her view, there was no question that she was destined to do so. For "Men don't worry a lot about women's affairs." Consequently, a woman's voice seemed necessary in the Assembly, at least "to keep men on the right lines".

Margaret Ekpo's nationalist ideology of Africa for the Africans (concept of gender equality) often found expression in her ardent advocacy for women's economic empowerment. For example, she strenuously defended the rights of Nigerian women to secure gainful employment. To this end, she campaigned against the subordination of Nigerian women's interests to those of European women. In brief, Mrs. Ekpo raised strong objection to the employment of European women (including the wives of colonial officials) in government and commercial establishments instead of African women. Arguing from the nationalists' ideology of Africa for the Africans, she insisted that African/Nigerian women, not European women, ought to be the rightful employees in all government and commercial enterprises. To do otherwise, she protested, was to deny African women their natural rights to economic well-being or empowerment.

Similarly of concern was the Christian missionaries' practice of retrenching married female schoolteachers, who were either pregnant, or nursing their babies-a policy that seemed rampant within the Roman Catholic Mission. To Margaret Ekpo, this was patently a bad policy, precisely because it signified gender-related job insecurity. Still worse, it was tantamount to marriage penalty. Therefore, arguing (correctly) that Nigerian working women had the right to retain their jobs when married, she proposed legislation against the policy. Political intervention ultimately brought this reprehensible to an end. (For discussions on this issue see Political Biography, p. 27; also *West Africa,* 22 August 1954, p. 773)

On the political front, too, Mrs. Ekpo was deeply concerned about the exclusion of women in political appointments. She, therefore, strongly campaigned for the appointment of women to the Eastern Region's Marketing Board. In British West Africa generally, Marketing Boards were statutory export monopolies, created by the colonial governments, and inherited by African governments at independence. They were responsible for the purchase of cash crops like palm oil, palm kernel, cocoa, cotton, etc. Because there was no competition whatsoever producers were consequently "in danger of exploitation." (See: P. T. Bauer, *West*

African Trade, 1963, p. 266) For Mrs. Ekpo, to be sure, the exclusion of women from the Eastern Regional Marketing Board was patently unfair and illogical, given that women, after all, were the producers of palm produce: they press or squeeze the oil, crack the palm kernels, and carry the produce to the market. Speaking therefore on this matter in the Eastern House of Assembly (1954), she charged that the non-inclusion of women in the Board smacked of blatant gender discrimination. For remedy, Mrs. Ekpo accordingly called for women's representation in the Eastern Regional Marketing Board, particularly insofar as Board policies by and large affected women directly. (See Nigerian National Archives, Enugu: *Parliamentary Debates of the Eastern House of Assembly,* 15 Dec. 1954; also *Political Biography, p.* 27) The agitation yielded handsome dividends, as reflected in subsequent government edicts:

> Committees and Boards formed following suggestions made at this meeting should [,] as far as possible [,] be composed of men and women who would give disinterested service and who would not draw any allowance for attendance. ("Minutes of a Meeting of Leaders of Thought of Eastern Nigeria ...23 ^{d} April 1960", p. 7. "Hereafter Minutes.")

To be sure, Mrs. Ekpo's concerns for women's empowerment were wide-ranging. For example, in 1988, she sharply chastised the Nigerian Military Administration for the non-inclusion of women in the Armed Forces Ruling Council, which, until 1999, was the military administration's policy-making body. In effect, women ought to be included at all levels of economic, political, and military services. (See *Business Tide,* Sept. 1988: 8) It is instructive to note that, in response to women's (particularly Ekpo's) agitation for inclusiveness, the NCNC leaders at the time of independence (1960) resolved that,

> All schemes of development [and administration] must take the womenfolk of the Region into consideration. The women are now awake and would no longer be satisfied with being expected to make a fall time job of their domestic chores. ("Minutes.")

Accordingly, more women should be appointed as NCNC Divisional Organizing Secretaries, inasmuch as "two of our women Organising Secretaries Mrs. Onyia and Afamefuna are doing quite a commendable job." ("Chairman's Address: N. C. N. C. East Regional Conference, 5'" Nov. 1960)

Still of concern, however, was rural women's economic handicap as reflected in the absence of improved transportation facilities. Speaking on this matter in the Eastern House of Assembly in 1954, Mrs. Ekpo drew special attention to the critical importance of improved road transportation facilities in the region. Indeed, her crusade for improved infrastructure, and particularly the provision of better roads, was certainly consistent with her commitment to women's economic advancement. For as she insistently argued, improved road transportation would invariably enable women to more conveniently carry their produce to the local markets, and ipso facto enhance their economic well being. Therefore, Mrs. Ekpo urged the Government to give priority attention to the improvement of rural roads, inasmuch as efficient transportation system, among other things, is a sine qua non for national economic development. The deterioration of most of the road system in the region by the 1950s gave increased impetus to the agitation for corrective action, especially as the poor condition of the roads created difficulties both to pedestrians and to lorries traveling on the roads. (Cf. Falola

2004) As Margaret Ekpo envisioned it, investment in basic infrastructure, as in roads, augured well for economic progress. In short, improved road transportation would serve a dual purpose: first, it contributes to the overall advancement of trade, and second, it enhances women's economic empowerment through increased income via trade. All told, Margaret Ekpo's zealous agitation for improved road transportation was aimed at ensuring women's economic and political emancipation. (See Mba, p. 117, footnote 2)

In furtherance of this objective or mission, Mrs. Ekpo directed a great deal of her political capital to campaigns particularly aimed at securing women's political empowerment. To this end, this shrewd politician and strategist founded several women's associations, whose basic aims were twofold: first, social mobilization, and second, political participation. In short, Mrs. Ekpo's efforts were geared toward increased women's political participation in local, regional, and national politics. Thus, in addition to the Aba Market Women's Association (AMWA), she founded the Aba Township Women's Association (ATWA), as well as the Aba Branch of the Nigerian Women's Union (NWU). Furthermore, she was the architect of the NCNC Women's Wing, which was formed in 1958. All of these associations, as it turned out, became potent forces in the Nigerian political landscape.

In particular, the AMWA and the ATWA became effective instruments of political reformulation in Aba, in the sense that the associations gave rise to women's political representation in the Aba Urban District Council. As elaborated below, the advent of women in politics effectively challenged the sociopolitical status quo in the city council. Established in 1952/53, the Aba Urban District Council was virtually dominated by men. By 1954, however, Margaret Ekpo felt that the time had come for women's voices to be heard in Aba city- politics. Hence the formation, in that year, of the ATWA, which eventually altered men's political monopoly. In the December 1955 election, for instance, Mrs. Ekpo successfully mobilized members of the association and encouraged them not only to become involved in politics, but also to contest in the election. The result was almost a foregone conclusion. Women now not only voted for the first time in city politics, but were also elected to the Aba Urban District Council, essentially because, "the majority of voters were women." (Mba, p. 117) Thanks to Mrs. Ekpo's political vision, therefore, women emerged henceforth as a force to be reckoned with in Aba city politics, and by extension national politics. In effect, the long-standing "edging out of the female from power discourses" could no longer be sustained. Put differently, the era of male political domination of Aba city-politics had virtually come to an end. In gratitude, Aba women could proudly and justifiably say to Mrs. Ekpo:

> You came.
> You pried open [our] silence.
> You reached out in sisterhood
> And [you] gave us articulation.
> (Modified from Grace E. Okereke's "Sisterhood," in Issue: *Journal of* Opinion (1997), p. 30)

Shortly after the Aba Urban District Council elections, the Council was dissolved because of alleged bribery and corruption connected with the system of allocating market stalls and lock-up shops. A Caretaker Committee, of which Mrs. Ekpo herself was a member, was thereupon appointed to run the affairs of the Council. In the subsequent election of 1958, Mrs. Ekpo was elected "unopposed" to the Urban District Council, thanks too, to the women's vote. As expected, she became a powerful voice in the articulation of women's interests and concerns. (For details see: Nwagum, p. 189; Mba, pp. 116-117)

Increased women's political involvement remained Mrs. Ekpo's political credo, which now resonates in feminist circles: "We consider that the feminist movement should be transformed into a political voice, because it is the only way equality of rights and opportunities will reach every woman." (Nelson & Chowdhury, 1999, p. 14) Thus, in 1958, Mrs. Ekpo initiated the movement for the formation of the NCNC Women's Wing in Eastern Nigeria, so as to ensure that women's political voices were heard loud and clear *in the inner circles of the NCNC*. As she reasoned, several men's NCNC "wings" existed in various parts of the country, such as the NCNC Youth Wing, the Zikist Movement, the Elders Vanguard, and so on. Since all these "wings" were mostly male dominated organizations, she, therefore, embarked on the campaign for the establishment of the NCNC *women's* wing in Eastern Nigeria, which would articulate women's interests and concerns within the party. After consultations with Mrs. Flora Azikiwe, wife of the National President of the NCNC Dr. Nnamdi Azikiwe (Zik), a meeting of NCNC women was convened at Enugu, in 1958. Here is part of Margaret Ekpo's "Address" to the women:

> Dear ladies, you're all welcome to the Coal City of Enugu. Before I do my main speech, it is my pleasure to introduce to you, distinguished ladies, the person for whom we're all gathered here today. I am talking about no less a person than the wife of our party President, Her Excellency, Mrs. Flora Azikiwe.

After all the pleasantries, she then explained the major objectives of the proposed organization, which included the promotion of women's interests and concerns within the party. The result was the formation of the NCNC Eastern Nigeria Women's Wing, with headquarters at Enugu. In deference to her position as the First Lady, Mrs. Azikiwe was elected as the National President, while Mrs. Ekpo was elected as the National Vice-President. However, in 1960, she (Ekpo) became the National President, following the departure of Mrs. Azikiwe (and her husband) to Lagos, upon Zik's appointment at Nigeria's independence as the Governor-General of Nigeria. (See Political *Biography,* pp. 19- 20) As sources indicate, the NCNC Women's Wing thereafter directed its energies to the campaign for women's political education and enlightenment, as well as to regional and national political campaigns.

It has been emphasized throughout this chapter that women's political empowerment remained central to Mrs. Ekpo's feminist agenda. Consequently, she and her mentor Mrs. Ransome-Kuti assiduously campaigned for women's political emancipation, and more particularly women of Northern Nigerian, who, until 1977, remained politically disenfranchised. Thus by the mid-1950s and early 1960s considerable effort was directed toward the political liberation of Nigerian women as a whole. The duo bemoaned the political marginalization of women at all levels of national and regional politics. They embraced the sociopolitical ideology that no nation can rise without its women being fully involved. Accordingly, the indefatigable feminists traveled widely throughout the country to raise women's political consciousness. And they urged women to become more forceful in the demand for increased female representation in both the federal and regional assemblies, especially given women's overwhelming numerical strength in the overall population of

Nigeria (over 50 percent). In addition, they asserted that women, not men, ought to be the chief advocates of women's causes. To this end, Mrs. Ransome-Kuti declared:

> Adequate representation of women in all legislatures should be guaranteed.... I am appealing to every woman in Nigeria to realize the importance and urgency of the need for the emancipation of our womanhood. We should be awake and accept our responsibilities by intensifying the contributions we are making towards the progress of Nigeria. (Johnson-Odim and Mba, pp. 102-103)

Of particular concern, as already noted, was the political disenfranchisement of Northern Nigerian women, attributed to the attitude of Muslims towards women, in general and their aversion to women's political participation. It was thus against this backdrop that Mrs. Ekpo and Mrs. Kuti launched a crusade for the political emancipation of women in Northern Nigeria. To this end, they petitioned the Northern Nigerian colonial administration demanding voting rights for women. And since women figured prominently in the population calculus of northern Nigeria, Mrs. Ekpo and Mrs. Kuti further warned that unless women were accorded voting rights, "the number of seats allocated to the Northern Region in the enlarged [Federal] House [of Assembly] should be drastically reduced...." (Ibid.) But sadly, the protests fell on deaf ears, until 1977, when finally women in Northern Nigeria were granted voting rights. (Ibid. p. 105; Okoujo, 1991, p. 27)

Yet problems remained. The early post-independence era (1960s), for instance, marked a period of political uneasiness and uncertainty. The results of the 1963 national census, for example, not only provoked considerable controversy but it also threatened the political stability of the country. According to the census figures, Northern Nigeria appeared to have comprised half the population of the country. To Southern politicians, this raised the prospect of Northern Nigeria inevitably dominating the federal assembly, given that political representation in the Federal House of Assembly was based on the population of the three major regions-Northern, Western, and Eastern Regions. Heated debates thus ensued over the census figures. Southern Nigerian politicians' opposition to the census was twofold: first, they viewed the census figures as being "blatantly inflated." Second, they were apprehensive that, if the "inflated" figures were accepted, the Northern Region would certainly wield a preponderant power in the federal legislature. What seemed even more ominous to feminists like Margaret Ekpo, was the prospect that the Northern People's Congress (NPC), dominated by conservative Muslims, who seemed virtually unsympathetic to feminist causes, would almost certainly disenfranchise women all over Nigeria. This was essentially the basis for her strong protest against the acceptance of the 1963 "inflated" census figures. As she explained:

> We the women of the South wonder what is going to happen to us if the representation in the Federal House will be on the basis of the inflated census figures.... [That will mean that,] I, Margaret Ekpo, Mrs. Mokelu and Madam Young [in the Eastern House of Assembly], will leave the floor of the House because women will not vote again. (Quoted in Mba, p. 272)

Alas, her fears never materialized, as women continued to serve in both the federal and regional legislatures.

ACCOLADES AND CONCLUSION

To most Nigerians, and particularly the educated elite, Chief (Mrs.) Margaret Ekpo remains a remarkable feminist and nationalist. Consequently, she has been (and continues to be) the subject of sociopolitical discourse in Nigeria. For example, she has been described variously as being "glamorous and stately," or as "a lady always with a bright smile," and as a feminist pioneer with "a quick skillful brain." Although now frail because of old age, yet she still retains some of her charm and sharpness of mind. When for example, I interviewed her by telephone hook-up from Kent State University (Ohio, U S A) on 9 September 1999,1 was pleasantly surprised to notice that she could still vividly remember details of her life, and particularly many aspects of her political career, as if it were yesterday. A Nigerian reporter, who interviewed her earlier, in 1996, when she was 82, had this to say of this seemingly ageless woman: "Age could be telling on her frame, but it has definitely not affected her intuition and intellect. The way she quotes dates leaves you wondering if she was 82 or 28." (Saturday *Punch,* 12 October 1996, p. 14) Equally remarkable, despite her advancing years, Mrs. Ekpo still retains some of her energy and humor, which characterized her political life. As she herself affirmed, "Yes, my dear, I still have [some of] my energy," adding, "I think my energy is hereditary. My mother [who died] at the age of 83 was very strong and my grandfather, the father of my mother, might [have been] 100 years before he died. So the energy I have is hereditary." Besides, "I was very active [during the political days], jumping from one soapbox to the other, campaigning. I think this is one of the things that contributed to my energy." (Interview 1999; also *Political Biography, p.* 51) It was this enormous energy that she usefully directed to nationalist and feminist causes. Nigeria, Mrs. Ekpo is still perceived as the embodiment of "perfect leadership, sacrifice, and service, not only to the nation and womanhood, but also to humanity." *(West Africa, 14* March 1953) Consequently, she has been showered with numerous national honors and awards. These include the Order of the Niger (ON), conferred on her by the Federal Government; Life Patron, bestowed on her by the Women in Nigeria (WIN) organization, and the National Council of Women's Societies (NCWS), respectively. Also in recognition of her extraordinary service to the nation, as well as her relentless advocacy for "the upliftment of women," she was awarded (along with two other women) the First Queen Amina Award in 1992. Queen Amina, who ruled in the 15th century, was the illustrious and legendary ruler of the pre-colonial Nigerian State, Zaria. (See the *National Concord,* 3 March 1992, p. 5) Upon receiving a certificate, a plaque, and the sum of N20, 000 (naira), she remarked with obvious excitement and gratitude: "And now I am having the last and best laughter."

In addition, Mrs. Ekpo was the recipient of honorary degrees from various universities in Nigeria and abroad, and these include the honorary degree of Doctor of Letters (D. Lit.) from the University of Calabar (1995). In the eloquent words of the Vice-Chancellor:

> The image of Hon. Chief (Mrs.) Margaret Ekpo has been so legendary, so ramifying, and so enduring that at no point would it be correct in her long career, to describe her as a politician, given what we now know of politicians... Being a wife, a mother, a grand-mother, an activist, and an ardent believer in equal rights to women, children, men and minorities, her rich plumage of honours will ever grow and groom with time. *(Nigerian Chronicle, 14* March *1995, p. 7)*

Similarly, Nigerian newspapers and social organizations have showered praises on this illustrious figure and quintessential feminist of the twentieth century. In its lead article of 3 March *1992* entitled "Honour to Women of Substance," the Nigerian *National Concord (p. 5)* observed:

> Mrs. Margaret Ekpo has been in the limelight for over *40* years now.... For many years she was the only female voice at the defunct Eastern House of Assembly where she was nominated as a special member. Mrs. Margaret Ekpo was a political juggernaut, suffering detention for her fearlessness in speaking against some of the obnoxious government policies.... On the international scene, Mrs. Ekpo's political dexterity saw her through many international inter-parliamentary sessions.... A mother of two sons and many grandchildren, Mrs. Ekpo is an executive member of the Nigerian Red Cross Society, National Council of Women Society and Society for the Prevention of Cruelty to animals.

More recently, too, the Nigerian *Vanguard* (newspaper), described her as "a great patriot" and "a warrior," and even compared her with the French heroine Joan of Arc *(1412*1431*)*. "Like Joan of Are, Margaret Ekpo also suffered arrest and detention, although while Joan was burned to death, Margaret Ekpo survived her detention [1966-70]. Still the two heroines had faced battle each in her own way alongside the men who were considered the traditional warriors." *(Sunday Vanguard, 30* May 2001, p. 3) As well, Mrs. Ekpo, described as the "doyen of feminist struggle in Nigeria," her feat has been likened to those of three other Nigerian predecessors: Queen Amina, Mrs. Ransome-Kuti, and Madam Tinubu. *(Nigerian Chronicle,* 28 March 1992: 7)

Now, at the age of 90 (in 2004), Mrs. Ekpo is evidently no longer in active politics. Yet her views on politics continue to be solicited. And quite characteristically, she does not seem to shy away from controversy. For instance, when asked in 1999 (?) to offer advice to the new breed of politicians in Nigeria today, the elder stateswoman cautioned: "whoever wants to go into politics must be prepared to rub shoulders, grow a thick skin; it is no joke. Especially these days, [politics is] not like in my days." With particular reference to what she calls the "politics of the stomach," so rampant in contemporary Nigerian politics, Mrs. Ekpo advised: "Whoever wants to go into politics must know that it is not for his stomach and his relatives alone, but for the people of Nigeria." And she further warned: anyone who wants to go into politics "should forget about himself, be selfless in serving" the nation, an admonition, which the reputable Roman Catholic Archbishop of Lagos, Anthony Olubumi Okogie, echoed.

> Selfishness, which has characterized our leadership and service, must give way to selflessness. Henceforth, our mentality must be changed from I to we, and, as in America, our concern should be what we can do for our country, and not what the country can do for us. (Quoted in Guardian News, 31 Dec. 1999)

But Mrs. Ekpo's disclaimer not withstanding, all was not rosy in the First Republic; selfishness, graft, and "politics of the stomach certainly prevailed in her political days." (For discussions of corruption or "politics of the belly," see: Jean Francois Bayart, 1993) After all, wasn't it corruption, coupled with mal-administration that led to the fall of the First Republic in 1966? As one Nigerian critic put it pointedly, the leaders of the First Republic "seemed more concerned with their own egos, political survival, and personal enrichment than policies to liberate the poor." (Falola, *Economic Reform,* 2004...) Certainly, corruption and unbridled ambition, as the military gang that overthrew the government in 1966 declared in a national broadcast, contributed to the collapse of the First Republic. In their words:

> Our enemies are the political profiteers, swindlers, the men in high and low places that seek bribes and demand 10 percent, those that seek to keep the country permanently divided so that they can remain in office as Ministers and VIPs of waste, the tribalists, [and] the nepotists.

Yet, given the current state of affairs in Nigeria, characterized by unprecedented social misery, mass unemployment, brazen corruption, and looting of the national treasury by the leaders, the "old regime" appears to have been "the age of progress." As Mrs. Ekpo herself avers, "what is happening in Nigeria today is bad. Nothing is working in the country today. No light, no water, no fuel. Nothing can survive. Mark you, in my days during the First Republic there was no oil boom, but the budget was sufficient. [Development programs were in progress]. Now everything has gone to the dogs.... God ... deliver us from the evil that is bordering us today." And she ruefully adds:

> This is not the Nigeria I planned for and worked with others to build. There is a lot of corruption. [There is now] a lot of distress. Everything has gone wrong with this country. From the policeman to the farmer and the housewife, people have changed; people are now all corrupt.... Things have changed. Now, with our economic strangulation people have become [too] greedy. (The African Guardian, 7 June 1993, p. 24)

A contemporary, M. C. K. Ajuluchukwu, agrees: "The Nigerian leaders who fought for the nation's independence did so without 'reward,' but with the sole aim of and vision of making Nigeria a great country. Today, the reverse is the case. Today it is a shame to be a Nigerian." And he sadly concludes:

> Today [2001] at 80, I feel saddened by the widespread decadence in our country. It is as though contemporary office holders have decided to embark on a deliberate enthronement of corruption in all facets of public life. Verily, verily, it can be said that only the uninformed may likely believe that the Nigerian government still belongs to the people. It is that bad! *(Nigerian Guardian,* 12 & 13 February 2001)

CONCLUSION: THE DARK DAYS IN THE LIFE OF A HEROINE

Sadly, Margaret Ekpo has not been immune to "the evil that is bordering [Nigerians] today." On the contrary, she now appears to be in dire financial straits. "These days," she wrote to this writer, "I can only afford to have a few meals" a day, due largely to the ever-increasing poverty of the masses. Even the house "I now occupy in Calabar," is "a gift from the Cross River State Government," her house at Aba having been destroyed during the Nigeria-Biafra War (1967-70). The government, she acknowledged, "built this house for me as a way of saying 'thank you'...for being the first woman in those days to organise and enlighten women and take part in politics and all that. So this is what they say I should take as a 'thank you' house." But while Mrs. Ekpo is obviously appreciative of the Cross River Government's largesse, she nonetheless deeply regrets that she no longer has her own assets, and has now to depend on the "benevolence of friends" to survive. After all, she reminisced,

"Had I played monetary polities ...I would [certainly] have been more financially secure." She elaborated:

> You know, in those days, I was not playing monetary politics; otherwise in those early days when Margaret Ekpo was Margaret Ekpo, there is no state in the federation where I would not have had some houses. By now, as I am sitting down, every month, I would have been sending something into my bank. (Saturday *Punch, 12* Oct 1996, p. 14)

It is indeed ironic that, at her advanced age, the pioneer feminist and nationalist, now relies on handouts from friends at home and abroad for sustenance. In a letter to me dated 15 September 1999, she wrote with amazing candor: "I am hereby enclosing my appeal for financial help.... If it is possible for you, kindly sent [sic] whatever you can." And she added elsewhere, "My regret in life is that I sacrificed myself politically for this nation and [thereby] forgot all about myself. I left all my children, my husband, my job and plunged very deep into politics, but here I am today [almost destitute]." (Political Biography, p. 51) Yet, despite her evident social misery, Mrs. Ekpo continues to look back with pride at her political accomplishments. "My proudest achievement is that I joined hands with those eminent Nigerians to fight for the independence of this nation." But she nonetheless laments the precarious life she now lives: Nigerians, "whom we fought for," have "forgotten all about us." True to form, she warned: "Nigerians of this present generation [should] not forget those women who are [now] playing deep into politics, [and] who are trying their best from where we left, to continue for the betterment of this nation." And while also encouraging women to continue the "good fight" bequeathed to them, that is, the struggle for women's sociopolitical empowerment, Mrs. Ekpo cautioned that, "Existing women associations should not create avenues for women to be lords to their husbands but make men recognize women's worth in building the nation." *(Political Biography, pp. 51-52; Business Tide,* September *1988, p. 8)*

To sum up, Mrs. Ekpo remains an illustrious figure in Nigeria's social and political history. Without question, her commitment to the "cause of feminism," as well service to the nation, has certainly immortalized her as a heroine and a nationalist par excellence. Indeed, because she has left an enduring mark on the Nigerian social and political landscape, she, therefore, deserves an equally enduring national recognition. And Nigerians have effusively done so, at least as mirrored in "Ekpo: A Salute to Grandmother of Progress." (Sunday Concord, 8 March *1992)* Furthermore, this tribute to the legendary Margaret Ekpo by the Secretary to the Government of the Federation, is equally apropos:

> Her participation in *politics* was self-sacrifice home out of an avid desire to improve the lot of the people.... *Politics,* to her, was service and a struggle for national emancipation not a business or an avenue to get rich quick- [Consequently her reward] resides in the appreciation of her efforts by her people and the nation, and the realization that the seeds that she [and] her contemporaries sowed years ago have now begun to yield fruits [evidenced] in the number of Nigerian women in elected and appointed political offices....

Finally, let me close this chapter with this epitaph that recognizes Mrs. Ekpo's never-ending social relevance and commitment to the cause of feminism:

> Margaret Ekpo was undoubtedly a courageous woman [, who fought] prejudice and oppression on two deadly fronts. She was at once a female liberationist leading the fight for

the emancipation of women and a nationalist fighting for Nigeria's independence.... [W]ith the heart of a Napoleon Bonaparte (1769-1821) [she] stormed the barricades of male dominated Nigerian politics by day and got in the trenches at night with Nigeria's freedom fighters to plot the overthrow of the Queen of England. Now living in almost undeserved obscurity, Chief (Mrs.) Margaret Ekpo has had no national or state institutions named after her. No currency note bears her picture; no commemorating stamp marks her great footsteps on the sands of Nigerian history. That's a pity because a nation, which fails to honour its heroes and heroines will soon find that it has none. (Sunday Vanguard, 20 May 2001, pp. 2-3)

REFERENCES

Books and Articles

Akpala, Agwu, "The Background of the Colliery Shooting Incident in 1949; *Journal of the Historical Society of Nigeria*, Vol. 3, No. 2 (Dec. 1965): 335-365

Bauer, P. T. *West African Trade: A Study of Competition, Oligopoly and Monopoly in a Changing Economy* (London: Routledge & Kegan, 1963).

Bayart, Jean-Francois, *The State in Africa: The politics of the Belly* (London: Longman, 1993)

Collins, Robert O. (ed.), *African History: Text and Readings* (New York: Random House, 1971.

Ekechi, Felix K., "Perceiving Women as Catalysts," *Africa Today*, Vol. 43, No, 3 (July-/Sept.1996): 235-249

--------------------, "Women and the Democratization Process in Africa," in *The Transition to Democratic Governance in Africa: The Continuing Struggle*, edited by John Mbaku & Julius O. Ihonvbere (Westport, Connecticut/London: Praeger, 2003), pp. 203-220.

Falola, Toyin, *Economic Reform and Modernization in Nigeria, 1945*-1965 (Kent, Ohio: Kent State University, 2004)

Interview with Mrs. Margaret Ekpo, 9 Sept. 1999. I wish to express my sincere gratitude to Mrs. Ekpo for the interview and for supplying a copy of her biography as well as other historical documents.

Iweriebor, Ehiedu G., *Radical Politics in Nigeria 1945-1950: The Significance of the Zikist Movement* (Zaria, Nigeria: Amadu Bello University Press, 1996)

Johnson-Odim, *Cheryl and Nina Mba, For Women and the Nation: Funmilayo Ransome Kati of Nigeria* (Urbana/Chicago: University of Illinois Press, 1997)

Koehl, Robert L., "Transplanting British Universities to Africa and India," *Journal of Higher Education*, Vol, XXXIX, No. 1 January 1968):.::

-------------------- -- " The Uses of the University: Past and Present in Nigerian Education Culture." Part I, *Comparative Education Review*, Vol. XV, No. 2 (June 1971): 116-131; also Part 2, Vol. 15, No. 3 (Oct. 1971): 367-377.

---------------------, *The Black Corps: The Structure and Power Struggles of the Nazi SS* (Madison: The University of Wisconsin Press, 1983).

Mba, Nina, *Nigerian Women Mobilized* (Berkeley: University of California Press, 1982).

Mezu, Rose U., *Women in Chains* (Owerri: Randallistown, MD: Black Academy, 1994).

Nelson, Barbara J. & Najma Chowdhury (eds.), *Women and Politics Worldwide* (New Haven: Yale University Press, 1999).

Nwaguru, J. E. N, *Alm and British Rule* (Enugu, Nigeria: Santana Press, 1973).

Ogundipe-Leslie, Molera, *Re-creating Ourselves: African Women and Critical Transformations* (Trenton, NJ: Africa World Press, 1994)

Okereke, Grace E., "Raising Women's Consciousness Towards Transformations in Nigeria: The Role of Literature", *Issue: A Journal of Opinion*, Vol. XXV (1997: 28-30.

Okonjo, Kamene, *Nigerian Women's Participation in National Politics: Legitimacy and Stability in an Era of Transition* (Boston University Working Paper, No. 221 (July 1991)

Onyche Susan, *Rights of Women: An Address delivered at Nwaorieubi Mbaitoli*, LGA (Owerri, 1982)

Sooryarmoorthy, R. and D. Renjini, "Political Participation of Women: The Case of Women Councilors in Kerata, India," *Journal of Third World Studies*, Vol. XVII, No ... (2000): 45-60.

Uchendu, P. K., *The Role of Nigerian Women in Politics: Past and Present* (1993)

Wiper, Audrey, "Kikuyu Women and the Harry Thuku Disturbances: Some Uniformities of female Militancy," *Africa*, Vol. 59 (1989): 300-337

Women in Nigeria, *Margaret Ekpo: A Political Biography* (Women in Nigeria, 1996)

Yusuf, Bilkisu, "Nigerian Women in Politics: Problems and Prospects," in *Women in Nigeria Today* (London: Zed Press, 1985).

ARCHIVAL SOURCES AND NEWSPAPERS

The African Guardian, June 7, 1993

Business Tide, Sept. 1988

Church Missionary Society (CMS) Archives: AF35149G31G4 & CMS: AF35/49 G3/G5

Nigerian National Archives: Enugu, Parliamentary Debates of the Eastern House of Assembly, September 15, 1954.

National Concord, March 3, 1902

Nigerian Chronicle, March 14, 1995

Nigerian Guardian News, December 31, 1999

Nigerian Saturday Punch, Oct. 12, 1996

Nigerian Sunday Vangard, May 20, 2001

West Africa, August 23, 1953

West African Pilot, November 18, 1949 & Nov. 21, Nov. 24, Nov. 26, and Nov. 29, 1949.

Women's Higher Education in Nigeria: A Shift in Cultural Paradigm

Mabel O. N. Enwemnwa
Prince George County Public Schools Board of Education
Maryland, USA

Introduction

The thought and belief, widely based on the Cultural Reproduction Theory with the implication that people forge their own meaning systems in response to the societal position that they are made to assume, are beginning to vary globally. While Production theorists suggest the existence of a potential for change in the structure, the Theory of Reproduction connotes invariant structures, (Enwemnwa, 1993). Meanwhile, Willis presents a picture of Cultural Reproduction, with its implication that people forge their own meaning systems in response to the societal positions they are made to assume. The same can be said to be true of Nigerian women and (higher) education in the twentieth/twenty-first century.

Background/Purpose of this Study

In a 1992 study (Enwemnwa, 1993), some specific objectives were aimed at, among others,

1. Examining some underlying factors in government policies and practices in the Nigerian educational system that had influenced and were still influencing the issue of women's limited contribution to and participation in government;
2. Finding out whether parents' and society's attitudes have changed: i.e. whether parents' perceptions influence their daughters' choices of higher education programs;

3. Determining the relationships between and among variables that seemed to impact upon Nigerian women's access to higher education;
4. Finding out the actual level of imbalance in educational attainments between the sexes; and
5. Arriving at findings that would lead to some useful recommendations that may inform future governments' educational policies and programs for all citizens, with regard to equal opportunities.

The questions that emerged, then, were as follows:

1. What educational programs have been made available by the government? How accessible were these to the women?
2. What were the implementation problems? Were these real or imagined?
3. Were there awareness programs in place? What were the driving forces?

Based on these questions, other questions arose. They were:

1. Is there still a causal relationship between the Nigerian women's access to higher education and their participation in national economic and technological development?
2. Are most Nigerian women with access to higher education strictly from higher Socio-Economic Status (SES)?
3. Is there still an inequitable distribution of educational resources and facilities and opportunities?

Many recent articles and surveys have focused on women's limited access to higher education and its effect on their participation in national development in Africa in general, and Nigeria in particular. These writings and other data which were obtained directly from primary sources have been studied and analyzed to identify some current trends that can be linked to these factors that had determined and are most likely to impact upon women's differential levels of participation in the overall development of their country. In most cases, societal attitudes, Socio-Economic Status of these women have continued to serve as the remote control buttons. Meanwhile, traditional beliefs, values and colonialism have all now been relegated to a more remote distance. They are no longer the immediate factors that were in 1993, (Enwemnwa, 1993). For example, it is no longer a strange idea when a girl declares her major as medicine, mechanical engineering, pharmacy or physics. Indeed, the majority of parents would now like their daughters to get into technical areas, because they are qualified and can compete favorably. Just as the earlier total control by Central government continues to wane, the Nigerian economy has become more capitalist. Thus, in the new dispensation, the tendency is for the women to be more economically and politically powerful, (Adeleke, 1990) Although Okebukola (1998), stated that there has been no serious efforts by government to lower admission standards to benefit the women, yet there is every indication that the Nigerian women did not allow educational opportunities to pass them by, (Odejide, 2003). According to Odejide, educational policy makers in Nigeria continue to face the enduring dilemma of promoting science and technology for national development, while advocating for closer attention to women's needs and interests by way of preparation for effective participation in such national development programs, (Odejide, 2003). Participation at higher levels, resulting from unequal access to higher education remains dominated by men. A look at the gender distribution of staffing for the higher institutions, as well as JAMB admission patterns, clarifies the picture, (JAMB admissions tables for UNIBEN). Factors that influence these patterns vary from region to region, thus helping to determine what goes to women and what criteria are used.

DISCUSSION

A simple random sampling was used, with a total of 52 questionnaires with the 3 open-ended questions administered to respondents in the University of Benin community. Fifty (50) of these were returned, giving a good 96% return rate. Although this result is high, it cannot be generalized to all Nigerian universities because of the sample size and the differences in demographic characteristics. However, it can be applicable to the other federal and Southern universities. It can also form a baseline since the University of Benin is federal and has a population that reflects the federal character—with students from all parts of the country. Also, there were a total of 10 interviews carried out: 2 with female professors, 2 department chairs, 2 non-academic staff administrators, including the registrar, and 2 graduate students. The undergraduate Respondents, who ranged from 19 – 25 years old, were in their 3rd or 4th years in the Social Sciences, Engineering Education and Medical Sciences. Of the 50 undergraduates, only 2 were Moslems; the others were Christians. Most of the students in Engineering and Medical sciences had both parents with at least a college degree. Those in Education and Social Sciences had parents that have at least a secondary school certificate.

Most of the interviewees in key positions, spoke candidly on the slow and arduous task of constantly working to prove themselves as being right for the job—always trying to justify their appointment. All the interviewees are also parents, who work and/or live on campus. The informal discussants were the University Staff Club officers and attendants, waiters, security officers and community members.

In an NTA (Nigerian Television Authority) question-and-answer session, televised on December 14, 2004, the Director-General of NAFDAC*3, Dr. Dora Akunyuli, the "Iron Lady" of Nigeria who has the arduous task of controlling the quality of drugs and beverages, explained how much she has to struggle and "fight" to prove that the confidence reposed in her by the executive was not misplaced. She virtually has to work thrice as much as her male counterparts, since she is constantly "stepping on male toes." Many pharmaceutical companies who "have something to hide," often try to discredit her.

The story was the same with Professor Grace Alele-Williams who was the first woman Vice-Chancellor in Nigeria. However, there have been a number of institutional arrangements made between the government and some agencies and some public institutions to boost women's participation through the creation of "new sites" for learning for women through in-service, part-time and "sandwich" programs. This is more common in education, but has spread to other areas like Banking and Finance, Law, and Public Administration. This has continued to improve.

The author of this article had gone into this study with the following assumptions:

1. There is a marked increase in the number of women completing higher education programs since 1993;
2. There is increased awareness among Nigerian women about higher educational opportunities and their benefits;
3. There is an increased and demonstrable determination on the part of the women to avail themselves of the existing opportunities.

This chapter focuses therefore on Nigerian women's increased access to higher education programs and their current participation levels in the economic and technological development in the country. According to Nigeria's first university vice-chancellor, Alele-Williams (1992), a lot has been discussed about the social, cultural and structural barriers against Nigerian women in higher education. She went on to propose a thorough examination of those factors and policies that could account for women's increased access, and subsequently boost their advancement and sustenance while in leadership positions in higher education, (Odejide, 2003). A surer way could be through increasing university admission numbers in favour of women. Odejide, (2003, p.4) further threw some light on this when she pointed out that while the 1999 Nigerian Constitution clearly made "provision for equality of women…", the issue still remains that in reality and practice, the said Constitution neither guarantees the rights nor does it protect the interest of women with regard to those cultural trends that negatively impact upon women's access. A quick look at the applications and admissions figures of the country by state, Odejide (p.8-11) finds that not much has been done to increase or reserve places for women for admission purposes. More emphasis is placed on giving admission to students from educationally disadvantaged zones, and to disciplines in the sciences. Since more women take arts than sciences, with a 40/60 ratio, any policy that promotes this reduces the chances of women who would have dreamed of getting into higher educational programs.

THE CURRENT SITUATION

Higher education has already been identified and recognized as providing the wherewithal for Nigerian women to question and so change their status. It has also been established that the Nigerian women's limited opportunities limit their advancement in many areas of life. However, there has been a major shift in cultural trends as they affect Nigerian women's determination to attain greater heights in the development of the country's economy. There has equally been a lot of attitudinal change by the parents and as such, the society regarding girls' career choices. Nigerian parents are now more inclined to support their daughters who choose to pursue science and more technological programs. This does not come as a surprise, when younger parents with higher levels of education are getting more involved and more supportive of their daughters' educational goals and choices, (Ndahi, 2002). There is therefore a strong correlation between the girls' career choices and parents' level of education and current job. Therefore, we can say that most Nigerian women with access to higher education come from higher Socio-Economic Status—especially with highly educated parents.

From the JAMB table (Fig.1), we see that the said shift in Cultural Trends has produced some results. For example, in every one of the 21 Federal Universities, there is a reasonable jump in admission figures between 2000/2001 and 2003/2004—even in the northern zones, where religious and cultural practices had tended to negate efforts. However, the overall picture still reflects regional differences. The enrollment gap between males and females at Ahmadu University, Zaria in the (Moslem) North is far wider than that between the two sexes at the University of Benin in the (Christian) South. However, the story is slightly different in the West, as can be seen from the figures for the Universities of Ife, Ibadan, Ilorin, Abeokuta and Akure. The practice of Islam and Christianity in Yorubaland is exemplary. It can be explained away by the fact that that particular group has shown a lot of cultural emancipation as Christianity, which came with Western education has long been established. The friendly coexistence of Christianity and Islam in the Western zone thus augurs well for women's greater access to higher education. Meanwhile, in Igboland (Awka, Abia, Nsukka, etc.), the trend was the reverse. The males pursued their goals differently, and conceded further and higher education to the females. Now, after some formal policy intervention, male enrollment is in line with rest of the country. Overall, the picture still shows elements of the North/South dichotomy.

It should also be noted that there is a consistent pattern of gender disparity in the figures as reflected above. Also, with the existence of local programs such as diploma, part-time bachelors and masters' degree programs as well as certificate courses, the trend in the disparity may become significant, possibly in favor of the females.

Conclusion

The issue of gender imbalance in access to higher education programs, especially in science and technology, and the resultant low female representation in policy and decision-making levels of Nigerian technological and economic development have continued to raise concern over gender parity. No doubt, there has been a lot of improvement. There has been some improvement, especially in the increase in admission figures (JAMB fig. 1). There is a very strong causal relationship between increased access and increased and higher level participation in development. From the JAMB admissions table, the upward movement for women between 2001 and 2004 is encouraging. From this table, there is a consistent pattern of gender disparity in the figures, and this trend becomes significant. But more importantly, admissions increased, and so chances of female enrollment and graduation will increase, thus preparing them for their future roles in development.

Meanwhile, cultural change does not happen in isolation. An understanding of the politics of educational policy-making is very crucial. Politics are needed to deal with policy. So women in particular must engage in the politics of education. Though some progress has been made regarding the number of Nigerian women in higher leadership (administrative), academic and technical positions, a lot still needs to be done. More role models are needed in strategic positions.

On a happy note, the following role players at the national level are women:

- Two (2) ministers of finance

- Director-General, Legal Aids Council
- Director-General, NAFDAC
- Director-General, Nigerian Stock Exchange
- Director-General, NICON
- Vice-Chancellors/2 Universities/2 Deputy Vice-Chancellors
- 7 Registrars; 25% of all tenured professors, etc..

Yet, more needs to be done! Some attention needs be drawn to the perennial problem of successive governments' tendencies to discontinue or reverse policies and projects initiated by their predecessors.

APPENDIX A

S/N	FEDERAL UNIVERSITIES	1999/2000 M	1999/2000 F	2000/2001 M	2000/2001 F	2001/2002 M	2001/2002 F	2002/2003 M	2002/2003 F	2003/2004 M	2003/2004 F
1.	A.B.U. ZARIA	N/A	N/A	8,200	4,800	9,500	5,100	10,100	6,500	11,600	6,600
2.	UNIV. OF MAIDUGURI	-	-	7,200	4,400	8,500	5,300	9,200	6,000	9,800	6,200
3.	UNIV. OF JOS	-	-	7,500	5,300	7,850	6,050	8,790	6,410	8,800	6,800
4.	UNIV. OF ABUJA	-	-	5,800	3,400	6,200	3,900	7,980	4,820	8,966	4,934
5.	B.U.K.	-	-	6,310	4,150	6,895	4,795	7,300	4,900	7,980	4,820
6.	UNIV. OF ILORIN	-	-	6,500	4,900	7,250	5,730	7,598	6,002	8,625	5,575
7.	ABUBAKAR TAFAWA BELEWA UNIV. BAUCHI	-	-	4,462	1,838	4,982	2,908	5,325	2,895	5,400	3565
8.	USMAN D. UNIV. SOKOTO	-	-	4,690	3,290	5,960	3,300	6,250	4,310	6,900	5,700
9.	FED. U OF AGRIC. MAKURDI	-	-	3,525	3,200	3,820	4,000				

Table 1: Admissions to Higher Education by Zone and Gender, 2000

REGION	FEMALE	MALE	TOTAL
North Central Zone	1,993	4,815	6,808
North East Zone	533	1,504	2,037
North West Zone	944	2,673	3,617
South East Zone	11,436	12,183	23,619
South West Zone	3,599	6,508	10,108
South South Zone	5,664	8,787	14,451
TOTAL	24,169	36,460	60,629

Source: Derived from Joint Admissions and Matriculation Board (JAMB) 2002.

Table 2a: Applications and Admissions statistics (UME/DE) by State of Origin and Sex, 2000/2001 Session, North Central Zone

APPLICATIONS				ADMISSIONS	
STATE	MALE	FEMALE	TOTAL	MALE	FEMALE
Benue	6,490 (64.9%)	3,509 (35.1%)	9,999	1,318 (70.7%)	3,509 (35.1%)
Katsina	1,584 (76.1%)	498 (23.9%)	2,082	248 (75.4%)	498 (23.9%)
Kogi	11,214 (63.3%)	5,965 (26.7%)	17,179	1,498 (68.3%)	5,965 (26.7%)
Plateau	2,787 (65.9%)	1,441 (34.1%)	4,228	376 (69.9%)	1,441 (34.1%)
Kaduna	4,416 (66.9%)	2,185 (33.1%)	6,601	633 (73.5%)	2,185 (33.1%)
Niger	2,328 (70.0%)	999 (30.0%)	3,327	447 (72.1%)	999 (30.0%)
Nasarawa	1,995 (71.8%)	785 (28.2%)	2,780	295 (74.1%)	785 (28.2%)
TOTAL	30,814(66.7%)	15,382(32.3%)	46,196	4,815 (78.7%)	15,382(32.3%)

Source: Derived from Joint Admissions and Matriculation Board (JAMB) 2002.
UME: University Matriculation Examinations
DE: Direct Entry i.e. Advanced Level, National Certificate of Education, National Diploma.

Table 2b: Applications and Admissions statistics (UME/DE) by State of Origin and Sex, 2000/2001 Session, North East Zone

APPLICATIONS				ADMISSIONS	
STATE	MALE	FEMALE	TOTAL	MALE	FEMALE
Borno	2,841 (68.7%)	1,295 (31.3%)	4,136	368 (64.3%)	204 (35.7%)
Gombe	1,310 (72.0%)	509 (28.0%)	1,819	279 (76.0%)	88 (24.0%)
Jigawa	1,283 (63.3%)	215 (26.7%)	1,498	187 (68.3%)	29 (31.7%)
Taraba	1,725 (76.1%)	542 (23.4%)	2,267	205 (78.2%)	57 (21.8%)
Yobe	1,416 (81.1%)	331 (18.9%)	1,747	114 (65.9%)	59 (34.1%)
Bauchi	1,511 (78.2%)	420 (21.8%)	1,931	351 (76.6%)	533 (26.2%)
TOTAL	10,086(75.3%)	3,312 (24.7%)	1,398	1,504 73.8%)	533 (26.2%)

Table 2c: Applications and Admissions statistics (UME/DE) by State of Origin and Sex, 2000/2001 Session, North West Zone

APPLICATIONS				ADMISSIONS	
STATE	MALE	FEMALE	TOTAL	MALE	FEMALE
Adamawa	2,929 (68.1%)	1,369 (31.9%)	4,298	358 (68.6%)	164 (31.4%)
Sokoto	1,394 (83.6%)	274 (16.4%)	1,668	345 (79.9%)	87 (20.1%)
Zamfara	1,331 (85.3%)	229 (14.7%)	1,560	258 (84.0%)	49 (16.0%)
Kebbi	1,094 (75.8%)	350 (24.2%)	1,444	264 (79.8%)	67 (20.2%)
Kwara	10,724 (64.1%)	6,014 (35.9%)	16,738	842 (71.4%)	337 (28.6%)
Kano	4,514 (73.2%)	1,655 (26.8%)	6,169	606 (71.6%)	240 (28.4%)
TOTAL	21,986(69.0%)	9,891(31.0%)	31,877	2,673(73.9%)	944(26.1%)

Table 2d: Applications and Admissions statistics (UME/DE) by State of Origin and Sex, 2000/2001 Session, South East Zone

APPLICATIONS				ADMISSIONS	
STATE	MALE	FEMALE	TOTAL	MALE	FEMALE
Abia	13,663 (52.0%)	12,869 (48.0%)	26,325	2,293 (54.1%)	1,944 (45.9%)
Anambra	19,452 (43.4%)	25,401 (56.6%)	44,853	3,224 (47.2%)	3,612 (52.8%)
Ebonyi	3,975 (66.2%)	2,031 (33.8%)	6,006	706 (69.5%)	310 (30.5%)
Enugu	11,167 (51.1%)	10,667 (48.9%)	21,834	1,878 (56.6%)	1,441 (43.4%)
Imo	28,043 (50.0%)	28,548 (50.0%)	56,591	4,082 (50.0%)	4,129 (50.0%)
TOTAL	76,300 (49.0%)	79,516 (51.0%)	155,609	12,183 (51.6%)	11,436 (48.4%)

Table 2e: Applications and Admissions statistics (UME/DE) by State of Origin and Sex, 2000/2001 Session, South West Zone

APPLICATIONS				ADMISSIONS	
STATE	MALE	FEMALE	TOTAL	MALE	FEMALE
Ekiti	10,409 (63.0%)	6,104 (37.0%)	16,513	677 (67.0%)	334 (33.0%)
Lagos	15,789 (58.0%)	11,455 (42.0%)	27,244	1,165 (58.8%)	815 (41.2%)
Ondo	15,315 (63.3%)	8,879 (36.7%)	24,194	1,299 (64.5%)	714 (35.5%)
Oyo	15,545 (67.8%)	8,399 (32.2%)	22,944	869 (69.5%)	381 (30.5%)
Ogun	21,855 (57.1%)	16,393 (42.9%)	38,248	1,506 (62.1%)	921 (37.9%)
Osun	17,549 (64.1%)	9,840 (35.9%)	27,389	993 (69.6%)	434 (30.4%)
TOTAL	96,462 (61.2%)	61,070 (39.0%)	156,532	6,509 (64.3%)	3,599 (35.6%)

Table 2f: Applications and Admissions statistics (UME/DE) by State of Origin and Sex, 2002/2001 Session, South South Zone

APPLICATIONS				ADMISSIONS	
STATE	MALE	FEMALE	TOTAL	MALE	FEMALE
Akwa Ibom	11,498 (54.8%)	9,479 (45.2%)	20,977	1,356 (69.0%)	903 (40.0%)
Bayelsa	4,678 (60.9%)	3,006 (39.1%)	7,684	623 (64.0%)	351 (36.0%)
Cross Rivers	5,150 (60.8%)	3,323 (39.2%)	8,473	876 (63.9%)	495 (36.1%)
Delta	25,699 (57.0%)	19,394 (43.0%)	45,093	2,480 (59.4%)	1,697 (40.6%)
Rivers	13,103 (57.0%)	9,882 (43.0%)	22,985	1,747 (59.0%)	1,216 (41.0%)
Edo	23,246 (58%)	16,818 (42.0%)	40,064	1,705 (63.0%)	1,002 (37.0%)
TOTAL	83,374	61,902	145,276	8,787	5,664

Table 3: Women in Management in Higher Education in Nigeria 1989-1999

POST	NUMBER	LOCATION	MODE OF SELECTION
Vice Chancellor	3	BENIN, LAGOS STATE, ABUJA	Nominated
Deputy Vice Chancellor	1	IFE (OAU)	Nominated
Registrar	2	OAU, FUTO	Appointed
Bursar	2	OAU, UNILAG	Appointed
Rector (Polytechnic)	3	IBADAN, ILORIN, YABA	Appointed
Librarian	3	IBADAN, OSU, OAU	Appointed
CMAC/Dir. Of Clinical Services	1	LUTH	Appointed
TOTAL 15			

Table 4: Women in Management in Higher Education in Nigeria, post 2000

POST	NUMBER	LOCATION	MODE OF SELECTION
Librarian	4	UYO, JOS, ENUGU, UNAAB	Appointed
Bursar	4	OAU, LASU, FUTO, UYO	Appointed
Deputy Bursar	1	OAU	Appointed
Chief Medical Director	1	National Eye Hospital Kaduna.	Appointed
CMAC/ Dir. Of Clinical Services	1	IBADAN	Elected
Director of Admin. Teaching Hospital	4	IBADAN, ILORIN, CALABAR, National Orthopedic Hospital.	Appointed
Dean of Students	1	UNILAG	Appointed
TOTAL 16			

Table 5: Male/Female Staff Strength University of Ibadan

CATEGORY	NUMBER	MALE	FEMALE
Academic Staff	1,332	78.7%	21.3%
Other Senior Staff	1,713	70.4%	29.6%
Junior	2,970	78.5%	21.5%
TOTAL	5,835	75.4%	21.5%
ACADEMIC STAFF BY CATEGORY			
Professors/ Readers	23.7%	88.1%	11.9%
Senior Lecturers	25.2%	78.2%	21.8%
Lecturer 1 and below	51.1%	74.5%	25.5%
TOTAL	100.0%	78.7%	21.3%

REFERENCES

Adeleke, M.R.A. (1990, Nov/Dec): Women in industrial development in Nigeria; *Management in Nigeria* 26.(6).

Alele-Williams, G. (1990): Major Constraints to women's access to higher education in *UNESCO, Higher Education in Africa: Trends and Challenges for the 21st century*, Dakar, UNESCO Regional Office, BREDA.

Awe, B. (!990): The role of Nigerian in management in the 90s, in *Management in Nigeria*. 26 (4).

Enwemnwa, M.O.N. (1993): *Women's access to higher education in Nigeria: the case of (former) Bendel State.* (Unpublished dissertation). University of Wisconsin-Madison.

Federal Republic of Nigeria. (1997): *Report of the Committee on the future of higher education in Nigeria.* (Nyadako Report) Unpublished.

J.A.M.B. Document/Report (2004): *Federal Universities Statistics* (Admissions).

Koehl, R. (1979): *Nigerian Universities in historical perspectives: A comparative approach to institutional transfer and Africanization.*

Lamptey, A.S. (1992): Promoting Women's participation in research and management in African Universities, in *UNESCO Higher education in Africa: Trends and Challenges for the 21st century*, Dakar, Regional Office, BREDA.

Makhubu, L. P.(1998): The right to higher education and equal opportunity particularly for women: The major challenge of our time. In *UNESCO, Higher Education in Africa : Achievements, Challenges and Prospects.* Dakar, UNESCO.

Ndagi, H. (2002): Gender inequality in Industrial and Technical Education in *Nigeria: Parents' perspective in the 21st century*.

Odejide, A. (2002, Feb.9-11): Women in Management in Higher education in Nigeria: The role of academic women's groups. *Paper presented at the Association of Commonwealth Universities and Institute of Education London*, Seminar on Managing Gendered Change in higher education, Johannesburg.

Odejide, A. (2003): Navigating the Seas: Women in Higher Education in Nigeria. *McGill Journal of Education* (Fall 2003, p.453-68)

Okebukola, P. (1998): Management of Higher Education with a special reference to Nigeria in *UNESCO, Higher Education in Africa: Achievements, Challenges and Prospects.* Dakar UNESCO Regional Office, BREDA.

Chapter 9

JOURNEY AS METAPHOR: THE PERSONAL STORY OF AN AFRICAN WOMAN IN EDUCATION

Precious O. Afoláyan
Lincoln Charter School, Venice
Illinois, USA

INTRODUCTION

Obiakor and Grant's recent work, *Foreign-Born African Americans: Silenced voices in the discourse on race*, is an interesting but encouraging anthology of testimonies stemming from some incredible experiences of foreign-born Black scholars and educators in America. Their stories spread over several decades of recent history. The book provides a model of personal narratives as effective tool for analyzing cultural experiences. I have borrowed this model to present this chapter. Using empirical personal experience and testimonial as evidence, I would like to argue that as long as women are willing to step out of their superficially constructed confining paradigm of societal expectation, there would be a breakthrough in their social standing and educational attainment in the developing world. In this chapter, I would like to narrate my experience from the time I left Nigeria, West Africa, for the United State of America through my struggles to complete my doctorate degree while raising a family. Here, I will use my journey as a metaphor for women's struggle. The conclusion is that though the journey may be long and windy, and the traveler may be footsore and weary, its end should be rewarding and fulfilling. This is a theme in line with both Drs. B. Robert Tabachnick and Robert Koehl's educational philosophy which in most essential ways, borders on education of self and for self actualization, and empowerment.

I have divided this chapter into five related sections. The first part is a statement to debunk the stereotypical image of the African woman as depicted in Western literature, both in academic and popular discourses. The second part deals with the start of my journey, from Nigeria to New Haven, Connecticut; the third part deals with my family and I moving from New Haven, CT to Davis, California, and then to Madison, Wisconsin; the fourth part talks about the point at which my family met Bob Tabachnick and his family, the struggles in raising a family, the multiple roles and functions that I had to perform in order to survive the mainstream America, keep my family and still move on in pursuit of academic excellence. This section also looks at the various ways Dr. Tabachnick helped to make the transitioning smooth and easy; the fifth and last part deals with our continued struggles as a family in trying to survive the American job market and the help we continue to receive from our wonderful friend, and mentor, Dr. Tabachnick.

THE MYTH OF THE WEAKER VESSEL

Elsewhere (Afolayan, 2004), I confessed that as an African woman who had spent a significant part of her professional as well as adult life in the Western world, and who is predisposed to western construction of knowledge, an aspect of cultural epistemology of the academia that has often interested me was the subject of feminism. While feminism has always been an effective, almost addictive, pedagogical tool in gender as well as ideological discourses, my "sixth sense," for lack of a better term, has often convinced me of a conflict, as well as a void, akin to an antithesis, between the Western notion of this subject on one hand, and the African sense of it on the other. I have long come to the conclusion that the African woman does not have a lesser status in her society than does the woman in any other parts of the world. Having looked in the traditional literature of African peoples, it is clear to me that the African cultures have a great place for their women, although the practitioners of the culture may not be as faithful as the culture demands of them. This has always been a topic of a growing interest to me. Yet, for an educator, and non-literary critic that I am, an avenue to vent out this kind of discourse rarely materializes. Thus, more often than not, the Yoruba cliché that, "The murmur and tremor and mumbling of sounds come and die in the belly of the pig" becomes an unfortunate truism. Except one seizes a moment to nurture and give thoughts of this nature a chance to thrive, one often faces the danger of killing them even before they were born. Thus, it is a great honor for me to have the privilege of telling my story as an African woman in honor of two of the world's finest and most outstanding and positive voices that have for decades hammered and echoed issues incidental to education of Africans, and especially women. Through my association with both Professor Bob Tabachnick and Bob Koehl in the 1980s through early 1990s, I have learned that it is okay to be a voice of dissent even when one's position is against prevailing currency.

Though far from being the purpose of this chapter, it is worth noting that there is an apparent contradiction in the discourse of feminism as it applies to women in Africa. This contradiction is inherent in the two lines of thoughts coming from Western or Western-trained intellectuals feminist theorists as opposed to those of African women who live the lives that are being theorized about. From the latter's experiences as expressed in the Yoruba culture, it is evident that African women are not as disenfranchised as the feminist literature would have us believe. In what follows, I will provide my story as one African woman who has lived through a difficult journey and yet has manifested a strong will and experienced a strong support from her family and friends and consequently survived the turbulence of the journey so packed full of life's vicissitudes.

COMING FROM NIGERIA

My journey from Nigeria to the USA started in January of 1983. I left Nigeria exactly five month after my husband came to study at Yale University, New Haven, Connecticut (CT). My husband left Nigeria two days after our wedding; thus, those five months of a long-distance conjugal relationship were pressurizing. Compounding it all was the fact that this was not the age of cellular phones or the Global System for Mobile Communications (GSM). All the letters that I wrote, which came to about an average of once a week, including the one I wrote when I found out we were expecting our first child, only started arriving one after the other two weeks after I had arrived in the United States, and of course, none of his arrived in Nigeria until after I left. The abysmal communication system did not ease the pain of the hasty "empty nest" syndrome which we ought to be feeling only after our children are of age and left home, but which we both felt as our family life took this funny course. Every one of my college friends thought it was crazy to let go of a husband of two days to America of all places where the cold weather would soon force him to seek the warmth and comfort of loose girls on the street, or who would soon meet the daughters of American presidents and millionaires especially in such a prestigious institution like Yale. Even people in my family questioned my wisdom. On the extreme end of the naysayers was a group which thought it was suicidal for me to go to America to join my husband since I had not completed my college of education degree. They had heard that all the women who went to join their husband in that category only ended up as janitors who would raise money for their husbands and make babies endlessly. They swore I would not return home without ever completing my college degree. For them, mine was a journey into servitude. My husband and I had a good laugh at this galaxy of paranoiacs after we reunited a few months later.

My journey to the United States started in Ibadan, the largest city in Nigeria, the night before I would board the plane for America. My brother-in-law and some of our close family members drove me to Lagos where we spent the night at the home of a relative. Every eye was on me as the "lucky one going to America." The following day, at 9:45pm, we left for the famous Murtala Airport, Lagos. I was warned of the need for an early arrival to the airport so as to take care of all the departure protocols. At the airport I checked my luggage in and waited to be boarded on board Pan-Am Airline. After what seemed like eternity, my plane took off at about 11:55 pm. I quickly found myself a fairly comfortable sleeping position and went to sleep shortly afterwards. The airplane flew non-stop and landed at JFK airport, New York, the second day. My husband was of course waiting to see me; I eagerly wanted to see him as well. He came with some close friends that he had hooked up with since getting to New Haven. We fell on each other's arms and exchanged news and pleasantries about home and family members. The airport terminal was one big human maze, and navigating our way out was almost impossible. Everywhere was parked full of cars. We had to go through many tunnels before finally getting out of the airport area and into the snow. Looking back to the past six months, I said to myself, "what a journey!"

SNOW: THE WHITE FLAKES OF THE SKY!

I must say, I had read and certainly heard all kinds of stories about the snow, but I never really experienced one until my arrival in January of 1983. As a Nigerian, reading about the snow and seeing the actual snow, are two different things. Watching the snow fall on me was just too overwhelming, to say the least. I could not help myself! I just had to get some handful of it against everyone's warning. That was a big mistake on my part as in a matter of minutes my two hands were as frozen as "*Oku Eko*," the infamous frozen fish of Nigeria. I quickly shook off the snowflakes and I put on the mittens which my husband brought for me. He ushered me into the waiting car and we started the journey towards New Haven. On the way, my husband introduced me to his friend and his wife, Susan. We all enjoyed a few stories of how my husband met this wonderful family and other friends. Susan and I talked about how my husband and I met while the two men talked about education, sports, family issues, religion, and the Reagan economics. I could not but enjoy the beautiful, breath-taking scenery outside the window.

AMERICA AND NIGERIA: TWO WORLDS, TWO PEOPLES

I had heard so many fascinating stories about this beautiful land, and now I was there. My reader should understand that most Nigerians knew America as the land of great wealth and opportunities, and that with little or no effort, a pauper could become a millionaire just in the twinkling of an eye! With this understanding, I braced myself for instant success. I had been brought up to believe that wherever I was I must not only survive but also succeed. Deep down within me, I had the feeling that this journey which had taken me from Nigeria, one of the most complicated nations of the world, to America, one of the most sophisticated nations of the world, would propel me into a new philosophical dispensation and usher me into a new social orientation. I knew this was a challenging journey in the making, I just could not predict how long it would be. This was my gut feeling, an instinct that was coated in a psychological and maybe, spiritual feeling. I could not wait to see my life behind this solemn but translucent veil of the new cultural and spiritual curtain. My feet were already on the road. Let the journey begin!

Nigeria of 1983 was a nation highly populated with people who for the most part were closely knit together by family ties, belief systems and communalistic philosophy. It was a nation that would come to be awarded the title of the world's happiest inhabitants. Today I wonder if the happiness was an illusion based on Fela Anikulapo-Kuti's characterization of Nigeria as a people "suffering and smiling," or Niyi Osundare's concept of people's "waiting laughters." Regardless of the characterization, I came to America with a strong sense of enthusiasm and a deep feeling of optimism. Nigeria is naturally divided into three parts, separated by its two great rivers - Niger and Benue. Nigerian colure and customs are a complex web. Falola (2001) provides a detailed description of that web. For the most part, Nigerians pride themselves in simply being Nigerians. Their achievements are measured by how much the community achieves, although, as I will explain soon, individual achievements did not go unnoticed either. The Yoruba people say, "Karin ka po, yiye nii yeni," in essence, "we are, therefore, I am," a contradistinction to the western sociological philosophy expressed in Descartes, "cogito ego sum," (I know, therefore, I am). I soon found out that the spirit of "ajosepo" or "agboole" or "egbejoda" (unity, or familiness, or togetherness) was very alien to my new American culture, and I found this out in more ways than one. Here, achievements or successes are measured by individual's personal attainments, and of course backed up by apparent hard work and relentless endeavors. Americans, I also soon found out, were casual and unceremonious. People hardly referred to themselves or each other by titles; you were called by your first name! Nigeria that I came from was very titular. There were in the academia titles of Professors, Doctor, Mr. Mrs., Miss, etc. It was very common to even conjugate the titles. Thus, one would run into names like "Chief (Professor) (Mrs.) Somebody," or Alhaji (Dr.) This or That" to refer to someone. If one made a mistake of referring to someone without conjugating his or her title, it would be construed as an effrontery. Not long after I left Nigeria, a new title was even introduced; people who went to technical colleges, polytechnics or studied engineering at the universities referred to themselves by the title, "Engr" denoting they were engineers. For me to come to the United States and be calling my husband's friends and professors by their first names was a culture shock! In what follows, I would like to say a little bit about the Yoruba people, the ethnic group that I belong in Nigeria and where my cultural journey began.

The Yoruba land is very rich in culture and it encompasses most of southwestern Nigeria as well as the people directly west of the Nigerian border in the independent countries of Benin and Togo. In Nigeria alone, the Yoruba people number up to 30 million people, according to the census of 1990. The Yoruba are in the states of Oyo, Osun, Ogun, Ondo, Lagos, parts of Kwara and of Edo states. Their major metropolitan cities include Ibadan, Eko (Lagos), Osogbo, Ogbomoso, Oyo, Ilesha, Ile-Ife, Ado-Ekiti, Abeokuta, Ilorin, Ondo, Okitipupa, Ijebu-Ode, Ijebu-Igbo, Saki, to name a few. The Yoruba ethnic group forms a formidable body polity in Nigeria. I am a Yoruba woman from Ilesha, Osun State and from one of the ruling families. Apart from my ethnic heritage, I am royalty. Though by virtue of my gender, I could not become the ruler, though I could serve as a regent in an interregnum period, just as the case is in most of Yoruba societies (see Afolayan and afolayan, 2004), yet, I hold an important position as a princess. I know I must achieve, as it is my destiny, and a journey I must undertake.

The Yoruba are a proud people, though not arrogant. From womb to tomb, they are driven by a push for success. Their upbringing often testifies to this unwritten code of belief. In every Yoruba family, the drive to succeed is impressed upon the child, regardless of gender or socio-economic status, as part of the daily ritual. The child hears all sorts of proverbs inexhaustibly expressed by the elders through oral education and hidden curriculum within the family. Afolayan (2004, 2005) spoke about this. Children learn various traditional lessons through family and non-family members, mostly, women. There is also a constant infusion of the pill of optimism by adult members to reinforce the notion of self-esteem in a child. This self-esteem helps the child to believe in the teachings of the elder and in him/herself and to be very strong and confident to want to succeed. The parents pound the doctrine of success in the ears of each child, making them to believe that success is achievable as long as one believes in oneself and leans on others. One must never give up but continues to try and see every opportunity as an indication to legitimize this drive. For me as a woman, a Yoruba, and from one of the most traditional families, there are certain traditional strings already sown into my personality. Yoruba society is very rich in culture and tradition and by this token, every one of its citizens is somehow generally wired into these fundamental cultural expectations. Understanding the cultural framework here is important for one to understand where the "self-imposed" stress came from. In my own biological family alone, there are expectations, different duties to perform to succeed. I was brought up like any other Yoruba, under the same guide, may be more, and have been made to believe that nothing good comes to those who wait or those who are lazy. Coming to America, a newly married woman, I was determined to do my best to make my biological family feel proud of the daughter they have raised. More importantly, I was resolved to make my new husband proud of me. I was also determined to do my best to make my country of birth proud. Last but not the least, I was resolved to making myself proud by working very hard and achieving the uttermost possible. The journey would be long.

FROM NEW HAVEN, CONNECTICUT, TO DAVIS, CALIFORNIA

About three months after my arrival in the USA, our son was born at Yale New Haven hospital. Olaoluwa "Daniel" arrived on April 27, 1983, weighing 6lbs.7oz, and 19 inches long. My husband was with me in the labor room. In-between contractions, he found time to write his first graduate examination in linguistics at Yale University, which he was allowed to take with him. One month after, he had to travel to Nigeria to go and collect data for his thesis. It was only three weeks after our son was born. One of my sister-in-laws that was at the time conducting a research in Boston, Massachusetts invited us over. We went to Boston to spend some time with her and came back to New Haven some three weeks after. I went back to work as a nurse's aide with a Home Health agency. I was working with this particular agency before my son was born. I also signed up with two other agencies to augment our income. They were Upjohn Healthcare Services and Tender Loving Care. Though I worked for both agencies, Upjohn Healthcare Services gave me a lot more hours than the other. I met a lot of people through these agencies whose lives touched mine and my life also touched theirs as well. Most had terminal illnesses. Some of these people became good friends later. Sad enough, though, most had long died.

FRIENDS IN NEW HAVEN

We were in New Haven, CT for a little less than four years. During our stay, we made many good friends. Some of these friends came through our associations with host families, our Churches, and others were just as a result of my husband being a graduate student at Yale. Frank and Alice, our host family couple, as well as Jerry and Elena, Fred and Susan, John, Stephen, and a few more, were all good friends with whom we were connected through Church. Dianne, now a professor and brilliant writer of children' literature in South Carolina, Blair an educator in California, Gloria, Thelma and Samba, were all close friends. Bob, still at Yale, "Skip," formerly at Yale, and now at Harvard, Ivan, Anthony, John (now deceased), Sylvia (now deceased), Sebastian, Rulon, Vincent, Ron, and many more were my husband's professors, mentors and also friends of our young family. Amazingly, some of these people still remain close to us this last quarter of a century, though we lost contact with others.

MY EDUCATIONAL JOURNEY

I had to attend various schools for upward mobility in my job as a nurse's aide, and also for academic growth. I first went to Southern Connecticut Community College in New Haven, for some time, and later transferred to Southern Connecticut State College (now Southern Connecticut University) and was there for one year before we moved to Davis, California. We were in Davis only for a short time before moving to Madison, Wisconsin. In California, I continued to work as a nurse's aide at different nursing homes in Sacramento, Davis, and as far as Modesto. My sister-in-law worked for the same agency and introduced me to one of her nursing supervisors who interviewed and hired me afterwards.

LIVING IN MADISON, AND MILWAUKEE, WISCONSIN

We moved to Madison, Wisconsin in January of 1986. Soon, our daughter, Ifeoluwa "Elizabeth" was born on April 21, 1986, weighing 8lbs 14oz, 21inches long. On arrival in Madison, I quickly set out looking for job. My husband and I knew we must get another job, especially with another mouth to feed on the way. Things became very difficult for us and raising our family was becoming a struggle. In Madison, I enrolled in an accelerated program with Concordia University Mequon. I was finally able to finish my program and received a Bachelor's degree in Management and Communication. In 1989, I applied for a Masters program in Educational Administration at the University of Wisconsin-Madison. To complete my admission process, I had to go through several evaluations of my credentials, which were at this point scattered through several institutions. All of my credentials from the United States passed without any challenge and I was on my way to being admitted into the program. After a prolonged time of looking at my credentials from Nigeria, I was told that I needed someone who was familiar with the Nigerian educational system to help clarify my experience. The admission officer asked if I could get one of the professors in School of Education. He sent me to Foreign Students' Office to talk to one of the advisors. It was at the Foreign Students' Office that I was directed to talk to Professor Robert Tabachnick. The following day I went to Dr. Tabachnick's office. He received me very warmly and after he offered me a chair. I told him my problem. He listened and explained to me what I need to do to get the problem resolved. I followed his advise, completed all the paper work, sent them to the proper channels and within five working days, I got the paper work back. I sent the paper work over to the admissions' office, and a few days after, my admission came through. This meeting with Dr. Tabachnick started a long and beautiful association with our family as well as his family.

While I pursued my academic interests, I also worked at various nursing homes to help pay the bills and fees. The first place I worked was at Oakwood Nursing Home. I was there for many years and later transferred to the University of Wisconsin Hospital and

Clinics (UWHC). Working in this establishment gave me schedule flexibility. My work was scheduled mostly around my classes and there was no conflict. In all my years of working at UWHC I gained valuable medical knowledge, and made friends.

For the most part, I worked in different departments. As time went on, I started noticing changes in my disposition and the patients that I took care. My family also noticed that I brought my work home, and this made them very uncomfortable. My phobic to issues of illnesses and diseases was getting a little bit out of hand. It was at that point that I told myself that it was time for a change of profession. I left the hospital and sought employment within the Madison Metropolitan School District. I had just finished my doctorate program and was employed as a classroom aide at one of the elementary schools. In this position I worked with little children with all sorts of disabilities. Their disabilities ranged from learning to emotional disability, physical to quadriplegic and many more. This was my first taste of special education 101. I enjoyed working with this population and their wonderful parents.

I left John Muir Elementary School, Madison and moved to Milwaukee, Wisconsin with my family. In Milwaukee, I started looking for job again and I found a teaching/administrative job with one of the public alternative high schools within the metropolitan school district. I worked with the school for about two years and was offered a teaching position with more pay and better benefits at one of the Milwaukee Public Schools (MPS).

In August of 1997 I started working for Milwaukee Public Schools (MPS) as a special education teacher. I was working in the school and was taking classes concurrently. I completed my certification program and was promoted as a certified special education teacher. I worked in this position for many years and also at many different schools with MPS until June 2003. In 2003, we moved from Wisconsin to Southern Illinois.

MOVING FROM WISCONSIN TO SOUTHERN ILLINOIS

We lived in the state of Wisconsin for almost 18 years, raised four healthy and awesome children. Within this time frame, I traveled to Nigeria with our three girls for 18 months purely for cultural orientation. Coming back to Wisconsin, my husband and I felt the need for a change. He applied for and got jobs as professor at different institutions. Both of us as well as the children felt that Southern Illinois University Edwardsville (SIUE) would fit our need more than the other institutions. We moved at the end of June 2003 after many visits back and forth for my own job interviews, and to search for accommodation. Our long time friends in Wisconsin were a significant part of our moving crew as we all traveled in a long caravan of multiple vehicles plus a jumbo size U-Haul which my husband, Michael drove with our mini-van hitched to it. How we were able to move from a five-bedroom house plus a full basement with two bedrooms of its own in Wisconsin into a two-bedroom apartment in southern Illinois still remains a marvel to me! But we did and lived in the two bedroom apartment for one full year; and amazingly enough, we did not cannibalize on each other for those twelve months! Our new place was not without the problems of its own. As noted above, we had lived in Wisconsin for a long time and had unconsciously accepted the frigid weather there. Thus, on arrival in Southern Illinois, I became sick due to the effect of the hot and humid weather, the like of which I never experienced, not even in Nigeria. The situation was quite awful as we had no medical insurance since my husband's job had not taken off. Nonetheless, I was taken to the hospital and received medical attention. We later purchased our house in Collinsville, Illinois.

In Southern Illinois, I continued to struggle in the American job markets. I came for several job interviews and was very excited about the prospect of getting one. However, things did not work out as planned. I was without employment for more than six months. The same common story of "over-qualification" was the drum beaten in my ears too often. Money was tight for the family, and the situation was getting worse, especially with the children's needs weighing heavily on my husband. The joblessness was excruciatingly painful for me. I thank God for my husband's efforts, love, and understanding of what I was going through. After what seemed like an unending nightmare, and with the help of some friends and mentors in the community, I was offered a part-time adjunct professorship at SIUE. I taught two graduate classes with an unbelievably ridiculous monthly salary which was less than 20% of what I got as a public school teacher in Wisconsin. Yet, I was so glad to be working at all. Adjunct professorship is a thankless job. You "do the work of a camel but given the reward of a dung beetle," to borrow the Yoruba phraseology. The thought of returning to Wisconsin for my old job crossed my mind several times but my husband did not see any logic in my decision. He kept reminding me of his late father's philosophy that "You do not go back to say 'good evening' wherever you already bade 'good night!'" He proposed intensifying job search in the area even as a substitute teacher. Having bought and moved into a new house, I signed up to substitute-teach with Collinsville School District, Edwardsville School District, and Triad School District, and with a bevy of new friends and learning to live daily by faith, I came to grips with the fact that life is a journey and my experience in America had only exemplified it. I am currently serving as principal for Lincoln Charter School in Venice, Illinois, where I first started as Dean of Students. I love the students and staff that I work with. This is what I really wanted, even though the reimbursement is not in any way at par with the energy that I put into it and the vision that I have for the school. However, as the old saying goes, "the journey of a thousand miles starts with the first step."

CONCLUSION

On a final note, I found interest and relevance in this topic because of the importance of the gender discourse in the education of people in developing nations. Men are often thought of as being tick! However, as my story has demonstrated, women are no less resilient. My story epitomizes this per excellence. I have come a long way. May be, I should actually say women have come a long way in their journey. This is more so for African women who have been wrongly slotted into the myth of inactivity and passivity as noted in the seminal essay of ben-Jochannan (1986). In all, we can borrow the words of Obiakor that in spite of this cumbersome journey, though footsore and weary at times, we can still turn "barriers into opportunities."

REFERENCES

Afolayan, M. O. (2005). Ààbò òrò: The indigenous language of education in Yoruba. In Falola T. and Genova A. *Yoruba creativity: Fiction, language, life and songs*. Trenton, NJ: Africa World Press. 165-182.

Afolayan, P. O. (2004). *The Non-feminist perspective of the educated African woman: Unpublished paper presented at the 10th Annual Conference of Midwest Alliance for African Studies (MAAAS)*, Southern Illinois University.

Afolayan, M. O. (2004). Defining and conceptualizing knowledge among the Yoruba. In Lawal N., M. N. O. Sadiku and Dopamu, A. (eds). *Understanding Yoruba life and culture*. Trenton, NJ: Africa World Press. 187-200.

Afolayan, M. O. and Afolayan, P.O. (2004). Obas in Contemporary Politics. In Lawal N., M. N. O. Sadiku and Dopamu, A. (eds). *Understanding Yoruba life and culture*. Trenton, NJ: Africa World Press. 283-296.

ben-Jochannan, Y. (1986). The African Contribution to Technology and Science. *A lecture delivered for the Minority Ethnic Unit of the Greater London Council, London, England, March 6–8, 1986*. It was addressed mainly to the African community in London consisting of African people from the Caribbean and African people from Africa.

Falola, T. (2001). *Culture and Customs of Nigeria*. Westport, CT: Greenwood Press.

Obiakor, F. and Grant P. (2002). *Foreign-Born African Americans: Silenced voices in the discourse on race*. New York: Nova Science Publishers.

Part III: Critical Challenges to Development, Research, and Training

In: Current Discourse on Education in Developing Nations   ISBN 1-59454-774-2
Editors: M. Afolayan, D. Jules et al. pp. 143-160   © 2006 Nova Science Publishers, Inc.

Chapter 10

ACTION RESEARCH AND TEACHER EDUCATION IN THE U.S. AND NAMIBIA

Ken Zeichner
University of Wisconsin-Madison
Wisconsin, USA

INTRODUCTION

In this chapter, I reflect back on my experiences using action research as an instructional strategy in a preservice teacher education program in the U.S over the last 20 years and in several years of work on a teacher education reform in Namibia. I begin when I first introduced the practice of action research into the teacher education program at the University of Wisconsin-Madison in 1984 as part of a broader strategy of developing the idea of an inquiry-oriented teacher education practicum that prepares teachers to work for greater social justice in education and society. I look at what we have learned and what we might have accomplished with 20 years of work aimed at integrating action research into our student teaching practicum. I also look at others' attempts to do the same thing at different universities and at what is known generally about the role of action research in teachers' professional development.

Although I strongly believe that genuine improvement in the learning of prospective teachers must involve much more than changes in techniques and strategies within existing structures of teacher education, I also believe that changes in the curriculum of teacher education toward more of an inquiry focus are necessary and must complement needed structural changes.

Between 1994 and 2000 I also worked on the Teacher Education Reform Project in Namibia that utilized a form of action research as one of the major vehicles for shifting classroom practice to a more learner-centered and democratic approach following the liberation of Namibia from colonial rule by South Africa. Following a discussion of my work with action research in Wisconsin, I will discuss the work in Namibia.

The Beginning: The 1980's

When I first went to Deakin University in 1986 to study the use of action research as an instructional strategy in the preservice teacher education practicum, I had only been working with action research with student teachers for about 2 years at my own university. Despite my experience with action research as a classroom teacher and as a teacher educator who studied and wrote about his own practice, I had been reluctant until then to teach prospective teachers about action research. I had included though as one of several approaches to teacher professional development in one of my doctoral level graduate seminars for teacher educators. To get this work started in the practicum was a bit complicated since as the program administrator I did not work directly with student teachers, only their supervisors and cooperating teachers. Through my graduate course where university supervisors often had the experience of conducting research on their own practice as teacher educators, I was able to interest a couple of graduate student university supervisors in introducing action research to their student teachers and worked with them as they dealt with the complexities of doing so.

At this time, there was no action research community to speak of in the Madison area and teachers were very skeptical of the appropriateness and usefulness of asking student teachers to use their time during student teaching to carry out a research project, even if it was focused on their own practice. Many teachers saw it as time taken away from learning how to teach and not an enhancement of that process. Although the teacher-as-researcher movements had been growing in the UK and Australia for over 10 years (see Elliott, 1991; Kemmis and McTaggart, 1988a), the U.S. teacher research movement was just beginning to become noticeable at the time we were getting started, and the idea of teachers as researchers was basically unheard of in Wisconsin except by a few people. Most of the resource material that we used with student teachers at that time, including examples of teacher's research, came from either the UK or Australia such as the widely used *Action Research Planner* (Kemmis and McTaggart, 1988b).

Why did I decide to introduce action research in the first place, and why did I choose the practicum as the site for its introduction? From the mid 1970's when I came to Wisconsin until 1984 when action research was first introduced, I had been trying with several colleagues to reconceptualize and restructure a very technically oriented and loosely structured student teaching experience into one that had inquiry as its basis. We wanted to redirect the focus in this practicum from only a demonstration and application of things previously learned to a more genuine occasion for teacher learning itself. We were very concerned with research that we had done that had shown our graduates to be very technically competent but very inarticulate about their own educational goals as teachers and ignorant of the social and political contexts of their teaching (e.g., Tabachnick, Popkewitz, and Zeichner, 1979). They gave very little thought to why they were doing what they were doing and hallmark for success for many students was only the assumption of independent teaching responsibility. We were very concerned to have our students begin to develop habits and capabilities during their initial education for teaching that would live on in further experience and help them continue to become better at teaching throughout their careers.

We introduced the notion of reflective teaching into the program in 1980 as a way of symbolizing the kind of analytic, thoughtful, and purposeful approach to teaching that we wanted our graduates to possess when they left our program after 4 1/2years of study (e.g., Zeichner, 1981; Zeichner and Liston, 1987)). At that time, before the work of Donald Schon on Reflective Practice had been published (e.g., Schon, 1983, 1987), we felt little need to clearly articulate what exactly we meant by the term reflective teaching, often speaking in very general terms and frequently quoting John Dewey's words about the importance of reflecting about purposes and consequences, about the reflective process and its relation to action, and about being open-minded and so on (Dewey, 1933). Over the years, as everyone in professional education no matter what his or her theoretical or ideological persuasion has claimed the banner of reflective practice as a major goal for their professional education program and the term by itself has lost any meaning, we began to more clearly articulate what kinds of reflection and about what things we were trying to encourage among our future teachers (e.g., Zeichner and Liston, 1996).

Action research was chosen as one of the majors vehicle for focusing the reflections of student teachers both about their practice and the contexts in which they worked because of my own experience with it as an elementary teacher and my strong desire to respond directly to what student teachers perceived to be their most pressing issues and concerns in the classroom while also working to help them see these issues from a variety of perspectives- to broaden their perspectives. Given the focus of our program on preparing teachers to teach all students including those who had backgrounds very different from their own (e.g., Zeichner, 1993), and our explicit concern to prepare teaches to contribute toward the building of a more just and humane society through their work in schools (e.g., Liston and Zeichner, 1991), I also strongly felt that the inside-outside approach to professional development (Cochran-Smith and Lytle, 1993) would be much more likely to win students teachers over to this cause than the typical top down and outside-inside approach that denies student teachers' current realities and pushes and drags them toward someone else's vision of best practice, sometimes kicking and screaming.

I think that one thing that we have demonstrated over the years is that by honoring and respecting where student teachers are when they come to us and by letting them maintain control over the focus of their action research, we are often able to help them broaden their perspectives on what are often initially perceived as only technical and instrumental issues to also consider the moral, ethical and political aspects of those issues.

Elsewhere, I have published a case study of my work in supporting the action research of one student teacher, Rachel. Bob Tabachnick and I facilitated the action research seminar in which she was a member and helped her confront and deal with the issues of race and social class that were embedded in her research issue but were initially ignored (Zeichner, 2003). We did this through our facilitation of a discussion of her research project in the weekly seminar and by our responses to her journal. In this particular case, the student teacher also read several articles (some of which were suggested to her by Bob and I) that helped her look at her situation from a different cultural perspective (Zeichner, 1997).

The usual approach in initial teacher education to student teachers' definitions of their realities is to deny those realities ("no, it is not really a classroom management problem") and to try to get them to adopt another more "enlightened" perspective on their issue. This top down approach often generates a lot of resistance among prospective teachers and, at best, only produces a surface and strategic compliance by student teachers, not a genuine commitment (Zeichner and Hoeft, 1996).

In addition to introducing action research into the practicum, we have also utilized a variety of other strategies as ways to stimulate reflective and thoughtful teaching by our students including, teaching portfolios, lesson study, peer mentoring, student teaching seminars, community field experiences, journaling, and life history and narrative inquiry. The idea was to make inquiry a normal part of what student teachers do when they are on their practicum-not an extra bit of work that diverts attention from becoming a better teacher, but as a way for teachers to approach their work on a daily basis.

Our early attempts to incorporate action research into the practicum resulted in very neatly packaged studies where students examined the effects of this or that classroom management approach or teaching method in getting students to do what they wanted them to do, usually some sort of behavioral compliance. These early studies considered such issues as getting more students to do their homework, improving students' reading comprehension skills and cooperation in small work groups and studying pupil reactions to different teaching styles and classroom organizational arrangements. They were very academic like and resembled very traditional kinds of positivist scientific research with mostly quantitative measurements, hypothesis testing, and so on. The student teachers wrote up reports of their research as they were required to do at the end of the semester and that was the end of it. The reports contained a finality and certainty that the problems had been solved the questions had been answered, but there appeared to be no internalization of the spirit of inquiry by the student teachers (Schildgren, 1993). I doubt very much whether any of the students in this early era of action research at UW-Madison carried the idea of teachers as knowledge producers with them into their beginning years or saw much difference between the assignment of an action research project and any other university determined assignment. They did what they perceived that they needed to do to be successful and get certified. We made no effort at that point to communicate with the cooperating teachers about what we were doing with the action research assignment and why.

We realized right away, as we initiated work that is still going on today examining our use of action research with student teachers, that one of the biggest mistakes that we made in these first attempts was to fail to take adequate time to help students reexamine their ideas about the practice of research, about knowledge and who produces it, about theory and practice, and so on, fundamental ideas they had been internalizing throughout their education (e.g., Noffke and Zeichner, 1987; Noffke and Brennan, 1991). It is not surprising that merely sticking an action research assignment into an existing practicum with a culture and set of expectations about what is to go on and what is important resulted in fairly conventional and self-contained studies that did not appear to result in the internalization of the habits and skills of inquiry that we had hoped for. I wasn't opposed to the idea of student teachers solving problems that they had set out to address. I was upset though by their failure to really explore in an open way the issues they took on and to become involved in a process of inquiry about their teaching that spirals outward as new questions keep emerging. If everything is neat and tidy at the end of one semester of inquiry and there is no messiness apparent, then something has gone wrong in my view.

We also realized right away that it was a big mistake not to involve the cooperating teachers in our efforts to engage student teachers in research. We immediately began to utilize some of the teachers who had been introduced to action research in my graduate class in the introduction of the idea to student teachers and to the local community of cooperating teachers. Pat Wood for example, was one of these original teachers. Pat is a 2nd and 3rd grade

Madison teacher whose action research studies have been cited worldwide (e.g., Wood, 1988).

A SABBATICAL AT DEAKIN UNIVERSITY

Soon after these initial attempts, I decided to accept an invitation from Deakin to spend a semester there as a visiting scholar. At that time Deakin University was one of the two centers in the world for action research activity in teacher education. The other was the University of East Anglia in the UK where John Elliott was located.

I learned many valuable things both about action research and its use in a practicum context during my semester at Deakin working as a "critical friend" helping Ian Rottobottom and Richard Tinning examine the use of action research in a Deakin practicum course for prospective teachers. One of the things that I came away most convinced of though was to stick to my determination to let student teachers choose their own research focus as opposed to the then Deakin policy of having practicum students select a topic from a set of predetermined topics carefully linked with campus courses and developed by Deakin staff (Robottom, 1988). I wanted to stick to my commitment to the idea of student ownership of their research and of having the research questions flow out of student teachers' practices, even given the tensions that often existed between our own developing views of the kinds of reflective practice that we wanted to promote in our program and our students choices about research topics. Specifically, there was often a gap between all of our goals to have our students reflect about their teaching broadly interns of its technical aspects, its moral and ethical aspects and its social and political dimensions and our students choices of what on the surface were very technical and instrumental issues concerned with controlling pupils (Gore and Zeichner, 1991; Zeichner and Gore, 1995).

Soon after I returned from Australia, two Australian graduate students Jenny Gore and Marie Brennan joined my student teaching program as university supervisors and worked with Susan Noffke and I in further developing our project of action research in the practicum. We worked on a number of specific things to improve the receptivity of both student teachers and their cooperating teachers to the idea of a focused self-study during student teaching. One strategy was to clearly have the supervisors model the process of action research for their students. Each semester the supervisors would collect data on some aspect of their teaching and mentoring (e.g., Gore, 1991) and provide a model for their students of the various aspects of action research such as exploring a problem, collecting and analyzing data.

Another change on our part was to broaden our conception of action research beyond the action research spiral to accommodate ways of conducting inquiry that are not typically found in the academy. The North American teacher research movement has developed since the late 1980's in the schools among teachers and although some of the research that teachers do resembles the research of academic professors (what Mary Kennedy of Michigan State University has called "researcherly research"), a large part of the research done by teachers in the U.S. does not resemble the research of academics ("teacherly research" according to Kennedy) (Kennedy, 1996)). The following quote from a recent book by Judith Newman on teacher research in North America, *Tensions of Teaching*, illustrates the different quality of some teacher research:

> The difficult thing about doing action research is that you have to override most of what you've learned about research as an activity. In a traditional research culture you begin by framing a question, setting up a situation which might provide some information, collecting data which bears on the question, then writing up results. Action research isn't like that at all. The research activity begins in the middle of whatever it is you're doing- something happens that you didn't expect... and you begin wondering about what's going on. . . . The dilemma in an action research situation is that you may not even realize something interesting has occurred that you ought to think about unless you're already in the habit of keeping a journal or reflective log... Unlike traditional research, action research begins not with a research question but with the muddle of daily work, with the moments that stand out from the daily flow (Newman, 1998; pp. 2-3).

Because of the developments in the teacher research movement in North America at this time, students and cooperating teachers began to exert pressure on us to broaden our conception of research to allow for the kinds of inquiry engaged by teachers that fall outside of traditional definitions of research in the academy. I would get questions like "Do I have to have a research question? Do I have to change my practice? Do I have to write up my a study as a chapter? Over the years, I gradually began to move beyond the action research spiral as the only way to approach self- study and beyond writing a study up as a chapter as the only way to represent research. Many of the student teachers and teachers that I work with choose to focus initially on improving their understanding of their practice through examining it more closely as opposed to selecting a question and investigating it with the immediate aim of improvement. I have also encouraged both student teachers and teachers to explore alternative ways to represent their research at the end of the semester. This encouragement has led to performances of research, videos, multimedia representations through art and music and last semester one teacher invented a card game to represent her inquiries.

During this early period, Bob Tabachnick and I also launched a major effort with two staff developers in the Madison schools Cathy Caro-Bruce and Jennifer McCreadie to begin to build a local community of action researchers in the Madison area. Cathy who runs a local teacher center for the school district had been to a conference and had heard about action research and wanted to start a program in the school district for interested teachers. Beginning with one group of 11 teachers in the first year, this program has grown and grown each year to where now over 800 local teachers have spent a year or more working on an action research project (Caro-Bruce and McCreadie, 1995). The district pays for teachers to be released from their classrooms one day per month to meet in groups with peers and each group is facilitated by two experienced action researchers usually classroom teachers. The teachers' studies are published and distributed throughout the district, are available on the web, and TV shows have been produced where teachers go on the air and talk about their research (Zeichner, Caro-Bruce, and Marion, 1998). For several years in the 1990s, Bob Tabachnick and I worked with staff in MMSD and other local districts in organizing a local action research conference where teachers from different programs in the area presented their research. Now it is very likely that when we place student teachers in Madison area schools that they will be working with cooperating teachers who have done action research themselves. This building of an action research community in which to immerse practicum students has created situations where cooperating teachers actively assist student teachers with their research and at times even join them in carrying out a collaborative research project. Action research is no longer perceived by teachers as just another university assignment that is designed to distract attention from learning to teach.

Pat Wood, the elementary teacher mentioned earlier, has argued that the quality of the conversations that she has with her student teachers is of a higher quality when the student teachers are engaged in an action research project (Wood, 1991). David Friesen of the University of Regina in Canada has also used action research as a critical dimension of the internship experience in his teacher education program and has confirmed Pat's experience by arguing that when action research is used in his program, it has promoted less hierarchical and more collaborative and inquiry-oriented relationships among student teachers, cooperating teachers and university supervisors. Friesen has argued as a result of systematic study of the action research experiences of teacher interns that the quality of discourse during supervisory conferences is of a much higher quality- getting into the subtleties and ambiguities of teaching- than when action research is not used as a focusing tool (Freisen, 1995). At the University of Pennsylvania, Marilyn Cochran-Smith and Susan Lytle's teacher education program involved setting up teacher research groups that included both student teachers and cooperating teachers who researched issues collaboratively (Cochran-Smith and Lytle, 1993).

INTEGRATING ACTION RESEARCH INTO THE PRACTICUM

What does it mean to integrate action research into the practicum? At my university, it has meant several things. First, student teachers for the most part do most of the things that students typically do on practicum - they plan and teach lessons and units, gradually assume more and more classroom responsibility over the 20 week period, conduct parent conferences, plan field trips, do a community project in which they learn more about their students' families and communities, and complete a period of at least 2 weeks where they are fully responsible for the classroom program. They are observed by both their cooperating teacher and university supervisor on a regular basis and assessments are made about the quality of their work in relation to a set of specific criteria that reflect the emphasis of the program. All of our students also compile an electronic teaching portfolio in which they put evidence that contributes to this assessment process.

The integration of an action research assignment into the practicum has meant though that throughout the semester, student teachers are also working on an issue or problem in a particularly intense and focused way. They identify and explore issues in their teaching that are of most interest or concern to them. Their exploration of the issues takes place both in the weekly seminars and in their journals where their supervisors respond on a regular basis. These inquiries are aimed at either better understanding an aspect of their practice or improving an aspect of their practice. Data are collected and analyzed related to the area of focus and sometimes action plans are developed and implemented to improve practice in the particular area of concern. Sometimes these inquiries follow the action research spiral (plan, act, observe, and reflect) and sometimes they do not. Oftentimes the question or issue that students begin with evolves and changes over the course of the semester as the issue is explored and seen from different angles. At the end of the semester, student teachers represent their research to others in some form. While some students have written conventional research reports, others have made oral presentations at the annual action research conference that was held for a number of years in Madison every spring. It is mostly the cooperating teachers who have been involved in making videos and in performances.

DEVELOPMENTS AND IMPROVEMENTS IN THE USE OF ACTION RESEARCH IN THE PRACTICUM

Over the years, we have tried a number of variations in engaging student teachers in action research in which we have tried to respond to some of the problems that have arisen. For several semesters, I moved from a background position of working with supervisors who work with student teachers to working directly with student teachers in supporting their research. One problem that we have dealt with all along is the competing demands on the time of student teachers during the practicum. Here we have gradually moved toward a position of making action research a central focus in the practicum rather than just another assignment (Liston and Zeichner, 1990) and in some cases, such as a recent project in science education, we have completely substituted an action research seminar for the regular student teaching seminar (Tabachnick and Zeichner, 1999). We have also tried to more directly link the clinical supervision that is provided to student teachers with their ongoing inquiries by using supervisors and cooperating teachers observations in part to collect data for students' research.

From the beginning, we have also had the problem of time. One semester is clearly too brief a time for student teachers to learn about action research, acquire some of the basic data collection and analysis skills needed, and to develop and carry out an action research project. We often now introduce the idea of action research to students before their practicum semester and try to prepare them to hit the ground running with their research when their student teaching begins. This more long term approach to the problem of developing student teachers' capabilities to inquire into their practice has been made easier in the Professional Development School program that I direct because students work with the same supervisors and in the same learning community over 3 or 4 semesters (Zeichner and Miller, 1997). In our regular program students have different supervisors and different seminar groups each semester and a lot of time is spent each semester building a safe and supportive environment in which inquiry can occur. By the time my PDS students get to their student teaching, they have already spent 2 or 3 semesters working with their supervisors, with me, and with the other cohort students and the conversations in seminar can operate at a higher level from the beginning because of the relationships that have already been formed.

For three years, I also worked in a year-long master's degree teacher education program (Ladson-Billings, 2001) which enabled me to work with student teachers in developing their research project over two semesters. This additional time made a big difference in the quality of the studies that student teachers were able to produce and in the impact of the research experience on the student teachers beliefs and practices (Zeichner, 1995).

Another area of tension involved with the use of action research in the practicum is concerned with the issues of grading and the compulsory nature of the assignment. Much of the research on action research and professional development suggests that it is important for involvement in action research to be voluntary (e.g., Zeichner, 1999). Giving a grade for action research also undermines the more democratic power relationships that are implied by the practice. We have tried to deal with these issues in several ways. First we have either listed action research as a choice of one or several inquiry modes that student teachers could choose from or have invited student teachers to volunteer for sections of the practicum where everyone would be doing action research. We have also moved to a contact type grading system for the projects that have either been pass/ incomplete or A/incomplete. Here if students produced certain things their research would be accepted and if they did not, they would not get credit until they did so. We avoided getting into judging the quality of the research reports (the products of the research) in a conventional academic way and have focused more on the process of acquiring the habits and skills of inquiry.

An interesting change has occurred over the years in the nature and quality of student teachers' research studies. As we have become more successful in making the research project a central aspect of the practicum experience, students have had more difficulty in quickly settling in on issues and questions for study. They explore their areas of interest more than before and at the end there is less finality to their conclusions. It is typical now for the process to be somewhat messy and for questions to arise during the course of the study that remain at the end of the semester (Cook, 1998). There is also more of a tendency now for the studies to more quickly get to an analysis of the teacher's role in relation to the area of focus. In the earlier studies, the tendency would be to focus "out there" on the students and their families, but to ignore a critical self-analysis. The kinds of things that I felt were missing from the earlier neatly packaged studies are beginning to appear now with more frequency.

Action research has been a part of preservice teacher education programs for over thirty years (e.g., Beckman, 1957; Perrodin, 1959). In addition to our 20 years of work in our teacher education program, many other teacher educators have also incorporated some version action research into their teacher education practicum. In North America, these have included institutions like the University of Florida, University of Pennsylvania, Trinity University, the University of Regina, Simon Fraser University (e.g., Cochran- Smith, 1994; Freisen, 1995; Poetter, 1997; Ross, 1987; Stubbs, 1989). It has reached the point now where I think most teacher education programs in North America now involve prospective teachers in some form of action research. It is not always during the final practicum, but it often is. This practice has also become widespread in the teacher education practicum many other countries.

Is all of this effort to engage prospective teachers in research a good thing? Our own research about the use of action research in the teacher education practicum has focused internally on the kinds of benefits that seem to be gained by student teachers from this practice near the time they are engaged in it. We have not done any systematic follow up of the long term impact of systematic and intentional self-study during the practicum except to note that some of the teachers who graduate from our program end up joining one of our local action research professional development programs in their first few years of teaching. While many have described the nature of action research in their teacher education programs, almost no one has reported any systematic investigation of the impact of these experiences on student teachers either in the short run or over time. It is often just assumed that it is a good thing to help teachers become researchers. While we have modified our approach at the University of Wisconsin-Madison over the years so that we now see more student teacher and cooperating teacher commitment to the research project and more of the tentativeness and grappling with issues and that we have been aiming for, we cannot say anything conclusive about the long term impact of this experience on our students, their practices in the classroom, or on the learning of their pupils. Despite this lack of data resulting from systematic study of the effects of conducting self-study research as a teacher at the preservice level in the practicum, there are data that have been accumulated in recent years related to the impact on teachers in general of conducting action research.

For the last few years, I have been analyzing and synthesizing data related to teachers' experiences in conducting research. First I conducted a two year intensive study of the action research program in the Madison schools, the one in which many of our cooperating teachers participate (Zeichner, Caro-Bruce, and Marion, 1998). Here we interviewed over 80 teachers who had participated in the program for at least a year and documented the practices of two research groups over a full year. I also recently finished a study for the U.S. Department of Education in which I synthesized work in which researchers have systematically studied the impact of teacher action research as well as teachers' own self-reports of the impact of the experience (Zeichner, 1999). Following is a brief summary of what we discovered in this work.

ACTION RESEARCH AS PROFESSIONAL DEVELOPMENT

It has been argued for many years and in many countries that teachers should become involved in conducting research about their own practices. We can see evidence of this call for teachers to become researchers as early as 1926. In a book *Research for Teachers*, Burdette Ross Buckingham argued that:

> The teacher has opportunities for research which if seized, will not only powerfully and rapidly develop the technique of teaching, but will also react to and vitalize and dignify the work of the individual teacher (Buckingham, 1926, p.iv).

These arguments have continued for the last 70 years and teachers' involvement in producing knowledge about teaching has often been associated with raising the status of the occupation in society. For example, Fred Erickson, of the University of Pennsylvania has argued:

> If classroom teaching in elementary and secondary schools is to come of age as a profession- if the role of teacher is not to continue to be infantilized- then teachers need to take the adult responsibility of investigating their own practice systematically and critically, by methods appropriate to their practice... Time needs to be made available in the school day for teachers to do this. Anything less than this basic kind of institutional change is to perpetuate the passivity that has characterized the teaching profession in its relations with administrative supervisors and the public at large (Erickson, 1986, p.157).

Over the years claims have been made that action research as a form of professional development has a profound effect on those who have done it, in some cases transforming the classrooms and schools in which they work. It has been argued for example, that practitioner research has helped teachers to become more flexible and more open to new ideas (Oja and Smulyan, 1989), that it has helped boost teachers' self-esteem and confidence levels (Dadds, 1995; Loucks-Horsley, et. al. 1998), that it has helped narrow the gap between teachers' aspirations and realizations (Elliott, 1980), that it has helped teachers understand their practices and students more deeply and to reexamine their personal theories of teaching, that it has helped teachers develop an attitude and skills of self-analysis that they apply in other areas of their work (Day, 1984), and that it has changed patterns of communication among teachers to more collegial interactions about substantive matters of teaching and learning (Selener, 1997).

Some have even gone so far as to claim that action research has fundamentally transformed the nature of instruction in classrooms of teacher researchers. For example, Marilyn Cochran-Smith and Susan Lytle (1992) have argued that:

> When teachers redefine their own relationships to knowledge about teaching and learning, they reconstruct their classrooms and begin to offer different invitations to their students to learn and know. A view of teaching as research is connected to a view of learning as constructive, meaning-centered and social... Teachers who are actually researching their own practices provide opportunities for their students to become similarly engaged... what goes on in the classrooms of teacher -researchers is qualitatively different from what typically happens in classrooms (p.318).

Despite the growing testimony in the literature about the positive outcomes associated with teachers doing research, there are a number of problems with drawing conclusions from these statements alone, about the value of action research as a professional development activity. First, many of the references in the literature to the value of action research are anecdotal in nature and are not the result of systematic and intentional exploration of teachers' experiences. Second, even if we accept the accuracy of the claims that have been made about the impact of teacher research, we are often provided with little or no information about the specific characteristics of the research experience or research context that are responsible for promoting this growth.

Action research has become very common now throughout the world and has been implemented in many different ways that reflect different ideological commitments and beliefs about teacher and student learning (see Elliott, 1991; Zeichner and Noffke, 2001). Similarly, conceptualizations of the process vary substantially, ranging from those that implement a particular structure of the inquiry process such as the action research spiral, to more open-ended approaches that enable researchers to choose from a variety of different approaches to doing research.

The contexts in which action research is conducted also vary greatly. For example, teachers conduct research alone, in connection with a research group, or as part of a whole school faculty, and the particular motivations for and conditions associated with teachers conducting research differ greatly. It is unlikely that all of the various forms of action research and ways of organizing and supporting it result in the kinds of positive outcomes for teachers and students that are often reported in the literature.

In my recent research, I have attempted to gain a better understanding of the particular aspects of organizing, and supporting action research for teachers that are associated with different kinds of teacher and student learning. While it is beyond the scope of this chapter to discuss these results in detail, I will briefly outline a set of conditions that appear to be associated with a transformative impact of action research for teachers and their students, a type of impact not often linked with professional development experiences for teachers.

If certain conditions are present: teacher control over the research process and focus, sustained dialogue over a substantial period of time among peers in a safe and supportive and intellectually challenging environment, the presence of rituals and routines that honor teacher knowledge and help build community, etc. there is clear evidence that the experience of engaging in self-study research helps teachers to become more confident in their ability to promote student learning, to become more proactive in dealing with difficult situations that arise in their teaching, and to acquire habits and skills of inquiry that are used beyond the research experience to analyze their teaching. Teacher research, under these conditions, also seems to develop or rekindle an excitement or enthusiasm about teaching and to provide validation of the importance of the work that seems to be missing from the lives of many teachers.

There is also evidence in my research of direct links between teachers conducting research under these conditions and improvements in students' attitudes, behavior, and learning. The experience of conducting action research under these conditions seems to help teachers move in a direction of more learner-centered instruction, to be more convinced of the importance of listening to and studying their pupils, and to be more wiling to use what they learn from this "student watching" to influence classroom events. These teachers begin to approach teaching more from the standpoint of their pupils and to give their pupils more input into classroom affairs.

Not all the programs that I looked at displayed the kind of general design characteristics that I have come to believe are important, and those that did, represented very different ways of putting these general principles into action. There were also a number of other factors such as giving teachers released time, having them write research chapters and follow the action research spiral that do not appear to be critical to producing the transformative outcomes noted above.

The professional development represented by those programs that exemplified these characteristics represents a long-term investment in building the capacity of teachers to exercise their judgment and leadership abilities to improve learning for themselves and their students. It is not a form of teacher education that will produce quick fixes for the complex and enduring problems of schooling or compensate for the unsatisfactory working conditions that many teachers throughout the world are forced to endure. In this era of educational accountability and standards, action research is not a tool that can be used by policy makers or administrators to externally impose particular changes on teachers although some have tried to do so.

In the end, the quality of learning for students in our schools will depend to no small extent on the quality of learning and opportunities for professional development that we provide for our teachers. While it is appropriate at times for policy makers and administrators to set directions for reforms and to provide teachers with the skills and content that they need to carry them out, there must also be a place in the lives of teachers for the kind of professional development that respects and nurtures their intellectual leadership capacity. As the late Lawrence Stenhouse of the University of East Anglia said:

> Good teachers are necessarily autonomous in professional judgment. They do not need to be told what to do. They are not professionally the dependents of researchers, superintendents, of innovators, of supervisors. This does not mean that they do not welcome access to ideas created by other people at other places or in other times. Nor do they reject advice,

consultancy, or support. But they do know that ideas and people are not of much real use until they are digested to the point where they are subject to the teachers' own judgment. In short, it is the task of all educationists outside the classroom to serve the teachers. For only they are in the position to create good teaching. (cited in Ruddick and Hopkins, 1985, p.104).

CONCLUSIONS ABOUT ACTION RESEARCH AS PROFESSIONAL DEVELOPMENT IN THE U.S.

There are a number of implications in this work for thinking about the use of action research in the teacher education practicum as a vehicle for promoting student teacher inquiry and reflection. First, and most important is the conclusion that action research under any conditions, is not necessarily a valuable professional development experience for prospective teachers that will set them on a path toward becoming thoughtful and reflective teachers who are disposed toward and capable of playing significant roles in the shaping of schools.

While it may not be possible to achieve in the teacher education practicum all of the conditions that seem to be important for teachers in general to gain the benefits of doing action research (the time frame of the practicum is one obvious constraint), it is possible to learn some important lessons from this work.

For example, the biggest mistake that is often made by some who seek to use action research as a way to focus the inquiries of student teachers, is to focus on the products of the research rather than on the process of acquiring the habits and skills of inquiry or on acquiring an orientation of teachers as learners and as educators who can and should assume leadership roles in school reform. Those who attempt to prepare student teachers as junior academic researchers, forcing them into preconceived and limited notions of what academic research should be, or expect to see major institutional changes result from the action research studies of student teachers, forcing the research to focus on some set of "progressive" educational topics, are emphasizing the wrong things.

The point of engaging student teachers in inquiry during the practicum is to set them on a course of learning that will continue to deepen as long as they teach. What student teachers actually produce at this point is far less important in the larger scheme of things than the vision of the teacher's role and the habits and skills they begin to acquire.

The test of whether one has been successful in doing this is not to be found in an analysis of the topics of student teachers' research or of their research reports. The true test of the success of this work is to be able to visit the graduates of these teacher education programs in their early years of teaching and see them engaged in inquiry about their practice and in developing their leadership potential. Has the teacher education program helped its graduates develop expanded visions of what teachers can and ought to do or are they still locked into the dominant view of teachers as passive recipients of others' visions of reform?

It is pretty clear that both the contexts of schools and of teacher education programs have done much to undermine a vision of teachers as learners and educational leaders. In this era of accountability, there are many who hold a dim view of the potential of teachers to assume leadership in schools.

The professional development school movement in the U.S (Abdal-Haqq, 1997) and similar structural revolutions in the practicum in other countries offer much potential for altering the context of teacher education so that the settings in which student teachers and teachers work will place more value on nurturing their development and leadership potential.

In my own work in Wisconsin, I am still continuing on the same general path that I began 29 years ago, trying to make the teacher education practicum a key site for fostering the development of teacher leadership. The structural context in which I now work, the professional development school, is much more suited to supporting this goal than the conventional practicum structure. In the end, it will be this dual focus on both changing the structural context and curriculum of the practicum that will enable the practicum to achieve its potential. Either type of change by itself is insufficient. There are a number of professional development schools in the U.S. where the structures have changed, but where the curriculum has not, as well as a number of instances where curricular changes are suffocated by the limits of outdated structural models. The kind of changes that are needed will not be easy to achieve, but I am more optimistic now than I have ever been about the future of the practicum despite the continued blindness of policy makers to the leadership potential of teachers and the continued low status of teacher education in colleges and universities.

ACTION RESEARCH AND TEACHER EDUCATION IN NAMIBIA

Between 1994 and 2000, I worked as a member of an international course team in the Teacher Education Reform Project in Namibia. In this project, a form of action research (Mayumbelo and Nyambe, 1999) was introduced to teacher educators in the four teacher education colleges and became a required part of the preservice teacher education curriculum. Before independence in 1990, teacher education in Namibia was part of the political agenda of the separation of the races to maintain social injustice (Cohen, 1994). The current national teacher education program, the Basic Education Teacher Diploma (BETD), emphasizes a set of democratic values that underlie post-independence educational reform in Namibia such as the promotion of gender and race equity and understanding and respect for cultural diversity, and developing school environments a that are responsive to the communities in which they exist.

One central component of the national educational reform has been the introduction of a form of action research, critical practitioner inquiry, into the preservice teacher education programs for basic education in the colleges of education. Additionally, teacher educators who participated in the TERP professional development programs for teacher educators conducted studies in their teacher education classrooms that were designed to further the broad goals of the reform (equity, democracy, etc.). Student teachers also conduct a variety of inquiries each year in their three-year program culminating in an action research project in their final year. With few exceptions (see Zeichner and Dahlstrom, 1999), the action research studies of student teachers represent inquiries that helped develop the disposition of student teachers to be reflective and analytic about their teaching and were not than full blown research projects.

Because most teacher educators experienced something other than the learner-centered and democratic education envisioned by Namibians for their schools, and only some participated in the professional development courses for teacher educators that were provided by TERP, there were some problems in the translation of the idea of critical practitioner inquiry into the preservice programs in the colleges (e.g., see Meyer, 2000). Despite these difficulties and the limited nature of student teachers' research studies, it is clear that critical practitioner inquiry as defined within the Namibian colleges has become a vehicle for teacher professional development that has set student teachers on a path of inquiry about their teaching. We have seen evidence of this inquiring stance toward teaching in our observations of the classrooms of graduates of the BETD program (Zeichner and Luecke, 2004).

From the beginning, there was never the hope that student teachers in Namibia could produce research reports that would have value beyond contributing to the professional development of the individual teachers who conducted them. There was hope however that the action research done by teacher educators could begin to develop a reservoir of locally produced knowledge that could contribute more broadly to the creation of a Namibian knowledge base about education and lessen dependence on knowledge produced outside of Namibia (Zeichner and Tabachnick, 1999). The emergence of action research studies done by teacher educators about aspects of learner-centered and democratic education in teacher education classrooms has led to several publications (e.g., National Institute for Educational Development, 2000) of the research of Namibian teacher educators that have been used as readings in both preservice teacher education courses and in professional development settings. One of the major lessons that I have learned through this work in Namibia is about the importance of adapting the meanings and methods associated with action research to fit into the cultural context in which it is being used. It was important that our Namibian colleagues conceptualized and developed the practice of critical practitioner inquiry drawing on the ideas from the outside that a variety of people offered them, but also changing and shaping these ideas to suit their own purposes. Despite the possibilities in action research for empowering teachers and teacher educators to play important roles in shaping an educational reform program, it can easily turn into a form of oppression and marginalize practitioner's contributions if it is imposed on them from the outside.

POSTSCRIPT

Bob Tabachnick has been an integral part of the work discussed in this chapter both in Wisconsin and in Namibia. I am extremely grateful to him for all that he taught me over the years about how to work with practitioners in ways that are respectful of what they know and can do but that also push and challenge them to question what they know and develop new ideas and skills.

REFERENCES

Abdal-Haqq, I. (1997) *Professional development schools: Weighing the evidence.* Washington, D.C.: American Association of Colleges for Teacher Education.

Beckman, D.R. (1957) Student teachers learn by action research. *Journal of Teacher Education 8*, (4), 369-375.

Buckingham, B.R. (1926) *Research for teachers..* New York: Silver Burdett and Co.

Caro-Bruce, C. and McReadie, J. (1995) What happens when a school district supports action research? In S. Noffke and R. Stevenson (Eds.) *Educational action research* (pp. 154-164). New York: Teachers College Press.

Cochran-Smith, M. (1994) The power of teacher research in teacher education. In S. Hollingsworth and H. Sockett (Eds.) *Teacher research and educational reform*. Chicago: University of Chicago Press.

Cochran-Smith, M. and Lytle, S. (1992) Communities for teacher research: Fronge or forefront? *American Journal of Education*, 298-323.

Cochran-Smith, M. and Lytle, S. (1993) *Inside/outside: Teacher research and knowledge*. New York: Teachers College Press.

Cohen, C. (1994) *Administering education in Namibia: The colonial period to the present*. Windhoek: Namibian Scientific Society.

Cook, T. (1998) The importance of mess in action research. *Educational Action Research*, 6, (1), 93-110.

Dadds, M. (1995) *Passionate inquiry and school development*. London: Falmer Press.

Day, C. (1984) Teachers' thinking, intentions, and practice: An action research perspective. In R. Halkes and J. Olson (Eds.) *Teacher thinking*., Lisse: Swets and Zeitlinger.

Dewey, J. (1933) *How we think*. Chicago: Henry Regnery.

Elliott, J. (1980) Implications of classroom research for professional development. In E. Hoyle and J. Megarry (Eds.) *Professional development of teachers*. London: Kogan Page.

Elliott, J. (1991) *Action research for school change.*. Philadelphia: Open University Press.

Erickson, F. (1986) Qualitative methods on research on teaching. In M. Wittrock (Ed.)*Handbook of research on teaching, 3rd edition.* (pp. 119-161). New York: Macmillan.

Freisen, D. (1995) Action research in the teaching internship. *Educational Action Research*, 3, (2), 153-168.

Gore, J. (1991) Practising what we preach: Action research and the supervision of student teachers. In B.R. Tabachnick and K. Zeichner (Eds.) *Issues and practices in inquiry-oriented teacher education*. (Pp. 253-272). London: Falmer Press.

Gore, J. and Zeichner, K. (1991) Action research and reflective teaching in preservice teacher education: A case study from the U.S. *Teaching and Teacher Education,7* (2), 119-136.

Kemmis, S. and McTaggart, R. (1988b) *The action research planner, 3rd edition*. Geelong: Deakin University Press.

Kemmis, S. and McTaggart, R. (1988a) (Eds.) *The action research reader: 3rd edition*. Geelong: Deakin University Press.

Kennedy M. (1996) *Teachers conducting research*. East Lansing, MI: National Center for Research on Teacher Learning.

Ladson-Billings, G. (2001) *Crossing over to Canaan: The journey of teachers in diverse classrooms*. San Francisco: Jossey Bass.

Liston, D. and Zeichner, K. (1990) Reflective teaching and action research in preservice teacher education. *Journal of Education for Teaching*, 16, (3), 235-254.

Liston, D. and Zeichner, K. (1991) *Teacher education and the social conditions of schooling*. New York: Routledge.

Loucks-Horsley, S.; Hewson, P.; Love, P. and Stiles, K. (1998) *Designing professional development for teachers of science and mathematics*. Thousand Oaks, CA: Sage.

Mayumbelo, C. and Nyambe, J. (1999) Critical inquiry in preservice teacher education. In K. Zeichner and L. Dahlstrom (Eds.) *Democratic teacher education reform in Africa: The case of Namibia.* (pp. 64-81). Boulder, CO: Westview Press.

Meyer, H. (2000) *Creating a Namibian definition of action research: A case study fromone Namibian college of education.* Unpublished doctoral dissertation. School of Education, University of Wisconsin-Madison.

National Institute for Educational Development (2000) *Namibian educators research their own practice: Critical practitioner inquiry in Namibia.* Windhoek: Gamsberg Macmillan.

Newman, J.(1998) *Tensions of teaching.* New York: Teachers College Press. Noffke, S. and Brennan, M. (1991) Action research and reflective student teaching at the University of Wisconsin-Madison. In B.R. Tabachnick and K. Zeichner (Eds.) *Issues and practices in inquiry-oriented teacher education*, pp. 186-201. London: Falmer Press.

Noffke, S. and Zeichner, K. (1987) *Action research and teacher thinking: The first phase of the action research on action research project at the University of Wisconsin-Madison..* Chapter presented at the annual meeting of the American Educational Research Association, Washington, D.C.

Oja, S. and Smulyan, L. (1989) *Collaborative action research: A developmental approach.* London: Falmer Press.

Perrodin, A. (1959) Student teachers try action research. *Journal of Teacher Education, 10,* (4), 471-474.

Poetter, T. *Voices of inquiry in teacher education.* Mahwah, N.J.: Lawrence Erlbaum.

Ruddick, J. and Hopkins, D. (1985) *Research as the basis for teaching.* London: Heinemann.

Robottom, I. (1988) A research-based course in science education. In J. Nias and S. Groundwater-

Smith (Eds.) *The inquiring teacher: Sustaining and supporting teacher research.* London: Falmer Press.

Ross, D. (1987) Action research for preservice teachers: A description of why and how. *Peabody Journal of Education, 64* (3), 131-150.

Schildgren, K. (June, 1995) *A closer look with student involvement with action research.*Unpublished chapter, School of Education, University of Wisconsin-Madison.

Schon, D. (1983) *The reflective practitioner.* New York: Basic Books.

Schon, D. (1987) *Educating the reflective practitioner.* San Francisco: Jossey Bass.

Selener, D. (1997) *Participatory action research and social change.* Quito, Ecuador: Global Action Publications.

Stubbs, M. (1989) *Training would-be teachers to do research: A practical account.* Research Report, No. 197 Wellesley, MA: Wellesley College, Center for Research on Women.

Tabachnick, B.R.; Popkewitz, T. and Zeichner, K. (1979) Teacher education and the professional perspectives of student teachers. *Interchange, 10* (4), 12-29.

Tabachnick, B.R. and Zeichner, K. (1999) Ideas and action: action research and the development of conceptual change teaching in science. *Science Education.* 309-322.

Wood, P. (1988) Action research: A field perspective. *Journal of Education for Teaching, 14,* (2), 135-150.

Wood, P. (1991) The cooperating teacher's role in nurturing reflective teaching. In B.R. Tabachnick and K. Zeichner (Eds.) *Issues and practices in inquiry-oriented teacher education* (pp. 202-210), London: Falmer Press.

Zeichner, K. (1981) Reflective teaching and field-based experience in teacher education. *Interchange, 12* (4), 1-22.

Zeichner, K. (1993) Traditions of practice in U.S. preservice teacher education programs. *Teaching and Teacher Education, 9* (1), 1-13.

Zeichner, K. (1995) *Action research as a strategy for promoting socially conscious and culturally relevant teaching in preservice teacher education.* Chapter presented at the annual meeting of the American Educational Research Association, San Francisco.

Zeichner, K. (1997) Action research and issues of equity and social justice in preservice teacher education. *Practical Experiences in Professional Education, 1* (1), 36-52.

Zeichner, K. (November, 1998) *The nature and impact of teacher research as professional development for P-12 educators.* Washington, D.C: U.S. Department of Education, Office of Educational Research and Improvement.

Zeichner, K.; Caro-Bruce, C. and Marion, R. (1998) *The nature and impact of action research in one urban school district: Final report.* Chicago: The Spencer Foundation.

Zeichner, K. and Dahlstrom, L. (1999) (Eds.) *Democratic teacher education reform in Africa: The case of Namibia.* Boulder, CO: Westview Press.

Zeichner, K. and Gore, J. (1995) Using action research as a vehicle for student teacher reflection:A social reconstructionist approach. In S. Noffke and B. Stevenson (Eds.) *Educational action research: Becoming practically critical* (pp. 13-30). New York: Teachers College Press.

Zeichner, K. and Hoeft, K. (1996) Teacher socialization for cultural diversity. In J. Cecilia (Ed.) *Handbook of research on teacher education, 2nd edition.* New York: Macmillan.

Zeichner, K. and Liston, D. (1987) Teaching student teachers to reflect *Harvard Educational Review, 57* (1), 1-22.

Zeichner, K. and Liston, D. (1996) *Reflective teaching.* Mahwah, N.J.: Lawrence Erlbaum.

Zeichner, K. and Luecke, J. (April, 2004) *A case study of the reform of teaching and teacher education in post-independence Namibia.* A chapter presented at the annual meeting of the American Educational Research Association, San Diego.

Zeichner, K. and Miller, M. (1997) Learning to teach in professional development schools. In M. Levine and R. Trachtman (Eds.) *Making professional development schools work: Politics, practice and policy.* New York: Teachers College Press.

Zeichner, K. and Noffke, S. (2001) Practitioner research. In V. Richardson (Ed.) *Handbook of research on teaching, 4th edition (pp.298-332)* Washington, D.C.: American Educational Research Association.

Zeichner, K. and Tabachnick, B.R. (1999) Participatory development and teacher education reformin Namibia. In K. Zeichner and L. Dahlstrom (Eds.) *Democratic teacher education reform in Africa: The case of Namibia.* (pp. 207-221). Boulder, CO: Westview Press.*http://madison.k12.wi.us/sod/car/carhomepage.html*

Capacity Building Effort and Brain Drain in Nigerian Universities

Bankolé Oni
NISER-Ibadan, Nigeria

Introduction

The advancement of the developed countries since the end of the Second World War has been through an aggressive development of capacity both human and institutional. Indeed, the globalisation phenomenon of the present age could not have been possible without the development and application of knowledge and the institutional capacity to sustain it. The examples of the United States of America and Germany, and of course, other developed countries reveal the critical role that universities, research centres, industries, foundations and government play in the institutionalisation of capacity building. Universities and research institutes in Europe and America demonstrate their social relevance not only through their esoteric research, but also through their contribution to meeting the needs of industry. An enabling environment for collaborative capacity building among the community of actors is important and the governments in these countries recognise their important role in this.

The underutilisation of existing capacity and the loss of it through brain drain have made Africa to remain underdeveloped. The countries of Africa constitute most of the poorest societies in the world as they show the lowest indicators of socio-economic development (World Bank, 1996). While the level of poverty in the continent has been attributed to many interrelated causes by different social science researchers and other scholars, the low level of capacity building indicators has, in the last decade begun to emerge in research as a major cause of Africa's underdevelopment (World Bank, 1998). It is also argued that the recent rapid economic development of the countries of Southeast Asia in the latter part of the 20th century has been due largely to their deliberate policy on capacity building through investment in human capital and institutional building. Development in Southeast Asia has been promoted through systematic and deliberate policies directed at capacity building both human and institutional.

In contrast, most African countries have displayed lack of attention to the relevance and development of institutional capacity building. This is not to suggest that African countries must follow the same development path to capacity building like the S.E. Asian countries as suggested recently by the Malaysian Prime Minister (see Mansell and Wehn 1998). The important lesson is that the Asian experience has confirmed the general view that human and institutional capacity building is critical to economic progress and development. In this context it is perhaps instructional and relevant to identify and analyse some of the critical constraints to capacity building (CB) in Nigeria.

As a starting point, one would like to argue that there exists a structural relationship between a society's human and institutional capacity building effort and the national ability to engineer social and economic development. A social system which places little emphasis on technology is less inclined to acquire technological capability and to achieve economic development. The link between building local capability and the ability to respond to challenges is usually brought about in the process of learning and co-operation between institutions. This is because without the cooperation among the ⬚community of actors⬚ and the necessary institutional framework for coordinating their activities it may be impossible for a country like Nigeria to develop the technological capacity that the country would require for the global competition of the 21st century (Oni, 1999b).

The main objective of the present discourse is to identify and analyse the determinants of the weak capacity building in Nigeria, the magnitude of the problem at the tertiary education level and the implications for Nigeria's future. Even though the Nigerian government recognises the development of science and technology as a matter of national policy, the existing research centres and universities are faced with problems that affect their performance. These problems are the products of the environment. In spite of this, there still exists within the country today a corps of internationally and locally recognised expertise and intellectual capacity that need to be harnessed to build the desired national capacity for development policy design, implementation, co-ordination and evaluation.

The requirements for human and institutional capacity building generally exist within the social and political environment; it is salient therefore to assume that the success or failure of any attempt to build capacity especially within the African context of development must be interpreted as the product of the structural relationship between the environment and the various institutions involved. Thus, capacity building (CB) in a broad development context implies a dynamic process that enables individuals and agencies to develop the critical social/technical capabilities to identify and analyse problems and proffer solutions to them. A conducive policy environment is therefore a *sine qua non* for the process of CB to thrive without hindrance. This is very critical for the technological sub-sector in the process of development. The policy environment for technological capacity building (TCB) should be multisectoral, involving government, universities, universities, research centres, the private sector and other stakeholders. This is important in any policy environment that is characterised by social and ideological heterogeneity.

Broadly defined technology is not necessarily hardware. It is the totality of knowledge and skills embodied in people and institutions that provide them with mastery over their natural environment. The role of capacity building in this context therefore is to harness the capabilities within the network of institutions and enhance organisational interactions to better manage the process of development and change, technology acquisition, diffusion, utilisation and skill development. A general policy environment that induces human and institutional interaction and collaboration is therefore necessary for effective policy management and capacity building.

Two critical social forces in the policy environment in Africa are the government and the bureaucracy. These two institutions are critical to the extent that well-intentioned policies may produce undesired outputs if the people charged with their implementation do not possess the necessary scientific background (Dahlman, 1989). Trained experts can only be productive within an appropriately designed institutional framework and not outside it. Such institutions can only exist in an appropriate policy environment where research institutes, university laboratories and the private sector are encouraged to build a network of information, knowledge and personnel exchanges.

Thus, the above suggests the intellectual relevance of a holistic approach that describes and also prescribes a structured and dynamic relationship between institutional networking for technological capacity building and the total environment. An appropriate policy environment would induce institutions to collaborate in building a network for the objective of strengthening national technological capacity.

Inherent in the present perspective is the possibility of lack of social cohesion within the community of actors (institutions), especially when resource allocators may not possess the critical minimum technical competence for prescribing standards to the experts within the relationship or when rewards or incentives generate conflict (Wohlmuth, 1998). However, if the machinery for decision-making is democratised, it should be possible to reduce the areas of conflict and promote social cohesion within the system.

The present emphasis on technology is deliberate; first, I have been involved in technology policy studies in recent times, (See Oni, 1999 b). Secondly, it is my sincere intellectual perception that technological capacity building (human and institutional) is critical to the integration of Africa into the global system. The term technology as used in the text does not imply just machine. Dahhman's (1989) definition that is adopted refers to technology as the inherent or acquired capability (skills) possessed by people and/or institutions that enables them to convert available inputs into desired outputs at maximum efficiency level. Thus the term technological capacity building is a dynamic and progressive process in which human and institutional capability is developed and sustained by organisations, communities and nations in order to benefit from economic interconnections within the global system (Lisk, 1996).

THE ISSUES

Africa as a whole has the resources and market for industrialisation (Green and Siedman, 1967) but the poor managerial capacity and weak technological institutions constitute major constraints (Richman, 1977). In a country where the education and training systems are not geared to the development of national capability, Richman concludes that more productive technology cannot be employed. The implication of this is that human resources development institutions must be strengthened to develop the needed capacity for African development. Such a policy should also incorporate a strategy for technological capacity building (TCB) as a continuous social process.

To develop this capability a nation therefore needs to have the appropriate policy, build the necessary institutions and structures that must be sustainable. But while many African countries are technologically backward they are still unable or unprepared to build the institutional/management structures for overcoming their problems. Hence Bell and Pavitt (1992) conclude that these countries are likely to remain without the necessary technological capability for entry into the global market, as they do not possess distinct resources such as technological skills, knowledge, experience and institutional structures and linkages designed to encourage the accumulation of technology. The integration of these components must be a policy objective of government, argue these authors.

Capacity under-utilisation and low retention due to brain drain constitutes another problem area in capacity building in Africa (Adubifa, 1990; Bossuyt, 1995). An evaluation of structural adjustment programmes in many African countries reflects a lack of capacity and management skills (Phillips and Ndekwu, 1987). Bad governance and instability can also decapacitate potentially efficient administrative machinery. Hence, Bossuyt suggests that capacity building issues particularly brain drain touch on many sensitivities which include governance, quality of leadership, management philosophy, workers' remuneration, resource allocation strategies etc.

Capacity building policies and programmes therefore should be grounded in an appraisal of the environment. Management weaknesses are usually not merely due to technical problems they generally manifest more pervasive and fundamental problems, which are generated through the structural relationships of these organisations with their environment. What lessons can the poor countries learn from the role of various institutions in TCB? While Africa may be looking up to Europe for models of TCB, the latter continent is concerned about its recent decline in TCB. In its recent report for the mid year 1998, the European Union (EU) is worried that it has not performed well in the field of science and technology. The EU attributes the continent's lower economic growth, lower employment and declining global competitiveness to its recent cutback policy on capacity building. As a major technological and economic power in the world today, Europe feels that it must promote long-term economic growth through aggressive investment in TCB if it must retain its leadership position in the world in the 21st century (EU; June/July, 1998)

The decade of the 1980s and 1990s in Europe created the awareness that the pre 1980 capacity building policies in these developed countries would not be able to cope with the global challenges of the 21st century. Future success, argues Rondinelli, would depend on creating stronger regional technological development capacity and a more complex and diverse institutional infrastructure to support technology-based industries. The management of what Rondinelli recommends for effective TCB in any nation requires complex interactions among stakeholders (Mansell and Wehn, 1998, p.49), that is, co-operation and co-ordination within the community of actors (Nelson and Rosenbeg, 1993).

These actors are the universities, research institutes, industry, foundations and government. While the role of each of these institutions in the developed countries is catalogised elsewhere (Oni; 1999b), the emphasis in the present chapter is to examine critically the objective conditions of the Nigerian University system as a capacity building structure, and their implications for the future.

THE NIGERIAN UNIVERSITY SYSTEM TODAY

The role of universities in human capital development, research and technological innovation cannot be underestimated. All over the world investment in university education is a critical component of national development effort. Nations today depend increasingly on knowledge, ideas and skills that are produced in universities (World Bank, 1997; OECD, 1996). As a nation's knowledge industry, universities increase the productive capacity of the labour force. In the developed countries university scientists are able to monitor global technology trends, assess their relevance to national needs and assist in developing the national technological capacity for economic growth. For example, a World Bank study of about 1000 inventors in the Indian subcontinent reveal that almost 90% of them had a university first degree; those with some graduate training among them were more than half and almost 30% had their Ph.D. (World Bank, 1998, p. 43). Since industry and the public sector demand high-level manpower the role of the university is to satisfy this demand.

All educational systems share three major universally accepted objectives. These are: (1) to socialise the recipient into the traditions, mores and values of his or her society; (2) to equip him with necessary skills that would ensure his livelihood, and (3) to help develop his powers to contribute to the development of his community (Shah, 1975). Even though this universality exists, yet the universities have their own distinguishing roles which are teaching, research, human resources development, storage and dissemination of knowledge and contribution to national, regional and international co-operation and understanding, that is, capacity building. But why focus on the university?

Nation states invest in university education because society expects it to contribute to national development in three principal ways (Oni, 1991). In the first place, society expects its university to produce the highly skilled personnel in technology, engineering, management and other professions. Secondly, universities have the responsibility of producing their own corps of academic personnel that is, the intellectual resource pool that will, through scientific research generate new knowledge and innovation to solve development problems. Thirdly, universities produce the teachers, administrators and managers for other levels of human resources development institutions. A university is able to perform all these complementary roles if it has the necessary financial resources, equipment and operates in an environment that is conducive to academic work.

Government in the developing countries must strive to achieve two apparently incompatible social objectives in the provision of university education. On the one hand access to higher education must be based on the principle of social justice in order to promote social cohesion in a culturally heterogeneous society like Nigeria. Simultaneously with the objective of social justice the university must produce the necessary high-level personnel for the management of the economy.

In the less developed countries, the university is the main agency for research and the creation of knowledge. The private sector is not strong enough nor does it possess the necessary incentives (private benefits) to create knowledge for public consumption. Thus the production of new ideas and skills in the less development countries requires institutional mechanisms beyond the capacity of the market (Conceicao and Heitor, 1998). Hence being public institutions, universities in the less developed countries are the major producers of knowledge. Through the performance of these multiple roles, the universities directly develop and sustain a country's knowledge industry on which future generations can build (Oni, 1991). For a university to generate knowledge and transmit same, it must have its pool of talent and students who must interact in the process of teaching, learning and research. Hence human resources (lecturers and students) constitute very important inputs in this process. This combination is critical because it has a structural and significant relationship with the society's capacity to innovate and manage its present and future development effort effectively.

The first university in Nigeria was established in 1948 at Ibadan with a total of 104 students who were enrolled in the four faculties of Arts, Science, Agriculture and Medicine. The number of universities in the country grew to five between 1960 and 1963. While enrolments in the five universities (Ibadan, , Nsukka, Lagos and Zaria) stood at 3,646, the number of academic staff was 680 in the 1962/63 academic session. The establishment of the sixth university in Benin City in 1972/73 brought total student enrolment to 20,889 with an academic staff strength of 2,655. There are 39 universities in Nigeria today (1999) with a student enrolment of 236,261 and 12,395 lecturers (Federal Office of Statistics (FOS), 1996)

A new development is that between 1987 and 1992, less than 20 per cent of the total number of applicants into the universities were offered placement partly because the rest did not qualify for admission and/or due to lack of facilities like lecture rooms, laboratories, equipment etc. This situation has not improved even with the establishment of state Universities in 10 States of the country between 1980 to date. Table 1 shows the disparity between applications and total admissions into the universities vividly between 1987/88 to 1991/92. What Table 1 shows is that the demand for university education in Nigeria is greater than the supply (Yesufu, 1996).

Table 1: Application and Admissions to Universities Through the Joint Admissions and Matriculation Board (JAMB) 1987/88-1991/92

Years	Applications	Number Index	Admissions	Number Index	as % of Applications
1987-88	210,252	100.0	32,839	100.0	15.6
1988-89	189,522	90.0	41,065	125.0	21.7
1989-90	249,164	118.4	36.616	111.5	14.7
1990-91	n.a.	-	48,168	146.7	-
1991-92	373,016	117.2	61,212	186.4	16.4

Source: F.O.S. Annual Abstract of Statistics 1994 Edition, Table 94-102
Note: n.a. = not available

When the total number of academic staff (12.395) is related to the number of students (236,261) Federal (Office of Statistics, 1996), a lecturer/student ratio of 1:19 should be considered much lower than the UNESCO norm of 1 lecturer to 10 students. Table 2 shows comparative lecturer/student ratios for five developing African countries including Nigeria, two middle income countries in Latin America as well as two developed countries in Europe. The ratio of 1:8 for Kenya and Zimbabwe is higher than the UNESCO norm, while Ethiopia, (1:18), Nigeria, (1:19) and South Africa (1:28.5) have ratios that are lower than the international norm.

Table 2: University Lecturer/Student Ratios in Selected Countries

Country	Lecturers	Students	Ratio
Ethiopia	1,440	26,415	1:18
Kenya	4,392	35,421	1:8
Nigeria	12,395	236,261	1:19
South Africa	13,326	380,184	1:28.5
Zimbabwe	1,618	13,045	1:8
Mexico	72,742	125,207	1:7
Brazil	172,828	1,716,263	1:10
United Kingdom	97,274	923,878	1:9
Germany	243,303	1,856,542	1:7.6
UNESCO Norm			1:10

Source: UNESCO Statistical Yearbook, 1997; Federal Office of Statistics, Lagos.

Using the above ratios as indicators of part of the responsibilities of university lecturers in the five African countries, it becomes obvious that the average university lecturer in Ethiopia, Nigeria and South Africa carries much heavier burden than his counterpart in Kenya or Zimbabwe. For example, the case of Nigeria may even be worse because of the constraints under which the academic staff in this country is forced to work (Mbanefoh, 1992; Bangura, 1994, Yesufu, 1996). When the Nigerian ratio is further compared with those of middle income countries like Mexico (1:7) and Brazil (1:10) or with those of the advanced countries like the United Kingdom and Germany that have ratios higher than the UNESCO standard, the enormity of the load shouldered by the Nigerian university lecturer can be further appreciated. The situation in the Nigerian university is probably worse than in most of the countries shown in Table 2 because of the problem of brain drain. A one time Pro-Chancellor of one of the Nigerian universities and Professor of Economics T.M. Yesufu, aptly describes the pathetic picture of the Nigerian university today when he says,

> ... The student-teacher ratios are worsening in virtually all disciplines. Laboratories are either non-existent or completely denuded of essential equipment and experimental consumables. Libraries cry out for updating with current books, periodicals and research findings. Teachers are grossly underpaid and many have had to resort to migration to other countries to seek how to keep body and soul together, and further their intellectual development. Many others have abandoned academics to the greener pastures of the private industry, the banks and consultancies. Part time jobs and moonlighting have become the rule than the exception (Yesufu, 1996, p. 207).

Consequently Yesufu concludes that the quality of graduates is so poor that their impact on the national economy in terms of productivity is generally below the required standard for a developing economy. As a result of lack of qualified academic staff the enrolment for graduate studies has also declined, concludes Yusufu (1996 p. 208). The loss of academic staff to the universities between 1992 and 1995 is later discussed below. No educational system can be better than those who operate it, that is, the teachers who constitute the intellectual resource pool which ensures that present and future human and social capacity can be developed, managed and sustained. Today, the Nigerian university system continues to suffer from intellectual hemorrhage created by the problem of brain drain (Mbanefoh, 1992). This is more so in the very critical fields of human medicine, pharmacy, computer science and engineering. The implication of this development is that because of emigration of technological know-how, the economy cannot grow. Many good students who probably would have enrolled for graduate courses in the critical disciplines to promote the necessary social capability in Nigeria have no teachers to guide their studies. Thus, the much needed intellectual capacity for the future cannot be built.

A critical look at Table 3 shows the decline in postgraduate awards by Nigerian universities from 5,149 in June, 1988 to 3,818 in June, 1992[2]. Nevertheless, one can safely conjecture that given the impact of the Structural Adjustment Programme (SAP) (1986-1993), inflation, attendant rapid decline in the value of the naira, and the attractiveness of off-shore employment opportunities for Nigerian scholars, the Nigerian universities have continued to suffer from serious intellectual hemorrhage. For the very few, who embark on graduate studies, the university does not offer them any attraction for employment (Oni, 1987, 1991; Yesufu 1996)

Table 3: Post Graduate Awards By Nigerian Universities (Year Ending June)

Discipline	1988	1989	1990	1991	1992
Administration	519	436	469	621	734
Agriculture	319	306	215	421	429
Arts	374	390	441	404	214
Education	1,751	2,055	1,229	1,972	1,062
Engineer and Technology	275	217	305	226	112
Environmental Design	267	170	210	199	41
Law	121	138	181	226	8
Medicine	141	152	157	200	77
Pharmacy	28	15	19	12	6
Sciences	420	474	620	491	276
Social Sciences	849	881	1,127	1,218	847
Veterinary Medicine	87	14	18	17	12
Others	-	-	-	918	-
Total	5,149	5,148	4,991	6,925	3,818

Source: National Universities Commission, 1998-1992

The relevant question is why would future workers in a critical knowledge industry (university) prefer to work outside the intellectual environment that has produced them? In other words, when it is recognised that inter-generational succession is a necessary condition for the maintenance of international competition in the knowledge industry, why is the Nigerian system unable to sustain itself? The answer is simple. The Nigerian university system today is unattractive to any young and ambitious man or woman. With lack of facilities for work, low pay and frustration in the context of rising expectation the Nigerian University lecturer is a cursed specie. As Oni. (1987:28) observed,

Through his or her experience, the Nigerian graduate student becomes aware of what goes on through his externalised analytic structure and his ego-centred cognitive map. The individual is able to interpret this map because he is located within it... it is this map that presents to him the configuration of (economic) opportunities. Thus, while the Ibadan respondents ranked university teaching post as fifth, it diminished into a non-desirable future career to be aimed at among Lagos university graduate student

The low ranking accorded university academic work by Nigerian graduate students has very serious implications for the future development of the university in Nigeria in the twenty-first century. This is because the graduate students of today are supposed to be the intellectual giants and scientific innovators of tomorrow.

Their preference contrasts sharply with the motivation for postgraduate studies among their peers in Britain and other European countries (Rudd, 1975), whose motivation for research and pursuit of knowledge is sustained by a long tradition of the search for new ideas and global competition.

The situation today is worsened by the inability of the Nigerian university system to retain even the very few academics it has got. This is due to the problem of brain drain earlier mentioned. This is reflected in Table 4 below. The total number of lecturers in the Nigerian universities was 12,977 in 1992. This total number declined to 12,064 in 1995. In other words, a total of 883 lecturers left the universities between 1992 and 1995. With an average separation rate of 294 per annum, the problem is very significant. Worse still is the distribution of the separation rates from the system between different disciplines.

Table 4: The Structure of Teachers in Nigerian Universities by Major Disciplines, 1992 and 1995

Discipline	(1) 1992	(2) 1995	(3)=(1-2) Difference	(4)% Difference
Administration	461	296	-165	-35,7
Agriculture	1,110	960	-150	-13,5
Arts	1,736	1.631	-105	-6,0
Education	1,108	1,111	+3	+0,3
Engineering/Technology	1,102	1,087	+15	+1,3
Environmental Design	549	452	-97	-17,6
Law	381	327	-54	-14,1
Medicine/Health Science	1,395	1,621	+226	+16,2
Pharmacy	211	215	+4	+1,9
Sciences	2,790	2,751	-39	-1,4
Social Sciences	1,132	1,154	+22	+1,9
Veterinary Medicine	329	279	-50	-15,2
Others	673	180	-493	-73,2
Total	12,977	12,064	-883	-6,8

Source: Columns (3) and (4) calculated from Federal Office of Statistics, Nigeria Annual Abstract of Statistics, 1996 Edition. P. 197, Table 138.

The most significant fall was in the disciplines categorised as others. Such disciplines cover non-degree programmes like certificate and diploma courses that are designed for capacity building for the working class and managers in the various sectors of the economy. A total of 493 lecturers in these other courses left the services of the universities either through staff rationalisation policies or voluntary separation.

The only significant gain of 16.2% was made in medicine, physiotherapy, nursing, etc. Engineering and Technology and Pharmacy made very insignificant gains of 1.3% and 1.9%

in the three-year period respectively. The total loss of academic personnel to the Nigerian university system is a colossal waste of resources. Of all the resources required by the knowledge industry, academic staff (researchers) constitutes the most crucial. It is this intellectual resource pool, which Nigeria is not able keep or generate that may constrain its capacity for competition in the global knowledge market of the next millennium. But what factors are responsible for the present situation? This question is answered in the next section.

CAUSES OF THE PROBLEM

The continuous process of the development of technology (human and institutional) in the poor countries is a major strategy in the struggle against poverty and underdevelopment (Adiseshiah, 1975). In this struggle, the historical achievements of the Nigerian universities have been impressive. From the establishment of the University of Ibadan half a century ago (1948), Nigerian universities have produced the leadership corps in all sectors of the economy. The graduates have made impressive contributions to the development and transmission of knowledge in the arts, agriculture, science, medicine etc. Among these are internationally reputable scholars and researchers in various fields. This is history. Today the Nigerian university is in the midst of serious trouble. Caught within bad political management and serious economic dislocation that seem to tear the Nigerian state apart, the university as an important structure within the stormy sea cannot remain an island insulated from the troubles.

Without doubt, it is government policy to increase enrolments in disciplines like medicine, engineering, computer science, etc. However, the present author concludes that the brain drain phenomenon has not helped matters. According to his study (Oni, 1991), the threat of staff rationalisation by the military government is a push factor forcing brilliant scholars to voluntarily take their exit from the academic world before they are forcibly ejected. The impact of this is the progressive loss of academic manpower needed to galvanise Nigeria into the next century. With the disinclination of most graduate students to take up academic posts, the danger is further reinforced that Nigeria would be unable to cope with the technological challenges and the knowledge explosion of the twenty-first century. The problem of brain drain from the university and lack of motivation for lectureship post among graduate students have several causes. Some of the causes relate to the low priority in budgetary allocation to education by the Nigerian government vis a vis countries like Kenya, South Africa and Zimbabwe. This is shown by the educational expenditures of these countries in Table 5. The percentage proportion of actual to budgeted expenditure was almost 100 percent in Zimbabwe in 1990 and 1993 respectively. This was followed by Kenya with 90.1% in 1990 and little over 94% in 1993 and 1995 respectively. The former apartheid South Africa also increased its actual to budget expenditure from almost 90% in 1990 to 94% in 1995. Nigeria on the contrary performed not only comparatively worse than these other countries but its ratio of actual to budget expenditure on education actually declined from 85% in 1990 to about 77% in 1993 and 1995 respectively. With falling investments in education particularly when alternative sources of funding have dried up due to the impact of the economic reform programme, the situation in the universities cannot be better than was described by Yesufu, an active participant in university administration in Nigeria for almost two and half decades.

Table 5: Budgeted and Actual Expenditures on Education in Selected African Countries, 1990-1995 in Million Dollars

	Budget			Actual Expenditure			Percentage		
Country	1990	1993	1995	1990	1993	1995	1990	1993	1995
Kenya	12.4	20.0	29.2	11.2	18.9	27.5	90.1	94.9	94.3
Nigeria	2.3	8.0	12.8	1.9	6.4	9.8	85.0	76.6	76.5
South Africa	17.1	26.3	32.3	15.3	23.8	30.5	89.0	90.6	94.0
Zimbabwe	1.7	2.9	-	1.6	2.9	-	99.2	99.2	-

Source: UNESCO Statistical Yearbook, 1997

Given the above scenario, it is not a surprise that the problem of brain drain, industrial strikes and decline in enrolment for graduate studies is the rule and not the exception in Nigerian universities today. Again this problem of declining finances to the universities is pervasive all over the African continent (African Development Bank, (ADB), 1998 p. 149) According to the ADB published report on African Development Indicators, the organisation concludes that the achievements of African universities are constrained by poor funding in the context of rising resource requirements and escalating inflation. This situation further explains part of the human capital flight from the continent (African Development Bank (ADB), 1998, p. 114.

The impact of the economic reform programme on the universities has been very grave. The human capital that is lost to the universities has been applied in other sectors of the economy (Bangura, 1994; Yesufu, 1996). The lecturers who left the universities have adopted a number of strategies to adapt to the impact of the reform. As a group of professionals they have, through their trade union the Academic Staff of Union of Universities (ASUU), expressed feelings of alienation and deprivation. They have often embarked on industrial strikes that have affected the lives of their students. These strikes have been over issues of salaries, fringe benefits, job satisfaction and self-actualisation. The government rather than negotiate with ASUU has often used the stick instead of the carrot; it has usually, in a characteristically military approach to workers' demand under dictatorships (Kester and Sidibe, 1997) resorted to the proscription by decree of the union, confiscating its assets, and subjecting the leaders to harassment, dismissal from work, arrests and detention.

As a result of their inability to maintain a decent standard of living with their salaries, some have resorted to voting with their feet to look for better opportunities in the private sector or as consultants to international organisations or government; while others have either migrated to other countries or engaged in trading. Under the military regime some have entered into the bureaucracy as ministers, special advisers to governors and heads of government parastatals. For the period 1988 and 1990 when the fall in government revenue was very low and inflation was high (41%) the National Universities Commission confirmed the separation of over 1000 lecturers from the universities (Bangura 1994).

The impact of the economic reform on the industrial sector did not provide the opportunity for industry to support the universities or collaborate with them, as it is the practice in many advanced countries. With a significantly high inflation rate of 72.8% in

1995, which declined substantially to 30% due to cutback in government expenditure in 1996 (African Development Bank, 1998, p. 90), the industrial sector has been severely constrained. The volatility of the oil price, low capacity utilisation and high exchange rates (Ariyo, 1996) have not permitted the industrial sector to play any meaningful role in the financing of university education.

A society's knowledge industry, mainly represented in the developing countries by their universities, which are critical to a nation's technological progress, has a direct and significant bearing on the quality of people available for managing its institutions. Unfortunately the objective realities in the Nigerian universities today reveal that apart from the serious problem of brain drain among the present generation of academicians, the future is very bleak because most of the present generation of graduate students does not want to remain in the university system.

Apart from the problem poor funding and lack of opportunities for self-actualisation, there is a general lack of motivation due to poor wages. Within the domestic labour market, Nigerian lecturers constitute the least paid workers. Table 6 presents comparative salary scales in the Nigerian economy as at September 1997.

Table 6: A Comparison of Average Salaries in Different Sectors of the Nigerian Economy

Sector	Salary per Annum in NAIA
Public Sector (oil)	450,000 - 600,000
Public Sector (Iron and Steel)	300,000 - 400,000
Nigerian Economy (Average)	100,000 - 200,000
University Academic Salary	**30,000 - 54,000**

Source: ASUU, National Secretariat Publication, 1997; (Exchange rate = 80 NAIA: 1dollar)

The wage differentials between the university and other sectors of the economy as seen from the table are a major cause of frustration and disillusionment among present and future generation of academic staff. Worse still is the comparative disadvantage suffered by Nigerian academicians vis-a-vis their peers in other African countries. This is shown in Table 7.

Table 7: Academic Staff Salaries in Selected African Countries

Countries	Academic Salaries per Annum (US $)		
	Lecturer	Senior Lecturer	Professor
South Africa	15,000	30,000	55,000
Zimbabwe	12,000	24,000	48,000
Ethiopia	3,600	4,800	6,000
Kenya	3,600	4,500	5,400
Ghana	1,800	3,000	4,800
Nigeria	**222**	**360**	**4,392**

Source: ASSU National Secretarial Publication, 1997.

The Nigerian academic staff pay package for a professor is about 1% that of his contemporary in South Africa, 7.32% (Ethiopia) and 9.15% (Ghana). Although allowance must be made for inter-country relative cost of living, wage policy etc., the Nigerian lecturer's pay is a major cause of out-migration to South Africa and the middle-eastern countries. Nation states invest in university education because society expects them to contribute to development in critical areas of national priorities. A university is able to perform these complementary roles if it has the corps of intellectuals in the right number, quality and composition. It is this important human resources requirement, which is inadequate at present that may be further depleted by the present conditions.

IMPLICATIONS FOR THE 21ST CENTURY

We started by observing that capacity building is critical to African development and that as a social process that must be sustained the university has an important role to play. There is also growing awareness that those societies, which are able to increase the productivity of workers in the knowledge industry, will control the economic wealth of the next century. Because of the obvious structural and dynamic relationship between higher education and a country's level of development, we can safely argue that a society's system of education has a direct and critical bearing on the types of people potentially available for the management of its institutions. Our examination of the objective realities of the Nigerian university system does not suggest that the country will be able to hold its own in the global competition of the knowledge industry in future.

Like in many poor countries, educational constraints or the underdevelopment of human resources with the critical skills often have a substantial negative impact on productivity, managerial effectiveness, firm operations and output. This is the position in which Nigeria is most likely to enter into the next century. With the lack of competitiveness in many economic spheres especially information management the only asset that Nigeria has and with which she can compete favourably in the global market is its human resources. Unfortunately, many of these are in other countries developing the social capabilities of their host nations. At home, the universities are in a state of crisis. The analysis of the problems confirms the hypothesis that a structural and dynamic relationship exists between the university system and the political and economic environment. It also further demonstrates the extent to which the use of resource allocation power can affect the performance of an entire system.

While some of these problems are endogenous to the universities, others are caused by exogenous factors. The continuous decline in the performance of the university is pervasive. It runs through absence of critical teaching/research personnel, lack of facilities, lack of textbook, poorly equipped libraries and laboratories. Poor motivation due to inadequate incentive for workers is also a major problem. In this very depressing situation, the process of teaching, research, publication and knowledge development has no relevance to the challenges of the next millennium or even the present global market. These are some of the implications of the realities of the present day university education in Nigeria.

For the Nigerian universities to have social relevance in the next millennium, the entire educational system needs to be overhauled. Beginning from the primary level, the entire citizenry should be exposed to education either formally or informally. For the older generation for whom primary education was too late, special literacy programmes must be organised at the village level and made obligatory by law. The content of the secondary school curriculum should be biased in favour of science. If this is achieved, tertiary education is bound to be similarly biased (Ozoro, 1982).

The success or failure of development policies depends on the quality of people who design the policies and manage the policy environment. Policies for capacity building in the knowledge industry during the next century will hinge on the existence of a well-educated labour force in the sector. Hence, to be effective, university education reform requires that the development of human capital through graduate education in science and technology should constitute the core of overall national development strategy (Verspoor, 1990). Through appropriate national economic policy package of incentives the migration stream of intellectuals can be damned, while return migration of high-level manpower can be further enhanced by the government.

Nigerian institutions must develop some specialised capabilities that are now missing: this is consultancy/research and development expertise that meet the needs of the growing oil sector, chemical industry and the machine tools companies. There is an urgent need to redirect the focus of some research institutes so that they can make their research facilities available to the universities in their area of location for the purpose of collaborative research to meet the need of industry. These new developments will require new policy co-ordination strategies between the departments of government concerned with the funding and supervision of the institutes and the universities.

Developing and sustaining the universities can require enormous amounts of financial resources, thus one of the prerequisites for ensuring this development is the adequate budgetary provision targeted at the advancement of knowledge in specific fields, but the government may not be able to provide all the resources required by the universities. This therefore calls for the adoption of specific strategies for exploiting alternative sources of revenue by the institutions themselves. Increased funding of the universities by the government should be a top priority in budget allocation. This will provide adequate resources for the maintenance of decaying infrastructures, procurement of new equipment, books, journals, chemicals and other learning inputs, the Nigerian government should address and review all the various policies that have triggered the migration stream of academicians from the universities. The frequent harassment, arrest, and dismissal from work of leaders of the Academic Staff Union of Universities, which was in vogue under the military government, should stop in a civilian dispensation.

The universities themselves should adopt a number of strategies within the campuses. Government alone cannot adequately fund the universities because of the lack of predictability in resource flow. In other words, the financing of the universities should not be tied solely to the revenue profile of the government. The universities should begin to aggressively market its research and development potentials to industry, government and other bodies. Each university should establish a University-Industry Research and Development Co-ordinating Unit. This unit would serve as a technology transfer link between the university and industry. Departments within the universities should also be encouraged to embark on consultancies in order, not only to generate revenue but also to provide exposure for the students to acquire practical experience. By getting necessary support form its external environment and combining the benefits with internal efforts to help itself the Nigerian university of the next century would be in a much better position to fulfill its statutory and social mandate to the nation, that is, build capacity and motivate its intellectuals to stay within the country.

REFERENCES

Adubifa, A., (1990), *Technology Policy in Nigeria*, Nigerian Institute of Social and Economic Research, (NISER) Ibadan.

Adiseshiah, M: S: (1975), Keynote Address. In *Higher Education and Development - a Selection of Chapters presented to the Golden Jubilee Seminar*, Association of Indian Universities, New Delhi, pp. I - xiii.

African Development Bank, (1998) *African Development Report*, Oxford University Press, pp. 90 -93.

Ariyo, A. (1996), Budget Deficit in Nigeria, 1974-1993: A Behavioural Perspective. In Ariyo, A. (ed), *Economic Reform and Macroeconomic Management in Nigeria*, Ibadan University Press.

Bangura, Y., (1994), *Intellectuals, Economic Reform and Social Change: Constraints and Opportunities in the Formation of a Nigerian Technocracy, Development and Change*, 25, 2, pp. 261-305.

Bell, M and Pavitt, K. (1992), Accumulating Technological Capability in Developing Countries. In *Proceedings of the World Bank Annual Conference on Development Economics*, pp. 257-282.

Bossuyt, J: (1995), *Policy Management Brief, No. 5*, September, European Centre for Development Policy Management, Maastricht

Conceicao, P. And Heitor, M.V: (1998), Sustained Society Learning: A discussion of the role of the university, in *Second International Conference on Technology Policy and Innovation*, Lisbon, August 3-5, pp3.11-3.18

Dahlman, C., (1989), Technological Change in Industry in Developing Countries. In *Finance and Development*, June, vol.26. No.2, pp 13 - 15

European Union, (1998), Europe S and T - The State of Play, *RTD Info*. 19, June-July.

Federal Office of Statistics, *Annual Abstract of Statistics*, 1994 edition.

Kester, G. And Sidibe, O.O. (e.ds.), (1997), *Trade Unions and Sustainable Democracy in Africa*, Aldershort, Ashgate Publishing Limited.

Mbanefoh, N., (1992), Dimension of Brain Drain in Nigeria: A Case Study of Some Critical High Level manpower Wastage in UCH, Ibadan, *NISER Monograph No. 8*

Nelson, R.R. and Rosenberg, N. (1993), Technical Innovation and National Systems, in Nelson, R: R: (ed.) *National Innovation Systems: A Comparative Analysis*, New York, Oxford University Press.

Nelson, R.R., and Romer, P. (1996), Science, Economic Growth and Public Policy, in Smith B.L.R. and Barfield C.E., *Technology, R and D and the Economy*, Brookings, Washington D.C.

Oni, B. (1987), *The Problem of Graduate Unemployment and the Demand Postgraduate Education in Nigeria: Case Study of Ibadan and Lagos Universities*, Ibadan, NISER Research report.

Oni, B., (1996), The Labour Market and Employment Planning in Nigeria, in Ariyo, A., (ed.), *Economic Reform and Macroeconomic Management in Nigeria,* Ibadan, University of Ibadan Press, pp 339-354.

Oni, B., (1999a), The Nigerian University Today and the Challenges of the Twenty-first Century, *Monograph, #60.* Institute for World Economics and International Management, University of Bremen, Bremen, Germany.

Oni, B., (1999b), A Framework for Technological Capacity Building in Nigeria: Lessons from Developed Countries, *Monograph No. 64*, Institute for World Economic and International Management, University of Bremen, Bremen, Germany.

Ozoro, O., (1982), Problem Areas in Nigerian Education: The School Curriculum - Technology in Secondary Schools, in *Nigerian Journal of Technical Education* 1, 2, pp. 5-11

Phillips A.O. and Ndekwu, E., (eds), (1987), *Structural Adjustment Programme in a Developing Economy: The case of Nigeria,* Ibadan, Nigerian Institute of Social and Economic Research, (NISER)

Rondinelli, D.A. (1998), Globalisation, Technology and Development Strategies for Regional Economic Growth, in *Second International Conference on Technology Policy and Innovation,* Lisbon, August, 3-5, pp. 5.1.1-5.1.14.

Rudd, E., (1975), *The Highest Education: A Study of Graduate Education in Britain*, London, Routledge and Kegan Paul.

Shah, A.B. (1975), Higher Education and Development, in *Higher Education and Development,* (ibid.) Pp. 9 - 19.

Verspoor, A., (1990), Educational Development: Priorities for the Nineties: in *Finance and Development*, March 27, 1, pp. 20-23

Wohlmuth, K., (1998), *Global Competition and Asian Economic Development: Some Neo-Schumpeterian Approaches and their Relevance* (forthcoming)

World Bank, (1996), *African Development Indicators*, Washington D.C.

World Bank, 1999*), World Development Report: The State in a Changing World*, New York, Oxford University Press.

World Bank, (1998), *Knowledge for Development: World Development report*, 1998/99, Washington, D.C.

Yesufu, T.M. (1996), *The Nigerian Economy: Growth Without Development*, Benin Social Science Series for Africa.

ON-LINE SOURCES

http://www.uneca.org/eca_resources/Conference_Reports_and_Other_Documents/brain_drain/word_documents/oni.doc More Results From: *www.uneca.org*

In: Current Discourse on Education in Developing Nations
Editors: M. Afolayan, D. Jules et al. pp. 177-191
ISBN 1-59454-774-2
© 2006 Nova Science Publishers, Inc.

Chapter 12

DEALING WITH THE GHOST OF THE COLONIAL PAST: SCIENCE EDUCATION IN NIGERIA

Toye J. Ekunsanmi
University of Wisconsin-Washington County
Wisconsin, USA

INTRODUCTION

Since science and technology are fundamental to all aspects of human living, their level of development has become the yardstick for a nation's development. A nation whose ideals and fundamental structure have been traumatized by colonialism stands on very slippery grounds. Such a nation is caught between recovering its identity and attempting to catch up with modern trends in science and technology. The concepts of science, science teaching and application of scientific principles in the modern world tend to be separated from culture. Whenever scientific principles are mentioned, the background of the teacher and the learner do not seem to be of much significance, if any at all. In fact, when the culture of science is mentioned, it is often synonymous with the western culture, in a manner which suggests that science is a characteristic of a particular part of the world, exclusive of some others. African countries seem to be told silently that they are receiving an untold favor by being exposed to "modern science and technology." Scientific facts are often taught as formalized, systematic ranges of facts, and all that pertains to scientific applications and usages are supposed to emerge from such formal knowledge. However, the history of modern science does not support this attitude. Rather, natural phenomena are universal operations in every part of the world. Does gravity, and therefore the laws of gravity and gravitation, apply on the North Pole as it does in Tropical Africa? Do green plants undergo photosynthesis in the same way in London, England, as they do in Lagos, Nigeria? Is the juice of a citrus fruit acidic in California as in Cambodia?

The factors which have made the teaching of science and technology to develop unevenly over the globe, and why the African culture has been erroneously portrayed as non-science oriented, or outright anti-science should be worthy of critical examination.. Since science is, closely linked with everyday living in any part of the world, it is practically impossible for any society to survive without its own form of science. Modern science is the backbone of human development especially as we know it today, because of its global, albeit uneven distribution. While some nations are busy with space travels, nuclear energy and genetic engineering, others are yet unable to process and distribute potable water to their populace. Others yet are trying to conquer space, while concurrently being unable to utilize science and technology for everyday convenience of the people within the same country.

The amphibious state of scientific development is in Nigeria is accurately expressed by and article of the Space agency Inc., on the 5th July 2001, which announced the setting up of a space agency in Nigeria, which will develop rocket and satellite technology, while mentioning that the same Nigeria is struggling to provide its citizens with roads, education and basic health services. Science is for better living. The development of science also requires better living, as is obvious in the case of Nigeria and other developing nations of the world. Lack of adequate facilities and basic amenities for most Nigerians has slowed down scientific development. There is, therefore, a vicious cycle of underdevelopment. The concept and pursuit of scientific advancement, at this time, is the farthest thing from the mind of many Nigerians, who are occupied by their struggle to have life's basic needs.

Obviously, various groups of people, including other nations, are interested in the scientific development of Nigeria. The ruling class, the educated people who are non-professional scientists, the science professionals (pure and applied), and the general public. The aspirations of these groups and their approach to how science should be developed differ in important details. Ultimately, however, the goal of scientific development must take into consideration how the people will be benefited by it.

Without any doubt, the government of any nation holds the key to the crucial factors of development. Economic development, development in science, technology, social life, and education to a large extent, are dependent on government policies and the execution of such policies. However, there are other factors such as the history of the nation, the attitude of its people, commitment of science professionals and the receptiveness of every member of the Nigerian public. All of these factors should be given equal importance. Nigeria's form of nationhood, its past and present economy, its history, its social structure, religion and culture have combined to produce a complex scientific tradition which almost defies definition. Suffice to say that its nature is unique, as would be expected. Hardly do any two nations of the world share the same pattern of scientific development. What is of concern is the degree to which Nigeria's science is of benefit to Nigerians. It also needs to be known if the nation is moving in the right direction in its mode of science education and applications to practical problems. No nation can live in scientific or economic isolation, but any nation that hopes to develop and earn a position among the developed nations of the world must go along a well-defined path of scientific and technological development. The degree of dependency on imported technology must be reduced.

This chapter takes a look at Nigeria's culture, history, economy as they affect its present level of scientific development. Some problems which confront the teaching and application of science at various levels of learning and some of the efforts which have been made in the past to make science meaningful to the people are examined. Some modifications which could help to improve on the present quality of science education are suggested. Emphasis here is on how science education could become more universal, be integrated into everyday lives of all Nigerians and produce an acceptable quality of living devoid of heavy dependence on extraneous sources. Suggestions are also made about how the Nigeria could adapt science to suit its culture and people, based on existing scientific principles and practices, as well as its cultural diversity.

PRE-COLONIAL AFRICAN SCIENCE

The entity now known as Nigeria is a conglomerate of a number of ancient civilizations, each with its developing science and technology appropriate for its needs. It is a well known fact that civilizations do interact with one another to change the direction of development. However, the influence of western education and science makes it difficult to predict the direction in which Nigeria's development would have proceeded.

The peoples of Nigeria had their own system of knowledge and practices. However, their often "mystical" and largely undocumented nature does not give it prominence in modern times. Nevertheless, no one could deny their impact on modern science, and the fact that it was deeply institutionalized. Weather forecasts were made, sometimes with great accuracy. Planting seasons were based on long accumulated observed patterns from several preceding seasons. Stars and other celestial bodies had specific names and relationships. Iziomon (2000) pointed out that the Africans practiced astronomy and space science, dating back to the ancient times and made skilful observation of the motions of the sun, moons, planets and stars. In the field of agriculture, the land fallow system and crop rotation were used effectively to preserve soil fertility. Different methods of food preservation were employed, including food fermentation, which also improved flavor, nutritional and medicinal values of foods. Food drying and processing techniques were used to preserve materials. Plant and animal breeding were practiced, and the characteristics of the different varieties were known and utilized. These practices were learned through an elaborate apprenticeship system or passed on from generation to generation, some of them being more exclusive than the others (Fafunwa 1974). The same author also described the apprenticeship system and the scientific practices, as well as the initiation rites of hunters, herbalists among others, as their admissions to higher levels of education. Further, he wrote: " Here the neophyte learns the secret of power (real and imaginary), native philosophy and *science* as well as the theology of animism, depending on the profession the young man wishes to pursue." (Italics mine).

There was an elaborate system of medical practices, including surgery and midwifery. The medical practitioners had a vast knowledge of an amazing variety of healing herbs, many of which are still in use till the present time. Not only did the medicine men know which tree or herb to use for specific purposes, they also knew what part the plant was most efficacious and what time of the day it had to be collected for maximum efficacy. The procedure for the study and practice of science in pre-colonial Nigeria would be described as *un*scientific (Cobern, 1996), by *Western* science, yet it was a form of science which worked for the survival of the people. Some of these practices still exist today in nooks and crannies of Nigeria. A lot of them, especially in the area of local healing, have been integrated into modern science, some might still be in future, but some may never be. For example cinchona alkaloids were originally derived from the bark of trees which have been used for the treatment of malaria for ages in Nigeria and other African countries (Woolman 2001). Mungazi (1996) commented on the "African tradition of observation and understanding of their natural environment which led to the discovery of healing techniques as an evidence of indigenous scientific observation and thought". Like any other forms of knowledge anywhere, there was a lot of room for improvement, which could have come in any form, including modernization. As would be expected, the advent of colonialism introduced many changes. Notable among these were governance, language, social structure, education and science.

COLONIALISM AND SCIENCE EDUCATION IN NIGERIA

Perhaps the reason there may never be an Isaac Newton or Albert Einstein in Nigeria or any African country is because modern science is of Western origin. The problems facing the teaching of science in Nigeria today are both basic and circumstantial. The origin and nature of Western Science create a fundamental problem to its teaching and comprehension in other cultures. Every society has its own way of thinking and this affects their way of understanding concepts. Ogawa (1995) recognized the uniqueness of the science of each culture, and on that basis proposed a multiscience system of science education. There has been a lot of lively discussions on multiscience and multicultural perspective of science education. There are definite merits and demerits to each point of view. None of them, however, denies the existence of the different "sciences" of various cultures. Not only does the Nigerian culture differ from those of the colonial masters, Nigeria itself consists of a variety of culturally diverse people. It is, therefore, a double dilemma trying to evolve a uniform culturally based curriculum for all Nigerian students, from the Western based science education. It is clear though, that the issue of cultural diversity among Nigerians is not as significant as the issue of the cultural difference between the Western culture and those of Nigerians. Yet it is deep enough to create its own problems. It is the view of Cobern (1996) that there is a link between the scientist and his or her scientific knowledge. According to him "If scientific knowledge is a meaningful construction based on the teacher's experience of reality, the learning of science could not be different". He argued further:

> "A classroom lesson seeks to make scientific sense of a scientific concept, but this becomes a cross-cultural activity when scientific sense does not automatically fit with the student's more global view of reality. One would think then that the further students are from the West, the more seriously one ought to address the relevance of culture in Science education. The learning of science is linked with the background of the student".

Thus, it must have been interesting to watch the faces of the first set of Nigerian science students during their first science classes. No doubt it must have been presented in the English language. The language of presentation, the background of the teacher, and the probably the subject matter would have produced some indescribable effect on the students. The results must have varied with individual students, but all their comments (if they could make any) must have been easy to summarize in a single word: "strange!" The issue of Language in teaching applies to this scenario. For example, one way of saying "I will soon be back" in Yoruba Language, if transliterated into English would mean "I am coming". Given the "novel" nature of English to a student whose first language is Yoruba, it is easy to see how the interpretation of situations as well as following scientific instructions could be an important issue to the teaching and learning of science in Nigeria even at the present time. Wilson (1981) noted that for science to be effective, it must take into account the culture of the society where it is based and exists to serve. It is certain that the presentation of science in the context of Nigeria's culture was the last thing on the minds of its former colonial master. While efforts were made to encourage the training of local artisans to serve the people's immediate needs, the primary goal of the colonialists was obviously not to teach science to their colonies, at least not the science to develop them. Uchendu (1979), cited by Woolman (2001), noted that the purpose of colonial education was the "subordination of Africans."

After the political amalgamation of the Northern and Southern protectorates to form what is now Nigeria in 1914, the first Governor-General, Lord Lugard, wanted Nigerians to "not to be so poorly trained that they could not meet the educational standards set for employment in either the modern British or "traditional" African bureaucracy, nor should they be so highly trained that they threatened to take over the responsibilities of British officials or native authorities" (Fafunwa 1974). While this was particularly relevant to administration, it was obviously applicable to all spheres of education of the Nigerians, especially the sciences.

Quite understandably then, science education in Nigeria started on the wrong pedestal. It was not intended to serve the people and was certainly not meant to make them independent. Rather, it was intended as a tool for the administrative convenience of the colonial lords. If such was the motive of teaching science, no regards could have been given to how much the students had learned effectively. This is probably one of the reasons why the slogan of "I hate science" is still so prevalent among Nigerian students today. If this kind of aversion to science is a global issue among most students, as is obviously the case, the fundamental issues of Nigeria's history, cultural difference from the West, and other problems discussed below, make it doubly knotty for today's Nigerian science students.

THE EMERGENCE OF POST-COLONIAL SCIENCE EDUCATION IN NIGERIA

As would be expected, more attention was given to social reconstruction than scientific or technological development immediately after independence in 1960. Woolman (2001) noted that education in Nigeria after independence was concerned primarily with using schools to develop manpower for economic development and providing indigenous manpower for the civil service. However, Fafunwa (1974) noted that in 1960, the training of graduate science teachers was given top priority. This was in recognition of the role science must play in the development of a young nation. The impact of such an effort on the long term development of science seemed to be weak indeed. One of the most spectacular post-colonial educational reforms was the National Curriculum Conference in 1969. The Decision Area VI of the recommendations dealt with "Functions of Science and Technical Education". This section addressed "the significance of science and technology in the individual and corporate life of Nigerians and how science and Technology concepts can be built into the education programme without destroying the fundamental values we live for". The recommendations recognized deterrents such as the rote system of learning inherent in the school system :"science and technical education require more than teaching facts and imparting information". It was recommended that science be taught, not only in schools, but also on "mass basis" to adults with little formal education. The need for science to prepare learners for life was also emphasized.

More government recognition of the role of education in promoting industrialization and modernization through emphasis on science and technology finally came in the 1980s. During this period, there were some spirited efforts on the part of the Nigerian government to encourage the teaching and learning of science at various levels. There were incentives for science teachers including what was tagged "Science teachers' allowance." This was a certain amount of money paid to science teachers, over and above their contemporaries in other disciplines. Science teaching seemed to enjoy a temporary boost, especially in well-established schools with trained teachers and good laboratories. Unfortunately this period was also characterized by the proliferation of schools. Schools were established with inadequate classroom facilities, and poorly equipped laboratories or no laboratory at all. The pattern was painfully uneven. Only a privileged set, who could gain admission into well established schools with enough influence to attract the relatively few qualified science teachers to their schools, were able to present an adequate science learning environment.

On the positive side, the establishment of the 6-3-3-4 system of education between 1977 and 1981 had shifted more emphasis on science and technical education. The Senior Secondary School core curriculum was dominated by Science, Mathematics and English, plus skill development. There were definite efforts to modify the science curriculum to make science more meaningful and attractive to students. More textbooks were published by Africans including Nigerians, with emphasis on Nigerian examples. The trend in junior secondary school Science became "Integrated Science" instead of the traditional "General Science". The Integrated Science curriculum attempted to teach unifying concepts of science, instead of placing separate emphasis on branches of science. Progress seemed to be on the way.

Unfortunately, most of what could have been the gains of the science and technology initiatives of this period were swallowed up by some politico-economic developments within the country. Perhaps one of the most tragic stoppers to Nigeria's progress, especially in the area of science and technology was the "oil boom" of the period discussed above. During this period, Nigeria enjoyed an unprecedented economic prosperity by exporting crude oil. It was therefore possible to import next to anything. There seemed to be no point in inventing anything. When machines were invented for use within Nigeria, they were invariably taken over by foreign investors in China or Japan, developed and sold back to Nigeria. The country was flooded with a large number of "toys". They were cheap, and most people could afford them. Concurrently, large amounts of money were also spent to import a lot of science and vocational training equipment. Unfortunately only a relatively small percentage of these items were ever put into any use for teaching, while most were left to rot away in sheds and storage rooms. The instruction manuals of most of them were never found, and nobody seemed to care. (It could produce fascinating results to ask if the instruction manuals ever came with them). Apparently some of the policy makers and those responsible for the purchase of those equipment were given the responsibility of getting schools equipped for the teaching of science and technical skills, and they simply ordered for whatever they thought was necessary and left it at that. Little or no attention was given to how the equipment would be put into practical use. The award of the contracts and the subsequent kickbacks", the grandiose commisionings and launchings were more important to the authorities.

There were instances where several power-operated items were delivered to villages without any form of electricity other than lightening and dry cell batteries. These expensive items were always invariably vandalized or stolen; nobody missed them. This was a time when the interest of many students in science could have been stimulated through the availability of visual and hands on materials. The missing link was the presence of enough trained personnel to put these pieces of equipment to use in all the schools, coupled with lack of power supply in the rural areas. It was a classical case of good intentions but poor planning. It was much profitable for businessmen to import and sell manufactured goods than to invest in the production of home made goods. Emphasis shifted to how much money could be made, and everybody wanted a share of "the national cake". It seemed pointless to study science. It was more fashionable to study courses which would result in positions in banks and other parts of the commercial sector. Scientific research suffered severe setback as the salaries of the average researcher was poor, and was not commensurate to the amount of money was in circulation and prevailing living standards. The economy was not in favor of wage earning, and even small businesses seemed to flourish. It was easy to set up an import and export business, or better still, win a government contract to construct or supply materials. Serious scientific endeavors were restricted to a few dedicated individuals. The result was an erosion of internal development of any serious scientific culture, a spurning of innovativeness and lack of respect, if not outright mockery for originality.

CURRENT STATE OF SCIENCE AND SCIENCE TEACHING IN NIGERIA

In this section, some attention is given to what the state of science is in Nigeria today. The appraisal of the state of science and science teaching in Nigeria has been aptly described by the summary of a UNESCO seminar on the state of Science Education, in Daily Trust of October 2001. Most Nigerian students of this generation hate or fear Mathematics and science subjects. Failure rate in Mathematics and science is on a steep increase. There is acute shortage of science and mathematics teachers, lack of instructional materials, laboratory equipment and training facilities as well as insufficient classrooms. The quality of science graduates is on a steady decrease. Most Nigerian-trained scientists and engineers are dubbed mere theoreticians (incapable of using both their hands and their heads!) but rather white-collar-job oriented.

The above picture sounds gloomy, but it is true. There has been a steady decay in the many sectors of the Nigerian education, and the most hard-hit is science. The materials required for the teaching of science include the teachers, well-equipped laboratories, consumables and textbooks. All or most of these are lacking in most Nigerian schools. Most existing science teachers, having been trained as theoretical scientists, can only teach theory, to the harassment of their students. Most Nigerian students take some science subjects because they are required to take them. With time, the cycle of memorization of scientific concepts has gone round and round, spinning out more theoreticians, who may never know the investigative aspects of what they memorized and may never recognize their application by sight and or ever apply them.

Most students at the secondary school level accept this as being normal, not having known anything better. While those at the tertiary level know better and lament about it, but are helpless to do anything about it. It is now commonplace for a students to study Biology in Secondary Schools without being able to use as basic an equipment as a microscope. In a number of cases, he or she has never seen one. The story is even more pathetic at the graduate level. Students at this level have sound awareness of the science they want to do, but are appalled at the science they have to do. What is required of them is enormous, but available materials are meager. Those who are lucky to procure study scholarships are able to work in laboratories abroad, but these represent an insignificant fraction of students. Moreover, the study of science subjects has not been encouraged by societal values. Onuora (1997) blamed lack of enthusiasm in science to the lack of respect for Nigerian scientists by Nigerians. For most Nigerians, a degree in pure science destines the recipient to a teaching career, which is poorly paid. Since, in Nigeria, a lot of importance is placed on the ability of adults to cater for their extended family members financially. The poor pay of a science graduate became a source of discouragement for students. Poor salaries were characteristic of teachers in all disciplines, including the sciences. As a result, there has been continual rounds of strikes in the Universities and other institutions of learning. Morale of teachers remained extremely low for more than 15 years, and University teachers have spent more time out of the classroom than inside during each academic year. Ejime's report of April 10 1996, is an example of the incessant strikes by University teachers, which could now be safely described as one of Nigeria's academic culture. It follows directly that scientists, both inside and outside the Universities, have spent much less time in the laboratory. Many are preoccupied with trying to make ends meet. Students are directly at the receiving end of this academic instability. Most of them depend solely on notes taken from their teachers, since they do not have access to current textbooks. The average cost of one science textbook is as much as a tenth of the minimum federal monthly wage and about a seventh part of the state monthly wage at the present time. Old editions of textbooks, whose contents have been overtaken by the rapid development in science, are still used, even by many teachers.

The research scientist in Nigeria goes through a daily mental agony of helplessness. The exceptionally lucky ones obtain research materials through grants or academic fellowships to study abroad. Equipment so purchased must be kept under locks and keys, with only a few trusted individuals being allowed to use them, for fear of robbery. It has become common to hear of cases of robbery of laboratory equipment worth thousands of dollars. Such articles are stolen and re-sold to some private laboratories, or even to other unsuspecting researchers. Projects which could be completed in only a few months or even days often take years to complete. Where equipment exists, they are usually outdated and not compatible with what other scientists use in similar experiments in other parts of the world. The Nigerian research scientists have been struggling unsuccessfully to keep up with the trend of things in their respective fields using these types of facilities where they exist. For example, while some laboratories in many parts of the world obtain de-ionized water from taps in the laboratory, many science laboratories in Nigeria fetch water in jerry cans from outside for laboratory use. Where there are minimal facilities for research, power failure makes a mockery of whatever research plans could be made.

Moreover, many research scientists do not have access to information on recent advancements in their fields, and access to the internet or any computer facility is limited. Word processing has to be done using commercial centers at high costs. Those who use the internet have to pay for such services as sending an e-mail to colleagues. Thus a vast majority of Nigerian researchers are, for most parts, isolated from their colleagues in other parts of the world. A vast majority of researchers have to depend on personal funds to publish the result of whatever they manage to accomplish. In many cases, it takes a substantial fraction of the researchers salary to send a manuscript for publication abroad.

The training of graduate science students has been a thorny issue in most Nigerian Universities. It has become increasingly difficult to produce graduate students in many science departments. There have been cases of professors refusing to accept graduate students because there were no materials to train them with. When graduate students are trained abroad, they return to the realities of the inadequate Nigerian economic situations. Frustration sets in speedily because the trainings they received do not match the situations in their home environment. The relevance of their acquired training to Nigerian needs is oftentimes questionable. As rightly noted by Lunetta and van de Berg (1995), available programs for the training of graduate students from low income countries are often not responsive to their special needs. This is expected, since these programs take place outside the countries of origin of the recipients and are often given en-masse without any cognizance to special needs. On the other hand, those Nigerian scientists who have been trained over the years are easily drawn away from the country to other countries for better economic and career opportunities in practicing their skills. This creates a worse shortage of trained manpower in diverse areas of science.

THE ROLE OF THE NIGERIAN GOVERNMENT

The role of the government in the development of science and technology in any country is so much so that many other factors are often overlooked. The foci here are on government educational policies, funding and execution of policies. Judging from the policies formulated over the years, it is clear that the various Nigerian governments and their organs concerned with formulation of policies which were, at least, well informed and well intended. From the "crash program" for the training of teachers, with emphasis on science in 1960, to the government education policy of the Obasanjo administration, considerable attention has been given to development in science and technology. In the most recent Federal Government Policy on Science and Technology, emphasis was placed on "achieving breakthrough with regard to some key projects such as on-going research and development supports for health care." Other areas of emphases include:

i. Honey Husbandry
ii. Upgrading Traditional technology to small scale level and patenting such technologies for adaptation in the informal sector.
iii. Acquisition of computer technology
iv. Acquisition and commercialization of Research and Development results.
v. Research into enhanced agricultural productivity.

As earlier discussed, it takes some basic features to execute such projects and the feasibility of most of these depends on the availability of constant power and water supply.
Funding has always been a major issue in the development of Education in Nigeria or any other nation. The Nigerian government has, for most part, given insufficient funding to science and technology. The appropriateness of the disbursement of funds has also been questionable. The suggestions below, like any other, are made with the assumption that there is willingness at all levels of governance in Nigeria to fund meaningful projects and give

other supports as found necessary. There has been a lot of talking and paperwork in the past with very little action to back them up. The provision of stable power supply and water facilities to all areas will bring about dramatic changes in the development of science and technology in all parts of the country, rural and urban.

SUGGESTIONS AND PROJECTIONS

It is hardly feasible for a nation to jump start its development depending mainly on technology and resources derived, as it were, from colonialism. When a nation does this, it is more than likely than not that there will, sooner or later, be a reversal of whatever gains might appear to have been acquired. Nigeria has been pampered to a state of mental lethargy by its habit of reveling in the technological achievement of other nations. Many suggestions have been made over the decades, some with seemingly positive results, but the fundamental problems have remained. Nigeria has a good crop of scientists who could help to restructure the nation's development in science and technology. There is the need to do some drastic "surgery" on existing science to effectively tackle the problems.

This is not to suggest that Nigerian scientists "re-invent the wheel". Poole(1968), cited by Cobern(1996), was of the view that "it is difficult to see how the less advanced societies can achieve the high living standards at which they aim without assimilating large portions of the Western conceptual system, not least those concepts of scientific significance". The area of learning methods which suits the African intrinsic learning characteristics should be predominant in the way science is taught. It has become more and more futile over the years to try to ignore this fact. The important issue here is not that of having assimilated the "Western conceptual system", it is more of the scientific need of the system, and teaching based on the culture and living style of Nigerians. It is important to stress here that the "Nigerian" in this context should not be interpreted to mean just the "executive" in one Nigeria's major cities like Lagos, Kano or Onitsha. It must consider the needs of the "Peasant Farmer" or "Blacksmith" in the rural areas. There is no doubt that Nigerians have, to a large extent, assimilated what Poole(1968) called the Western conceptual system, especially in science. How could what Nigerians have learned over the years first be integrated with those inherent in Nigeria(ns) and be fully adapted to benefit all Nigerians and the whole world? If any suggestion on Nigeria's scientific development would be meaningful, it must ask a fundamental question of "What do Nigerians need, and how could the needs be met by Nigerians?" Nobody knows the needs of Nigerians more than the Nigerians themselves, and nobody could be held responsible for the needs of Nigerians except Nigerians. If Nigeria is to develop its science, the responsibility must lie with the Nigerians scientists. As earlier discussed, the Nigerian scientists do face extreme problems. But Owuo (2002) observed that the continent (Africa) will never develop if its professionals spend much time complaining and passing the blame to "others" The report encouraged African professionals to "get down to real work and make a positive difference" and to stop being experts at "why things cannot be done". Quite obviously, there is a lot to complain about by the Nigerian scientist, and there are many who deserve to be blamed for the poor situation of science and technological education, but a lot of responsibility still lies on the him to make a "positive difference" even in the face of these obvious hardships.

The science curriculum needs to recognize the ability of younger scientists to carry out science projects outside the classroom. It is an erroneous assumption of the present system of science teaching in Nigeria, to limit serious science projects to higher levels of learning. Enough opportunity should be given to young learners to demonstrate their ability to explore nature, develop their initiatives and satisfy their curiosity. Given the proper guidance, it is possible to unleash the vast mental resources inherent in Nigerian children. The natural potential of the Nigerian children could be developed through scientific inquiries, and their interest would be stimulated to learn science and not see it as a dreaded subject. Erinosho (1997) compared the choice of science subjects among female students in the first year of their senior secondary school with those of their male counterparts in some parts of Nigeria. There was a definite correlation between what the pastimes these students engaged in and their choice of science subjects. It is a well established fact that exposure to manipulation of physical objects by students is a strong stimulant of their scientific interest in early life (Johnson, 1987), cited by Erinosho (1997).It is, therefore, desirable that students be encouraged to use locally available materials to develop their manipulative skills and increase their scientific potentials. Moreover, learning methods based on indigenous reliance on field experience, active discovery and close observation reflects a progressive pedagogy and is more promising in promoting learning retention than classroom-based book and test method that is characteristic of Western schooling (Woolman 2001).

Another way by which Nigerian scientists could make a change is to focus more on people-oriented research projects, not with a narrow view of publishing in the "International Journal of this and that." A lot of research works have been done in various University departments and government research institutes with locally applicable results. More of these should be encouraged, and more investment could be made to commercialize the outcome of such research by promoting them to small industries. A remarkable development is the establishment of research centers to promote this concept. As far back as 1956, the Federal Institute of Industrial Research (FIIRO), in Oshodi, Lagos was established. Originally named The Institute of Applied Technical Research, the institute carries out research and development on local food and Agro-Allied resources for the purpose of promoting their industrial uses. The institute has made a lot of progress over the years in achieving its state objectives. The production and nutritional values of certain fermented food such as *Gari* and *Ogi* are some of the more recent works carried on at this institute. Trainings and workshops have been organized to transfer research results to small scale industrialists and the public. As noted earlier, lack of necessary infrastructures, especially in the rural areas has prevented the widespread distribution of these improved methods. The government of the East Central State established the Project Development Agency (PRODA), in 1970. The objectives were "the provision of recognized outlet for the promotion and establishment of new industrial projects utilizing local raw materials and indigenous manpower through laboratory and pilot plant investigations to the actual construction of large-scale commercial plants". The institute's major concern was to adapt known processes, plants and technology to local conditions using a new approach to the problems of industrialization of under-developed economies. Also there have been efforts on the part of some None Governmental Organizations (NGOs) to increase awareness in science and technology. An example is the Foundation for African Development Through International Biotechnology, located in Enugu. This institute has undertaken the training of sub-Saharan Africans in biotechnology and related science. Doubtless, the goals of these institutes are in line with the needs of the country in the area of applied science and technology. However, more of such similar institutes are needed in order to reach more people, especially those who do not attend the trainings and workshops for only academic reasons. The existing ones could be expanded and further decentralized to reach many more Nigerians, and new ones could be established. Funding the existing ones should be given top priority by the Nigerian Government.

As earlier mentioned, it is not feasible to jump off the bandwagon of technological revolution sweeping the whole world at the present time. It should be remembered, however, that the present state of science at the global level has its humble beginnings. Where necessary, Nigerian scientists should not hesitate to take things "from the first principles" and go ahead from there. In this respect, collaboration among experts in different aspects of science is of great importance. India has, for a long time, embarked on what may be described as the "indigenization" of its science and has groomed itself to a state of scientific non-dependence. Nigeria is capable of doing such if not more. There are now many journals of science in Nigeria with increasingly competitive credibility. The *Nigerian Journal of Science* is a good example. Some international journals also accept papers of different cultural backgrounds. Thus, it is now easy to get well published doing the type of research required for the immediate needs of Nigeria. Moreover, where Nigeria based journals are not available, they could always be established. It could be astonishing to know the number of Nigerians who are involved as editors of journals in their fields, based in other countries. Nigerian scientists should not isolate themselves from other parts of the world. Rather, they could use their expertise to deal with local situations as a matter of priority. It is unlikely that a Nigerian scientist would gain any true recognition for their accomplishments if his or her country remains underdeveloped in science and technology. As much as possible, projects should be undertaken within the communities they are intended to benefit. With this approach of community-based research results, it should be easier for the people to benefit from whatever results are obtained. "Elitist science education" needs to give way to functional science education.

When a pattern of "Science of the people, by the people and for the people" has been put in place, a strategy for the utilization of research outcomes needs to be established by the government and local entrepreneurs. If Nigerians continue to scoff at locally invented or locally manufactured goods, any effort at producing them would be a waste of time and money. Co-operation with foreign investors should be encouraged, but care should be taken to ensure that they do not control the sole technology behind major operations during production. If science is to become meaningful to the average Nigerian student, especially at the foundation level, the current mode of presentation must change drastically. Science teaching must take into consideration the background of the students. It is important too that those who teach science to people in the rural areas must themselves know what life is like to people in such areas. It will take some supernatural insight for anyone who does not have the experience of living in the rural setting to visualize how a rural dweller feels, thinks and understands concepts. Teachers may be capable of sympathy with the rural situation, but this does not go a long way to identify with the minds of the students and comprehend their way of understanding. Thus, it will be worthwhile to fish for talented people at the different settings, train them and send them back to teach science in the those parts of the country which match their own backgrounds.

The mass media is a convenient way of disseminating scientific knowledge. At present only a relatively small proportion of Nigerians have access to scientific information which have direct bearing to their everyday lives. The radio and television industries in Nigeria have made some efforts in the past of disseminating scientific information. Some newspapers also have regular science columns. To ensure that rural communities have access to these sources, community centers could be established under the supervision of teachers to provide these services at no cost to the citizens. Many Nigerians are capable of reading materials written in their first language without being able to read English. Instead of dubbing such people "illiterates", who are destined to eternal ignorance, their capacity to read their own language should be used to introduce them to science. This will, in fact "demystify" science and provide those who do not read the English language more insight into the world around them. English could continue being used to teach science to those who speak it, but not being able to speak English should not preclude Nigerians from learning science. This is especially true of the science that is relevant to their lives.

Grandy (1995), commented that the teaching of science in the past tended to present science as "monolithic and an unerring guide to truth". This rigid approach to science teaching tends to present science as an exclusive area and this could be a serious impediment to the learning of science in such a setting as that of Nigeria. There is no doubt that modern science, despite its sophistication, is abandoning this straitjacketed approach, and is giving way to a broader approach. One obvious impediment to the teaching and learning of science to most Nigerians is strict adherence to the traditional approach of what has been called "the scientific method". While not contesting the merits of the traditional procedure in studying science, it should be noted that many landmark discoveries were made without following it. Examples are the discoveries of penicillin, gravitational pull, the principle of flotation and a host of others. Some discoveries have been made while in the course of other investigations which had no bearing with what was being investigated. *Penicillium*, the fungus which produces the antibiotic penicillin, was a contaminant on Alexander Fleming's agar plate, while he was on a different investigation altogether. The application of "the scientific" method often applies to further investigation, but not an absolute prerequisite to the initial discovery. Science teaching should be more focused on activities and inquiries without the usual contempt for the unconventional approach to discovery.

SOME CONCLUDING REMARKS

Similar statements to "It is impossible to teach or do science under these situations" are becoming the slogans of most Nigerians scientists. Conferences and workshops are becoming increasingly meaningless. In a UNESCO report of April 29th 1999 entitled "African Scientists voice skepticism on conference outcome" African scientists doubt that such conferences would make any difference to the development of Africa. A Nigerian scientists was quoted as saying " I have been to meetings like this for the last 40 years, and we've said the same things. But nobody ever listens and nothing has changed". This is an example of how frustrated Nigerian scientists have become with the situation of science and science teaching in Nigeria. Nigerians have long lost confidence in Nigerian scientists.

Most of the past Nigerian governments seemed to pay mere lip service to science, technology and science teaching. The Nigerian government (as at the time of this writing) seems to have a positive attitude to science education and technology judging by the stated

"Policy on Science and Technology. The execution of any such policy is what could make any difference from the previous sad history. A recent report of the space news agency reported the announcement of $22.7 million to the development of rocket and satellite technology with an additional $22.4 annually in the next three years with the aim of becoming self financing. The National Council on Space Science Technology is to be headed by the President. The same report described Nigeria as one of the world's poorest countries, with a per capita income of $300. Here again is an issue of "surface technology". The transfer of advanced technology is desirable, but with the realization that it must be adopted in a manner to ensure that it is sustained. Sustenance depends very much on the provision of well trained Nigerian personnel, solid research and development infrastructure and availability of locally produced raw materials. While it is important for Nigeria to keep up with global developments in science, grassroots development needs urgent attention, as a solid scientific foundation cannot be laid without it. The teaching of science in a way to make it more meaningful to the students and community in which they live must take precedence over technologies which are relevant to only a few Nigerians, and whose sustainability is questionable. Care needs be taken to stop the trend where Africa's own industrial minerals (Nigeria inclusive) continue to propel other parts of the world to industrial prosperity, while Africa remains underdeveloped (Masood 1999). The same source cautioned: "It is time that Africa developed levels of expertise commensurate with its material resources so that both may serve the African people and their destiny."

Given the existing tradition of natural curiosity and activity, plus more than one century of formal science education, Nigerians are ripe to handle Nigeria's scientific needs. Should this is not be so, steps should be taken to make corrections by re-orientating science education curriculum, science teaching and science projects. Failure to do this will allow external factors to continue dominating most vital areas of the country's infrastructures and technology. The result will be an indefinite dependence with consequent chronic underdevelopment. The situation could change in a short while, but a lot has to change first. The Nigerian government must be truly motivated to fund science and science teaching. Teachers must be trained for science teaching and should have a sense of mission to train people to be functional scientists. Basic materials to facilitate the teaching of science need to be available. Nigerian government, Nigerian science and scientists are able to transform the nation through science and technology with adequate commitment.

REFERENCES

African News Service: *Daily Trust* (2001). UNESCO Seminar on State of Science.

Cobern, Wm. W (1996). Constructivism and Non Western Science Education Research. *International Journal of Science Education.4* (3): 287-302.

Costa, Victoria B (1995). "When Science is Another World" Relationships between Worlds of Family, Friends, School and Science. *Science Education 79*(3) 313-333.

Ejime, P. (1996).Teachers' Strike Paralyses Nigerian Universities. Pan African News Agency. April 10, 1996. *http://www.prairienet.org//acas/96D10072.html* August 6, 2002

Fafunwa, A. B.(1974) *History of Education in Nigeria*. Pp 30, 114, 239 London, George Allen and Unwin Ltd Federal Government of Nigeria (1999). Nigerian Economic Policy (1999-2003) December 8th 1999. Retrieved from *http://nopa.net/useful_information/economic-policy.html* August 5, 2002.

Erinosho, Stella(1997). Scientific Experience as a Predictor of choice among female high school students in Nigeria. *Researches in Science and Technological Education 15*(1) 1-7.Retrieved from EBSCOhost. UW-Washington Co. Library West Bend, Wisconsin. *http://web6.epnet.com/citation.asp?tb=1and_ug=dbs+0+fic+0+ln+en%2Dus+sid+B75 98A17%/* Aug 9, 2002.

Grandy, R. E (1995). Expertise and the critical non- expert (Comments on Norris) *Science Education 79 (2):219-221*

Good, R (1995): Comments on Multicultural Science Education *Science Education* (3):335-336.

Iziomon, M. G. African Skies-4 Promoting Space Science Education in Africa: Practical Initiatives. Retrieved from *http://www.saao.ac.za/~wgssa/as4/iziomon.html* August 5, 2002.

Lunetta, V. N and Van Den Berg (1995): Tailoring Science Education Graduate Programs to the needs of Science Educators in Low-Income countries. *International Science Education. 79 (3):273-294*

Masood, E.(1999). African Scientists voice skepticism on conference outcome.UNESCO World Conference Outcome, Nature World Conferences. April 29, 1999. *http://www.nature.com/wcs/a26.html* Retrieved on August 5 2002

Mungazi, D.A.(1996).*The Mind of Black Africa*. Lond: Praeger. Cited by Woolman D.C.(2001) I*nternational Journal Education Journal 2*(5) *http://www.flinders.edu.au/education/iej*

Owuo, O (2002) African Science. Science and Development in Africa. Science First and why Africa's professionals must wake up. Retrieved from *http://www.sciencenewsdev.co.ke /science.html.Retrieved* August 5 2002.

Ogawa, M.(1995). Science Education in a Multiscience Perspective. *Science Education. 79*(5): 583-593.

Onuora, L. I. (1997) If Nigerian Astronomers can still do research under the conditions they face. Imagine what they could achieve if they had world- class facilities. *Mercury* Magazine. July/August 1997. Retrieved from *http://www.aspsky.org.mercury/mercury/ 9704/nigeria.html* August 5 2002

Uchendu, V.C (1979) Education and Politics in Tropical Africa. NY: Conch Magazine Woolman, D.C. (2001). Educational Reconstruction and Post-Colonial Curriculum Development: A comparison of four African Countries. *International Education Journal 2*(5):27-46.

WCCES Commission 6 Special 2001 Congress Issue *http://www.finders.edu.au/education/iej*

Chapter 13

SCHOOL REFORMS IN POST-INDEPENDENCE GHANA: TRENDS AND ISSUES IN SPECIAL EDUCATION

Anthony M. Denkyirah
Southern Illinois University Edwardsville
Illinois, USA

INTRODUCTION

Ghana, formerly called the Gold Coast, obtained political independence from Britain in 1957, becoming the first sub-Saharan African nation to obtain political independence from its colonial master. The British ruled this colony for a little over a century and developed a system of education that prepared school leavers mainly for white-collar jobs. Additionally, the British bequeathed to the newly-independent Ghana a divided nation in which almost all of the major educational institutions were sited in the southern part of the country (Mfum-Mensah, 2003), a situation which did not augur well for nation-building. Though, all of Ghana's post-independent governments have attempted to address these disparities by investing massively in education in the northern sector of the country, yet the inequalities in educational opportunities have persisted over the years. For example, since independence, successive governments in Ghana have introduced different plans intended to reform the colonial educational system so as to improve the social, economic, and manpower needs of all the ten administrative regions of the country. Specifically, in the first two decades after independence, fee-free education for school children in the northern sector of Ghana sometimes included free meals, free school uniforms, free school supplies, free tuition, and subsidized transportation to any other part of the country for the purpose of attending college. In contrast, fee-free education for school children in the south meant free school supplies and free tuition only. One area, however, of Ghana's education system that the British colonial masters failed to address and which has seen a remarkable degree of improvement under post-independence governments in Ghana is special needs education.

A BRIEF OVERVIEW OF GHANA'S POST-INDEPENDENCE SPECIAL EDUCATION SYSTEM

After Ghana attained independence from British colonial rule in 1957, educational reforms became the highest agenda of the new all-Ghanaian government (Eyiah, 2004). Post-independence programs in education expanded an earlier drive at increasing literacy rates in the country which started in 1951 under Dr. Nkrumah's Accelerated Development Plan (Eyiah, 2004; McWilliam and Kwamena-Poh, 1975). Post-independence expansion in education in Ghana was necessary for many reasons, among which was a desire to address educational inequalities and disparities between the north and south of the country.

The development of educational programs for individuals with special education needs has become a major priority for most governments worldwide (Abosi, 2000), and in Ghana, such programs have remained a major priority for all post-independence governments. In fact, Ghana is one of the few African countries that, historically, have offered educational programs for their citizens with disabilities. In addition, post-independence Ghana has offered to train several general education teachers (McWilliam and Kwamena-Poh, 1975) and special education teachers from other African countries (Abosi, 2000; Gadagbui, 1998; McWilliam and Kwamena-Poh, 1975). Countries whose early special education teachers trained in special education teacher training institutions in Ghana include Botswana (Abosi, 2000; Gadagbui, 1998), Zambia, Malawi, Nigeria, Tanzania, Kenya, Togo, Lesotho, and Zimbabwe (Gadagbui, 1998). Additionally, Ghanaian special educators helped begin special schools and programs in many parts in Africa, a role Ghanaian special edcators continue to play even today.

Educational services for individuals with students with special needs in Ghana started in 1945-46 when the Basel (now Presbyterian) and Methodist missions jointly opened the first school for the blind at Akropong-Akwapim, in the southern part of the country (Torto, 2002). In a period of twenty years after the school enrolled its first students, special education services had become part of a wider non-governmental and governmental agenda for educational expansion. For instance, the First Republican Government of Ghana passed the Education Act of 1961 which made public education free and compulsory for all children of school-going age, including children with disabilities (McWilliam & Kwamena-Poh, 1975; Torto, 2000). Also, in 1958, the Methodists opened a second school for the blind at Wa, in the north-west of the country while the government opened schools for persons with deafness and other forms of hearing impairments in all the ten administrative regions of the country in the 1960s and 1970s. McWilliam and Kwamena-Poh wrote that two females, who were totally blind, enrolled at an all-female teacher training college in 1961, thanks to the Education Act of 1961. Schools for individuals with significant cognitive disabilities were opened in the late 1970s and early 1980s.

Schools for students with special education needs in Ghana, as mentioned earlier, were started by missionaries and other not-for profit organizations, a pattern similar to those in other parts of Africa (Abosi, 2000; Chitoyo and Wheeler, 2004). However, unlike countries such as Zimbabwe and Zambia (Chitiyo and Wheeler, 2000; Csapo, 1986, 1987), special needs education programs were accessible to all Ghanaians and non-Ghanaians living in Ghana free of charge.

The first schools for persons with disabilities in Ghana were residential schools and remain the main special education service delivery system in the country. The trend in special needs education in most developed nations like Canada, Britain, the United States (Chitiyo and Wheeler, 2004), Italy, and countries in the Scandinavia has been toward inclusion. In Ghana, the rate at which special education policy-makers and administrators are embracing the concept of educating students in inclusive settings is extremely slow. All that one can talk about with regards to inclusive education for students with special education needs in Ghana will be a few schools selected as inclusion pilot projects (Avoke and Hayford, 2000). Also, in Ghana, special education is synonymous with the education of individuals with visual impairments and blindness, hearing impairments, and significant cognitive disorders (mental retardation). For instance, whereas many countries, such as the United States of America, recognize as many as thirteen disability categories (Kirk, Gallagher, and Anastasiow, 2003), Ghana's special education system caters for only three categories of disabilities - mental retardation, visual impairments, and hearing impairments.

SPECIAL EDUCATION POLICY IN GHANA

Despite many years of special education practice in Ghana, the country has no official policy on disability issues. In a 1996 study cited by Asamani (2000), teachers and administrators admitted their work did not follow any laid down policy guidelines. In 1998, Dr. Koray, who represented the Ghana Society for the Blind at Ghana's first national conference on special education, expressed his disappointment and frustration about how special needs education and services for persons with disabilities were offered without any clear-cut guidelines (Asamani, 1998; Koray, 1998). Kwaku (1998) also wrote about the lack of a national special education policy in Ghana as follows:

> Special education operates on an extension of the legislation of the general education system. There is no separate legislation governing the education of children with disabilities. It is expected that the special education division will interpret and implement general education policies with minimal modification. (p. 13)

It is interesting to note, however, that over the years, government officials in Ghana always promised far-reaching reforms and policies to guide special education practice and service delivery. For example, in 1998, the First Lady of Ghana, Mrs. Konadu Rawlings, and the Minister of Education, on the same day and at the same forum declared the official government's plan to outdoor a comprehensive policy on special needs education and services. After eighteen years in power, the three different Rawlings governments did not outdoor or promulgate any such policy into law. In most recent years, special education advocates, special educators and organizations have kept the pressure on the Kuffour administration to come out with the long-awaited policy. There are brighter indications that such a policy will become law soon because the government has submitted the proposed policy to the Fourth Republican Parliament for consideration (Agbeke, 1998).

It is clear that the situation has persisted over the years because successive post-independence governments have consistently failed to implement major special education reforms as part of all major educational reforms since the 1961 Education Act was passed.

Asamani (2000) cites two examples of such minor reforms in special education and services as the Education Amendment Act of 1962 and the Dzobo Committee Report of 1972. Asamani further points out that both the Education Amendment Act of 1962 and the Committee Report 1972 only addressed a few of the issues that disability organizations and advocacy groups had requested.

The implications of the lack of a special education policy include a situation where educators and administrators who have little or no background experience in special needs education make major decisions that affect the area of special education. For examples, until 2001 all the directors of the special education division in Ghana, who were appointed by the Director-General of the Ghana Education Service, had little or no background training in special education. In such a situation, the heads of the special education directorate were naturally not able to provide direction that special educators and related staff needed. Secondly, some government departments took over major components that traditionally were under the area of department of special education. For instance, education and training of individuals with orthopedic impairments are offered by the Ministry of Employment and Social Welfare. This could mean that many individuals with orthopedic impairments would not receive special education services because services provided in rehabilitations centers target mainly vocational education.

INTEGRATION OF INDIVIDUALS WITH DISABILITIES IN GHANAIAN SCHOOLS

The integration of students with special needs into general education has attracted diverse opinions (Abosi, 2000; Asamani, 200; Avoke and Hayford, 2000). Some investigators report that many general educators perceive classroom adaptations for students with disabilities as desirable but not feasible (e.g., Abosi, 2000; Asamani, 2000; Schumm and Vaughn, 1991) whiles other researchers (e.g., Farrell, 2000) report that some general educators consider integration of students into general education settings as both desirable and feasible. Interestingly, many more general educators than special educators show a more positive inclination toward inclusion (Agbeke, 1998). Issues concerning the inclusion debate become even more complex when they apply to a developing country such as Ghana (Ainscow, 1997), where superstition, lack of training opportunities for personnel, lack of teaching and learning materials, and a long-standing history of a segregated system of education for individuals with disabilities remain part of the special education culture. Ainscow, as well as other investigators (e.g., Avoke and Hayford, 2000; Avoke and Ocloo, 2000) explain that, though it may not be a peculiar problem to Ghana, many people who make decisions that affect special education in Ghana prefer segregated system for educating students with disabilities to integration. Several reasons may be advanced to explain this phenomenon. For instance, many parents of children with disabilities may be temporarily relieved of problems (shame, frustration, disappointment, etc.) that are associated with caring for a child with disabilities when their child with a disability is enrolled in a special residential school. Besides, once a child is enrolled in a special residential school, parents are assured that the state would take care of all the cost for educating their child, and thus allow the parents to make additional income (Agbeke, 1998).

In the early 1990s, the Special Education Division of the Ministry of Education selected a small number of public basic schools in the Eastern Region and Volta Region to begin what is now called unit schools for the deaf. At about the same time, *Sight-Savers International*, a not-for-profit organization began a similar system in a few schools for children with visual impairments and blindness. These schools that cater for children with deafness and blindness, respectively, are the closest that Ghana's special education system has come with regard to inclusion in basic schools. In both cases, only a few students who are deaf or blind are served in integrated settings, most of them remain in segregated institution-like boarding facilities. In both the units for the deaf or general classrooms that serve children with blindness, Agbeke (1998) found very limited levels of integration practices on the ground. According to Agbeke, lack of adequate preparation for classroom teachers was cited by more than ninety percent of the respondents in his study as the main reason for the disappointing integration outcomes.

Population of Students in Special Schools for 2003/2004 Academic Year per Category: Enrollment in Schools for Students with Visual Impairments during 2003/2004 academic year

INSTITUTION	STUDENT ENROLMENT		
	Males	Females	Total
Akropong School for the Blind	162	111	273
Three Kings-Blind Unit	10	5	15
Wa Secondary School	4	2	6
Presbyterian Training College	9	6	15
Bechem Blind-Unit	4	2	6
Wa School for the Blind	114	67	181
Wenchi Secondary School	14	8	22
Cape Coast School for the Deaf-Unit	9	2	11
Wa Training College	5	2	7
Total	338	205	543

On the contrary, students with visual impairments and blindness have been successfully integrated into general classroom at the college level for nearly half of a century. For example, McWilliam and Kwamena-Poh (1975) mentioned that two female students who were blind were enrolled in a teachers training college in 1961, soon after the 1961 Education Act was passed into law. Thereafter, many students with visual impairments and blindness in Ghana have successfully pursued college/university programs to become economists, lawyers, psychologists, teachers, administrators, and secretaries. Several colleges and all public universities in Ghana serve students with visual impairments and blindness. Because of the successful integration of students with visual impairments and blindness at the post-high school level, there are only two main residential schools for the blind in Ghana, located at Wa and Akropong-Akwapim, respectively. Seven other schools with sizeable numbers of students having visual impairments are either integrated in regular schools or are part of unit schools for the deaf. This contrasts with schools for children with mental retardation and hearing impairments. For instances, there are more than ten residential schools for students with hearing impairments and five or more units for the deaf spread all over the country. In addition, there are six residential schools for students with mental retardation, three of them having been started by private individuals and later absorbed by the special education division. It is clear then that, integration has been least successful with children with mental retardation and hearing impairments because opportunities for segregation are much more readily available than opportunities for integration for these children.

Enrollments in Schools for Students with Hearing Impairments during 2003/2004 Academic Year

INSTITUTION	STUDENT ENROLLMENT		
	Males	Females	Total
Koforidua Unit for the Deaf	88	61	149
Savelugu School for the Deaf	191	82	273
Volta School for the Deaf	134	79	213
Ashanti School for the Deaf	170	153	323
Bechem School for the Deaf	184	128	312
Salvation Army School for the Deaf	25	31	56
Cape Coast School for the Deaf	152	137	289
Kibi School for the Deaf	107	56	163
Wa School for the Deaf	118	82	200
Gbeogo School for the Deaf	86	54	140
Mampong Demonstration School for the Deaf	153	107	260
State School for the Deaf	145	77	222
Sekondi School for the Deaf	149	101	250
Total	**1702**	**1148**	**2850**

Enrollments in Schools for Students with Mental Retardation during 2003/2004 Academic Year

INSTITUTION	STUDENT ENROLMENT		
	Males	Females	Total
New Horizon	89	43	132
Sharon School for the MR	60	28	88
Twin City Special School	66	33	99
Battor Three Kings	55	41	96
Dzorwulu Special School	78	67	145
Garden City Special School	96	46	142
Castle Road	25	11	36
Koforidua Special Class	19	7	27
Volta Special Class	21	13	34
Wa Deaf Special Class	18	15	33
Kpando Inclusive	37	34	71
Total	**564**	**338**	**902**

Enrollment of Students at the Mampong Deafblind Center during 2003/2004 Academic Year

INSTITUTION	STUDENT ENROLMENT		
	Males	Females	Total
Mampong Deafblind Centre	9	1	10
Total	9	1	10

TEACHER EDUCATION

As mentioned earlier, Ghana was one of the first African countries to train its own special education personnel and to share its experience with other African countries (Gadagbui, 1998). The training of teachers for students with hearing impairments and deafness in Ghana started in in the early 1960s at the Deaf Education Specialist Training College, Mampong-

Akwapim. Many of its graduates have served and continue to serve in Ghana and different parts of the world as speech therapists, audiologists, and classroom teachers. The training of teachers for students with visual impairments and blindness locally, however, started as a department of the Presbyterian Training College (PTC) Akropong-Akwapim in the early 1980s. Prior to this time, teachers for students with visual impairments and blindness trained overseas at the Royal School for the Blind, England. In 1986, the Deaf Education Specialist Training College, the PTC department of blind education, and a department of the mentally handicapped were amalgamated to create a 3-year diploma awarding college – the College of Special Education at Mampong-Akwapim. In December, 1992, the three departments were moved to the University of Education, Winneba which then became the Department of Special Education.

The Department of Special Education at the University of Education trains teachers for individuals with one of the three disability categories traditionally catered for in Ghana, namely; visual impairments, hearing impairments, and mental retardation. Gadagbui (1998), dean of the Division of Professional Studies in Education of the university wrote:

> The Department has a unique role of training (special) teachers for the visually impaired, hearing impaired, and the mentally handicapped. The Department trains its products or graduates to function in the following areas: segregated special schools for individuals who are blind, deaf or mentally handicapped from nursery to senior secondary school, integrated/inclusive settings, community based rehabilitation (CBR) programmes, peripatetic services (regional and district special education coordinators), hospital schools, assessment centres, and resource centres. (p.1)

The opportunity to broaden special education service delivery to include students with other disabilities will, therefore, be difficult to achieve since the main teacher training university in Ghana is perpetuating only the three traditional categories of special education. The Department, through its school attachment program, has been identifying and supporting children with reading, mathematics, spelling, and behavioral problems in thirty-two basic schools (Avoke and Hayford, 2000). This may eventually lead to the training of teachers in the other categories of special education. As Avoke and Hayford rightly observed, "... a key issue in promoting inclusive practice must be a reappraisal of the training provided to teachers and other professionals." (p. 6)

TECHNOLOGY AND SPECIAL EDUCATION

Assistive technology (AT) has made teaching and learning easy for all categories of children (Avoke and Ocloo, 2000). For example, it is possible for a student who is blind to get his or her speech transposed into print or Braille, and vice versa, with the use of a computer designed for that purpose, and a student with multiple orthopedic and mental impairments to move around his or her classroom without being supported by other people (Kirk, et. 2003). Though, AT is very useful in the education and training of individuals with disabilities, its rapid expansion can result in increased budgetary problems for developing countries such as Ghana. In addition, special educators and general educators have little or no training in AT as applied to special education service delivery. As a result, students with disabilities in Ghana continue to use outdated equipment for learning. For instance, Avoke and Ocloo found that special schools for students with visual impairments in Ghana lacked basic supplies of learning equipments. In addition, these authors found that equipments that were available (e.g., Braille machines, slate and stylus, magnifiers) were very old. These authors did not find equipment like close circuit televisions and computers and therefore concluded that the "state of the art in terms of technology for students with visual impairment and low vision is still at the rudimentary level." Also, the only Braille press in the country is for the greater part of the year, out of service due to frequent breakdowns and lack of supplies (Agbeke, 1998).

The ailing economy of Ghana, like other sub-Saharan African countries, has made the use of AT in special education look like a luxury. This view is supported by Avoke and Ocloo (2000) who point out that it has never been the priority of any government in Ghana to allocate funds for the purchase of AT equipment for students with disabilities.

The University of Education, Winneba, has launched an information communication technology (ICT) program which is aimed at creating access to the thousands of junior secondary school students in Winneba and its environs (Anamua-Mensah, 2004). The ICT program will be replicated in other parts of the country, thanks to the government's nationwide ICT program for all schools in Ghana. This new development in information technology is expected to benefit students with disabilities. Besides, special education teacher-trainees in the University will be able to apply the knowledge and skills from the ICT program when they graduate.

DISTANCE EDUCATION AND SPECIAL EDUCATION

Distance education programming is now a core component in all public universities in Ghana. At the University of Education, Winneba, distance education coursework includes special education and rehabilitation. There are many ways that the distance education program offered through the University of Education, Winneba, will positively impact special education in Ghana. First, the university offers regular distance education classes through its outlets across Ghana and this allows teachers to obtain certificates and degrees without having to leave their regular classrooms. Secondly, the University's distance education programs offer an opportunity for related services staff attached to schools to update their knowledge and skills. Thirdly, the program is designed to provide extension services to support parents of children with disabilities so that they would be able to stimulate their children with disabilities outside of school, and to develop a home-school collaboration school staff.

A successful distance education program that will cater for the needs of students with disabilities and their families in Ghana will depend upon several factors, three of which are discussed below. First, distance education, through the ICT program, will require computers and accessories that must be maintained regularly. This may pose the greatest danger to the successful implementation and sustenance of the program, considering the poor economic situation of the country. Second, there is a lack of personnel to support the program, both within the university itself and the numerous outlets where courses are offered. Since ICT is a new concept in Ghana, a greater section of the teaching staff at the university and those running off-campus programs does not have the knowledge and skills to participate effectively in the distance education program by the ICT medium. Third, since most students with disabilities in Ghana attend special residential schools, they are separated from their families for long periods of time. Parents would be unlikely to avail themselves to the distance education program when they cannot find an immediate use for the knowledge and skills they would learn.

CONCLUSIONS

Special education in Ghana has seen remarkable growth since the first school for the blind started over fifty years ago. More schools for students with disabilities have been established, and more teachers have been trained, but many more areas have seen no changes over all those years. Integration of students into general education classrooms should be pursued vigorously because it is the preferred practice worldwide and sometimes, is more cost effective. In addition, a policy on special education is long overdue. The use of information communication technology and distance education programming will help to bring the much needed changes in special education in Ghana. Both the Special Education Division of the Ministry of Education and the University of Education, Winneba plan to expand their services for individuals with disabilities. The plan is to go inclusive. Also, it is in the plan of the Ghana Education Service and the University of Education, Winneba, to start preparing teachers for children who have learning disabilities and deaf-blindness, respectively.

Special Education in Ghana is beset with many challenges. The major challenge is lack of equipment or resources. Many of the equipment used in special schools in Ghana are imported and are expensive. In this respect, attempts must be made to find out how some of the equipment can either be manufactured or assembled in Ghana. For example, in 1981 Volta Aluminum Company and Accra Polytechnic, both with resources to make plastic products started manufacturing mobility canes for the blind. Other manufacturers can be part of this business too. Staffing for the schools remains another problem. Teachers are turned out every year to work with students with disabilities but the schools still lack teachers because there is a high attrition among special educators in Ghana.

REFERENCES

Abosi, C. O. (2000). Trends and issues in special education in Botswana. *Journal of Special Education, 34*(1), 48-53.

Agbeke, W. K. (1998). Inclusion of students with visual impairments in Ghana: Prospects and problems. *Ghanaian Journal of Special Education, 1*(3), 25-32.

Ainscow, M. (1997). Toward inclusive schooling. *British Journal of Special Education, 24*, 3-6.

Anamua-Mensah, J. (2004, May). *University of Education, Winneba: UEW's commitment to African universities initiative.* Speech delivered at the launching of the African Universities Initiative (AUI) Project of the World Computer Exchange (WCE) at the University of Education, Winneba, Ghana, May 14th, 2004.

Asamani, C. A. (2000). *Developing special education needs (SEN) policy in Ghana: A silver lining in the clouds for children with special education needs.* International Special Education Congress: Including the excluded. Manchester, 24th-28th July, 2000.

Avoke, M., and Hayford, S. (2000). *Promoting inclusive education in basic schools in Winneba Circuit: The role of school attachment programme.* International Special Education Congress: Including the excluded. Manchester, 24th-28th July, 2000.

Avoke, M., and Ocloo, M. (2000). *The use of instructional technology in teaching children with low vision in Ghana.* International Special Education Congress: Including the excluded. Manchester, 24th-28th July, 2000.

Chitiyo, M. and Wheeler, J. (2004). The development of special education services in Zimbabwe. *International Journal of Special Education, 19*, 41-52.

Csapo, M. (1986). Zimbabwe: Emerging problems of education and special. *International Journal of Special Education, 1* (2), 141-160.

Csapo, M. (1987). Special education in sub-Saharan Africa. *International Journal of Special Education, 2* (1), 41-67.

Eyiah, J. K. (2004). *Brief history of state-organized education in Ghana.* Retrieved January 12, 2005 from the Worldwide Web:
http://www.ghanaweb.com/GhanaHomePage/features/artikel.php?ID=54812

Farrell, P. (2000). The impact of research and developments in inclusive education. *International Journal of Inclusive Education, 4*, 153-162.

Gadagbui, G. Y. (1998). *Education in Ghana and special needs children.* Accra: City Press.

Kirk, S. A., Gallagher, J. L., and Anastasiow, N. J. (2003). *Educating students with disabilities.* Boston: Houghton Mifflin.

Koray, B. I. (1998). Policy trends related to special needs education in Ghana reviewed from an international perspective. *Proceedings of the first joint national delegates conference on persons with disabilities.* Winneba: University College of Education, Ghana.

Kwaku, M. (1998). Review of the state of special education programme/services in Ghana. *Proceedings of the first joint national delegates conference on persons with disabilities.* Winneba: University College of Education, Ghana.

McWilliam, H. O. A., and Kwamena-Poh, M. A. (1975). *The development of education in Ghana.* Hong Kong: Longman Group Ltd.

Mfum-Mensah, O. (2003). *The impact of non-formal basic education programs: A case study of northern Ghana.* Unpublished Ph.D. dissertation. University of Toronto, Canada.

Schumm, J., and Vaughn, S. (1991). Making adaptations for mainstreamed students: General classroom teachers' perspectives. *Remedial and Special Education, 12*(4), 18-27.

Torto, E. O. (2000). The *history of special education in Ghana.* Accra: Ghana Education Service.

Part IV:
Lessons from the Industrialized World

Chapter 14

HEY DUDE! IT'S NOT THE COMPUTER: TECHNOLOGIES, CURRICULUM AND GOVERNING THE SELF*

Thomas S. Popkewitz
University of Wisconsin-Madison
Wisconsin, USA

INTRODUCTION

Technology has a polysemy of meanings. One relates to the physical entities that act as an interface with people's work and communication. These might be the emergence of the printing press to make possible mass book publishing; the invention of the lead pencil, ballpoint pen or the typewriter for writing, and more recently the handheld calculator and the computer. Each physical technology has importance as it moves into social/cultural practices with long histories in the school. I will not retell any of them. My interest in technologies is with the cultural practices that govern the self - the assemblage of ideas, institutions and authority relations that generate principles about who we are, should be, and who is not that "we" – the child who is located as outside the boundaries inscribed as normalcy and thus "at-risk." This notion of technologies is found in the cultural turn of Marxism in the 20th century by the Frankfurt School, Althusser, Gramsci, and in the "linguistic turn" of social theory which inverts the Marxist concern with labor to that of knowledge as a material practice. The latter is exemplified in Foucault's (1988) notion of *the technologies of the self* "which permit individuals to effect by their own means or with the help of others a certain number of operations on their own bodies and souls, thoughts, conduct, and way of being, so as to transform themselves in order to attain a certain state of happiness, purity, wisdom, perfection, or immorality" (p.18). This second sense of technology has less to do with machines or "hardware" and more to do with the assemblage of practices that are to inculcate virtuous habits and the self discipline that enables one to feel empowered, given voice, and self-actualized with the proper education.

Using this second notion of technology, my focus is to consider the computer within the assemblage of cultural practices in the current restructuring of education. One curriculum and two research practices in contemporary school reforms are examined as technologies of the self. One site is a curriculum project of online teaching. The other two sites are about school research: a National Council of Research report on education science and the professional journal *Educational Researcher*'s issue devoted to research as design. The choices of sites are not as a "sample" but to think about the system of reason that circulates among what otherwise seem as unrelated. Central to this overlap is the use of "design." Design is a word that appears across the sites and provides a thread to think about the principles of action and participation. The problem of design is told as giving voices, agency and empowerment to those selected. Yet I want to argue that that is not only what is going on. Design is a technology of the self that administers the freedom of the individual and thus is an effect of power.

To think about the technologies of the self in pedagogy and research, I draw upon American cultural history by bringing in another notion of technology - the technological sublime. The technological sublime enables me to consider how the designing of the child and research in this vein engage a sense of beauty, awe and fear in who the child is and should be. The sublime of the contemporary pedagogy and research that I examine involves the designing of the self as the fulfillment of a future vision that has qualities of The Third Coming. I speak of later in this article as The Third Coming to focus on a historically particular narrative of salvation and redemption other than earlier Puritan notions of the utopian world given by God reclaimed in the New World of the 18th century, and the Second Coming of redemption brought by the train and the harnessing of electric power at the turn of the 20th century. The sublime of the Third Coming is embodied in the designing of the figure of the lifelong learner. That individual works for the future in a continuous, lifelong engagement of communication, innovation, active learning, and flexible decision-making. If this was all there were to the technological sublime and the technologies of the self, then there might be little to discuss in this design of an updated Enlightenment figure. But the habits and dispositions of action and participation embodied in the design projects are not universal and generate principles of inclusion and exclusion.

THE TECHNOLOGICAL SUBLIME:
THE FIRST, SECOND AND THIRD COMING

If I look to American historical studies at the turn of the 20th century (Nye, 1999, 2003), the stories that describe how the technological marvels of railroad, electricity, bridges, and skyscrapers are made into elements of a cultural dialogue. The new technologies that transformed the world embodied the national or manifest destiny. The technological changes were viewed as the apotheosis of reason and an expression of the fundamental hopes and fears of the nation (Nye, 1999). Particular natural sites (Niagara Falls) and architectural forms (the skyscraper) were given a transcendent significance in the popular literature of the time. Utopian visions and national narratives were woven into discourses of a new prominence, progress, and expansion. The building of the railroad, for example, was not merely a system of transportation. The railroad entered into national imaginaries. It was seen as a sign of western expansion and progress that celebrated the power of human reason, and the special privilege of engineers and inventors that would continually innovate and transform the world.

This sense of awe and wonder given to the railroad or the skyscrapers produced a *technological sublime* (Nye, 1999). That sublime was not only about the present but also of a future invested with a particular hope, sense of beauty and awe that connects the nation and its people. Nye calls this *The Second Coming*. The earlier 17th century Puritan narratives told of The First Coming, the redemption in the Promised Land that recaptured the past Garden of Eden and the settlers as The Chosen people. Salvation was found in the New Worlds, unblemished by the corruptions of Old Europe. A Second Coming was told as the new technologies of the 19th century were placed into narratives of the nation as the Promised Land. Unlike the First Coming that looked to the past in recapturing the pastoral world of God, the Second Coming looked to the future. The technological marvels of the railroad, electricity, bridges, and skyscrapers were not only related to the social consequences of economic and political forces. These technologies embraced an essentially religious feeling aroused by the confrontation of impressive objects, such as the Niagara Falls, the Grand Canyon, and later, the New York skyline (Nye, 1999, p. xiii). The railroad and bridge were triumphs of art and a token of the liberation of the human spirit to be realized by the young republic.

The technological sublime in the U.S. was different from European narratives about technology. The U.S. established a relationship to the cities and its physical landscapes by inverting the conditions of cities to the countryside so that the enterprise of the city made possible its existence and settlement (Nye, 2003, p.35). The technological foundation narratives explained historical events and fused them with cultural values that differentiated them from earlier salvation narratives. New foundation stories told about Americans transforming a wilderness into a prosperous and egalitarian society whose landscape and people had a transcendent presence through its technological achievements (Nye, 2003, p.5). Mechanical force was taken as axiomatic, making possible new landscapes, boomtowns, sudden profits, personal success, and national progress. The foundational narrative was not about the individual hero such as those told of the American Revolutionary War. The technologies of the axe, canal, or railroad were narrated in as a (causal?) chain of events in an inevitable developmental process. The marking of the chosen people in the technological sublime also inscribed those who were not chosen- the people who could not be or were not civilized and thus part of the American civilization. The sublime was both a reaction to science as well as a furthering of the romantic images that enabled science to proceed. Today, that sublime is different from The Second Coming, involving different technologies of the self that I speak of as the Third Coming.

AN EXCURSUS ON DESIGN

One way of thinking of the technological sublime is through the word "design" that appears in the Second Coming and again in today's literature. Today's reforms and research talk about children's *designing* their own learning, science as involving rigorous *designs* to develop causal knowledge, and research itself as *a design problem*. Design is a process that generates principles for human agency. It orders and normalizes the rules and standards by which teachers, children and researchers are able to intervene in the order of things and transform that order in the name of progress. Design is a word that is used to talk about change, progress and a future utopia that redeploys the term "engineering" from the turn of the 20th century. Design embodies the technological sublime in the technologies of the self.

Design was a word that spoke of what God gave to human affairs as part of the First Coming. That notion of design moves from the Heavenly paradise to the City of Man [sic] that harkens (from?) the earthly progress of the 18th century philosophers (see, e.g., Becker, 1932). Design is now about the planning of the modern nation, the city, and the modern person. The individual has a design given by nature, and that nature is no longer spoken about as a thing ordered by heavenly intervention. Into the early 20th century, though, it was not uncommon for pedagogical interventions to be thought of as completing the latent design of God within each child, the family and the citizen. In 19th century Sweden, for example, the educator Rudenschöld placed the notion of design in the Ståndscirkulation, the outer technological side of an evolutionary process that will inaugurate Christian values and life forms on earth (Hultqvist, in press). The evolutionary process embodied a national Exceptionalism. That Exceptionalism was the individual's heritage of certain virtues like modesty or freedom from vanity and overlapped with the Lutheran heritage of individualism and the practices related to salvation. The virtues and characteristics of the saved *self* later were embodied in the Swedish welfare state during the post War II-period. The state, society and the individual were open to change, but change was contained by the idea of a pre-designed universe.

The design of the individual in the name of future progress appears in the political movement of American Progressivism and progressive education. The design of the self involved a new urban professional expertise that was put into *the service of the democratic ideal,* to use the language of the early social sciences. But that democratic ideal was conceived of in terms of the psyche in which participation had social significance and thus moved from external structural criteria (such as class struggles) to a psychology about personalized alternatives to changes in life and situation (Sklansky, 2002, p.162). For the progressives, the problem of design embodied the triumph of cooperation over competition as the natural destiny of human progress (Sklansky, 2002, p.161). The technologies of design were captured in new scientific psychologies. The new psychologies, for example, envisioned the empirical building blocks of selfhood as of deliberate design rather than of something related to a static, metaphysical soul (Sklansky, 2002, pp.148-9). William James' notion of a pragmatic psychology placed a premium on habit formation as the main means of acting in accord with one's designs (Sklansky, 2002, p.146). Design was a key technology of education to reach into the interior of the individual as *the great panacea to equality.*

THE PROPHESY OF BEAUTY AND AWE: THE DESIGN OF ONLINE LEARNING

A recent book (Maeroff (2003) on online learning by the director of the Hechinger Institute on education and the Media at Teachers College, Columbia, provides another telling of the Third Coming through the child's design of his or her own learning. The book begins with an invitation to revolution (the title of the first chapter). That revolution is where the physical technology of computers makes possible the individualization of learning so that "one-on-one education may be closer at hand than ever before. (p.1). As with the foundational stories of the nation told through the stories about the train, bridges, and power plants at the turn of the 20th century, online learning is a 21st century foundation narrative of the technology of the self. Online teaching embodies the prophesy of the new beginning and a design of one's life that "will be an enabling one, as printing presses have been to the production of books" (Maeroff, 2003, p. 3).

The prophecy is about progress through regulating the present. Progress is a performance embodied in creating a delivery system for education. The technology of the computer is "thing," a sovereign object that serves to fulfill human purposes and desires. "What has developed, courtesy of the Internet, is the possibility of offering learning on a scale more far-reaching than previously imagined...The push to breach classroom walls has accelerated...These programs, with their ability to transcend state lines and even national borders, circumvent geographic barriers that were often used in the past to protect campus-based education from competition (p. 4).

But the prophecy is also about who the child is to become. The online teaching offers a foundation narrative about a new cosmopolitanism that the Enlightenment philosophers could have only wished for: the globalized individual who travels as a lifelong learner. The unfinished qualities are also narratives of a new individuality. Time/space are unfinished and always in the making. The self is a cosmopolitan traveler with no attachment except attachments to the process and design. That cosmopolitan lives in unfinished ways of life that is a continually reworking one's self. Individuality is ordered through the overlapping of cognitive skills and dispositions that make innovation and choice the characteristics of one's potentiality. The future is the potentiality of the present, but also is the mean of regulating it.

To design one's self through online learning is to become a continuously self actualizing individual. The unfinished cosmopolitan is produced through the individualization and the making motivation. The *individualized instruction* is a technology to produce children who desire to make education more convenient (p.76), have greater achievement and satisfaction (p. 83), and assume a self responsibility and motivation (p. 95). Design is how "students create choices in completing tasks; lets students have some choice in the difficulty levels of assignments or tasks that they complete; and give students some discretion about when they complete particular tasks (p. 102). The child's design of education is for the self-discipline of the student and promotes comfortableness with academic tasks.

The design of one's life is assembled by the inscription of motivation. Motivation is the key tool that enables the autonomous individual to design a life of choices. This autonomous self is rhetorically placed in relation to policies of a free-market approach. As online learning interjects "more choice into the system, advocates reason, the richer the offerings and greater the benefits to consumers (students and their families) (Maeroff, 2003, p.4).

But the motivational psychology of the unfinished cosmopolitanism is not only about the self. It is given legitimation in current social policy about markets, but that intelligibility would not be there but for the earlier child-centered pedagogical reforms of the 1970s that made the decentralized child (Hultqvist, 1998). The child of the progressive pedagogies of the 1970s was one whose life was composed of a continuous self realization through the making of choices.

The designing of the interior of the child to create desire and motivation is not new to psychology or pedagogy (Danziger, 1997). It entails an early shift in the social and psychological sciences to make daily life and experience as an object of administration. The early psychology of Wundt or Titchner, for example, did not think of psychology as providing an explanation of everyday conduct. The emergence of mass schooling produced an interest in early American psychology to understand children's "fatigue" so that it could be treated through calculating and influencing will, motives, interests, needs and desire. This treatment of the inner "thought" was part of a larger concern of the American social sciences with social control and engineering. Psychology focused on the inner characteristics of the child as a potential object of external influence. Motivation became a key player in this administration. Rather than abstract from inner experiences, motivation became a term for making the interior of the child calculable and administrable. The portrayal of online learning as motivating children to design their own modes of living is one re-calibration of that administration of the self.

But, as in the early psychology, the agency of the child who learns online inscribes its opposite, the "nontraditional student" whose inner characteristics are not cosmopolitan. The non-traditional students are the part time college student and employed students, as well as those in the public schools." They are "students who live in inner-city neighborhoods so besieged by crime that travel between school and home is a threatening ordeal. The chance to stay at home and attend virtual classes might provide some relief. As it is, crime, violence, and drug dealing have forced school systems in some urban locales to consider holding classes in community rooms at housing projects so that children would not have to venture onto unsafe streets. (216)

While social and cultural distinctions are recognized in how internet technologies are used in the classroom ("While poor children drill on the computer, higher-achieving students have more chances to work with data bases, spreadsheets, and graphics, for example. (Maeroff, 2003, p. 221), the distinctions are easily solved. Teachers need more professional training! And with this solution is a plan of rescue. The non-traditional students gain power through individualization. "part of the lack of progress of some struggling students has stemmed from their feeling that they lack any power over their own learning. Online courses might offer a breakthrough, a way to put them in control for the first time. Online learning in the security of their own homes, shielded from peers who scoff at academics, could offer an opportunity that other measures have seemed unable to provide" (Maeroff, 2003, p. 218).

The social and cultural distinctions and differentiations elide the divisions that are made in the continuous project of the making. Agency is both individualized and placed in a psychological register. To effect change lies in the inner qualities and characteristics of the child that instruction is to shape and fashion under the rubric of "learning" and development. The notions of students "lacking" power, the idea of progress, and individual control function as technologies of administrating the self.

The technological sublime embodies a particular rhetorical style of American politics and the broader juxtaposition of degeneration and progress of modernity. The 17th century Puritan sermons of Jeremiad's about the fall of the temple and then the finding of grace through change are given in a new pulpit. The degeneration or fall is bound to existing school systems. It is a "system that has often been inflexible and reluctant to change" (Maeroff, 2003, p. 18); and the teacher who does not embrace the prophesy of technology is thus not able to bring the future into the present. "Instructors who in coming years ignore the potential of web-based embellishments will be as remiss as their peers in past years who did no expect students to enrich their learning by consulting sources beyond their books" (Maeroff, 2003, p.

3). To rise and prevent the fall is to have the vision of the new delivery system. Such a shift will require a vision of educators who recognize that education can be education regardless of its form of delivery (Maeroff, 2003, p. 3). Online learning is a governing in the name of a utopian logic concerned with reforming people. But that utopian logic evokes the future as a practices of governing of the self in the present.

THE TECHNOLOGICAL SUBLIME IN EDUCATIONAL RESEARCH: TWO GENRES OF DESIGNING THE CHILD AS THE EMBODIMENT OF THE THIRD COMING

The technological sublime of online learning is morphologically related to the educational sciences. Science is historically tales of redemption and salvation of the future as it embodied the seductive reasoning of modernity. The narratives and images of science assert themselves as objective and detached, the *sin qua non* of modernity itself that imposes the Enlightenment philosophical claim that human beings gain knowledge about the world by distancing themselves from the world (see, e.g., Wagner, 2003). But that distancing for self-reflection also embodied inscription devices that render the thought of a child visible and amenable to governing (for see, e.g., Foucault, 1991; also see, Latour, 1986; Popkewitz, 2004, Rose, 1999). The inscriptions of science are made into design problems in contemporary educational research. While the notion of design has different configurations in the two exemplars of research below, they inscribe a technological sublime in the continuous flow between science, everyday life and change.

DESIGN AS RESEARCH METHODS: THE NATIONAL RESEARCH COUNCIL COMMITTEE OF SCIENTIFIC RESEARCH IN EDUCATION

The Committee Report (2002) is a response to Congressional legislation related to *No Child Left Behind* and seeks to outline the foundations of all sciences for the educational science. (For a discussion of the assumptions of this report, see the special issue of Journal of Qualitative Inquiry (forthcoming, Spring, 2004)). The Report is high profile in the U.S. context, consecrated by the National Research Council, related to national legislation, and overlaps with other efforts of the government to provide a particular instrumental focus to the study of schooling and educational reform. A central assumption is that research can empirically demonstrate "what works" for school improvement. The argument of the report is that there is a unity among all social and natural sciences, including medicine. This unity across all sciences is reminiscent of the Logical Positivists who came to this country from Vienna in the 1920s. The ostensible influence of the Logical Positivism was short lived. But its spirit lives in the Report that views sciences as an administrative project "to reengineer schools in effective ways" (p.12).

Like the sciences of progressive movements a century earlier, the unity of science is, placed in a language of research that serves democratic ideals. It is to secure the future of the nation through the present education of the child. Its warrant is "the nation's commitment to improve the education of all children requires continuing efforts to improve its research capacity" (The National Research Council, 2002. p. 21). The science of education provides the expertise in which public policy and private choices are made. The science is to provide politicians, citizens and school systems "hard evidence," "impartiality," and "reasonable, rigorous, and scientific deliberation (The National Research Council, 2002, pp.12-13). Scientists describe reality and what works for others to use. "The scientist discovers the basis for what is possible. The practitioner, parent, or policy maker, in turn, has to consider what is practical, affordable, desirable, and credible" (The National Research Council, 2002. p. 49).

The design problem of this science is to *rigorously* order and stabilize contexts and individuality so as to enable their "re-engineering." That re-engineering is called reform and innovation. The designs of research, for example, "offer stable explanations for phenomena that generalize beyond the particular" (The National Research Council, 2002. p. 3). Whereas design in the online learning was the fulfillment of what was naturally in the child, the research design is the rigorous use of the techniques of data collection to successfully re-engineer the teacher and child through, for example, identifying causal relationships, conducting randomized field trials, estimating populational characteristics, and developing adequate maps of the mind and thought.

The rigorous design in research meant "to re-engineer the school, the teacher, and the child, brings together the vocations of science and of politics, to draw on the language of the turn of the 20th century German sociologist Max Weber. Science moves into terrains where expectations are formulated through seers and prophets--dispensers of sacraments and revelations that merge the vocation of science with the vocation of politics. But these sacraments of the sublime also universalize the inner characteristics of the child, talked about in this report as "volition" or as stable populations groups that are randomly assigned to some treatment.

The designing of the procedures and methods of research are not only about descriptions and explanations of schools and learning. The design problem of research is a utopian project to make overt government necessary through a self government. The reforms of human beings are to provide a secure world through the shaping and fashioning a secure knowledge of the world. That world is to improve how we do things through the designing of desire and motivation of the child. The objects of intervention are the inner qualities and characteristics of the child. The science spoken about makes the child an empirical "entity" that can be re-engineered through the application of psychological theories of learning, motivation and individualization.

The unity of science is invoked with a principle of equity, calling for an education that serves *all* children. Evoking the equity principle as such, the exemplars of good science relate to testing achievement and to assessing for disabilities. In both instances, the assumption of normalcy in populational characteristics is central and assumed. This assumption is important as it creates a global and universal system of characteristics from which difference is formed and normalcy inscribed.

The normalcy is not only about what is included but also about exclusions. The inclusion and exclusions are not in the categorical labeling of deviance but in the establishing of a normalcy from which deviance is inscribed as the inner characteristics of the self. I will return to this later when I discuss the uses of the new phrase of equity in schooling "*all* children," here only saying that the design procedures to unify science with the earlier discussion of motivation does not discover what is natural to the child but constructs a continuum of values about who the child is, should be, and who is not that child.

DESIGN AS RESEARCH

A recent issue of the American Educational Research Association journal, *Educational Researcher* was devoted to "the role of design in educational research." Whereas design in the online learning was for a student to administer what was thought of as natural to the individual, the National Research Council placed design as the procedures in which to explicate the natural order of things that science finds and (or, in other words,...)as a research strategy that brings complexity theory to the classroom. "The educational system may be described as open, complex, nonlinear, organic, historical, and social" (Kelly, 2003, p.3). Design research orders the complexity of the classroom into a continuous monitoring system and feedback loops that take into account individual actions and context to bring practices into a relation with the unidentified "interests" of the intervention system called state reforms. The quality of the system of people and organization is one of continual flexibility, adjustment and adaptation that enable ongoing "innovation." As with online learning, design is to order and generate principles of an unfinished cosmopolitanism that embodies the continuous process of supervising, theorizing, and intervening in a lifelong process that makes and remakes the self.

The notion of design is seductive as it brings together two sacred values of modern progress – science and democracy. Design utilizes "the scientific processes of discovery, exploration, confirmation, and dissemination" to develop theories about the interventions in the metacognition of the child and the teacher (Kelly, 2003, p.3 and 5). Similar to the design functions of the National Research Committee Report, design research talks about reengineering as impartially changing the practices of schooling. Science both brings "the values and problems of the society that supports it and sets its goals and... educational researchers [to use their professional language] to generate distinctions and descriptions for the system. The distinctions and descriptions themselves, and interventions designed from them, make the system's actions relevant to its own evolution and improvement" (Kelly, 2003, p.3).

The democratic ideals are spoken about through the use of the phrase, *anchored instruction*. Using mathematics teaching as an exemplar, "learning should be contextualized, and of ideas that mathematics learning should be more closely tied to students' experience" (The Design-Based Research Collective, 2003, p.5). Design research brings agency to the teacher and child through a system through "design and engineering [that is] generative and transformative" (Kelly, 2003, p. 4).

In one sense, design research has found the Philosopher's Stone that is earlier centuries was to find the elixir of life. It both captures reality by getting closer to the actual perceptions, attention, and dispositions that order the classroom, and has the tools to change that reality to produce *evolution and improvement*. This relationship of science and change, as the pragmatism of Progressivism, joins elite knowledge with a populism of local citizen participation. Design research is to "close the credibility gap between unscientific research and detachment of researchers in which there is incompleteness of knowledge. Design provides a closer relation in the "interactions between intervention and setting" (The Design-Based Research Collective, 2003, p.5).

But *to capture* something as reality is to elide the manner in which the intellectual tools of science construes and constructs its objects of study. Whatever the merits of the different approaches to classroom observation and cataloging, they are never merely descriptive of some natural reasoning of the child, idiosyncratic to a particular classroom, or descriptions of good teaching practices. The procedures of data collection and interpretation embody particular sets of rules related to intellectual traditions for ordering who the child and teacher are and should be. The intellectual traditions that shape the design research are themselves cultural practices and effects of power. There is no structuring or coding of experience without prior mediating structures of thought (see, e.g., Fendler, 1999; Britzman, 1991).

Such interventions, however, are placed as abstract ideals about democracy and participation that have no historical qualities about the constitution of the rules and standards that are authorized for action. Whatever the democratic rhetoric about participation and collaboration, the design research is an operation to order conduct and ways of being. The technologies of the self as design research are different in focus from that of the National Report or the child's design of online learning. But design research is a technology of the self. It involves a close relation of the expertise of science with the forming and transformation of individual's interpretative tools. "Micro-analysis of student interactions with activities based on that principle enabled redesign and refinement of activities, and ultimately refinement of the underlying interest-drive learning framework. Thus, emergent behaviors of students in response to activities drove development of the intervention and development of theory" (The Design-Based Research Collective, 2003, p. 6).

This empowerment embodies a paradox as registers of administration and freedom are joined. The sublime in this context is a procedural democratic theory in which science continuously orders everyday life to mold the self to what is relevant to *the evolution and improvement of the system*. The transformative action is continuous innovation *to provide stability and consensus to the future of change:* "Sustainable intervention requires understanding how and why an innovation works within a setting over time and across setting." (The Design-Based Research Collective, 2003, p.6). The complexity of design is presented as suggesting a particular reality, serving as truthful statements that need no further exploration as they stand as unquestioned objects of action in relation to a natural, and ahistorical " values and problems of society" and its "goals." The only thing that is natural to the self in this design research is the continuous administration of choice.

The educational site of online learning, the design procedures of science and design research are historical trajectories in the formation of the modern nation and the modern school in the nineteenth century. The self-governance of modern pedagogy replaces the older Puritan notions of instruction. Whereas the Puritan converting ordinances related to evangelizing works to bring one's salvation, school subjects functioned as providing a calculated design to save the soul through the works of science. The design research is one recent reassembly of these technologies that connect the scope and aspirations of public powers with the personal and subjective capacities of individuals. The connecting of the social and the person are now embodied in the relation of "social interactions" and "metacognition" (p. 5) whose "refinement brings the goals of society to the child ("the interest-drive learning framework" (The Design-Based Research Collective, 2003, p. 6).

GENERATING PRINCIPLES OF QUALITY AND INEQUALITY

The different educational sites above express the commitment to equity that appears in the reiteration of the phrase *all* children – *all* children will learn, programs for *all* students, the imperative to provide *all* children with high quality programs, and so on. The reiterated phrase *all* stresses the inclusiveness of teaching for "improving the academic performance of disadvantaged children" (Bush, 2001, p.2). The distinctions and divisions through class, race, gender, and disability, among other social/cultural factors, in schooling no longer matter.

The phrase "*all* children" appears as a political and social principle and commitment carried into action. But the phrase is not only that. It inscribes differentiations about human kinds that the school operates through its educational research and policy. (See, e.g., Hacking, 2002 for discussion of human kinds; as related to curriculum, Popkewitz, in press).

The *all* in *all children* differentiates the capacities and capabilities of the child who does and does not belong to the space captured in the phrase, *all* children, from a different human kind, the *disadvantaged* – a phrase used in standards based reforms and research. Maps are drawn in the discussions of two different human kinds that require different technologies of the self. The child who "fits in" the spaces and is not left behind is the child who participates, problem solves, and continuously innovates as a lifelong learner. The other human kind is *the disadvantaged child* who needs rescue as that child does not embody the inner characteristics and personhood for action and participation.

If I relate the various uses of design of instruction and research to a prominent standard for mathematics education reform published by the National Council of Teachers of Mathematics (2000) *Principles and Standards*, the two human kinds are easily apparent. There is the "all children" who problem solve as the embodiment of the unfinished cosmopolitan discussed earlier. And there are "some children" whose capabilities do not match up with the particular characteristics of the classification "*all* children" and these children are *left behind*. That latter child does not problem solve, psychologically has "low expectations," and if I go back to the online learning, is the child who is not motivated. From these different determinate characteristics is a particular human kind that is called the disadvantaged or the urban child who embodied these missing psychological qualities of motivation, individual expectations, self-esteem, among others.

What is interesting as one goes further into the various texts that talk about inclusion of those excluded, the psychological qualities of the child left behind is re-assembled with social characteristics to *make* a particular human kind who needs redemption. That human kind with low expectations travels with categories of children "who live in poverty, students who are not native speakers of English, students with disabilities, females, and many nonwhite students [who] have traditionally been far more likely than their counterparts in other demographic groups to be the victims of low expectations (National Council of Teachers of Mathematics, 2000, p. 13). The children who do not embody the norms of self improvement and collaboration are also "students who are not native speakers of English, for instance, and may need special attention to allow them to participate fully in classroom discussions ... [as] students with disability may need increased time to complete assignments, or they may benefit from the use of oral rather than written assessment" (National Council of Teachers of Mathematics, 2000, p.13).

When thinking of the assemblages and connections of these distinctions as forming a distinct human kind, the overt purposes of the narratives are to recognize an important social commitment of equity that includes the excluded child. But the inscriptions are of the normalizing pedagogy (see, Popkewitz and Lindblad, 2000). The distinctions of policy that states that *all children learn* entail a continuum of value that differentiates, classifies and divides. The division includes the child who is in perpetual preparation for being part of the all but who never achieves the norms of "the average" (see, e.g., Popkewitz, Tabachnick and Wehlage, 1982, ch. 4).

THE TECHNOLOGICAL SUBLIME OF SCIENCE

The technological sublime in online teaching and research are seductive narratives about saving or delivering the nation through the education of the child. They embody different themes about democracy, equality and economic progress of the nation in the new global world of a knowledge-based society. The technological sublime is presented as secular ideas of progress and democracy that redeems and empowers the self-actualized individual. My discussion is not to discard such salvation stories but rather to interrogate the contemporary field of cultural practices in which they are deployed.

The salvation stories of the Third Coming are technologies of the self. The renovation of the reform strategies of education embody an active sense of "self whose emotional bonds and self-responsibility are circumscribed through networks in which the classification of affiliation and belonging are being reworked --the family, the locality, and the community. The struggle is for the inner dispositions and moral being that is to become the autonomous learner. That child and the citizen are continuously involved in self-improvement and ready for the uncertainties through working actively in "communities of learning.

Freedom is talked about as the empowered individual who continually constructs and reconstructs one's own practice, and the ways of life through a perpetual intervention in one's life through working actively in "communities of learning. Life becomes a continuous course of personal responsibility and self management of one's risks and destiny as a problem-solving lifelong learner. The child's future is of the citizen and the worker who are tourists and/or consumers in the world that seems to beckon as so many enticing paths.

Progress is embodied in the pedagogy of the decentralized individual. The decentralized individual is an unfinished cosmopolitan who continually makes choices as a "lifelong learner. The lifelong learner is flexible, continuously active, and works collaboratively. These inner characteristics are cosmopolitan in the sense of an individuality that can chase desire and work in a global world in which there is no finishing line. The desires and will to learn of the child and teacher who relish change for the sake of change. The child is someone who can choose to refuse allegiance to any one of the infinite choices on display, except the choice of choosing. A child is, to use recent discourses about the reformed child, one who is flexible, ambitious, and motivated in a learning society. The location of responsibility is no longer traversed through the range of social practices directed toward a single public sphere--the social--but in diverse, autonomous and plural communities that constitute the common good. Change, contingencies and uncertainties of daily life are without author or history to form the common good.

But the unfinished cosmopolitanism is not unbound. The technologies of the self and its sublime of progress and self-actualization are embodied in fields of cultural practice and cultural production that give intelligibility to what is already there, and what serves in social contexts as foundational and 'preexisting facts that seem to live beyond them, often surviving empirical refutation' (Schram and Neisser, 1997, p.5). While the reform oriented research seems to offer the solutions to all problems and, at the same time rooting out of all evil, it brings into play particular enclosures and internments that cannot be taken unproblematically.

My focus on the technologies of the self embodied in the different sites also raises double questions about the interpretative "tools" that are to consider the internments and enclosures produced. The de-emphasis on structural categories such as class in the formation of subjectivities does not mean that governing is not there or that social exclusions do not exist. Rather, it suggest that the problem of governing that has preoccupied social theory since the late 19th century needs to be rethought and different sets of categories invented as ways to interpret agency. The intellectual move of this discussion places resistance, agency and social action, and the politics of schooling in a non-Hegelian field of thought. To poke holes in the seeming causality and propaganda in the conduct of modern life is the possibility of opening up alternatives to existing frameworks for change and agency. My strategy of analysis is diagnostic of the technologies of the self and a way to historically and sociologically interpret issues of technology. To consider the assemblages and connections in which action and participation are ordered is to consider how *thought* plays a part in holding together the contingency of social arrangements and thus to contest the givenness of social life.

REFERENCES

Becker, C. (1932). *The heavenly city of the eighteenth-century philosophers.* New Haven: Yale University Press.

Britzman, D. (1991). *Practice makes practice: A critical study of learning to teach.* Albany: State University of New York Press.

Bush, G. W. (2001). *No child left behind.* Washington, DC: Department of Education, U Government Printing Office.

Committee on Scientific Principles for Education Research. (2002). *Scientific research in education.* Washington, DC: Center for Education, Division of Behavioral and Social Sciences and Education, National Research Council.

Danziger, K. (1997). *Naming the mind. How psychology found its language.* London: Sage.

The Design-Based Research Collective (2003). Design-based research: An merging Paradigm for educational inquiry. *Educational Researcher.* 32/2: 5-8.

Fendler, L. (1999). Making trouble: Predictability, agency, and critical intellectuals. In T. Popkewitz and L. Fendler (Eds.), *Critical theories in education* (pp. 169-190). New York: Routledge.

Foucault, M. (1991). Governmentality. In G. Burchell, C. Gordon and P. Miller (Eds.), *The Foucault effect: Studies in governmentality* (pp. 87-104). Chicago: University of Chicago Press.

Foucault, M. (1988). The political technology of individuals. In L. Martin, H. Gutman and P. Huttan (Eds.), *Technologies of the Self* (pp. 145-162). Amherst: University of Massachusetts Press.

Hacking, I. (2002). *Historical ontology.* Cambridge, MA: Harvard University Press.

Hultqvist, K. 2004. Fremtid som styringsteknologi og det paedagogiske subjekts opdigtede inderlighed (The governing of the future and the fabrication of the inferiority of the pedagogical subject). In *Pædagogikken og kampen om individet Kritisk pædagogik - ny inderlighed - selvets teknologi. Seks essays om pædagogik og senmoderne uddannelse*, (pp. 159 - 188) J. Krejsler, ed. Köpenhamn: Hans Reitzel förlag.

Hultqvist, K. (1998). A history of the present on children's welfare in Sweden. In T. Popkewitz and M. Brennan (Eds.), *Foucault's challenge: Discourse, Knowledge, and power in education* (pp. 91-117). New York: Teachers College Press.

Kelly, A. (2003). Research as design. *Educational Research.* 32/1: 3-4.

Latour, B. (1986). Visualization and cognition: Thinking with eyes and hands. *Knowledge and Society*, 6, 1-40.

Maeroff, G. (2003). *A classroom of one: How online learning is changing our schools and colleges.* New York: Palgrave Macmillan.

National Council of Teachers of Mathematics. (2000). *Principles and standards for school mathematics.* Reston, VA: Author.

Nye, D. (1999). *American technological sublime.* Cambridge, MA: MIT Press.

Nye, D. (2003). *America as second creation: Technology and narratives of new beginnings.* Cambridge, MA: MIT Press.

Popkewitz, T. (2004). The alchemy of the mathematics curriculum: Inscriptions and the fabrication of the child. *American Educational Research Journal*, 41 (4): 3-34.

Popkewitz, T. S., and Lindblad, S. (2000). Educational governance and social inclusion and exclusion: Some conceptual difficulties and problematics in policy and research. *Discourse*, 21(1), 5-54.

Popkewitz, T., Tabachnick, B., and Wehlage, G. (1982). *The myth of educational reform: A study of school responses to a program of change.* Madison: University of Wisconsin Press.

Rose, N. (1999). *Powers of freedom: Reframing political thought.* Cambridge, MA: Cambridge University Press.

Schram, S. F., and Neisser, P. T. (Eds.). (1997). *Tales of the state: Narrative in contemporary U.S. politics and public policy.* N.J.: Rowman and Littlefield.

Sklansky, J. (2002). *The soul's economy: Market society and selfhood in American thought, 1820-1920.* Chapel Hill, NC: University of North Carolina Press.

AUTHOR NOTE

NB: This paper is drawn from a draft presentation given at the Seminar on Technology, London Institute of Education, Melbourne University, and University of Wisconsin-Madison. 2-4 October, 2003 in Madison, School of Education, the University of Wisconsin-Madison, Wisconsin. As earlier version of this paper appears in M. Nikolakaki(ed (2004) *Globalization, Technology and Paideia in the New Cosmopolis*, Atrapos editions:pp. 231-250

Epilogue

I write this after being in the Department of Curriculum and Instruction since 1970. As I begin to put words to talk about my career in the department, I find "career" an odd phrase to use as I had no notion of a career when I started my doctorate or when I came to Wisconsin. I was the New Yorker of the New Yorker magazine cartoon whose horizon spanned the Palisades across the Hudson River and not much more. I went to Wisconsin because they invited me and my advisor told me it would be a good place for me and that was all I needed without knowing what "good" meant. It was the right choice by whatever accident it came about. And that right place had an awful lot to do with Bob Tabachnick. He was the person who hired me, who cared over my finding a place in the faculty, encouraged me to intellectually find my place, and who over the years supported me in ways that were extremely important institutionally and intellectually. And I learned a lot about respecting and giving to people from Bob. He was always looking out to make sure that fairness was the rule of living in the department that had no distinction between faculty, staff and students. I think that he succeeded in this in his own way of living. But as important, Bob was instrumental in making the intellectual qualities of openness to competing ideas, and the social and cultural qualities of collegiality and fairness as part of the department's quality of life. And from those early days, Bob and Jeanne were also thought of as my friends.

In different and probably more distant ways I came to know the "other" Bob Kahl over the years. Through doctoral students and other contexts over the years, I came to admire his intellectual and personal integrity and insights.

Chapter 15

FORDHAM AND OGBU MEET MISS RUBY: ACTING WHITE VERSUS ACADEMIC SUCCESS

Marguerite W. Parks
University of Wisconsin Oshkosh
Wisconsin, USA

My teacher's name is Mrs. Ruby and I like my teacher. She is a nice teacher to everyone. Mrs. Ruby is the second and first grade teacher. Mrs. Ruby has 60 children in her class-room. I like my school, too. And I like Mrs. Ruby. Mrs. Ruby is a nice lady. She is the best teacher a black child could have. (Third grade student at Holy Cross-Faith Memorial, May 1991)

INTRODUCTION

Recent events have brought the idea of what it means for African Americans to "Act White" back to the forefront. Bill Cosby raised the issues when he recently spoke at Jesse Jackson's 33rd Annual Rainbow/PUSH Coalition. It was central again in the keynote address at the 2004 Democratic National Convention when Illinois Senate candidate Barak Obama approached the same ideas but with a different tact. Few, however, have examined the issue to the extent of John Ogbu and Signithia Fordham.

Looking at the large educational picture of the academic success of African Americans, the issues seem insurmountable in today's society. But when we look at individual teachers who uphold high expectations of their students, both academically and morally, children of color in today's schools can achieve academic success. This paper looks at one such teacher; one amazing woman who for 64 years told her students that academic success was just that, academic success, not "acting white."

Mrs. Ruby Middleton Forsythe (Miss Ruby)[1] was an African American educator whose teaching career spanned 64 years. Trained to teach during a time when few African Americans received any formal education, Miss Ruby remained an educator until cancer claimed her in May of 1992. Over a period of two years, I was fortunate to spend six weeks in

---

[1] As was common in the South the term "Miss" was used as a sign of respect. Throughout the time I knew Mrs. Forsythe, everyone called her "Miss Ruby." Therefore, throughout the paper, this is the title used.

Miss Ruby's school, Holy Cross-Faith Memorial School at Pawleys Island, South Carolina. While there I observed, assisted, taught and learned more about being a teacher than my years in an inner city high school ever taught me.[2] The focus of this paper, however, is specifically on what I learned from Miss Ruby about the issue of "Acting White" and why this issue was never present in her school.

FORDHAM AND OGBU

According to Fordham and Ogbu (1986) "...one major reason black students do poorly in school is that they experience inordinate ambivalence and affective dissonance in regards to academic effort and success" (p. 177). They continue this argument by saying the poor school performance of African Americans is partially the result of whites assumptions of black intellect and black doubts of academic capabilities. The result is the definition of "academic success" as something white people do and that African Americans who strive for academic success are trying to be like white people, or "Acting White (1986)." This theory has come under attack by some, so a close examination of Miss Ruby's school, teaching methodology and moral expectations of her students serves to further the discussion. This paper will examine the absence of "acting white" at Miss Ruby's school and its relationship to her students' academic success.

A major component of the acting white theory of Fordham and Ogbu revolves around the difference between immigrant minorities and castelike minorities (1986). According to Fordham and Ogbu, the difference between the two groups and their experiences has an enormous impact on how each view schooling and the ability of the educational system to be a source of success:

> ...*immigrant minorities*, [sic] came to America more or less voluntarily with the expectation of improving their economic, political, and social status, and subordinate or *castelike minorities* who were involuntarily and permanently incorporated into American society through slavery or conquest. (Fordham and Ogbu, 1986, p. 178)

The major difference arising between these two groups is immigrant minorities see the structure of society as welcoming and an opportunity to get ahead. Castelike minorities, however, view society as discriminatory and oppressive because historically this has been their experience.

When the theory is expanded to include the educational system, Fordham and Ogbu claim that within the ecological structure of African Americans, three things happen: 1) black Americans have "been provided with substandard schooling, based on white Americans perceptions of the educational needs of black Americans (Ogbu and Fordham, 1986, p. 179), 2) black Americans face a job ceiling and 3) "in response to substandard schooling and barriers in the adult opportunity structure, black Americans developed several survival strategies and other 'coping mechanisms'" (Ogbu and Fordham, 1986, p. 179). Because of the presence of this ecological structure, African Americans form a collective identity which is in

---

[2] The complete research can be found in the PhD dissertation of Dr. Marguerite W. Parks on file at the University of Iowa, Iowa City, IA.

opposition to the dominate culture. Part of this collective identity for adolescents is the perception of academic success as part of the white domain:

> School learning is therefore consciously or unconsciously perceived as a subtractive process: a minority person who learns successfully in school or who follows the standard practices of the school is perceived as becoming acculturated into the white American cultural frame of reference at the expense of the minorities' cultural frame of reference and collective welfare. (Fordham and Ogbu, 1986. p. 183)

IDENTITY

Working with adolescents one has to recognize the importance of peer pressure and the misperceptions adolescents attach to what is "in". Adolescents believe there is either a right or a wrong. Adolescents see only the right hair, the right clothes, the right language and the right friends. The issue of group identity versus individual identity becomes paramount in the child's mind. According to Beverly Tatum (2003) people of color do not have the luxury in America of choosing their group, because society does it for them:

> Why do Black youths, in particular, think about themselves in terms of race? Because that is how the rest of the world thinks of them. Our self-perceptions are shaped by the messages we receive from those around us, and when young Black men and women enter adolescence, the racial content of those messages intensifies. (p 53-53)

These ideals are closely associated with the idea of "fictive kinship." Fictive kinship refers to "a kinshiplike relationship between persons not related by blood or marriage in a society, but who have some reciprocal social or economic relationship (Fordham and Ogbu, 1986 p 183)." The concept of fictive kinship can be found in all cultures, but in American society it is especially present in African American youth as they move through identity development. Identity development for adolescents places a high loyalty on membership in a group. The stakes are raised, however, when the group identity impacts on academic success, as is being argued by Fordham and Ogbu.

At his keynote address to the Democratic National Convention, Barack Obama stated: "... children can't achieve unless we raise their expectations and eradicate the slander that says a black youth with a book is acting white" (http://www.wahingtonpost.com/wp-dyn/articles/A19751-2004Jul27html). Overcoming adolescents' misperception is at the heart of the issue. It can be done in many ways; by role models, by getting people of color into the media, by publishing books by people of color about people of color and encouraging everyone to read them. It can be accomplished by presenting facts as Henry Louis Gates did in his editorial response to Obama when he stated:

> Reality check: according to the 2000 census, there were more than 31,000 black physicians and surgeons, 33,000 black lawyers and 5,000 black dentists. Guess how many black athletes are playing professional basketball, football and baseball combined. About 1,400. In fact, there are more board-certified black cardiologist than there are black professional basketball players (*The New York Times,* August 1, 2004).

The major questions arising from all of this are 1) does eliminating the idea of acting white happen when you remove the three major blocks of the ecological structure presented by Fordham and Ogbu, 2) if the three major blocks presented by Fordham and Ogbu are not there, is academic success possible? and 3) is this what happened at Holy Cross-Faith Memorial School.

HOLY CROSS-FAITH MEMORIAL

Holy Cross-Faith Memorial was an all-black school within the grounds of Camp Baskerville, an Episcopal outreach facility at Pawleys Island, South Carolina. The relationship between Holy Cross-Faith Memorial and the Episcopal Church used to be quite strong, but in recent years the school functioned on a mostly independent level. When Miss Ruby first began at Holy Cross-Faith Memorial in 1937, there were three teachers who taught grades preschool through 11th grade, a terminal grade in South Carolina at that time. The Reverend Forsythe[3] taught the upper grades, Miss Ruby taught the middle grades and Mrs. Motry Martin taught the lower grades. During this time the academic curriculum at Holy Cross-Faith Memorial followed the strong academic philosophy of Avery Normal Institute where Miss Ruby received her teacher certification (Drago, 1990). When school desegregation occurred in the area, Mrs. Martin left to join the public school system. The Reverend died in 1974 and the diocese discussed closing the school but the parents fought to keep the school open. The grades dropped to eighth and "a gentleman" came to help. When he left after a year or two (both times were mentioned by Miss Ruby) Miss Ruby kept the school open for preschoolers, or "The Little Ones," (4year olds) through 4th grade only. This is how the school remained until Miss Ruby's death. Following her death, parents, community members and alums tried to keep the school open, but it closed after a few years.

MISS RUBY'S CURRICULUM

> ...allright. What will that education do for you? The reason why you are in school? Education is suppose to teach us how to live, how to do, and how to help us in ourselves. Every girl and boy today should have a self-esteem, o.k., if you don't go to school day by day, and try to get everything that your teachers are telling you, for your own good, for the future, you are going to be worse than the people who were in slavery, that sounds bad doesn't it...[4]

The academic curriculum at Holy Cross-Faith Memorial reminds one of what has become known as the "old classic curriculum." According to Larry Cuban, children learned "fundamental verbal, writing, reading and mathematics skills" in both rural and urban schools at the turn of the century (Cuban, 1984, p. 198). Students at Holy Cross-Faith Memorial had several "dominant" subjects. "Math, we do Math everyday, all right, now, everyday, They got

---

[3] Reverend William Forsythe was an Episcopalian minister and Miss Ruby's husband who she always referred to as "The Reverend." According to the Bishop Payne Library Archives now held by Virginia Theological Seminary, William Forsythe graduated from Bishop Payne Divinity School in 1925.

[4] Recorded by author during a talk Miss Ruby gave a visiting middle school.

to know their multiplication, yes sir, everyday.[5]" Reading was only four days, but "English" was taught separately. English appeared on the curriculum for two days and consisted of grammar worksheets and grammar books. Spelling was taught on Mondays, Tuesdays and Fridays. Once a week students studied science, social studies, health and "Bible." The fourth graders also studied Black History on Fridays. In addition, two community volunteers taught singing and music and the older students learned to play the recorder. In the schools early years, the Reverend also taught students Latin, Greek, Trigonometry and Calculus.

Miss Ruby seriously viewed her role as a teacher and the teacher as a professional. One can see this philosophy reflected in the training she received at Avery Institute under Benjamin Cox. The philosophy of "social uplift" present at Avery Institute during the "Gilded Age" of the school was continued during the tenure of Benjamin Cox. (Drago, 1990. p 172). Miss Ruby attended Avery during the Cox Era and the school's educational philosophy dominated her teaching. Cox attempted to "mold his students into cultured, learned, and responsive citizens who would involve themselves in the community and serve as examples to their members" (Drago, 1990. p 139). In addition to high academic standards, Miss Ruby emphasized the development of the entire student. Her school centered on academics, building self-esteem, responsibility, understanding self-worth, and the importance of community outreach:

> The most important thing for any child before they can accomplish anything, they are going to have to discipline themselves. And from that disciplining themselves, they are going to have to begin feeling, have a feeling about themselves that they can. That's the next thing. Nothing will be accomplished if that child doesn't have that feeling – "I can."

The idea of "Never say I can't, Always say I'll try" was the guiding philosophy of Miss Ruby's teachings. She felt students needed to believe in themselves in order to be successful in schools:

> But as long as they are nobody, I tell them, you are all nobody now, some of you are dependent on someone else to do for you. When you get to the place when you can depend on yourself, then that makes a difference. (Miss Ruby in an interview with Carol Hanley, 1990)

Miss Ruby modeled, taught and required high standards of behavior and academic excellence from her students at all times.

Defining academic success is a difficult task. Defining successful teaching is just as difficult because everyone has a different idea of what equals "success." To define academic success at Holy Cross-Faith Memorial time was spent with Miss Ruby going over all of the graduation programs from 1937 to 1990. Of the students Miss Ruby could trace, all of them had either graduated from high school or received their GED. Some were still in school and some she did not have information on. Many had become doctors, ministers, nurses, and teachers. One young woman had recently entered The Air Force Academy, and one graduate of the school was a Bishop. Many of their children and grandchildren were enrolled at the school when I was there. The teaching assistant, Mrs. Wallace was a graduate of the school and a grandparent of several of the students. Even though the information gathered from Miss

---

[5] All quotes from Miss Ruby are from personal interviews conducted by the author in 1990 and 1991 unless otherwise noted. Many of the quotes can be found in the original dissertation research.

Ruby is not statistically comparable, there is obviously a difference in the academic success of the students from Holy Cross-Faith Memorial and the 55 percent nation wide graduation rate of African American children (Holland, *www.heartland.org*).

ADDRESSING 'ACTING WHITE' AT HOLY-CROSS FAITH MEMORIAL

The relationship between Fordham and Ogbu and the Fordham and Ogbu research on Acting White (1986) and Miss Ruby and her educational philosophy is a strong one. By eliminating the three major parts of the ecological structure presented by Fordham and Ogbu, substandard schooling, job ceilings and coping strategies, Miss Ruby created an environment where academic success was associated with just that, academic success. African American students at Holy-Cross never viewed education as acting white and were allowed to value education for the future it provides for all students.

SUBSTANDARD SCHOOLING

According to Fordham and Ogbu (1986) the first structural barrier to the academic success of African American children is the historically substandard schooling present in segregated schools. In *The Education of Blacks in the South, 1860-1935,* James Anderson presents the history of African Americans' education, and the philosophical struggle of the Hampton-Tuskegee model and the ideals of W.E.B. Dubois (1988). The Hampton-Tuskegee model supported vocational training for African Americans. In contrast, W.E.B. DuBois called for the same academic liberal arts education provided to White America. Teacher training institutes also reflected different educational philosophies. Normal schools at that time had an increased academic emphasis for teacher training. Anderson states that:

> During the early twentieth century states began to require a high school diploma for admission to the normal schools. This step automatically put the normal schools on the college level and led to higher academic and professional standards for training teachers (p. 113).

As a graduate of Avery Normal School in Charleston, South Carolina Miss Ruby was educated in the liberal arts philosophy of W.E.B. Dubois. She entered Avery after completing the 6th grade at a private Quaker school. The curriculum of Avery at that time shows she most likely studied Economics, Languages, Methods of Teaching, Literature, Mathematics, School Management, Natural Philosophy and Physiology (Drago, 1990). She also claimed to have sung in the choir, performed in Shakespearian presentations and played volleyball and basketball. Although I never spoke with Miss Ruby about the specifics of the education of Reverend Forsythe, Miss Ruby did mention he taught Greek, Latin, Calculus, Trigonometry, Algebra and Physics to the older students. Also, when I spoke with older members of the community commented "ditch diggers" in the area would speak to in Latin or Greek because they had attended Holy Cross-Faith Memorial. The result of this is that substandard schooling was never an issue at Holy Cross-Faith Memorial. The education of the students at the school until its close remained a rigorous academic curriculum with high expectations. The curriculum and text used when I visited the school in 1990 and 1991 followed state requirements and when recent students entered the public system in the 5th grade their performance, according to Miss Ruby, was standard or above standard.

A JOB CEILING

The second structural barrier impeding the success of African American children according to Fordham and Ogbu is the issue of a perceived job ceiling. Similar to the idea of a "glass ceiling" when discussing gender issues, the job ceiling implies that:

> even when they [African Americans] achieved in school in the past, i.e. had good educational credentials, they were not necessarily given access to jobs, wages, and other benefits commensurate with their academic accomplishments." (Fordham and Ogbu, 1986 p. 179)

One thing Miss Ruby stressed over and over again to her students was that they could be anything they wanted to be:

> There's a group that's waiting to see whether they can turn you this way instead of that. And it's easier to fall this way than it is to fall the other way. Every one of you should have an aim, say, to yourself, what do I want to do? Who am I? I am somebody. There is nobody here exactly like you, I told these boys and girls the other day. But if you don't have an aim, or you're not looking out there for something, you ain't going to find it, but don't blame a soul but yourselves, all right, you listen girls and boys, cause there's a hard world waiting out there, for you and if you are going through school you got to try to get what these teachers are telling you, you got to feel and think that you are somebody to do something, an you got to try. The more you try, the higher you climb. But when you say "I can't," you put a big block right there and you are giving your brains and your mind to somebody else.[6]

The process Miss Ruby used to push her students to excel at anything they wanted is similar to the ideas of Janie Ward when she talks about "raising resisters (1996)." The idea presented by Ward (1996) is that "Healthy psychological resistance fostered through a liberating truth telling has a transformative quality. It helps children to grow strong as a resister on the individual level and empowered by their sense of belonging to a group whose very survival has been dependent upon the collective ability to resist (pg 97)." This philosophy was prominent at Holy Cross-Faith Memorial.

Miss Ruby talked to her students about what they would face in "the outside world." She worked hard at teaching them how to rely on themselves while still participating in community activities. She pushed them to be proud of their academic success and "the journey it took" to get there. She discussed issues they were going to face as African Americans and how people would treat them because of the color of their skin. She told them to "stand up" for themselves and what they believed in. And over and over again, I heard her tell the students they could be anything they wanted as long as they worked hard. Students at Holy Cross-Faith Memorial never envisioned a job ceiling, because Miss Ruby never allowed

---

[6] Recorded by author during a talk Miss Ruby gave a visiting middle school.

them to believe it existed. Miss Ruby held up alumni of the school as role models for the students by continually sharing their stories of success.

ACTING WHITE AND ELIMINATING COPING STRATEGIES

According to Miss Ruby, students at Holy Cross-Faith Memorial had a distinct advantage over public school students in that their school was a private, all black school. The private school issue gave Miss Ruby a control over her students the public school system did not allow. Because the school was private and all-black, Miss Ruby was able to create an environment supportive of African American history and culture. The presence of these two aspects also allowed an atmosphere where eliminating the issue of acting white becomes more possible.

Holy Cross-Faith Memorial started during the time of segregated schools. Miss Ruby claimed she and The Reverend stayed at Holy Cross-Faith Memorial following desegregation because transferring meant giving up some control of the school. Miss Ruby also told me she felt desegregation harmed the African American community because they lost their leaders. According to Miss Ruby, when the black students went to the white schools they became followers. She felt her students, because they were in an all-black school, had "a sense of themselves as Negroes" before they entered the public schools.

The opportunity for students at Holy Cross-Faith Memorial to create a sense of collective identity not interfered with by the white community becomes essential to avoid "acting white." According to Fordham and Ogbu "subordinate minorities also develop an oppositional cultural frame of reference which includes devices for protecting their identity and for maintaining boundaries between them and white Americans" (1986, p. 181). Circumstances at Holy Cross-Faith Memorial and Miss Ruby's teaching philosophy made possible the elimination of this oppositional cultural frame of reference. Fordham and Ogbu go on to say that:

> Thus subordinate minorities regard certain forms of behaviors and certain activities or events, symbols, and meanings as not appropriate for them because those behaviors, events, symbols, and meanings are characteristics of white Americans. At the same time they emphasize other forms of behaviors and other events, symbols, and meanings as more appropriate for them because these are not a part of white Americans' way of life. (Fordham and Ogbu, 1986 p. 181)

In his address before Jesse Jackson's 33rd Annual Rainbow/PUSH Coalition conference in Chicago this summer, Bill Cosby questioned several behaviors of African American youth. In his talk he addressed their language, their reading and writing skills, their lack of value of education, and their lack of self-respect. Looking at the attitudes identified by Fordham and Ogbu as "Acting White" several of the issues presented by Cosby appear. The major issue discussed by Fordham and Ogbu is that black students who pursue academic success are seen by other African Americans as being "braniacs," "oreos," "wannabees," and as "Acting White."

Long before I read my first article by John Ogbu I experienced this phenomena in the classroom. As a white high school teacher in a predominately black inner city high school I heard my students using these terms but never understood them. I watched students tease those who were academically successful and talk about them behind their backs. I watched smart students purposefully not participate or study, and wondered why. One of my drama students wore penny loafers and a madras plaid shirt one day and was consistently harassed for being a "preppy white guy." The next day, he was in baggy jeans with a hairpick in his Afro, and an attitude towards me I had not seen before. The attitudes and behaviors identified by Fordham and Ogbu shed light on what happened. My student adapted "coping strategies" to fit in, to be one of the brothers and to not be associated with the established system, me. Fictive kinship became more important than academic success.

Some of the coping strategies, or attitudes and behaviors, identified by Fordham and Ogbu as white are: speaking standard English, spending a lot of time in the library studying, working hard to get good grades in school, getting good grades in school and being on time (Fordham and Ogbu, 1986 p. 186). Although these are just a few of the coping strategies, they show a direct link to a student's ability to be academically successful in school. These particular strategies were also chosen because of their strong link to Holy Cross-Faith Memorial. Looking closely at Holy Cross-Faith Memorial and the methodology and philosophy implemented by Miss Ruby, one can see that the issues listed by Fordham and Ogbu are not present because Miss Ruby never associated those behaviors with "acting white." She associated them with responsibility, self-respect and a desire to succeed in life.

Holy Cross-Faith Memorial started every morning at 9:00 A.M. Students were expected to be in their seats and ready when Miss Ruby started class. Although there was not a formal dress code, students were required to be neat, shirt tails were to be tucked in, shoe laces tied, girls in dresses, and no "Christmas trees"(Miss Ruby's name for hair with a lot of beads and barrettes) were allowed in girls' hair. Since only some classes occurred on certain days and the students did not have lockers, it was expected they would remember what was due and have with them the books required for that particular day. If they did not have either their homework or their books they would be disciplined. One day I loaned some students pencils and Miss Ruby took them all back. She felt this was all part of teaching the students responsibility. She did not view completing work or being on time as "White," she saw it as being responsible. She passed these ideas on to her students.

Upon arrival, students would stand by their chairs and recite their prayers, including one of five memorized psalms, kneel for the Lord's Prayer and then "Get to Work." Students were required to have their homework neatly finished. They were expected to be prepared. If she had assigned reading, the child should be ready to read it out loud to her. They should not stumble or pause, the reading should be practiced. That was part of homework, and Miss Ruby expected it to be right. She did not expect it because it was "white," she expected it because it was what was needed to be successful. If the child's work was not complete or prepared, Miss Ruby did not grade it down, she sent it back to be completed correctly. Students were going to do their work until it was done right. She did not accept "adequate," it had to be right.

Throughout the day, Miss Ruby expected students to be attentive, responsible, hard-working students. Academically she expected them to be high achievers. She recognized not all of the students were going to be straight A students, but throughout the day you could see her pushing each and every child to perform at the highest level they were capable of. Many lessons were individualized to the child's level, reading levels varied, spelling lists were different, but all were challenging for the individual child. When students completed their work early you could hear them practicing their multiplication tables. They were constantly challenging themselves and each other.

These expectations were not only in academics, but in personal behavior. Students were expected to use Standard English, address each other with full names (no nicknames) and to use Please, Thank you, Excuse me, and Ma'am and Sir to visitors. Miss Ruby was very particular on behavior and language. She viewed this as a sign of self-respect as well as respect of others. Students who used a "bad" word would get "the bottle:"

> I got a little mixture here that I keep in a bottle and I put it in their mouths and make them hold it there until it starts bubbling. It's nothing but peroxide, Listerine and water, but they think they're going to die. That peroxide starts working with that water and then all these white bubbles start coming down and I won't let them spit it out! They start crying right off as soon as they see me getting the bottle. That'll cure all bad languages. (Lanker, 1989)

Listening to Miss Ruby tell stories of her expectations of students and her methods one can see the twinkle in her eye. She obviously loved working with children, but demanded high expectations. Once again, none of these behaviors were expected because there was a link to white behavior, but because Miss Ruby wanted her students to act in a manner she felt all people should act. She stressed studying hard, responsibility and discipline. At Holy Cross-Faith Memorial students strove to *be* the top students, not to ridicule them.

Miss Ruby felt parents were an integral part of the child's education and that they learned their behavior from their parents. At Holy Cross-Faith Memorial parents were required to be involved in their children's education. Miss Ruby expected them to be as responsible as the students. Miss Ruby eliminated the coping strategies presented by Fordham and Ogbu by stressing, hard work, responsibility, self-reliance and by requiring high expectations academically and morally of both parents and students. Sharing one of her favorite stories shows her expectations for her students, their parents and the community:

So she came here to see me one day, she had one small one she wanted to register. "Miss Ruby can you take my child?" I said, "How old is it? "Oh, be five soon." And I said, "Well, mam, " I didn't know if it was a girl or a boy – so I said, "Well what do you do?" That be the question I asked her, and she looked at me as much as to say you fool – that's right – "What do you do?" "I don't do nothing. I don't have to work, I get my check the first of the month." I said, "Well, honey, everybody here has to work, I sure can't take your child," I told her. She asked me the other night, "Miss Ruby, you think you can take my child next year?" I said, "I don't know about that," I said, "We still have to work here." I said, "Parents have to work, they have to keep the building clean, take their turns, they have to come here, scrub those toilets that their children use, "I said, "But you said you don't have to work, so you don't belong here." She lets the welfare check come. She has those five children, and you see she's getting a good welfare check, and she asked me as much as to say, you fool, what I'm gonna work for, I get my check the first of the month. You see, well you see, I don't believe in that. The littlest one come here they gonna do something if they have to scratch on a piece of paper. Like me, I can't understand what some of them gonna do, but they scratch, and they gonna give me that paper before they go in the yard. Understand, as little as they are, you wouldn't understand what they write, it could be one or two, but, down in this little group, but they're gonna scratch it. So if she doesn't have to work, everybody here has to work, her child doesn't belong here – um, um. If they's willing to take responsibility and our help, I take their children. But you see, the full responsibility of the student is on us.

CONCLUSIONS

Miss Ruby felt the three areas of Ogbu's ecological structure were pertinent to her school. We spent an afternoon talking about the theory and its impact on African American children. Miss Ruby did not believe the areas were present at Holy Cross-Faith Memorial. She acknowledged, however, that as a private school she had more control and was able to eliminate the issues easier. She stressed the importance of her students having a sense of themselves as African Americans and as scholars. She did not say that being in an all-black school eliminated the problems proposed by Ogbu's theory but she did feel that in her school the students did not adopt the strategies presented. She felt strongly that the school should remain segregated. When we discussed the idea of "acting white" she felt too many African American children misinterpreted the behaviors she felt were simply behaviors everyone needed to be successful. She strongly believed in the power of education to "lift up her people."

Looking closely at Holy Cross-Faith Memorial one can see the three areas of Fordham and Ogbu's theory are not present. Historically the school never provided "substandard schooling," but had a highly rigorous academic program that persisted throughout the years. Students at Holy Cross-Faith Memorial did not perceive a job ceiling because the role models who graduated from the school show success in college and the workforce is possible. And students at Holy Cross-Faith Memorial do not view academic success as "acting white" but as a goal to strive for personal fulfillment. At Holy Cross-Faith Memorial there is a presence of academic success. It is the presence of this academic success that draws one to take a closer look at Mrs. Ruby Middleton Forsythe. It is the belief of this author that if one looks closely at any program where students of color are academically successful such as Marva Collins or Jamie Escalante or any one of the incredible teachers currently working in the school system, one will find the presence of these three areas to be virtually nonexistent.

Martin Haberman, in his article, *The Ideology of Star Teacher of Children of Poverty*, says "Stars are different from other teachers in that they are aware of the connection between their behavior and their ideology, and they accept this challenge because they believe the purpose of schooling is to form good people who are knowledgeable (Haberman, 1992 p. 126). This was the guiding philosophy of Miss Ruby, to form intelligent, responsible, good people who achieved, not because it was white, but because in order to be a successful person, these are the skill one needs. She did not associate academic success with "acting white," and she did not associate behavior with "acting white." They were "acting right" (Auten, n.d.). The result? A teacher who achieved what all teachers want to achieve; academic and personal success for over half a century of students:

> Once they feel that they can do, it starts building something, by doing it and being encouraged, then, that child gets a joy, and it makes him try to do a little better each time. He climbs. He climbs…I always tell my children, "Never say 'I can't,' always say 'I'll try." So that's what I believe in.

REFERENCES

Anderson, J.D. (1988). *The education of black in the south; 1860-1935.* Chapel Hill: The University of North Carolina Press.

Auten, R. (n.d.). Acting Right, Not White. *The Austin Chronicle.* Retrieved September 9, 2004 from http://www.austinchronicle.com/issues/vol17/issue10/pols.tales.html

Comer, J. P. (1988). Education poor minority children. *Scientific American,* 259,(5). pp. 42-48.

Cuban, L. (1984). *How teachers taught: Constancy and change in American classrooms 1890-1980.* White Plains: Longman Inc.

Drago, E.L. (1990). *Initiative, paternalism, and race relations: Charleston's Avery Normal Institute.* Athens: The University of Georgia Press.

Escalante, J. & Dirmann, J. (1990). The Jamie Escalante math program. *The Journal of Negro Education,* 59(3), pp. 407-423.

Fordham, S. (1996). *Blacked out: Dilemmas of race, identity, and success at Capital High.* Chicago: University of Chicago Press.

Fordham, S. (1988). Racelessness as a factor of Black studetnt's school success: Pragmatic strategy or Pyrrhic victory? Harvard Educational Review 58(1). pp. 54-84.

Fordham, S. & Ogbu, J.U. (1986). Black students' school success: Coping with the "Burden of 'Acting White.'" *The Urban Review,* 18(3), pp. 176-206.

Gates, H.L. (2004, August 1). Breaking the silence; [Op-Ed]. *The New York Times.* (Late Edition (East Coast)) pg. 4.11.

Haberman, M. (1992). The ideology of star teachers of children of poverty. *Educational Horizons,* 70(3), pp. 125-129.

Hanley, C. (1990-1991) Personal interviews with Mrs. Ruby Middleton Forsythe.

Helms, J.E. (1990). *Black and White racial identity: Theory, research, and practice.* Praeger: Westport, Connecticut.

Holland, R. (January 1, 2003). High School Crisis: 3 in 10 Drop Out. *School Reform News.* The Heartland Institute.

Lanker, B. &Summers, B. (1989). (Ed.). *I dream a world: Portraits of black women who changed America.* New York: Stewart, Tabori & Chang.

Morano, M. (2004, July 2). Bill Cosby to Blacks: Stop blaming 'the white man.' *CNSNews.com.* Retrieved September 20, 2004 from http://www.cnsnews.com

Obama, B. (2004, July 27). Transcript: Illinois Sentate Candidate Barack Obama. *Washington Post.* Retrieved September 21, 2004, from http://www.washingtonpost.com

Ogbu, J.U. (1974). *The next generation: An ethnography of education in an urban neighborhood.* New York: Academic Press.

Ogbu, J.U. (1978). *Minority education and caste.* New York: Academic Press.

Ogbu, J.U. (1983). Cultural discontinuities. *Anthropology & Education Quarterly,* 13(4), pp. 290-305.

Ogbu, J.U. (1990). Literacy and schooling in subordinate cultures: The case of Black Americans. In K Lomotey (Ed.). *Going to school: The African-American experience.* New York: Albany, pp. 103-112.

Parks, M.W. (1993). *Miss Ruby: An island in the sun.* Unpublished doctoral dissertation, University of Iowa: Iowa City, Iowa

Tamarkin, C. & Collins, M. (1991). *Marva Collins' way.* (2 ed.). Los Angeles: Jeremy P. Tarcher.

Tatum, B.D. (1997). *"Why are all the black kids sitting together in the cafeteria?" and other conversations about race.* Basic Books: New York.

Ward, J.V. (1996). "Raising resisters: The role of truth telling in the psychological development of African-American girls," in B.J.R. Leadbeater and N.Way (Eds.), *Urban girls, Resisting stereotypes, Creating identities.* New York: New York University Press.

In: Current Discourse on Education in Developing Nations
Editors: M. Afolayan, D. Jules et al. pp. 237-255
ISBN 1-59454-774-2
© 2006 Nova Science Publishers, Inc.

Chapter 16

TAKING AMERICAN STUDENTS FOR A CULTURAL PLUNGE INTO JAPAN AND AVOIDING THE TOURIST EXPERIENCE & RETURNING TO JAPAN: INITIAL CULTURAL CHALLENGES

Scott Johnston
Osaka Jogakuin College, Osaka, Japan

INTRODUCTION

This chapter examines two instances of cultural immersion into Japanese culture. In the first, U.S. college students experience Japan in a 3-week program, and in the second the author reflects on his cultural challenges on returning to live and teach in Japan about two years after leading the group of students to Japan. One examines how others respond to a different culture while the second considers how the author himself reacts to initial cultural challenges and how these challenges, while initially stressfull, soon are all but forgotten.

PART I: TAKING AMERICAN STUDENTS FOR A CULTURAL PLUNGE INTO JAPAN AND AVOIDING THE TOURIST EXPERIENCE

"How can a 3-week program in Japan become an opportunity for students to develop cultural sensitivity towards the Japanese people and their culture and not be a mere tourist jaunt?" This was the question that I asked myself while developing an undergraduate course for a college's short-term overseas program. In this program, faculty members utilize their individual expertise and create off-campus experiences for students. I developed a course for ten participants, which included a semester of meetings followed by a three-week immersion in Japan during May 2002. I endeavored to avoid the overseas "tourist" experience in which programs often reinforce stereotypes and view the people in the country as THEM. This stereotyping, I believe, is more common in developing countries or in countries such as Japan, where the language and lifestyles are quite different from that of western countries. The course immersed the students in homestays, school visits and interactions with Japanese college students. This chapter examines the three-week immersion aspect of the course in Japan and in what ways the participants' beliefs changed. Did they become more culturally sensitive? If so, what is it that they learned?

Calls for providing students and new teachers with more global perspectives are increasing (Anderson, Nicklas, and Crawford, 1994; McFadden, Merryfield, and Barron, 1997; Merryfield, 2000). One way to challenge students to develop multiple perspectives is to create experiential opportunities. McFadden and others (1997, p. 17) say:

> Opportunities for sustained cross-cultural experiences and ongoing reflection should be integrated in teacher education for the demonstration and implementation of goals of multicultural and global and international education.

Cross-cultural encounters are viewed as means of supporting students to develop multicultural and global competencies. Tran, Young and DiLella (1994) found that opportunities of cultural immersion were conducive to students rethinking stereotypes. The word "cultural plunges" described these opportunities (Wade, 2000, p. 21). Short-term courses abroad are one type of cultural plunge. However, merely taking students overseas will not necessarily challenge their biases, stereotypes, and views towards people in that country. Students need to step outside their comfort zones in order to challenge their long held beliefs concerning schooling, culture, and the world. They need to "reposition their perspectives" (Sleeter, 1995) so that they become culturally sensitive. Sleeter says, "Repositioning one's perspective requires recognizing that one is situated in an unequal context, and one's perspective grows partially out of one's situation" (p. 417). Repositioning perspectives may lead to becoming more culturally sensitive to others in a social context where the "other" is the cultural expert. Preservice students need to challenge their own beliefs about why people act the way they do, and they need to try to see the world from the other's perspective(s). In this way, the students are actively involved in the process of knowledge construction (Sleeter, 1995). Sleeter adds:

> This is different from having students write traditional papers; papers are usually private experiences students share only with the teacher and require students to seek published knowledge from 'experts' rather than actually creating their own interpretations (p. 431).

By being involved in constructing knowledge of other groups, students learn from each other and the people in that community. What they are learning is more than what a teacher could present in a classroom. The three-week course immersed students in life in Japan through homestays, interaction with Japanese college students, and visits to Japanese schools. Through the numerous experiences in Japan and reflecting on those experiences, they had opportunities to construct knowledge of Japan and reposition their perspectives about the people and society.

Data-Sources, Methods, and Limitations

The large question posed was: How did the students make sense of the cultural experience? Because the nature of the question pursued the students' own beliefs and perceptions, open-ended qualitative research tools were used (Miles and Huberman, 1994). While in Japan, the students talked about the cultural plunge in focus groups. They also gave speeches on critical episodes at the Japanese college to students and staff that were videotaped. The students wrote final papers on key learning experiences in Japan after returning to the U.S. Finally, in September they answered a survey about the May experience. The videotapes, focus groups, final papers and surveys were analyzed for key themes. Some of the students were then contacted to discuss these preliminary results, in order to determine if my analysis seemed to fit with their own perceptions of the experience. In addition, most of the results were self-reported, and thus described the participants' perceived influences. Thus, though the results of this paper cannot be generalized to any other short-term overseas program and their participants, this description of the Japanese experience can help educators understand how students respond to cultural plunges and how they might benefit from such experiences.

Course and Context

The program was composed of a semester long pre-departure course and three-weeks in Japan. In the pre-departure course, students gained some practical use of the language, and they studied the education and culture(s) of Japan. This was accomplished through readings, discussions, and watching videos. The Japan component included visiting school and work sites, three-week home stays, visits to historical sites, and a link to a Japanese college. Homestays allowed students to develop an understanding of one Japanese family's life through becoming a member for a short period. These homestays were arranged though a Japanese colleague at a Japanese college. Through this arrangement, the students had access to a classroom, computers, seminar house and Japanese college students. Following is a brief overview of the activities the students were engaged in during the plunge into Japanese life. This is necessary to understand the context of the students' immersions as they began to reposition their perspectives.

In Japan, we rode on public transportation or walked to schools and work places in the Yokohama area. We visited one preschool, a public elementary school, a public middle school, a public high school, a private girls' high school, an international school in Yokohama, as well as classes at a Japanese college. On our first day in Japan, still struggling with jet lag, we visited a preschool and watched the children play outside for over an hour. They were swinging on bars, chasing each other, falling down, scrapping knees, and resuming chases. The students enjoyed interacting with children, but the students' facial expressions revealed their shock at the roughhousing of the children. After all, according to many U.S. media reports, Japanese children should already be overwhelmed with their academic studies. And what about the legal concerns about swings and falling? After a group discussion about Japanese preschools and the social context, it was obvious that, even struggling with jet lag, the students were already recognizing that schooling and views about what occur in schools were both similar and different from their expectations.

In the elementary, junior high and senior high visits, the principals often divided us into two groups, and we observed two or three different subjects. In the public elementary school, one group visited a mathematics class. Three students were at the board working out solutions to questions while other students had their hands flailing in the air trying to get the teacher's attention. In the public junior high school, we first went to a special education classroom of three students. They sang a song to us in English, after only one month studying English at the school.

The public high school's classes were much more structured with the teacher standing in the front and directing all learning. In one English class, the teacher even apologized to us, the visitors, that he was teaching grammar because it was required!

At the private girls' high school, there was more interaction going on in the English class. Students were actively answering questions. The homeroom class was particularly enlightening because the girls led a discussion about the teachers. This was the beginning of the school year (school begins in April in Japan), and students complained about the teaching styles of several teachers. The class secretary was taking notes that would then be passed on to the homeroom teacher. At the international school in Yokohama, the students observed elementary classrooms in which resources were abundant and students were on the floor in groups working on mathematics projects. Hands-on learning in action!

After most of the visits we were able to discuss the school's education with the principal and some teachers. A translator, many times the author, was always available. This was a great opportunity for the U.S. students to learn more about how the administrators and teachers viewed the role of school in educating and socializing students. On our last weekend in Japan, our group and some Japanese college students stayed two nights at the college's seminar house in a resort town about two hours south of Tokyo. Here, the faculty and organizers stepped in the background as the students enjoyed themselves at the beach, playing cards, and just talking. In fact, the students shopped for food and the Japanese and U.S. students took turns cooking the meals at the seminar house. This type of cross-cultural interaction would not have been possible without this close link between colleges. As a result of these numerous interactions, the U.S. students had many opportunities to plunge into Japanese life. While these experiences were positive, the interactions with Japanese were an initial concern for many of the U.S. students.

Students' Concerns About Being Accepted

Before leaving for Japan, I held some concerns about the students' cultural sensitivity to the homestay families and their reaction to not understanding the language around them. In fact, in the students' papers and presentations, they also spoke of fears of fitting in. One student stated in his oral presentation, "When I first came I was a little scared about fitting in, eating food and if I would be accepted." Another student added, "Before coming I was worried about people accepting us and if I would be able to adjust...My host family helped make me comfortable and helped adjust. I not only got to know our host family but the extended family."

Similarities Highlighted

Another student talked about her fears before arriving in Japan and her perspective at the end of the course, "Before we landed in Japan, I was afraid of so many things, of the food, the area, and of course how we as Americans would be accepted in a country so different from ours." She adds:

> I found it extremely interesting to talk to my host family as well as my new Japanese friends and get to know them on a personal level and create special relationships with them. I learned so much about their own beliefs as well as what they want in life. For the most part, we had similar goals and ways toward life.

This student's comments elaborate both on the initial fears and the view at the end of the course that similarities stand out. This was a common theme among the students, developing new perspectives that focused on similarities between their experiences in Japan and those in the U.S. Another girl added, "I came into the country expecting to be awed by all the differences and everything, but I'm going to leave valuing the similarities that I have experienced."

This student interviewed her homestay sister for an assignment, and through this interview, she learned how similar youth in the two countries are:

> Throughout this interview, I began to feel a stronger attachment to Aya and Japan in general. I am going through the same struggles in my life that Aya goes though in hers, and it was astonishing for me to find so many similarities between her and myself. I came to Japan expecting everything to be different from anything that I had ever known, but what I found was that the similarities were so astounding that several times I found myself forgetting I was in Japan.

Another student touched on similarities:

> I was prepared for a world completely different than I am used to. At first I noticed that food, people, phones, smells and customs are very different. But like all the others, we found a home here—very many similarities to our home in America. The same things they do for fun I do at home.

Students also perceived similarities in schools. One student commented in her paper:

> There were many similarities that I noticed with the students that I observed. Before coming into the school system, I was prepared to see students that were very attentive, and involved in the class discussion and lectures. I was surprised to see that the teachers in Japan have the same struggles of keeping the attention of the upper class students.

Another student highlights the purpose of this type of course by saying, "I have seen videos of Japanese schools, but nothing compares to being there and experiencing it for myself. There were differences and likenesses in everything from the physical features of the classroom to the teaching methods."

Developing Self-Confidence

I also discovered that many participants gained self-confidence in traveling overseas. In their speeches, focus group and reports, they espoused how they felt they could go abroad now without the structure of a course. In a report, one student wrote, "I've learned that I can do things that seem scary at first. I also learned that traveling and being in other cultures is something that I want to do again." Another student commented, "I have learned about myself that I can be independent...I have learned that I can do anything that I put my mind to it. I am even considering going back to Japan to study even longer." Most, like the last student, were contemplating future excursions to other countries or Japan again. In fact, two of the students actually completed part of their student teaching in Yokohama during the Fall 2003 semester.

Benefits for the Japanese College

The benefits also accrued at the Japanese college. The Japanese coordinator pointed out that around one hundred Japanese students attended at least one of the activities for the U.S. students, including lectures, discussions, student presentations, school visits, and the overnight retreat. He added, "We have several foreign students who came from other Asian countries on our campus, but there have been no students from English-speaking countries. Therefore, it was a precious opportunity for our college."

A staff member at the college, who put in a great deal of time supporting our group, added, "I was surprised that the students were so sensitive and thoughtful. Through mass media, our Japanese knowledge about America was something different. It comes as a fresh reminder that we are all in the same boat on the earth." This staff member also served as a host family. This 3-week encounter was reshaping her views of American students.

Generalizing Experiences

While this short-term experience did stimulate the students to understand the world from others' perspectives, this also led, in some cases, to the development of new stereotypes. For a couple of students, they now felt that they knew Japan through their interactions with their homestay families and the visits we made to schools and businesses. They were generalizing from their limited experiences with Japanese to all Japanese. For example, one student interviewed her family and noticed that the boys went to college and then acquired jobs, whereas the girls took a somewhat different path. She wrote in her paper, "I have been wondering if it is understood that when women marry, they are to be housewives." This student is drawing on one experience and generalizing to the whole population. Another student found that crime was low in Japan, and after arriving back in the U.S. found statistics to support this idea. However, this student then came to the conclusion that this was due to:

> ... The diversity issue in Japan and the separation in social-income levels. The first issue is that Japan is not a very diverse country. The majority of the people in Japan are Japanese...The Japanese people have a great sense of togetherness and unity. I am not

saying that there is no racial prejudice in Japan, but it is just not as common as in more diverse countries.

This student came to several conclusions about Japan that may just be new stereotypes. Particularly, this student connected limited diversity with a lack of racial prejudice. This view of diversity was based on three-weeks in Yokohama as well as a thinking of diversity only in terms of his concept of "Japanese". While this student has gained more knowledge about Japan and its people, stereotypes have merely been reshaped, not truly transformed.

Thus, though this immersion experience has helped students think about their own thinking, it has not eliminated stereotypes. Yet this type of plunge might be just one step towards gaining a more cultural sensitive perspective. Indeed, a major transformation in beliefs in just three weeks could not be expected.

Is this Cultural Plunge for Everyone?

Students, staff and faculty involved in this Japanese experience gained a greater awareness of similarities between people rather than the differences. The students' cultural plunges put them in a context in which they needed to make sense of the world through interacting with Japanese and connecting this to their own experiences. That many of the students highlighted the similarities and not the differences suggests that they have started the process of renegotiating meaning and developing cultural sensitivity.

Short-term international programs, whether in Japan or other countries, could have very positive impacts on future teachers. Teacher education programs that promote multicultural and global perspectives need to seriously think about such cultural immersions. Many readers may be thinking, "It is too expensive!" This cultural plunge into Japan cost each participant $2300 for the course including homestays, most meals, and international and domestic transportation. While not cheap, it is quite reasonable and such overseas immersions might be created as alternatives for some students.

The key component of such a program is the contact person in Japan. This was a program to help U.S. students begin to understand another country and the people. Thus, it is only fitting to conclude with a quote from one of the students that concisely expresses what many students did take away from this course in Japan: "I told my friends [back in the U.S.] that I went to another country, not another planet."

PART II : RETURNING TO JAPAN: INITIAL CULTURAL CHALLENGES

Notes on Returning to Japan:

As I revise this segment of the chapter, I am sitting in my 10 feet by 9.5 feet study with a typhoon swirling outside and the wind and rain blowing in once in a while. Looking outside, I see trees bent over and water spraying against the window. It is a bit exciting, yet also somewhat scary. At least school was cancelled so I didn't have to take the train to downtown Osaka, with the possibility of finding myself stranded in the city if the trains stopped due to the storm. This is the reality of living in Japan. While I have read about typhoons in Japan and lived through some, at this moment the actual experience is much more overwhelming. Past experiences often loose their immediacy as my typhoon experience will soon fade away. In articles and academic books I read, I assume that the authors also have had such experiences during their research, writing or teaching overseas.

Though published articles can not highlight the typhoons of life abroad, these and our daily encounters help shape how we interpret what we observe. Yet, how often do we consider how we, as visitors, adapt to life in the country where we are carrying out research or teaching? While the researcher/teacher must adapt in any country, there are probably more challenges in developing countries or in countries, such as Japan, where the language and aspects of daily life may be quite different from the home country.

This segment of the chapter highlights some of my initial encounters when moving back to Japan to teach at Osaka Jogakuin College (OJC), a small liberal arts college in February 2004. While I, like many researchers/teachers, have read about the country and known that I must adapt to daily life in order to become a member of that society, both within and outside of schools, the reality of the experiences is more challenging. I found that I was not quite as ready to deal with issues as I had thought I was. This became apparent to me as I struggled to acquire an appropriate visa, find a place to live, move my family, and learn to communicate in culturally appropriate ways with my new neighbors. I realized that other teachers/researchers pursuing international experiences face similar situations. This section of the chapter, drawing on my fresh and emerging memories, presents some of the challenges I faced when first arriving and how I have coped with those challenges after six months.

Cultural Challenges: Expectations and Reality

My return to Japan to teach and live was a re-immersion into Japanese society and education. My framework for examining the initial challenges draws on research into culture shock, coping with stress, and multicultural education. The role of how cross-cultural encounters influence people are most often raised in books on culture shock (Ward, Bochner, & Furnham, 2001). Most theoretical frameworks that examine traveling to another country assume an assimilation perspective over time. Culture shock is used to describe the tensions when moving to a new, unfamiliar area—often a foreign country. Lustig and Koester (2003) suggest, "...culture shock is said to occur when people must deal with a barrage of new perceptual stimuli that are difficult to interpret because the cultural context has changed" (p. 165). The traditional view of culture shock was developed by examining emotional reactions at different points while in the foreign country (Oberg, 1960). In this stage theory there is a honeymoon phase in which the person is excited, followed by a crisis stage in which frustrations arise, then a time of learning, and finally an adjustment stage where the individual is happy again (Ward et al., 2001).

When considering how people react to cultural differences faced abroad, one factor to consider is the type of cultural traveler. Ward et al. (2001) suggest four groups: tourists, sojourners, immigrants, and refugees (p. 19). The sojourners include international students, business people, and teachers, such as myself. According to Ward et al. (2001), "Sojourners voluntarily go abroad for a set period of time that is usually associated with a specific assignment or contract" (p. 21). I was returning to the country where I had lived for ten years. As a "returning sojourner", I faced somewhat different cultural challenges than a person coming to Japan for the first time. Many of my episodes involved an unconscious, "Oh yeah, I remember that now" on my part. The culture shock perspective seemed to deemphasize initial feelings of discomfort or confusion that may not have long-term impact, yet do influence the teacher at those particular moments.

The stress and coping framework, on the other hand, "…highlights the significance of life changes during cross-cultural transitions, the appraisal of these changes, and the selection and implementation of coping strategies to deal with them" (Ward et al., 2001). This view suggests that the sojourner's own past experiences interact with the context of the experiences in the country and that this causes stress which results in the sojourner drawing on coping strategies (Berry, 1997). In this approach, the individual's own experiences and knowledge shape how he/she will respond. This approach also allows for a different response than the typical culture shock highs and lows. Indeed, the initial encounters in a country can lead to higher levels of negative emotions than might be anticipated in the culture shock model (Ward, Okura, Kennedy, & Kojima, 1998).

In the Japanese college classroom, ways of adjusting to new, or in my case previous teaching methods, were shaped by experiences in the U.S. In the U.S., I had taught multicultural education with a goal of preparing my students to be teachers in classrooms with diverse groups in terms of factors such as ethnicity, gender, social economic status and language (Brown and Kysilka, 2002; Cushner, McClelland, & Safford, 2000). I aim to make these students aware of the needs of minorities in the classrooms by emphasizing constructivist learning and knowing the learners and the ways they might learn best. Thus, I realized the importance of knowing my students and their prior knowledge and experiences. Yet, as this chapter highlights, knowing and acting can be quite different. As Brown and Kysilka (2002) clarify, "Knowledge of cultural learning and communication styles does not guarantee application" (p. 87). While my knowledge of Japan and past experiences helped me adjust to life in Japan once again, I still faced cultural discomforts. When highlighting how I react to individual experiences, it must be remembered that my personal episodes are unique to me and should not be generalized. As Mabuchi (1995) points out:

> It is not wrong to bring up personal experiences or write about Japanese culture or society, because these experiences and fresh ideas can be useful and should be appreciated. The problem is, as it was mentioned before, that the authors very easily slip from experience to generalizations (p. 40).

My initial challenges when returning to Japan were less cultural shock, as depicted in the literature, and more with juggling my anticipated expectations with a conscious grappling with reality and change. From past experience I had memories and knowledge of teaching in Japan, but when faced with these realities the episodes became revisited cultural encounters. These were initial challenges in my life rather than a lack of knowledge, skills and attitudes about teaching and living in Japan. They were created by a change in a current context to a different one. These challenges occur even when moving to different schools in your home country, but we do not think of them as cultural encounters, just differences.

In this segment, I describe some of my experiences as I perceived them initially and several months later. I do not deeply analyze my teaching or my experiences in Japan, rather I present encounters that I had not anticipated for the reader to grasp the difference between knowing and acting. The experiences are very subjective. Yet, this is a positive aspect, as it is my interpretations of the experiences rather than the experiences themselves that are remembered. As a result of this purpose for writing, a less "academic" style of writing is employed, but more fitting in order to highlight cultural understanding in progress.

Returning to Japan: Daily Life

This was not my first experience in Japan. Indeed, I had lived in Japan for more than ten years in the past, teaching in Japanese high schools, a junior college, and colleges. However, this time my family and I had plans to stay for an extended period of time.

There were several reasons for returning to Japan—three to be exact. In the past, I had enjoyed living in Japan, where I had constantly been faced with new challenges—many concerned with my understanding of Japan and myself. My wife and daughter were the other two reasons. My wife is Japanese and she would be returning to her birthplace, where she could speak in her first language and be closer to her family and friends. Our daughter, as she calls herself, is "half." She is twelve, and almost her entire education has been in the U.S., except for one year in Zimbabwe and a one-month summer experience in a Japanese 3rd grade classroom. While we had occasionally traveled to Japan, these trips did not facilitate my daughter's development of her academic skills and knowledge in Japanese. Now she was at an age where, in Japan, she would be entering junior high school, the equivalent of U.S. 7th grade. This would provide her with the opportunity to become bilingual and bicultural.

Thus, in the summer of 2003, I was searching for teaching positions on the worldwide web. Unexpectedly in June, while my wife and daughter were in Japan for a brief visit, I located an announcement for a position in Osaka, with the deadline the following day. After hurriedly emailing out the application and resume, I departed for a weekend camping trip. Upon returning, I found several emails waiting concerning the position and asking me to come for an interview by the end of the week! Following hurried emailing and phoning, I arranged a phone interview on Thursday and boarded a plane for Tokyo, Japan on Saturday. Arriving on Sunday afternoon, I met my wife and daughter at the airport—they were returning to the U.S. the next day—and we were able to discuss the prospects of this new job face-to-face that evening. On Monday at 7:30 a.m., I was relaxing on a bullet train headed for Osaka. The two days in Osaka remain a jet-lagged blur, but it was a time of filling out documents and signing agreements after being hired. On Wednesday, I was flying back to the U.S with a new job starting in April.

Preparing to Move

Although Osaka Jogakuin College arranged the shipping of our goods to Japan, we did not send furniture; most would have been too big to fit in a Japanese apartment. The size differences in the house we were moving from to an apartment needed to be considered ahead of time as well as our American mission-style furnishings fitting with the potentially bland walls in our future Japanese apartment. Our house, which we had sold, was three bedrooms with a basement. In Japan we were looking for a three bedroom apartment. So far, it sounds similar. However, the area of the house was about 114 meters squared while an apartment would be around 82.5 meters squared. My new study could have held our bed, but it would have left no room for a desk and bookshelf. While many of our friends in the U.S. were surprised that we did not ship all of our mission-style furniture, at least in this respect, we had anticipated correctly that it wouldn't fit, either physically or aesthetically. As a result, we sold, or in many cases gave away, our living room furniture, cooking ware, and bedroom furniture. That was the easy part. Deciding on which books and journals to send was a long, stressful experience. I still find it hard to believe that I actually gave away so many books before leaving the U.S., especially at times like the present, when I could use some articles for citation.

Settling in

After shipping our goods, we departed for Japan in search of a place to live. Osaka Jogakuin College was once again very helpful in settling my family into an apartment. They arranged nine nights in a hotel during which we secured an apartment and signed the housing contract. Before returning to Japan, we had searched on the web for apartments, but we needed to actually see the communities and the apartments before choosing one. Fortunately, we had contacted a realtor in Japan through a friend, who had examined apartments fitting our requirements, and he had selected some that he thought would be appropriate. The realtor drove us to four possible apartments, of which one met our needs. Up until this point, there was little difference from apartment hunting in the U.S. However, a difference was soon to emerge. In Japan, the landowner must approve of any new tenants. Many times, realtors or landowners do not want non-Japanese tenants because of the possible cultural and language barriers. Fortunately, we did not have that problem. Our problem concerned money. The landowner approved of us and our offer for rent, a bit lower than the listed rent. Here is the shocker; in Japan, renters often pay what is called key money. Key money is a combination security deposit and thank you money, thank-you-for-renting-to-me-money, which in our case was about ten thousand dollars! While I am sure there are ways around this system, for a newcomer, we did not have time to bicker. We needed a place to live.

Even though my wife had read on the web about the amount for key money, she was stunned when we actually paid the money and reflected on how much higher it was than in the Tokyo area. Only when we were in the position to have to pay the money, did the amount really hit home. Once again, this experience highlights that knowing something in "theory" is different from actually experiencing it. On the bright side, we should receive about three thousand dollars when we move; the remainder is the 'thank you money.' Quite a "big" thank you.

After paying the money through a bank transfer—personal checks are not used in Japan—we were ready to claim our new apartment. We actually live in what is called a 'mansion,' an oxymoron, if you have ever seen the size of these mansions. In Japan there are many borrowed words from other countries, which do not seem to fit quite right. Mansion is one of those words. According to Webster's New World Dictionary (Neufeldt and Guralnik, 1988), one definition of a mansion is, "a large, imposing house; stately residence" (p. 824). Ours was a three bedroom apartment on the fourth floor of a six floor building, with no lights, no refrigerator, and no stove, not much of anything. So moving into the apartment involved expensive trips to appliance stores and the local department store with a liberal use of our credit card. In a positive light, the sales people are extremely friendly and polite and provide impeccable service, so at least you feel good when you give them your money!

Price Shock

Moving into a mansion was the beginning of price shock. Although I had remembered that meat and other consumer goods were expensive in Japan, when we moved back and I started shopping again the reality hit me of what "expensive" really meant. For example, the cost of vegetables was shocking. One stalk of celery costs about $1.50. Let me emphasize, ONE stalk. Three carrots cost $1.50. Other food was not cheap either: a SMALL box of cereal required $3.00, and a dozen donuts costs around $15.00. The cost of items surprised us during the first few weeks as we readjusted to living in Japan. However, I did find that there are more stores now than eleven years ago that sell daily goods. For example, I was especially happy to shop at 100 yen shops. (100 yen is about 96 cents). I became a frequent visitor to buy pens, pencils, staplers, and paper.

Acquiring a Visa

With a place to live, furniture to be delivered and paper and pencils, I was ready for an extended stay in Japan. I only needed a work visa or, in my case, a spouse visa to begin teaching. Since my new college was accustomed to hiring foreign teachers who were already in Japan, it was not familiar with procedures for obtaining a spouse visa for a new hire from abroad. Thus, I entered Japan on a ninety day travel visa with expectations of obtaining a spouse visa soon afterwards. That expectation immediately evaporated at the immigration office while presenting my request to change my visa from travel to spouse. The set answer was, "It takes three months to process the change." My response followed, "But I start teaching in April." The bureaucrat replied, "We process the applications in the order we receive them. You will receive a letter when yours is ready." After going around and around, it became apparent that there were no more answers. I left, wondering if I would be able to teach in April. This story ends happily with my letter arriving at the end of March and a return visit to immigration to obtain my visa before school started in April. This was fortunate, as it meant I could be paid! However, while the story ended happily, the several weeks spent worrying if I would receive the visa become overshadowed. Those weeks involved worries that did interfere with daily life. Yet, in retelling this episode those worries become limited to a sentence. That is one of the prices to pay in retelling emotionally charged episodes. As in my daily life, these emotional experiences occurred in my new school.

(Mis)-Assumptions About Teaching

Teaching and learning in schools is universal. Yet, how this actually happens in schools varies. The U.S. and Japan have liberal arts colleges. However, organization and teaching within these institutions vary, both within countries as well as across countries. For example, unlike liberal arts colleges in the U.S., many small Japanese colleges do not have numerous departments, such as Education, History, Biology, etc. Osaka Jogakuin College, a small liberal arts college, has both a two-year and a four-year school. The four-year school has just one department, the Department of International and English Interdisciplinary Studies. Rather than teach English, the college aims to teach through English. The curriculum is content-based with areas of study in peace, science and religion, human rights and crisis of life (global issues). OJC is different from many colleges in Japan, as it integrates three freshman courses of reading, writing and discussion in the areas above (Swenson, Chihara, & McKay, 2001). This reinforces the students' learning in English and in content areas. While excellent for students, course scheduling is not flexible. As a result, the full-time teachers have little to say in terms of time and day of teaching. This all makes perfect educational sense but coming from a college in the U.S. where the department faculty sat down and picked times to teach, I was at first shocked. The schedule also informed me that my "research days" were Thursdays and Saturdays. With Saturday a designated research day and only Sunday off, I knew I was no longer in the U.S.

As I started teaching, differences in classroom interactions emerged from what I was used to in the U.S. I found myself, as I did when teaching at junior colleges in Japan from 1988-1993, speaking slowly and simplifying my words. Yet, when it came to assignments this was not successful. To offset this, I often explained more, when the initial problem was that the students just did not understand some of the words I was using. Speaking more probably just confused the students.

One of the initial challenges was overcoming my assumptions about prior knowledge, particularly concerning classroom English. I soon realized that I assumed the students knew English concerning classroom instructions. When I said, "Read pages 25 through 30 and do the questions on page 30", students read the pages. They did the reading, but they were confused when I asked them to hand in the answers to the questions. They had not written the answers down because I did not tell them to write the answers. I had merely told them to, "Do the questions". As a result, I have had to introduce a great deal of classroom English such as hand-in, submit, first draft, revise, and edit.

In a discussion class early in the first semester, we studied the meaning of peace and there was misunderstanding about the assignment. The assignment was to interview five people about the meaning of peace using questions in the text. Some questions included: Is Japan a peaceful country? Why or why not? Do other Asian countries think Japan is dangerous? Why or why not? and What should Japan do to keep world peace? These survey questions provided students with the opportunity to be actively engaged in their own learning and to reach out to the community for knowledge. The activity seemed sound in terms of constructivist learning. The directions for reporting back, however, indicated, "Report the results of your Peace Interview activity. Homework: Prepare your answers to the following questions." As per instructions, students wrote phrases for answers. Walking around class, I soon noticed that students had difficulty orally discussing their responses because they could not put their answers in sentences. In order to make this a more successful assignment, I reassigned the homework with instructions to write out their answers in full sentences using appropriate language for reporting information and giving opinions.

On the second day of a writing class, I assigned a semester-long assignment for students to exchange journals weekly and to read, respond and pass back the journal to continue the process. Two weeks into the course, three fourths of the students were still giving me blank looks. The blank looks were themselves dilemmas. In the U.S., I was always able to locate two or three students whose faces I could successfully read. If an assignment was not clear, their expressions informed me. Here I had no idea. That skill is obviously culturally dependent. While the explanation of key classroom instructions has helped reduce some miscommunication, making assignments clear to the students remains an ongoing challenge for me. With my multicultural teaching background, I am well aware that the culture of the classroom is based on the students' experiences in their school lives. At this point, we were in the process of constructing a classroom culture that promoted open discussion of varied ideas. As I am constructing a classroom culture, I am also finding that the faculty, of which many are new, is learning about how to cooperate and collaborate on issues of teaching, curriculum and research.

Colleagues at the College

At the beginning of the school year in April, I had many opportunities to interact with colleagues around writing, teaching and learning. As I began writing this article, I sent out an email to Japanese and foreign colleagues for pertinent research. Immediately, I had five responses that led me to numerous articles and books related to the topic, as well as colleagues with whom I discussed my ideas.

Since the four year college was just established in April, there are many new teachers. Though they have not moved from abroad, we still face similar challenges in understanding the students, the school culture, and the classroom culture. We have had many conversations around improving students' English speaking and writing skills, as well as how the college operates.

By May, the committees were beginning to meet. I am a member of the Integrated Unit Committee, which aims to improve the three integrated courses in reading, writing and discussion. I was working closely with two other members revising the unit's discussion section. We discussed changes and were exchanging drafts of new ideas. Already early in the year, there was a lot of collaboration among faculty members.

Six Months Later

Up until this part of the chapter, I have examined the initial challenges in my life and school. In the next section, I discuss life in Japan from a perspective of July, around six months after arriving. Let's fast forward to July 2004. Now, I have been living in Japan for about six months and teaching for around four months, about to finish the first semester. Initial cultural challenges have come and gone. Life and school seem to be flowing in regular routines. Our past experiences living in Japan seemed to have softened the initial cultural discomforts that are now behind us. Prices no longer are shocking, new inexpensive stores have been discovered, and our mansion has become home. Actually, looking back at what I wrote earlier, I want to say, "It wasn't that bad." Yet, I know that at the time, the lived experience was not easy and worries about housing, visas, and life in general in Japan were constantly on our minds.

Family Adjustments

Flourishing is an appropriate word to describe my family and life after six months back in Japan. I actually expected that this would happen from past experiences and knowing about cultural and language immersion. Yet, when the family adjusted and I came to understand my students better it was a surprise of sorts. I knew it would happen, but I was surprised when it did. A gap had existed between expectations and realizations.

My daughter is attending a private Japanese junior high school. She is not just learning Japanese; she is immersed in the language and the culture all day. I realized that this immersion was enhancing her Japanese language skills when she comes home speaking Osaka dialect with the express purpose of confusing me. At the dinner table, she complains when I do not speak Japanese, saying, "It is not fair. We speak Japanese, but you don't. You are in Japan now, so speak Japanese." On another day I needed to make a telephone call to the city office and asked my wife to do it. My daughter overhead this conversation and pointedly said in colloquial Japanese, "I have to speak Japanese in class everyday. You don't even try!" I made the phone call. She is obviously settling into life in Japan and "helping" me to do so as well.

My wife, though missing her friends at work in the U.S., is settling into life in Osaka. Her family and Japanese friends are much closer. Her family lives in Yokohama, about a two hour bullet train ride. Now she can speak in her first language, enjoy the Japanese food she was raised on, and easily travel around Japan on the trains.

As for my daily life, I relish the daily cultural encounters through observation or my favorite interest: people watching. I am amazed at how young ladies can apply makeup inside crowded rush hour trains. With people shoulder to shoulder, I have witnessed young ladies holding a tiny mirror with one hand and applying lipstick or eyeliner with the other. And they are very adept at it. In the same way, I marvel at how people can maneuver in crowded shops or on train platforms staring at their cell phones while reading/creating email messages and NOT bumping into anyone.

I also had a positive experience due to my own negligence. As I often do, one day I was studying Japanese on the train on the way to work and was using my electronic dictionary. I got off leaving my dictionary on the train, a $200 device. I called the Lost and Found office the next day, and it had been turned in. These types of experiences, both interesting and heartwarming, keep me intrigued with the every day life of life in Japan. My classroom experiences were also becoming more engaging.

Teaching and Learning: Drawing on Prior Knowledge

As I am here longer, I realize that the college students are very much like college students in the U.S. in many ways. Many of the initial cultural challenges involving the classroom are fuzzy memories. In each of my courses, I have located students whose faces can be read. It may be less explicit than in my U.S. classrooms, yet I can determine if they understand. I have even created a classroom culture in which I can shake my hide sideways or up and down and get a few to send a nonverbal signal. When I say, "Do you understand?" these students slightly shake their heads sideways if they do not understand. I just need to be more aware of the degrees of non-verbal communication that may differ between my students in Japan and those I had in the U.S.

I have also reverted to what I did more often in my U.S. classes, drawing once again on the multicultural skills I had taught my pre-service students to use. After getting over the initial cultural challenges, instead of trying to survive in the classroom and treating all students the same-something I told my students not to do-I was teaching in a way to support student leaning. For example, after teaching the students new classroom vocabulary and, importantly, reinforcing the vocabulary, I also write on the board each day's objectives and homework, using the new classroom English. Students here have homework calendars in which they write the assignments. Now that I am aware of this, and the students know the classroom English, assignments are seldom a problem.

My knowledge of the students' own school experiences is helping me teach. After having realized that many students in the college had taken a high school English course in composition that actually means translating sentence by sentence, I am astonished at their progress. Classes just finished in July, and students wrote well organized five paragraph essays on topics such as cloning, organ transplants, creation theories, and views on religion.

In the discussion course, students have advanced from hesitating to talking about themselves and/or their weekend activities to participating in group presentations on topics in the areas of science and religion. Using posters and visuals, students taught other students about cloning, organ transplants, in vitro fertilization, and religious beliefs on life after death. One group drew on large poster paper the steps in cutting out a kidney for transplanting, and then explained the process in English. Another group presented ideas on organ donors in the format of a humorous quiz show. Students have begun to blossom in terms of talking and drawing on their own creativity.

It is not just the students who are learning. My students have taught me a great deal. In my second year class, I required students to come to my office in twos or by themselves to talk about current event topics discussed in the course. All students came, and some came and stayed to talk. One student, who talked about a North Korean issue, informed me that she had gone on a school trip to North Korea by ship. Even though I knew this student was a Korean living in Japan and had attended a Korean high school, I had not realized that students could visit North Korea.

In the classroom, I realize that, as in the U.S., I as a teacher need to be flexible and to listen to the students. Their prior knowledge is key. When I first came, I tended to focus on my own needs of fitting in and tended to ignore the students. I was overwhelmed with what at the time seemed to me to be major cultural miscommunication and how I felt, rather than draw on my knowledge and skills of teaching in the U.S. and Japan as well as what I had learned in my Ph.D. program in Education. Only after the initial cultural challenges subsided could I become the teacher I knew that I was.

Committees and Colleagues

At the beginning of the school year in April, I mainly interacted with colleagues around writing, teaching and learning. By May, the committees were meeting regularly. I continued working as a member of the Integrated Unit Committee towards revising the curriculum, as well as in several other committees. In the Liaison Committee, as the new Writing Liaison person, I have helped to create and revise syllabi for writing courses. This committee endeavors to create a college-wide curriculum that is not fragmented, and thus we examine not only the course descriptions but also the content and evaluation processes in courses. This is not micromanaging courses, but rather an effort for continuity in courses and the evaluation process.

I also attend a committee involved in identifying universities abroad that our students can attend during their third or fourth years. OJC has a program to encourage students to study abroad for one semester in their major areas. Because of my experiences supporting international exchanges in the U.S., I have had positive input into this committee.

I still find time to pursue my own research agenda. Currently, I am working with a colleague at OJC, who used to be high school principal, on ways to improve the teaching of English in high schools. We have had discussion about how to support teachers and determined to start by offering our help at one school. We have met with two teachers and the principal and will be working more closely with the school after summer break. With this as a starting point, we hope to create a support group and an on-line website where we can hold discussions and provide teaching ideas connected to the curriculum and textbooks to provide practical ideas to use in their classrooms. Another OJC colleague and I are researching the effectiveness of the new Writing Center at OJC that opened in April 2004. We created a questionnaire and are currently analyzing the data. Thus, at OJC I have become very involved in curriculum development while able to pursue my own research.

Initial Cultural Challenges: Revisited

Sitting in my study with 30 degrees Celsius temperatures (86 degrees Fahrenheit) and high humidity, I am sweating at this computer. I could use some wind from a typhoon now. I have adjusted to life in Japan. No longer do typhoon winds swirl around my study or my life. I just hear the sounds of cicada buzzing outside in the morning heat as I reflect on "initial cultural challenges."

When I moved from Michigan to Wisconsin in 1999 for my first college teaching position, I was surprised not to see Mejiers Stores, a large discount store, since we shopped there so much. In Wisconsin, we faced the challenge of purchasing a house, getting a new drivers license, and learning about the community. These are all challenges, but they are taken for granted and not viewed as major cultural encounters. When we go abroad, these then become cultural challenges. When we become sojourners abroad, even with knowledge of the country and past experiences, somehow these challenges take on greater impact because they are unexpected and unique, for example the key money paid for our apartment. We face cultural encounters everyday. How do we handle daily expenses, transportation, classroom management, and human interactions? While we address these issues daily, wherever they may be, they do not stand out because we take them for granted. When we engage with cultures quite different from our daily encounters, whether within the U.S. or elsewhere, these everyday issues can no longer be taken for granted when we first encounter them. We must then consciously grapple with these differences because our accustomed ways of interacting no longer function appropriately. As these cultural challenges slip into the past, their impacts at the time need to be kept in mind.

Returning to Japan and keeping a journal of the experiences for the purpose of writing this chapter has highlighted how we tend to erase or diminish a sojourner's first encounters. If I had not written about the experiences, I might have downplayed stressful encounters. I would probably argue that it was easy since I was just returning to Japan. However, due to keeping this journal and writing this article, I know better. The cultural challenges disrupted my life in Japan and teaching. Problems now seen as "fixed", such as reading faces or acquiring a visa, were concerns that disrupted my life and teaching. These disruptions were mountains, not hills, at that time.

Cultural challenges overwhelmed me in such a way that my academic and experiential knowledge of Japan did not eliminate stress for cultural encounters in school and in society. While I knew that key money would be high, having to pay it was shocking. While knowing that teaching would involve changing my teaching style, having to change appropriately was difficult. While my knowledge of Japan and previous experiences were helpful, initial cultural challenges still occurred and obstructed my goals of teaching.

This section of the chapter reminds teachers and researchers about the initial weeks or months in different cultural contexts and how our efforts to adapt should not be underestimated. Prior knowledge and past experiences do not preclude discomfort and anxiety. Seasoned sojourners need to be cognizant of these potential cultural challenges when going abroad to carry out research or to teach.

CULTURAL PLUNGES AND CHALLENGES

These two articles on cultural encounters underscore that experiences differ depending on the reasons for going abroad. In the 3-week cultural plunge, students—with little Japanese experience—quickly shifted from concerns about the interactions towards understanding similarities between themselves and Japanese students. On the other hand, the author—long experienced with living in Japan—faced more initial "shocks" when resettling in Japan. However, if he had not kept a journal, these cultural bumps might have passed and been forgotten when, in fact, at the time the bumps were more like mountains. In both instances, however, the cultural encounters seem to have been opportunities for growth. Indeed, the author continues his encounter.

REFERENCES

Anderson, C., Nicklas, S., & Crawford, A. (1994). *Global Understandings: A Framework for Teaching and Learning.* Alexandria: Association for Supervision and Curriculum Development.

Berry, J. W. (1997). Immigration, Acculturation and Adaptation. *Applied Psychology: An International Review, 46,* 5-34.

Brown, S., & Kysilka, M. (2002). *Applying Multicultural and Global Concepts in the Classroom and Beyond.* Boston: Allyn and Bacon.

Cushner, K., McClelland, A., & Safford, P. (2000). *Human Diversity in Education: An Integrative Approach* (5th ed.). New York: McGraw Hill.

Lustig, M., & Koester, J. (2003). *Intercultural Competence: Interpersonal Communication across Cultures* (4th ed.). Boston: Ally and Bacon.

McFadden, J., Merryfield, M., & Barron, K. R. (1997). *Multicultural and Global/International Education: Guidelines for Programs in Teacher Education*. Washington, DC: American Association of Colleges for Teacher Education.

Merryfield, M. (2000). Why Aren't Teachers Being Prepared to Teach for Diversity, Equity, and Global Interconnectedness? A Study of Lived Experiences in the Making of Multicultural and Global Educators. *Teaching and Teacher Education, 16*, 429-443.

Miles, M., & Huberman, M. (1994). *Qualitative Data Analysis: An Expanded Sourcebook.* (2nd ed.). CA: Sage Publication.

Neufeldt, V., & Guralnik, D. (Eds.). (1988). *Webster's New World Dictionary* (3rd ed.). New York: Webster's New World.

Oberg, K. (1960). Cultural Shock: Adjustment to New Cultural Environments. *Practical Anthropology, 7*, 177-182.

Sleeter, C. (1995). Reflections on My Use of Multicultural and Critical Pedagogy When Students are White. In C. Sleeter and P. McLaren (Eds.), *Multicultural Education, Critical Pedagogy, and the Politics of Difference*. Albany: State University of New York Press.

Swenson, T., Chihara, T., & McKay, T. (2001). Integrating Courses across the Curriculum. *Osaka Jogakuin Tankidaigaku Kenkyuu Kiyou, 32*, 1-12.

Tran, M. T., Young, R. L., & DiLella, J. D. (1994). Multicultural Courses and the Student Teacher: Eliminating Stereotypical Attitudes in Our Ethnically Diverse Classroom. *Journal of Teacher Education, 45*(3), 183-189.

Wade, R. (2000). Service-Learning for Multicultural Teaching Competency: Insights from the Literature for Teacher Educators. *Equity and Excellence in Education, 33*(3), 21-29.

Ward, C., Bochner, S., & Furnham, A. (2001). *The Psychology of Culture Shock* (2nd ed.). East Sussex: Routledge.

Ward, C., Okura, Y., Kennedy, A., & Kojima, T. (1998). The U-curve on Trial: A Longitudinal Study of Psychological and Sociocultural Adjustment during Cross-cultural Transition. *International Journal of Intercultural Relations, 22*, 277-291.

PART V:
TRIBUTES TO THE BOBS – INTELLECTUAL, PERSONAL AND REAL

Chapter 17

TEACHING AND RAISING THE TABACHNICKS

David Tabachnick
Muskingum College, New Concord
Ohio, USA

I remember as a kid being lured to Bob Tabachnick's desk, piled with books and chapters, so he could try out an idea. At the seminar on the occasion of his retirement, people debated a little of this and a little of that and then he turned to me and asked, "So what do you think, David?" Hoping I'd respond with an instant aria. Afterwards someone asked me, "Is that what you had to contend with growing up?" Rapid response training paid off particularly well in my job as assistant to a judge. We'd hear something complicated, go backstage for a moment, "So what do you think?" I'd speak with the confidence of the possessed and try to figure out later what I said.

Maybe if my father had been a writer like H. Rider Haggard or Edgar Rice Burroughs or Joseph Conrad you would say "Africa" and I would answer "diamonds" or "jungle" or "Mistah Kurtz—he dead," but for me Africa is intertwined with education - mine and everyone else's. In 1974, encountering hostility towards imperial Westerners at Fourah Bay College, Sierra Leone, I asked a fellow student, Boubacar Njai Bah, who was President of the student body and wrote political poetry, whether he thought my father's work promoted an imperialist agenda. "Oh no," he said. Boubacar wrote an ambiguous poem suspicious of neocolonialism in which a schoolboy celebrates his African heritage but fervently wishes "Lord let me go to their schools." Boubacar read this poem at a school event and was scolded for its ending by a Kriol writer with an Oxford accent.

Years later, I attended my father's class at the University of Wisconsin on educational planning in poor countries. Students studied a fifteen year plan for the Sierra Leone education system, a plan my father consulted on while in Sierra Leone. A student complained that the plan was a typical product of Western imperialists. That was puzzling. "What do you mean, Westerners wrote the plan? The plan is the work of Sierra Leoneans."

The student explained, "Whenever I read something like this, I look at the names of the authors. They all have English names. Hardly any Sierra Leoneans were involved." He had mistaken Sierra Leonean Kriol names like "Coker" or "Smart" for the names of Western experts.

Dad and I once drove into a rural village in the Mende area of Sierra Leone and attracted a crowd ranging from school kids to moms to elders. We assembled under the village tree, the school kids in green and white uniforms translating for us: "How important is education to you?" "Very important." "Would you like a school to be located in your village?" "Sure." "If a high school were located nearby, would you send your children to it?" "Yes." "Would that create a problem, as the children would not be available to do work in the village?" "Oh no, we would just produce more children!"

The great thing about Bob Tabachnick's international career is I got to tag along for much of it. His large and public career became my small and private career. With his help, I obtained my own international education. Nigeria was my grade school, Kenya my high school and Sierra Leone my college. As a family we traveled around, but the United States, in its way, was traveling too and added its momentum to ours leaving only Madison's hometown timelessness as an anchor.

Bob Tabachnick worked with colleagues to develop ways to educate students that emphasized student inquiry and deemphasized rote response of the group to teacher stimulus. He told a story of how when he first learned to handle a classroom, he would stay up to eleven at night designing plans for keeping busy thirty or so eight or nine year olds divided into groups working on separate tasks. While he was learning to do this, he met a man from Italy who exclaimed that teaching was easy—they give you a textbook and you make the students repeat after you everything in the book. I was in Japan recently and spent time with a professor of education, Koji Kato, who has worked with Bob Tabachnick. After attending a class in which Koji Kato discussed playful alternatives to lecture oriented teaching, I asked the graduate students in the class how many of them had experienced teaching that stressed student inquiry rather than straight lecture format: none of them had. Koji pointed out that despite initial interest in alternatives to Japan's traditionally rigid education, as Japan's economy stagnated the media blamed unconventional approaches to education for harming the international competitiveness of Japan's students. Back to the basics! This reminded me of the United States, where increasingly no child is left time off from reading and math drills to do art and music.

Is an ever more interconnected and internationally competitive world doomed by globalization to an ever more obsessively rote and narrowed education? Probably not, if one looks at Bob Tabachnick's experience in Africa! Nigeria in the 1960s combined medieval with more modern technologies but was particularly weighed down by a poor imitation of the less desirable aspects of European education. My father's job was to unsettle this parochial world. He did so by escaping the parochialism of the professional educator's research methods of the day which stressed statistics over qualitative narratives. One can only be an artist of education, as my father is, when the individual matters. He carried out, with the help of Nigerian graduate students, research into a day in the life of a girl and a boy in a Nigerian village. The study was published in Nigeria under the title: *Two Children--Two Days: a day in the lives of two school children in North Central State*. In discovering and writing up the story of the girl, Magajiya, and the boy, Shuaibu, he found a way back to an early dream: to write fiction. Instead of making fiction out of reality, one explores the fiction of reality.

George Spindler's courses at Stanford inspired Bob Tabachnick to think about how ethos energizes culture and how case studies in the form of ethnographic narratives can be effective social science. *One Boy's Day* by Roger Barker and Herbert Wright offered a model for the study of two children in Nigeria. The teacher treated Magajiya and Shuaibu like automatons with no ability to make decisions for themselves. "Stand! Sit!" And in school they responded like automatons. But outside of school they led a rich, active life. Magajiya spent hours spinning cotton or would take things to the market to sell for her mother. In the evening, Magajiya loved to dance. School suppressed all that lively self direction. Perhaps, in a dystopian future squeezed imaginatively dry, Nigerians will make their way to the United States to unsettle its parochialism, saving American education with the help of ideas transplanted in the 1960s.

In sixties Madison I, like my sisters, detached myself from conventional public school to experience a "free" school. Just one thread held me to the old institution: French class. My father, rather than fight this change, went with me to convince the Principal that I should be allowed to continue on in French. Then I'd bike or ice skate from the west to the east side of Madison for my other classes. A man who went on to publish several successful novels taught my favorite class, creative writing. Teachers like that just did not exist in the old school.

After a year of this freedom, my father took a job in Uganda that turned into a job in Kenya, thanks to the violent dictator Idi Amin, who boasted that Uganda produced the best refugees in the world. Before my father left for Africa, we discussed where I might do my senior year in high school. Paris? That's cool, my Dad thought—like Hemingway!

Moving to Paris and to classes taught in French was like being taken to live in a city underwater. The French language rushed over me and I lived in its sound, without understanding much, for about three months. But then, like a fish, I started to breathe in French. In these complicated times, the Vietnam War dragging agonizingly on, I was pulled out of Paris into thoughts of life in an African village. After one semester I left my chambre de bonne below the mansard roof of a French apartment building, milk cartons cooling in the winter air on the ledge outside the window, Bunsen burner for a stove, large bed, sink, wardrobe, toilet down the hall and enormous heating pipes hanging from the ceiling. A few months later I volunteered to teach seventh and eighth grade in a Harambee school in a village near Malindi on the Kenyan coast. I lived in a mud hut, palm thatched roof, bed shrouded in mosquito netting, Bunsen burner for a stove, kerosene lamp, no sink or toilet.

I have a black and white picture of me in action teaching twenty or so eighth grade students ranging in age from thirteen to sixteen years old. As I talked at the students, my hand on the closest student's desk, one can see the half dozing look on his face. What was I saying, what did I have to say about subjects such as U.S. history, curiously required by the syllabus, or algebra? I was seventeen, had of course not graduated from high school myself, and I dressed for work in flip flops, jeans and a yellow paisley cotton shirt. I was helped by the obliviousness of youth, a wide-eyed wonder at everything, the knowledge that if I wasn't there the students would have no teacher to replace me, and finally by my father's classroom visits, encouragement and advice. He sat in on a muddled lecture about 19th century robber barons and a desperate attack on the idea of an equation and how to solve for X. Strangely, he thought I was much clearer in explaining how equations work, although in retrospect I can understand how my talk of robber barons and industrial monopolies must have fluttered around like exotic butterflies before heading straight out the window.

Years later, when I entered a Ph.D. program, my father's coaching truly became invaluable. He read first each chapter of the dissertation, encouraging me to keep moving. Once again he sat in on classes I taught. He helped me understand the need for transparency, for explaining to students why the class is structured as it is. He took notes on demeanor—too many uhs and ahhs. He pushed me to get off the page and trust to my knowledge while fully engaging students. We cooked up small group assignments even for large lecture classes of a hundred students. He encouraged me to frame a class with an introduction and conclusion and connect back to where the class had come and forward to where the class was going. Build a class around a coherent story, or a select few issues, and when assigning readings, less is more! No matter what conflict occurred, he urged me not to reduce the class to me versus them. At the same time, no matter how empathic the teacher, one is unlikely to be universally loved.

In 1979 Dad visited the French sheep farm where, with assistance from my parents, I was living and working on a documentary film portrait of two farm families. We decided to go for a picnic in the Pyrénnées poking up on the farm's southern horizon. First we shopped for all the good things I had learned about. A light gold sparkling sweet wine called Chateau Septy Monbazillac. Several kinds of *saucisson sec*, *patés*, *rilletes*, goat cheese distilled into *crottes de chevre* and crisp *pain de campagne*. We loaded all this in the car and drove into the hills. Forested slopes rose up, speckled with fields of hay, gray stone barns and farmhouses sometimes alone, sometimes clustered in villages. I followed a road that became a path into an isolated valley lit up by the summer sun. The car just made it over a crumbling bridge, the path petering out by the bank of a clear and very cold stream. We chilled the wine in the stream, unwrapped meats and cheeses and cut up the bread. I had been homesick for my father's visit, but this perfect day in the country justified my time in France. I felt like a music student who wows them at the end of year recital.

I hope I have illuminated Bob Tabachnick's approach to education by telling about his involvement in my education, formal and informal. My father allowed me my adventures. That was brave teaching. In what follows, I will provide what I call, for lack of a better term, Dad's social history.

A Social History of Robert Tabachnick

My father's parents came from shtetls in the Ukraine. His mother, Sarah learned to stitch fur caps when she was five. His father, Harry, was an accomplished shoer of horses as a boy and taught younger children the ABCs of Hebrew. Harry decided to seek his fortune in New York and walked across Europe in the Jewish youth migration from Tsarist Russia to Manhattan, thus missing the drama of the First World War, the Russian Revolution, 1930s Stalinism and finally the Nazi holocaust that broke all links between family in New York and family in Russia.

When Harry met Sarah they were both working in the garment industry. Harry decided the future was not in horses and worked his way up in the clothes business, taking apart a Singer sewing machine and putting it back together, learning how to cut patterns from a friendly older man. Sarah worked in fur, a nice job in the early 1900s. Sarah liked to go to public lectures in Harlem with her girlfriends for an evening out. Tolstoy, Dostoyevsky, Chekhov, Sholom Aleichem--she read all those old stories. Harry told me that when he first took Sarah out, they sat on a bench in a park and he asked if he could give her a little kiss. Sure! He also told me that when Dad met my mother, Dad said "Pop, she's so beautiful in the morning!" My parents' story was that they met and fell in love by the monkey house in the zoo.

Dad was the third of three brothers. Sarah wanted a girl so badly that she dressed her youngest son as a little girl for a photograph when he was four years old. He had long curly hair and sat in a swing in the photographer's studio. At this time he was as fluent in Yiddish as in English. Milt and Joe, Dad's older brothers, told stories about rock fights between Jewish and Italian kids in the Bronx, the younger kids fetching ammunition for the older kids. Dad could always count on his older brother Milt. He once taunted a bully, knowing Milt was coming up behind. Milt saved him but told him not to do that again.

By the time Dad was in high school, Harry had started his own factory in New Paltz, New York. Harry would walk through the garment district and the department stores of Manhattan, taking an idea from this design and from that, then go back to his factory and make his own clothes. Somehow the clothes business has gotten along quite well without the copyright protections that are the obsession of the music and movie industries.

Harry had a religious education but he decided not to join a synagogue and raise his children as religious Jews. Why did he do this? Sarah said he always wanted to be a Rabbi, but apparently the secular, independent spirit of his times led him to break with American Judaism. Harry explained it like this: As a young man in New York he had no money, but he wanted to hear a famous cantor on the holiest day of the year. The synagogue would not let him in unless he bought a ticket. This so outraged him that he decided never to set foot into an American synagogue. So my father never learned Hebrew and did not have a bar mitzvah. Sarah, though, took Dad to a service once and he was called up to read from the Torah. The Rabbi divined that Dad could not understand a word and whispered each phrase for Dad to repeat out loud. Sarah beamed.

Dad edited the school newspaper and had dreams of writing. He won a Regent's scholarship and departed for Syracuse University to study English. He roomed with Harvey Jacobs, who would go on to write short stories and novels and make a living in advertising. David Soyer was another college friend. David, for whom I was named, was the son of the painter Moses Soyer. Years later, out in California, Moses would paint my mother when she was nude and nine months pregnant.

That moment of truth--what should one do for a living?--came after graduation from Syracuse and Dad realized writing short stories was not the answer. Neither did he want to work in Harry's factory. The perfect answer, combining performance with curiosity and invention, was teaching. Dad began his teaching career pursuing a Master's degree at Columbia. His first job was in a school in Harlem, a different Harlem from the days when Sarah and her girlfriends spent the night out listening to a lecture. Sometimes Dad would bring his guitar to class and play folk songs. Once a boy stopped him in the hall and asked him if he was going to sing that day. This was surprising, as the boy was not in Dad's class. It turns out the boy sat in the last row of the class next door. He would lean his chair back and listen to the music through the wall. Dad's next job after Harlem was a school in Scarsdale. The contrast between the two schools just about summed up public schooling in America.

Mom could not imagine raising kids in New York and so, pregnant with their first child, she and Dad decided to move to California, to Palo Alto, where Dad would complete a Ph.D. at Stanford. Palo Alto, back then, was a place where a young couple could afford to buy their first house. They have a picture of me dressed in a cowboy outfit and playing hide and seek behind the chimney on the flat roof of their little ranch house. I'd crawled up the ladder while Dad was cleaning the gutters.

At Stanford, Dad met his partners in creativity, Rod Fielder and Millard Clements. Together they published a book full of ideas for teachers. Rod ended up on a filbert farm in Oregon and wrote lumberjack tales while Millard taught at New York University, creating a program in environmental education.

The University of Wisconsin eagerly recruited Dad, although Mom was not so eager to go. She thought she had escaped the Midwest when she left Ohio for New York and New York for California. But of all the Midwestern states, Wisconsin was to her the most bearable. The road trip from California to Wisconsin was our first great family adventure. We stopped in national parks and camped out on the way.

Things we liked to do as a family: try to carry a tune as Dad sang and strummed folk tunes, camp in tents and sleep in bags waking to drink hot cocoa on cold mornings the rain rattling the leaves of the trees, canoe a Wisconsin river sandbar to sandbar, scramble up granite rockslides to the bluffs of Devil's Lake, ride long hours in a station wagon to visit our relatives in Chicago or Philadelphia or New York or Cincinnati. This Midwestern idyll ended for me after third grade. Doctors pumped us full of vaccines and we set off across Europe to Africa, to the dry, amethyst encrusted red earth of Northern Nigeria. Mom learned how to photograph. We learned how to leave the familiar and enjoy foreign mysteries such as the incomprehensible speech of cockney London.

Northern Nigeria introduced us to the Harmattan, a wind that coats everything with a fine dust that puffs into the air when you kick a bush. Since the colonial era, West Africans have battered the fragile dry soils with peanut plants producing pyramids of groundnuts and lakes of peanut oil. I never tasted a peanut so fine as the dark brown roasted nuts set out in dishes at the faculty club of Ahmadu Bello University in Zaria.

My parents got to know an international coterie of poets and scientists at Ahmadu Bello University in that brief mid 60s calm before the Biafran crisis. The scientists helped us create a little backyard zoo with baby warthogs, duikers and parrots. Hausa traders would knock at the door around dinner time and slowly unwrap cloth bundles revealing statues, masks and swords. Dad was accused by some of the other expatriates of paying too high prices and driving up the market

Mom was out photographing one day when she encountered a mob with machetes that Hausa politicians had organized to attack Ibos. The Biafran crisis had come to Zaria. Some of the men actually stopped to pose for her and then went on to smash up a gas station owned by an Ibo.

Mom went home and saw another group of men with bows and arrows and machetes come up the driveway to the house. They wanted to go inside and take our servants, who they had mistaken for Ibos, as the servants came from the east. Mom stood in the doorway and refused to let them in. Finally a Hausa man ran up and said he knew our servants were not Ibo. He convinced the men to leave. In the meantime, Dad had gone out in the car to collect us children from school. He also picked up an Ibo man who hid at our feet in the back while Dad drove him to the police station that offered refuge to any Ibo that could make it there. He remembers sadness on the faces of Nigerians he met, the disappointment and shame at the violence.

Nigeria started my mother on a career documenting people going about their lives in Africa, Asia and the United States. Wisconsin became a home base from which she and Dad could recuperate and then launch further international adventures. In addition to Africa (especially Nigeria, Kenya and Sierra Leone), they spent several years living in and exploring Indonesia. When I was working on the documentary film about French farmers, I met a man who bought a farm in the south of France on a dry lavender growing plateau. He had worked as an agronomist in Madagascar before focusing on his own little patch of earth. He explained to me that the more he traveled, the more he realized how ignorant he was, and he lost the desire to travel. Travel that involves you deeply in another culture humbles you in this way, but rather than be daunted by your expanding ignorance you can feel refreshed. My parents taught me their nomadic skill at enjoying new campgrounds, arriving gently curious into the world.

Chapter 18

ROBERT L. KOEHL: OUR FATHER

Stefan, Jeremy and Sarah Koehl
USA & Canada

Our father, historian and teacher Robert L. Koehl, taught us to observe closely, read widely and think critically. From him we learned that ideas are much more valuable than things and that beneath and beyond popular conceptions lays the complex truth about our world and our societies. He has always been an inquisitive man, unafraid to march to a different drummer, whose interests range from history to politics to stamp collecting to science. Through his example and words, he conveyed the dignity and equality of all people and the possibility of building a better life for people everywhere by drawing upon a thorough understanding of what has happened in the past. Altruism is not enough, he would tell us, the road to hell is paved with ill-informed, good intentions. We share our dad, Bob, with his students, for whom he also cared deeply. May his scholarship and idealism continue through them too.

BOB KOEHL: THE TEACHER

Mabel O. N. Enwemnwa

At first, I literally "saw red!" I had taken a number of courses in Educational Policy Studies—from Professor Koehl and others—and I had an idea what he expected from the students. However, nothing really prepared me for the next phase of my life, under his tutelage! In the Spring of 1992, it was time to fulfill the departmental requirement for me to continue with my doctoral program. Having earned my first Masters degree in Educational Administration by examination and a paper, I needed to submit a Masters thesis in Educational Policy Studies. I chose my topic and got through all the other stages with little or no problems or surprises. Then it came to the actual writing, and I began to see the real Bob Koehl!!

In fairness to him, he had "told" me to expect different "colors of pen" with the different drafts of my paper. Yet, I was devastated when I saw the "corrected" paper of the first draft of the first chapter! I quickly put the paper back in my mailbox in the department. Someone else was walking by and I didn't want anyone to see the screaming redness of my paper! Every single line was coated with red. Some of the little punctuation marks I had taken for granted, were highlighted. All the comments in the margin were in red. I felt so embarrassed that I never showed it to anybody. How could I? My thoughts ran helter skelter. Did I really need a doctorate degree in Educational Policy Studies? Why not just return to my position as a high school principal in Nigeria?

Feeling downcast and actually ashamed, I summoned enough courage to go and wait for Dr. Koehl's office hours that afternoon. He caringly asked me what the matter was, seeing I was distraught; and without saying a word, I pulled out my "red paper" from my bag and showed him. I was expecting him to ask me why I thought I should remain in the program. But he simply said: "Oh, I think you should go on with the second draft—take note of the corrections". I couldn't believe my ears! Was this normal?

Then I remembered! He had explained to me during our initial conferences what his style was: he would use red for the first draft, purple for the second, and black or pencil for the final!! This was indeed my first draft! I never got over that first shock. Much later in the program, I summoned enough courage to share this with my friends and fellow advisees of Bob's. They too had had the same experience.

Meanwhile, he saw me through that and future phases of my program, with the same level of patience, understanding and encouragement. Many times, I would wait for his office hours, with one reason or the other, regarding my possible decision to quit the program. Bob would always have an anecdote to share from his experiences. Having spent time working on the "Wisconsin Project" in Nigeria, it was as if he had known me and my problems, from the very first day.

BOB KOEHL: THE PERSON

Bob was ready for me—exactly the way he had put it in that first letter they usually write to prospective students of the department—even before you left your home country! Bob Koehl was more like my guardian. Though a grown woman, wife and mother of five, I still cried to him and he would literally wipe away my tears of frustration. He always found words of encouragement. The best part was preparing for the Ph.D. orals. Bob prepared me for every detail, as you would for a wedding rehearsal. Everything happened the way he had advised!! He kept reminding me that I was the "expert," and so should be on top of things at the defense. Each time I looked at him across the room, I drew some fresh inspiration and courage. Bob Koehl surprised me when he and his wife, Jane, attended my 50th birthday thanksgiving service—almost five years after my graduation. He had kept in touch. He danced to the altar with me. I will never forget. No Christmas passes without Bob sending me a Christmas card!

THE OTHER BOB!

Right from my first semester, I knew the two Bobs as always working together. Of course, they were in the "Wisconsin Project" together. So, I did not have to look far to find my next committee member. Bob Tabachnick was equally understanding and caring—knowing where I was coming from. What touched me the most was that he had to cut short his European trip, in order to make it to my oral defense!! He even called me the moment he got into the country—to let me know he was back and that everything was as planned. He was ready for me. I could not have asked for more from these two loving and caring teachers and mentors!!!

Chapter 19

TEACHING EDUCATIONAL DEVELOPMENT AND CURRICULUM PLANNING IN THE 21ST CENTURY: DISCURSIVE RUPTURES IN THE CONVERSATIONS ABOUT PLANNING FOR MODERN CITIZENSHIP THROUGH PUBLIC EDUCATION

Marianne Bloch
University of Wisconsin-Madison
Wisconsin, USA

INTRODUCTION

I should warn my readers right from the outset that my tribute to the Bobs and the main thrust of this chapter are one and the same. I am currently a professor in the Department of Curriculum and Instruction at the University of Wisconsin-Madison. At the time of writing this chapter (2004), I am completing my *first quarter* century at the university. While this seems as though it is a long time, when my colleagues Robert (Bob) Tabachnick and Robert (Bob) Koehl retired, they had each been at the University of Wisconsin-Madison teaching for at least 35 years each. This is a long time to "make a mark" on a generation of future researchers and graduate students from the United States and from many countries of the world. When they began teaching in the early 1960s, they were pioneering members of their respective departments of Curriculum and Instruction and Educational Policy Studies. In fact, when they both began, Bob Tabachnick was in a unified Department of Education (now we have five separate departments within the School of Education), and subsequently became a Professor in the Department of Curriculum and Instruction with a joint appointment in Educational Policy Studies, and a program affiliate of the African Studies Program at the University of Wisconsin-Madison. Bob Koehl was in the Department of Educational Policy Studies with a joint appointment in the Department of History and program affiliation in the African Studies Program. They both had strong backgrounds and appreciations for the complexity of educational research and the value of a critical theoretical, comparative, and historical approach to educational policy issues. When I arrived, they were co-teaching a course, *Curriculum and Instruction/Educational Policy Studies 963: Educational Planning and Curriculum Change in Developing Countries.*

When they had each come near to the point of retirement, I was asked to co-teach with them for one semester; I made "three" teachers in a class of at least 24 master's and doctoral level students, the majority of whom were split between the Departments of Curriculum and Instruction and Educational Policy Studies, with a few from the UW-Madison Ph.D program in Development Studies. Before they were nearing retirement, I had known both men for many years, and had done extensive research and collaboration with Bob Tabachnick on earlier projects, some of which are cited as examples here (e.g., Bloch and Tabachnick, 1994; Tabachnick and Bloch, 1995; Bloch, Beoku-Betts, and Tabachnick, 1998). We were/are all of Euro-American, white background; they are men, and I am a woman. We shared regional experience in Africa, and a strong interest in comparative and international education. My research had focused on early and elementary education in and out of schools, women and development, gender, work, and child care, and gender and education than had been traditional foci in the course under the two Bobs. I had also spent somewhat more time exploring the intersections of post-structural, feminist, and post-colonial theories, while they were somewhat more focused somewhat on critical structural theories of empowerment, neo-Marxist analyses of state, class, race, and gender, Freirian ideas of critical liberatory pedagogies, and local, democratic and participatory educational reforms, including action research in their framings of issues in the class, and in own research experiences. The mixing together of the three of us for one semester enriched the class in several ways, I thought, and I enjoyed collaborating in course planning, co-teaching seminars, and I learned from Bob Koehl and from Bob Tabachnick in terms of content, ways to debate different issues, selection of literature for the course, and the ways in which they worked their own strengths and those of students into the discussion an debate oriented class. As some former graduate students who have taken their classes are writing in this volume, I expect the richness of their graduate experiences will be well-documented, beyond my experience.

However, when they had both retired, I began to teach this course alone; the rich interchange of multiple professors co-teaching the class was gone, and the different frameworks that I brought to the co-taught course now were reduced to some extent to my own integration of theory, empirical literatures they had introduced, and that I wanted graduate students to discuss in the class I was organizing. Without modesty, in my own opinion, I can say that the course has never been as good as the time that we all co-taught the course, and this is certainly a compliment to them. Fewer students from educational policy studies came to take the course without Bob Koehl and Bob Tabachnick teaching it; therefore, there were more from Curriculum and Instruction, and fewer with comparative and international educational policy interests. However, new students took the class because of my better known foci on early and elementary education, and my background in feminist, critical and post-structural as well as post-colonial theoretical literature. By the time I began to teach the class in the mid-1990s, there were shifts in arguments about "transitional states." While in the co-taught course, we had used Carnoy and Samoff's (1990) text titled *Education and Social Transition in the Third World*, which had a clear neo-Marxist, and socialist framework, by the time I began to teach, the Berlin wall had fallen, and there was a greater emphasis on how former Communist bloc nations would make a transition toward market economies and democratic governments. The literature we used included: Bob Tabachnick,

Josephine Beoku-Betts, and my own edited volume *Women and Education in Subsaharan Africa* (Bloch, Beoku-Betts, and Tabachnick, 1998), Arturo Escobar's *Encountering Development* (1995), Linda T. Smith's *Decolonizing methodologies* (1999), Edward Said's *Orientalism,* Robert Young's *White Mythologies* or his *Colonial Desire,* Akhil Gupta and James Ferguson's *Culture, Power, and Place,* Nick Burbules and Carlos Torres, *Globalization and education* (2000) as well as Tom Popkewitz's *Educational Knowledge* (2000). These volumes, and examples from different World Bank and US-AID, as well as UNICEF, OECD, and UNESCO documents, and a variety of articles, allowed us to look at different theoretical lens and ways of analyzing the spread of modern schooling around the world. We used world systems theory, illustrated by Ramirez (2004) and Scriewer (2000) in conjunction with ways of analyzing local/global relations and hybrid patterns (Anderson-Leavitt, 2003; Bhabha, 1994). These gave a somewhat different theoretical focus to the course, while also facilitating continuing critique and presentation of multiple "narratives" of development and educational reform and planning, as the original class had always done. Students' projects were flexible and required explanation of theoretical frameworks along with analyses of curricular and educational policy development projects, in relation to the region of greatest interest to them.

However, as I will discuss further in later sections, the new times that often call for new ways of thinking about instruction, different theoretical frameworks, and the intersections between theory, methods of research, and approaches to policy and action, also create different instructional and pedagogical environments. New instructors are not the same as older ones, but, as I hope I was able to do, instructors and students integrate ideas, making new hybrid spaces for the pedagogies of instruction. New instructors necessarily bring their own complex identities, ideas, and experiences into teaching, and integrate with those, the identities and differential experiences of graduate students who are in different classes.

In the first section of this chapter, I discuss the ways in which my work was both integrated with as well as was influenced by my research, writing, friendship, and teaching with Bob Tabachnick as well as Bob Koehl. In the next section (Section 2) I follow with some additional autobiographical notes about how I took from their work, as well as my own, to forge a new hybrid course that would question the notions of "Curriculum Change and Educational Planning for Developing Countries" in different ways than had been done previously. I discuss to a greater degree different questions I have asked myself and graduate students in my courses, and working on theses with me since Bob Koehl and Bob Tabachnick have retired; I don't do this as a "diary" of one instructor's teaching of a course, but as a narrative about the issues we might debate about international education, curriculum change, and educational reform as we move further into the 21st century. In order to do this, in the third section of the paper (Section 3), I discuss different discourses that circulate to form the debates of teaching such a course in the United States in higher education and comparative education. Finally, in the fourth and final section, I bring in voices from graduate students with whom I've worked in the classes, as we question together how to co-construct pedagogical spaces at an American or non-American university, and different ways to consider decolonization of research, while also situated in an American academic institution.

AUTOBIOGRAPHICAL NOTES: SITUATING THE CONTEXTUAL VALUE OF WHERE AND WITH WHOM ONE BEGINS AN ACADEMIC CAREER

I was the fourth woman to be hired in the Curriculum and Instruction (CandI) department at UW-Madison in the fall of 1980, either because of my gender, or because I was "well qualified," although as with anything else, the definition of "qualified" depends upon the interpretive meanings and the discourses that surround these.

When I initially interviewed for the assistant professor position in early childhood education in CandI, I was worried because I had just completed my second field research project in a rural part of Senegal (the first in 1976, and the second in 1979) on women, work, and the organization of child care and its impact on child development. I had done extensive field work, with the help of an interpreter who spoke fluent Lebou, and all of the research had been done outside any institutionalized western school context. While I had my Ph.D. degree in Early Childhood Education, my interests at the time were focused on studies of comparative human development, using qualitative and quantitative methodologies to study education in and out of institutional and western school settings. I had entertained teaching in a department of anthropology, or in the field of anthropology and education, but the position at UW was to teach undergraduate and graduate courses in curriculum and instruction in early childhood education, with a focus on kindergarten curriculum in the USA at the undergraduate level. While I felt appropriately anxious about teaching "traditional" early childhood education methods classes at UW-Madison, I was "qualified", and was offered the job by the then chair of the department, B. Robert Tabachnick.

My interview at UW-Madison's CandI department, in the spring of 1980, had been unusual; faculty appeared to appreciate my international experience, and asked me challenging questions about how I would use my experience to bring cultural issues into my classroom teaching; these questions challenged me, and were different than those at other universities where my different backgrounds seemed to bother many faculty and students. It helped me to see that Madison was an unusual place when I wandered, nervously, into the Chair's office for the traditional applicant interview with the Chair. I immediately saw photographs by Jeanne Tabachnick of African children (from Nigeria and/or Kenya) as well as other African tapestries positioned as art on the Chair's (Bob's) office walls; he knew many of the researchers with whom I'd done work in graduate and post-graduate studies. I left my interview feeling that it was possible that UW-Madison was a rare place to live and learn, as well as to do research and teach. I felt that my odd ideas related to early childhood education and child care, and my interests and experiences related to gender and education, as well as in international work might be appreciated, and even extended in this environment. I was hired as an assistant professor; I accepted; and I was right that it was a rare and good environment to learn and live, personally as well as professionally.

During my interviews, and in subsequent discussions with faculty across the university, there was nothing "normal" or normative about the questions I was asked. It appeared that the Curriculum and Instruction department was not "normal" and that international as well as interdisciplinary work, which seemed abnormal elsewhere, was appreciated in Madison. I found the context in Madison enriching my own learning, always challenging the ways I'd been thinking, and doing research. I liked the intellectual and often critical challenges to my past training—at empirically rigorous institutions, but inadequate in terms of "theoretical" training, one colleague suggested. While I'd indeed had rigorous "research" empirical training in both statistical/quantitative and qualitative/ethnographic research methods, my training in the theories (human capital, positivist, critical, etc.) that framed much of the work of my colleagues at Madison had been less than I needed. Life in Madison and at the University and Department were never dull; I affiliated with the African Studies Program as well as Women Studies; I liked the constancy of new things to learn, as well as different ways to think about research and teaching that were consistently presented to me by my own colleagues, doctoral students in courses, as well as through my cross-campus dialogues.

I was able to begin to teach and learn not only "how" to do research, but to publish it—a much harder endeavor for me, in order to get tenure. Drawing on Butler's notion of gender and performativity (Butler/Gender Trouble, 1992), I can honestly suggest that I performed, in specific contexts, the multiple, complex, identities of being woman, professor, mother, wife, mentee, mentor that many do during their pre-tenure years; in short I combined my professional interests in gender, work, and child care, with my personal life of work in the office and at home doing child care with my economist husband and our two young children (see Bloch, 1998).

Twenty-five years later, many of the faculty colleagues that I "grew up with" at Madison are now retired, or close to retirement; these include my long-term friends and colleagues, Bob and Jeanne Tabachnick, and Bob Koehl. In addition, I have collaborated with multiple others at Madison over my years there. Our CandI international "team" included Professors Tom Popkewitz, Michael Apple, Carl Grant, Michael Streible, Gary Price, Ann DeVaney, Ken Zeichner, Gloria Ladson-Billings, and Bernadette Baker. From Educational Policy Studies, our cross-department international and comparative education collaborators were/are enlarged by Professors Andreas Kazamias, and Amy Stambach. Over the years, Bob Tabachnick mentored and collaborated with most of us in the Curriculum and Instruction department in relation to our international research, writing, and teaching. Small groups of us, at different times, have participated on research as well as gone together on international exchanges and projects in Africa, Russia, Sweden, England, and the United States. We continue to collaborate now on exchanges, research, some writing, and just now through conferences, collaborative research with international colleagues, as well as international exchanges over the internet and through the use of videoconferencing. This leads me toward a discussion of the global and the local in educational discourses and the cultural pedagogies of teaching a course on development and curriculum planning, educational reform and knowledge.

TEACHING EDUCATIONAL PLANNING AND CURRICULUM CHANGE IN DEVELOPING COUNTRIES

"What do we know and How do we Know it?"

In this section, I want to highlight some of the theoretical debates I've had with myself and with students in the past few years as I've continued to teach the course originally pioneered by Koehl and Tabachnick as a team-taught Educational Policy Studies and Curriculum and Instruction course. The first issue is the name of the course.

When I first began to teach the course by myself, I became concerned about the title of the class. I included a reading by Arturo Escobar, *Encountering Development* (1995) as one of the early readings in the class in order to construct and deconstruct the discourses of *development, third world, and education*, as well as the discourses of *planning* and *curriculum change*. In brief, I was uncomfortable with almost every one of the words in the title of the class. One might wonder why I chose to teach a course with such a degree of discomfort with its title; but I had far less discomfort with the goals of the course, the general content that had been in the course, and I was also interested in offering a course that was decidedly focused on education in nations outside of Europe and the United States. In addition, the course was important to a variety of students who otherwise often felt that the curriculum at UW-Madison in the School of Education was oriented primarily to problems in the USA (and Europe). The study of "others", often exoticized as different, or abnormal, or in need of development, through western education, for example, to enter the "modern" world, was a topic that needed to be included in the curriculum, and critiqued. There had to be one or many more than one "place" where international students (including those from the USA) could share the knowledge and experiences they brought with them, often at great personal and financial sacrifice, to come to the United States for their graduate studies.

The problematic of global discourses of mass education, exemplified most recently in the reforms related to the UN's call for action for "Education for All", was also a topic that required critical study, and should provide a foundation for important questions about educational reform world-wide—the history as well as the direction of reform. In the current political climate (2004-2005), when it continues to appear to be the privilege of the United States of America to transfer its ideas of "freedom" and "liberty" to other nations, through schooling, media, and an exportation of political discursively constructed ideals about justice and liberty for all, it is even more important, or at least equally important, to critique the discourses of globalization of knowledge, curriculum, and pedagogy than it seemed in earlier years. It is critically important to examine different cultural constructions of freedom, liberty, social justice, and the different meanings and practices associated with the universalized term "democratic education" in terms of what local meanings might be important to different nations and people around the world. It is important to recognize that ideas that appear as "universal truth", as part of the desirable modern, civilized world, are and have been fabricated, that power in relation to knowledge must be understood as the nexus of power/knowledge relations that circulate to construct reason, regimes of truth, policy, pedagogy, and learning (see Bloch and Vavrus, 1998; Popkewitz, 2000).

The discourses of "educational planning" and "curriculum change" in "developing countries" then offered me a new opportunity to discuss these issues within different critical theoretical frameworks, including the multiple theories of post-structuralism, post-colonial and feminist theories. While it is important to recognize the reality of the spread of schooling around the world (Anderson, 2004; Coombs, 1968; Ramirez and Boli, 1987; Meyer and Ramirez, 2000), as well as the construction of the desire for modern schooling world-wide, it is also important to deconstruct the ideas of modern schooling as these frame the discourse of who is educated and who is not, which nations are developed, and which are not, which constructions of schooling should be understood as normal, and are considered abnormal and in need of interventions from the outside, or outsiders.

The course that I inherited from Bob Koehl and Bob Tabachnick then offered me an opportunity, as it had offered to them before me, to critique the philosophies of modernity and modern education that are embedded in the spread of, and desire for, westernized conceptions of schooling. The course required acknowledgement of the ways in which instruction in the United States, and at the University of Wisconsin-Madison too often privileges western rationalities and knowledge over "non-western" rationalities, knowledge, or cultural histories. The course and the dialogue with students from many nations of the world allowed for the disruption of commonly taken for granted ways of doing research that included, again, the privileging of western research, western notions of science that historically objectified the other as different, and western research that privileged itself over indigenous education and methodologies (Smith, 1999). Finally, the course and our discussions allowed for discussion of different rationalities/irrationalities related to education for citizenship. Was the western notion of education or schooling for citizenship a universal "good" that could be translated or transferred elsewhere, or, rather, was it a historical and cultural construction of an imagined citizenship for an imagined nation that embedded notions of autonomy, rationality, and independence as ideal, while collective dialogue, irrationality, emotionality, subjectivity, and dependence were made to appear abnormal? Indeed, using a post-structural, post-colonial, and feminist lens, one wondered why the questions were posed as dichotomies, and understood as hierarchically organized ways of knowing that privileged western philosophies, histories, and languages of logic, science, and progress, and meaning over those of other peoples, cultures, language groups, and nations (Willinsky, 1998; Mignolo, 1995). Moreover, if development and progress were to be constructed as good, why does it still seem increasingly important in 2005 to question the developmental "good" and progress embedded in neo-colonial practices of the new Empires that still take place as educational ideas from the west become discursively constructed as "best practices" and evidence of modernity and development in many other nations of the world? Why these ideas are still embedded in most western educational development and planning assistance programs and projects, including the fabrication of new "American style" democratic schools in Afghanistan and Iraq, most recently? Why must "girls education" be developed as a reform in all places and in all countries, unless local networks of women and girls have collectively formed ideas about what curriculum is important, and how different schools for girls might be constructed (see here, for example of different debates, chapters by Bloch and Vavrus, Stromquist, Mbilinyi, and Tabachnick in Bloch, et al., 1998).

It also remains important to acknowledge the importance of local education that takes place out of institutionalized school settings, and to study local as well as global understandings of what it might mean to be an "educated" subject as well as to distinguish the educated subject from the construction of the "schooled" subject (Bloch and Vavrus, 1998; Fendler, 1997; 2001). Using this framework, discourses of educational deficiency, underdevelopment, or being "at risk" due to a lack of schooling, come to be deconstructed, whether in the USA, or in another country where the less schooled are also normatively constructed as abnormal, less developed and modern, as well as generally less educated. In my own work, I draw on Foucault's notion of governmentality (Foucault, 1991) and power/knowledge (Foucault, 1980) to discuss the construction of subjectivities about ourselves as well as those constructed as "others", "abnormal", and in need of educational (or other) interventions (e.g., Bloch, 2003). In a recent article, I examined discourses of modernity, development, and who and what was considered educated, modern, civilized, and developed in the context of a comparative study of discourses that circulate in Senegal, Hungary, and in the United States. I also use Foucaultian theory to question the construction of differences, in general, the ability to "empower" others through transferring reforms, such as critical reflection or liberatory or "democratic" education to other nations. At the same time, I examine different ways in which post-structural notions of power/knowledge relations are *circulating* rather than directional as played out in the terms "transferred", oppressor/oppressed, or emancipation/liberation. Using post-colonial, post-structural and feminist theories, in our class, we discuss the differences between a post-structural framework that uses the notion of power/knowledge as a system of cultural reasoning that circulates globally, and locally, and power and knowledge that serves to reinforce existing power relations between, for example neo-colonial powers or richer nations and those who are dependent upon, and/or made to desire new reforms from abroad. These discourses of power/knowledge as disciplinary knowledge systems are contrasted with theoretical framings embedded in the work of the German Frankfurt School's critical theories, Gramsci's notions of hegemonic and counter-hegemonic discourses, and Freire's critical pedagogies, as we search for multiple, and complex ways to understand the relations between the global and local ideas, and "experience" (see Burbules and Torres, 2000; Scott, 1992). The need to examine how discourses flow and "settle" or become translated between and within richer and poorer nations, reproducing or producing sites of power/knowledge, resistance, and/or oppression becomes clear. I and the students who want to explore post-colonial theories of hybridity and translation investigate Bhabha's (1994) notions of hybridity as global and local discourses and identities move, collide, and become translated (O'Malley, 1998). We examine Chakrobarty's (2000) notion of knowledge as "provincial", when it is given that knowledge emanates from Europe, the USA, or the "west". We use Linda T. Smith's push for indigenous methodologies to explore the ways in which the "master's tools" (e.g., definitions of science and good research in the western countries) "can never be used to dismantle the master's house" (Lorde, 1984); we also question which tools can be used—especially as the class held at the University of Wisconsin-Madison is truly a site of critical reflection, but one in which the privileges of western researchers, publications, English as the language of instruction and reading, and research methods are used as truths that must be learned and tried, to some extent, in graduate research and education (see, for one example, Jankie, 2003).

The contradictions raised by the above discussion, I believe, are important for discussions, and as frameworks for analyses by students in the class I now teach. They are difficult ones for some class members who are new to these debates (e.g., Bhabha's *The location of culture* is a book some want to pore other, and others find immensely and too difficult). In addition, as it is often a personal as well as financial struggle for international students to come to the University of Wisconsin-Madison (or other universities in the USA or Europe) to get their graduate degrees, and the critiques undermine the idea that "western" universities are the best locations for training for research, or that the "master's tools" should NOT be privileged or held up as ideals.

In these discussions, Bourdieu's notion of distinction (1979/1984), cultural capital, habitus, and field become important to discuss (e.g., Bourdieu and Passeron, 1977/2000; Boudieu, 1991; see also Bloch and Vavrus, 1998 as one published example of such a discussion held in class), as these help us to recognize the importance of certification, the symbolic power associated with degrees from western universities, and, at the same time, the importance of "indigenous" knowledge, the need to deconstruct power/knowledge relations, and to open up new spaces for discussion, research, and collaboration.

As we re-examine new educational reforms proposed by international agencies such as UNESCO, UNICEF, the US Agency for International Development, or the World Bank, for example, in the class we distinguish between the ideas of human capital, economic capital, and cultural and social capital as used by Bourdieu (Bourdieu and Passeron, 1977/2000). We play with the idea of deschooling, and examine with great seriousness indigenous methods of education that try to integrate or hybridize local indigenous knowledge with globalized discourses of knowledge that are promoted as important for citizens in the 21st century. We examine ways in which local actors and activists in educational reforms offer different narratives of what is valuable to learn in relation to how power and knowledge relations between nations and different groups and individuals are constructed (see Breckenridge, Pollock, Bhabha, and Chakrabarty, 2002; Hardt and Negri, 2002?; Matua and Swadener, 2003; McCarthy, 1998; Smith, 1999; Willinsky, 2001). International students, in dialogue, with students from the USA, represent themselves, their experience, and the ways in which they have felt represented as the "other" or different in their own schooling, in relation to the curriculum at UW-Madison, or in relation to their own cultural value system. We discuss the false dichotomy built into the notion of "indigenous" or "native" and outsider by reading Kirin Narayan's (1993) essay in the *American Anthropologist* "How native is the native anthropologist" that complicates the essentializing notion of who is native, and who is othered.

Finally, we discuss the discursive construction of "experience" (Scott, 1992), as well as the concepts of global/local knowledge that are formed as hybridized notions of community, education, truths, and national as well as citizenship identities (Anderson, 1991; Bhabha, 1990). We look to the newer idea of a globalized discourse – universal democratic education, "modern" schooling for all, the rise of discourses of "life-long learning" and the knowledge society (see, for example, Hargreaves (2003), in relation to the rise of the risk (Beck, 1992) or the network society (Castels, 1996/2000). These concepts and constructs make it appear that we are all on the same playing field, but with unequal access to be chosen as players. These ideas suggest the necessity and desirability of abandoning "old" ways to take on more modern technical knowledge systems and skills required for a globalized, cosmopolitan, "knowledge" society and citizenry, which is at the same time uncertain and filled with risk. We examine the traveling (O'Malley, 1998) discourses of democracy and a "free" market society for all that embed assumptions that *all* appear to have free choice in an open market place of knowledge to consume the "valuable" knowledge that seems available, but that these ways of reasoning appear inclusive, while excluding many. We acknowledge that official knowledge must always be troubled.

Section IV: One example of an exchange that privileges "indigenous experience" and decolonizing strategies while acknowledging the importance of global/local and hybrid relations.

In 2001, I participated in a symposium on "Decolonizing research in education" organized by Kagenda Matua and Beth Blue Swadener at the American Education Research Association; they eventually published many of the papers, and additional ones in a volume titled *Decolonizing research: Critical personal narratives* (2003). I was to collaborate on a chapter with two former doctoral students from the University of Wisconsin-Madison, Dudu Jankie, and Miryam Espinosa-Dulanto about some of the issues raised in earlier sections of this paper; both had been in the Curriculum and Instruction 963 class, and both had worked with Professors Koehl and Tabachnick, and me at various points during their doctoral programs; in fact, Miryam completed her master's with Bob Tabachnick shortly before he retired. I served on both women's doctoral committees, and knew that we could raise certain issues about teaching and learning in the American academy that could be important.

Unfortunately, and fortunately, I was unable to participate in the final publication, though I gave the AERA paper by myself, as Dudu Jankie could not afford to attend AERA due to time and money that year. Miryam was asked to collaborate on the joint paper after the original presentation. In the end, Matua and Swadener liked the work of Jankie (a citizen of Botswana who is also an assistant professor at the University of Botswana) and Espinosa-Dulanto (a Peruvian citizen who is an assistant professor at the Pennsylvania State University) enough to offer them individual chapters in the volume, an act of generosity, and recognition of the value of their research and knowledge. These invitations, however, also broke apart our collaborative chapter.

I had a family member who was extremely ill; the deadline was drawing near. It was clear to me that the two former students of *mine* (note my colonial desire to possess!) would benefit from writing their own chapters, as the need to "publish or perish" was important to them, as to most assistant professors. I let go of my own contribution, and fretted with them about completing their own; I needn't have worried, as each was extremely capable, and only needed the opportunity to express their own ideas. Quickly, each expanded a small portion of one chapter that we were all to have written into two independent full chapters (see Espinosa-Dulanto, 2003 and Jankie, 2003).

I was asked to participate in the original symposium at the American Education Research Association about decolonizing research; one might wonder why. Before the symposium, I asked two former students, both of whom who had been in the course discussed above, to collaborate on a paper with me for presentation, and eventual publication. The two graduate students, now Dr. Dudu Jankie, at the University of Botswana, and Dr. Miryam Espinosa-Dulanto, at the Pennsylvania State University, decided they would write a chapter with me that would help to examine the different ways a professor of a course at UW-Madison, and two international students saw some of the issues in the course, and, more generally, saw learning to do research in the United States in relation to issues of importance to them in education and educational reform in their own countries.

In the AERA paper we did collaborate on, I began with a quote taken from Leila Ghandi's (2001) book, an *Post-colonial Theory: A Critical Introduction,* that was to speak to the issue of international students' desire to come to western universities for graduate degrees, their desire, and motivation for learning the newest research methodologies and educational reforms, and the expectation that some of these new "knowledge" or truths and skills would return with them to their home countries—a desire to import western knowledge expressed through the giving of national fellowships to send students abroad for their doctorates, for example.

Ghandi (2001) wrote: "The forgotten content of post-coloniality effectively reveals the story of an ambivalent and symbiotic relationship between coloniser and colonised. (P. 11). She also referred to Albert Memmi's argument that the lingering residue of colonisation will only decompose if, and when, we are willing to acknowledge the reciprocal behaviour of the two colonial partners. The colonial condition, he writes, 'chained the coloniser and the colonised into an implacable dependence, molded their respective characters and dictated their conduct' (Memmi 1968, p. 45) (in Ghandi, L. Post-colonial Theory: a Critical Introduction, p. 11)

"(It is) really an attempt to understand the puzzling circulation of desire around the traumatic scene of oppression. The desire of the coloniser for the colony is transparent enough, but how much more difficult it is to account for the inverse longing of the colonised. How, as Memmi queries, 'could the colonised deny himself so cruelly...How could he hate the colonisers and yet admire them so passionately?' (1968) p. 45" (Ghandi, ibid, p. 11).

I began my own part of the AERA presentation with this controversial quote from Memmi, and selected by Ghandi, because it troubled me that we perpetuate a colonization of knowledge and methodologies every time we have international, "third world" students enter into our doctoral programs, and our courses. The contradictions in speaking about decolonization, and the realization of my own, and my former students' desires and pleasures of working together in courses, in doctoral research, and in writing were apparent; they puzzled and troubled me. In what ways were we all, and particularly me, participating in colonization through my teaching of European theories (Foucault, Gramsci, Bourdieu, for example), and methodologies that emanate, whether qualitative or quantitative, largely from the west? What were we missing by not being able to read articles or research published in other languages, in not including unpublished manuscripts by leading researchers in other countries, beyond the "English-zone"? To what extent did my inclusion of post-colonial theorists, largely writing in the west, despite their topic and their birth or citizenship, perpetuate a privileging of "western" knowledge, despite my desire not to be doing so. Did I have a right to do research in other countries, as I'd done for most of my career? What should be my *new* ways of teaching and researching, if I didn't want to participate in colonial or neo-colonial practices?

But what does it mean to be teaching post colonial theory, or to be using western theories to deconstruct largely western knowledge? When do we stop being colonized by the discourses that surround us? Can we get to a point where we are "pure,"and not colonized by others' truths? How do our ways of reasoning represent power/knowledge relationships that discursively construct what we "desire" to know, who we think we must "be" and become, what identity we want, and "the conduct of our conduct" (Foucault, 1977)?

I began to think more about the symbiotic relationship between colonizer and colonized that Memmi and Ghandi highlighted, and that I felt was embodied in the relationship between a University Professor and her/his international graduate students from abroad. There was a pleasure and a desire on all of our parts to work together, despite reading critiques from post-colonial theory, despite wanting to write about the need to decolonize research. Could it be possible? If so, how?

Nikolas Rose writes about the construction of desire that becomes embodied through cultural reasoning systems he refers to as "governing our (own) souls" (Rose, 1989, 1999). Drawing on Foucault, he speaks about technologies of the self that relate to the acknowledgement of desire and conduct that is discursively formed, through contingent historic and cultural moments and spaces. The ideas that the Master's House can never be dismantled with the Master's Tools, a powerful point made by Audre Lorde in 1984, and repeated by many, did not take account of forces of globalization, the circulation and hybridities of knowledge, the difficulties of deconstructing one knowledge system from the other—as though one could find "indigenous knowledge" or native knowledge that had not been influenced by discursive patterns of the past and present.

When we (Jankie, Espinosa-Dulanto, and I) talked about our stories and ideas, we spoke of the contradictions and complexities of the ways in which current global/local discourses govern "the souls" of the educated subject. Jankie's research showed that she was unable to "regain" the position of native researcher in Botswana once she established she was engaged in her doctoral work at a western university. She wrote of the dilemma of doing western research as a "native"/and "other", and the inability to not be anything but a hybrid native/other in the research (see also Narayan, 1991). Her desire to do good research, using the tools she had learned at UW-Madison, despite a good dose of post-colonial theory, highlighted the conflicts within the notion of decolonization of research, or the impossibility of indigenous researchers, once educated in the west, of being "pure" or innocent—without tarnish from western regimes of truth. As Linda Smith also acknowledges, western tools of research are valuable parts of cultural as well as instrumental capital, as is, at times, a degree from a western university. Jankie's continued research in Botswana on the value of learning Setswanan languages along with English, and her ability to problematize as well as to use multiple critically reflective theories and methods in her research may demonstrate the possibilities of hybrid knowledge systems. She can no longer escape or do away with her former desire to come to the University of Wisconsin; she cannot go back in time and undo her knowledge, and, in fact, when asked, she doesn't desire this. The inverse longing of the colonized for the knowledge of the colonizer may lose sight of the complexity of relations in power/knowledge regimes, and the need for all of us (whether "colonizer" or "colonized") to understand our global/local and circulating rather than directional relations.

While for her article, Espinosa-Dulanto wrote a story about the children of "Pinky Times" (Espinosa-Dulanto, 2003, p. 45-47) in Peru who were invaded by "progress-and-changers" who lead to modern changes that eventually killed many of the native customs, ruined the environment (represented by Tellervo the tree that gave shade and friendship to the inhabitants of Pinky Times before the invasion of the progress-and-changers. Her article, however, was not about those who would have been pristine without "development", but about the inevitability of change, and shifting, multiple and mixed identities. As the progress-and-changers stayed and intermarried with the citizens of Pinky Times, there was no longer a clear way to speak of the indigenous "others", and the new comers. Her article illustrated, again, the need to complicate instruction and narratives of change with an acknowledgement of multiple, complex, discourses that come to govern, and to include some ways of reasoning about development and change, progress and the purity of remaining "untouched" or "native". Her article again illustrates the need to go forward with the ability to critically reflect in research, to have a multiplicity of strategies to use in research and writing, to use narrative, poetry, and autoethnography/autobiography to illustrate different ways of seeing, of doing research, or understanding others. Her research acknowledges the damage and unequal relations between and among groups, and nations; her research acknowledges the environmental as well as educational damage that can be done in the name of "progress-and-change".

We used multiple personal examples, as well as different dialogues from our own research projects that helped us to see the complex entangled positions of teachers/students growing up in the late 20th century, where schooling is wide-spread, and to achieve graduate standing in an American university, you have learned to want to be "modern" or perhaps even "post-modern". Jankie's and Espinosa's stories were critical to my learning, as something in the discussions we'd had throughout their years of graduate school had some impact upon them (undoubtedly sometimes positive; sometimes negative). I am the token "colonial" researcher in the group. But then we get to our questions, beginning with Kirin Narayan's and

Joan Scott's two articles on the idea of the "native anthropologist," and the one on experience as a discursive constitution of self.

While their questions and experiences of being Native/Other are better expressed in their own articles, my own questions begin with problematizing my own past and current roles as teacher of "scientific" research and western knowledge, while understanding that I have always privileged the indigenous knowledge of anyone considered "other," even to the extent of romanticizing indigenous knowledge over western school-based knowledge. But my mind is colonized with the knowledge I have been taught, and my "soul" and bodily constitution of self and desires as teacher/researcher are based on my discursively based "experience", my own graduate education, the academic world I live in and its expectations for "good scientific" educational research and publication. It is very difficult to pull myself away from some of these truths, while I attempt to deconstruct myself/my own knowledge systems, and "teach" toward new possibilities.

As a post-structural feminist researcher, I feel strong in trying to deconstruct narratives related to the constitution of "good research" (see, for example, Bloch, 2004). But I still try to understand why I privilege schooling, and worry about whether or not to romanticize indigenous cultural systems of knowledge, when those constructed often as indigenous "others" need to learn the "codes of power" through more schooling to have any chance to succeed in this world as it is constituted currently (Delpit, 1995).

I have different ways to decolonise my own bodily desires to "research others", and to "save the world" at home and abroad (from what?), but it is a difficult and contradictory task. How do I do my bodily desire of international work with others in an ethical way; how do I continue to teach international students; or do I stop.

Dudu Jankie who talked to one of my classes after the students had just read Smith's *Decolonizing Methodologies: Research and Indigenous Peoples* (1999), was asked how she felt about western research as an "indigenous" researcher? I saw her startled reaction, as the term "othered" her/while supposedly privileging her non-discursively formed natural "voice." She provided her own text of questions in our original AERA paper that I can end this paper with; thank you Dudu. While finishing her doctorate at UW Madison, studying and using post-colonial literature, she asks the following:

- How does the relationship between indigenous research methodologies and globalization provide complexities, contradictions and (im)possibilities for indigenous, native, and those who are native and other?
- What are some ways in which post-colonial researchers can write/present their data that will do justice to the participants' voices?
- What role do participants play in the reporting of the data?
- How can we deal with the complexities of 'double consciousness' when indigenous or native researchers more than often use colonized knowledge, including western languages like English and French to "dismantle the master?"
- In what ways does post-colonial theory provide (im)possibilities for dealing with the ethical and political challenges and complexities brought about by the 'colonized knowledge' native researchers have attained as part of their western education or training?

- As a native researcher, is it not possible to take some issues for granted and ignore or miss their meanings?
- Does researching a phenomenon that is based on the researcher's 'experience' suggest objectivity on the researcher's part? How can that 'experience' best be discursively and critically/reflexively used in the doing and writing/publishing of research/with/on others?

While Dudu was unable to be here to present at AERA this year, we join together to interrogate our own identities as "oppressor" and "oppressed," "non-indigenous" "colonizer," and "indigenous" "researchers" to understand the continuing postcolonial relationships and the "desire" or admiration of each for the other, in many of the different identities we have each "held," as well as the continuity of the colonially formed western schooling within much of Africa, as well as a persisting need for or "desire" for schooling in the west.

What does it mean to "be" post-colonial? Clearly, one of the problematics present within the notion of the post-colonial subject is the condition of time passing and the colonial being "past." Within multiple theoretical and empirical writings, this point has been questioned. Whether it be in past literatures that embodied the language, the publication forum, or the power relationships, it has been clear that "to be educated" has often depended upon knowledge of and ability to use the language of the "oppressor," and often has involved acceptance of the regimes of truth expressed within Western institutions, and required mastery of them in order to take on the certification (for example, the Ph.D.).

Dudu: To be post-colonial, or to read postcolonial theory are different activities and/or identities. It is very clear to both of us (Dudu and I) that post-colonial writings speak to both of us–albeit from different lens–but then we all bear and wear different lens as we look at readings, select what to appreciate, and how to value the "counting" of truth. I have offered Dudu (and others) my interest in reading post-colonial theory from the vantage point of someone who is a professor, has engaged in long-term research and maintains interest in Africa as a continent, with specific interests in research in the past (how do I and others evaluate now my past research and writing) and the types of research I might engage in the future. Dudu has offered me her own interest in looking at post-colonial theory as some of the current theory and literatures that speak to her own study of educational reform in Setswanan languages at the secondary level of schooling within Botswana. She, too, is a professor of Setswana languages and of teacher education at a university. Through her Ph.D. and publications, particularly if these appear "in the west" she may advance her career in Botswana, as well as internationally. Thus, in order to ask questions about postcolonial theory as well as our respective ideas of "knowledge," we must look at our identities, our differences in identity and the "lens" with which we take things into our subjective souls; we must look at our relationships–past and present-- and the history of governing that has formed the good citizen/scholar as a "western/colonial" (male) subject. We must try to critically analyze the embodiment of our personal/professional "desire".

My story is about my memories of work and research in Senegal, the Gambia, and in Guinea in West Africa at different periods from 1975-1994. In addition to my own memories, I will intertwine those of other writers "on Africa" both from within and without. In the end, I will try to make some "sense" by talking about (im)possibilities and possibilities as I see these in my own and others' futures.

I am heartened at this AERA meeting that an author I have come to enjoy and find challenging to me has chaired and organized her own symposium on some of these issues–Lynda...Smith, an indigenous researcher/teacher from New Zealand, who in her book......challenges other "indigenenous" researchers to decolonize their minds, and recognize the strengths of their own "sciences", "knowledge systems", and ways of thinking about research in education, and numerous other areas. When I turn to my own session related to similar issues, as a producer of Western knowledge about the "other" –in my case, generally in West Africa, but sometimes of others in the United States, I wonder at the reproduction of western ideas that I am complicit in, and for whose benefit and interest. I wonder at the requirements for participation in research on "others", and how I have come to, with good intentions, be a "coloniser" of knowledge, a spreader of lies, and in the name of "science". How can I dare to "teach" my sisters from Africa about "Education in the Developing World"? How do I answer the questions we raise in my courses: What role does a white American have in doing research in third world settings? As we proceed to spread our female "seed" and educate others, help to get them jobs in prestigious universities, and learn to publish, how are we engaging in the production and reproduction of colonization.

Theory: In claiming the authority to teach a class on "Third world" X , or to publish a volume (which I did) on "Sub-Saharan Africa, Women and Education", what knowledge can I claim. I draw on post-colonial writers to interrogate the knowledge of the coloniser while, in my class, we question our role, but gain and give credit for completion of a course on these issues. IN my post-modern self, I can never reach closure, I have unending uncertainty. And, yes, despite interrogating and deconstructing the discourse of (economic and child) development, I do not believe that I am "politically correct" nor sufficiently active to simply question the relationships of power/knowledge imbued in the terms we use, or the actions of our selves or others.

Once when I got tenure at the University of Wisconsin-Madison, someone said to me, "Aren't you proud" of all that you've written? I looked at a pile of papers that were about to be sent up to the Tenure God in the Sky for his judgment as to whether I was worthy of staying for Thirty! More years at this August western institution (to teach others), on the basis of my 6 years of writing and publication, and I thought of the poverty of so many I'd worked with in West Africa, and walked away saying, I'd done nothing. My memories of accomplishments after twenty years of teaching in the same institution leave me with similar regrets, painful memories of how I've helped a few, but had so little I had "done."

Reading theory with a capital T on post-structural feminism, post-colonial theories, theory, theory, and theory leaves me with an intellectual "high" that most empirical work and research fails to give me these days. But why? I am learning some more to help me be a better teacher of others to help them be better researchers and writers about "others". If I wanted to, I could justify my existence simply as a scholar who entered the academe with some naiveté and is doing what the academy allows–exploring narcissistically our own interests, and at times involving ourselves in some applied work that may "help". First my theoretical readings are used to elevate our discussions about the ideas of studying and working with those who are different, who are "othered". Second, my "seed" goes out and produces new theories, new research, and new ways to look at "others". Even those from, for example, Africa, use much the same methodologies, and concepts of "good research", worth of "science" propagated in the west, now with a sense of collaboration between west and being "native", with the complicity of multiple identities, with the fear of becoming "educated" and different, colonised while studying post-colonial theory.

I will return to theory with a capital T, but let me talk about the west, science, the notion of the "educated subject" that has been pushed onto Africa. What roles have I played in this push? What are the complications with an interrogation of my negative role? Why did I play the player roles that I did? What did I learn–who represented what to whom? Was I complicit? What was impossible to think? What new possibilities did I enable, IF ANY? What new possibilities are there now as I think back? And forward?

REFERENCES

Anderson, B. (1991). *Imagined communities*. London: Verso.

Anderson-Levitt, K. (Ed.). (2003). *Local meanings, global schooling: Anthropology and world culture theory*. New York: Palgrave.

Bhabha, H.K. (1994). *The location of culture*. New York: Routledge.

Bloch, M.N., Beoku-Betts, J., and Tabachnick, B.R. (Eds.) (1998). *Women and education in Sub-Saharan Africa*. Boulder, CO: Lynn Reinner.

Bloch, M.N., Holmlund, K., Moqvist, I., and Popkewitz, T.S. (Eds.) (2003). *Governing children, families, and education: restructuring the welfare state*. New York: Palgrave.

Bloch, M.N. and Vavrus, F. (1998).Gender and educational research, policy and practice in Sub-Saharan Africa: Theoretical and empirical problems and prospects. In Bloch, M.N., Beoku-Betts, J., and Tabachnick, B.R. (Eds.) (1998). *Women and education in Sub-Saharan Africa*. Boulder, Col: Lynn Reinner Publishing Co, 1-24.

Breckinridge, C.A., Pollock, S., Ghabha, H.K., and Chakrabarty, D. (Eds.). *Cosmopolitanism*. Durham, N.C.: Duke University.

Burbules, N.C. and Torres, C.A. (Eds.). (2000). *Globalization and education: Critical perspectives*. New York: Routledge.

Carnoy, M. and Samoff, J. (1990). *Education and social transition in the third world*. Princeton, N.J.: Princeton University.

Chakrabarty, D. (2000). *Provincializing Europe*. Princeton, N.J.: Princeton University.

Escobar, A. (1995). *Encountering development*. Princeton, N.J.: Princeton University.

Espinosa-Dulanto, M. (2003). Silent screams: Deconstructing (Academia) the Insider/Outsider Indigenous Researcher Positionalities. In Matua, K. and Swadener, B.B. (Eds.) (2003). *Decolonizing research in cross-cultural contexts: Critical personal narratives*. Albany, N.Y.: State University of New York, 45-52.

Gupta, A. and Ferguson, J. (Eds.). (1997). *Culture, power, and place: Explorations in critical anthropology*. Durham, N.C.: Duke University.

Jankie, D. (2003). "Tell me who you are": Problematizing the construction and positionalities of "Insider"/"Outsider" of a "Native" ethnographer in a postcolonial context. In Matua, K. and Swadener, B.B. (Eds.) (2003). *Decolonizing research in cross-cultural contexts: Critical personal narratives*. Albany, N.Y.: State University of New York Press, 87-106.

Lorde, A. (1984). *Sister "outsider": Essays and speeches*. Freedom, CA: Crossing.

Matua, K. and Swadener, B.B. (Eds.) (2003). *Decolonizing research in cross-cultural contexts: Critical personal narratives*. Albany, N.Y.: State University of New York.

Mignolo, W.D. (2001). *The darker side of the renaissance: Literacy, Territoriality, and Colonization.* Ann Arbor, Mich.: University of Michigan.

Smith, L.T. (1999). *Decolonizing methodologies: Research and indigenous peoples.* London: Zed.

Chapter 20

CHILDREN'S BOOKS ABOUT AFRICA AND THE AFRICANA BOOK AWARD

Patricia Kuntz
Madison Metropolitan School District

INTRODUCTION

Robert Koehl and Robert Tabachnick as Africanists and educators were the major faculty advisors of the African Studies Outreach Program (HEA Title VI-funded African Studies Center). They had both worked in various Nigerian schools and universities with funding from USAID in the 1960s. Upon their return, they were concerned about a lack of African content in Wisconsin schools. This situation led to their involvement with outreach staff from 1973-1995 in building a lending library of quality materials and in hosting K-12 teacher workshops and institutes. During the 1980s, Tabachnick facilitated the move of the "African Studies Outreach Collection" to the University of Wisconsin CIMC (education library at the Teacher Education Building) to make the collection more accessible to student teachers, teachers, and education staff. I interacted with these two scholars on various projects, first as an outreach assistant (1974-1978), and later as an Outreach Director (1987-1995).

In addition to my professional relationship with Koehl and Tabachnick, I earned several degrees under their direction. While an undergraduate, I took my social studies methods course with Tabachnick. As a graduate student, I enrolled in a master's program with both Koehl (Educational Policy Studies) and Tabachnick (Curriculum and Instruction). Tabachnick subsequently became a member of my dissertation committee. Their knowledge about Africa and pre-collegiate education inspired me to become a co-founder of the Children's Africana Book Award (CABA) in 1990.

PICTURE BOOKS

Although the CABA addresses books for several different genres, this paper will focus only on the award-winners for picture books for early elementary students about which Tabachnick was most interested. Picture books are a particular genre of literature designed for pre-school to grade 3 children. Nodelman summarizes the concept of picture books:

> Because they contain illustrations, picture books offer a form of pleasure different from other types of storytelling. Because they contain words, the pleasure they offer is different from other forms of visual art. (132) .... we must consider not only their beauty (pictures) but also how they contribute to our unfolding knowledge of the story that is a part of. (133)

Of course, each child has a particular cognitive ability and interest level for this genre. A story must be engaging and focus on children and not adults. Typically, these books comprise 32 pages (unpaginated) with illustrations on every page. The text is limited; however, it tells a story or gives information. Because the books are so short, they do not contain chapters. They often are enclosed in a dust-jacket and thematic end-pages.

For the purpose of this paper, picture books are those published or distributed in North America and designed for a North American audience. Although an earlier version may have been produced by an African publisher, the North American edition meets the requirements of the North American book market in terms of paper quality, font size, ink, binding, and color. In addition, these books must be readily available to North American teachers in U.S. currency for immediate purchase.

The marketability of picture books is critical for the author and publisher. Consequently, book reviews are essential promotional devices. Content, pedagogical, and reading-appropriate reviews can be found in databases such as the Comprehensive Children's Literature Database, Africa Access Review (Randolph), H-Net AfricaTeach (Michigan State University), TeachingBooks.net, and ICDL (icdlbooks.org). The Internet is also a source of books reviews such as those found at Amazon.com, Borders.com, and BarnesandNoble.com. Journals contain book reviews.

African Content

During the past 30 years, several picture books about Africa have received awards. Four titles have obtained a Caldecott (American Library Association) award for illustrations. Of these, three are folktales and one is an alphabet book. Dial has published three titles while Charles Scribner published one. All books deal with a general African setting. One book has been challenged for its reference to "God" being "black" (West).

Caldecott Honor Books have comprised five titles. Muriel and Tom Feelings published their two bilingual titles with Dial. Three other books portray folktales. Authors of the honor books commonly address life in specific countries of west, east, central, and southern Africa. In addition to ALA awards, African titles have received awards from other organizations such as the Coretta Scott King Award.

CHILDREN'S AFRICANA BOOKS

The Children's Africana Book Award (CABA) is the African Studies Association's (ASA) award for excellence in children's and young adult literature about Africa published in North America. Although African Studies (Higher Education Act-Title VI 1965) Outreach Directors (Kuntz 1979, 1997; Randolph-Robinson 1984; Schmidt 1981, 1979, 1974) have reviewed children's picture books about Africa since the early 1970s, their critiques appear to have had limited impact upon authors and publishers. Consequently, the directors have created an award that would highlight accuracy and appropriateness to offset stereotypes, inaccuracies, and derogatory labeling (Hall 1977, 1978; Rich 1974, 1976). In addition, these directors have encouraged more publications to help K-10 students become familiar with the continent. The award has been given since 1992 (Randolph 2002, 2003).

Submissions vary in type and publisher. The committee members solicit from publishers for free copies of books. Some publishers send copies while others do not. Some distribute only one of several African titles and other send only one volume of a set. Therefore, the committee considers only books which publishers submit. This policy places the burden on the publisher to be actively involved in the award-granting process. Reviewers accept any title which contains a text with more than 50 percent dealing with Africa. Over the past 13 years, the committee has reviewed over 200 titles.

The reviewers comprise ASA members with experience in pre-collegiate education and expertise in an African discipline. These reviewers are North Americans and Africans who hold an appointment for two years. Their reviews can be read on Africa Access Review and the Comprehensive Children's Literature Database and in *MultiCulture Review* or *Sankofa*. In addition to sending books to the award committee, books are distributed to other ASA members for in-depth, content-related reviews to be posted on H-Net (AfricaTeach). Consequently, there are now many locations to read reviews of children's picture books about Africa.

CABA PICTURE BOOKS

After 13 years of reviewing books for the CABA, the committee has awarded 26 children's picture books. (Appendix A) Several variables have been designated for analysis of this collection including country setting, topics, character, author, illustrator, and publisher.

Country

The setting for the books ranges from a generic African presentation to town specific. For the most part, Anglophone countries of West, East, and Southern Africa are the most frequently represented. These countries include: Ghana (2), Nigeria (2); Ethiopia (2), Tanzania (5), Uganda (1), South Africa (6), and Zimbabwe (1). Texts written in English are essential for U.S. publishers. In contrast, the representative Francophone countries are Benin, Cameroon, Madagascar, Mali (2). Titles set in Lusophone countries are rare perhaps because of the past political situation and lack of translators. Only one award-winning books portrays a North African country, Sudan. This situation may reflect the fact that most picture books set in North Africa portray Ancient Egypt rather than contemporary countries.

Topics

The topics of the text vary from alphabet, body parts, and counting books to ones dealing with disabilities (1), schooling (1), celebrations (1), childhood (5), history (1), markets (3), and economics (2). Biographies (2) and folktales (4) are also among the winners. Since publishers find folktales an easy sale, they dominate the literature field. Two books are non-fiction texts describing textile production and families from different countries. Two of the books are bilingually designed in English and an African language. The reviewers would like to see more bilingual books to promote African languages and cultural tolerance. Books about contemporary situations are increasing. Those books that focus on the child and portray the contemporary life seem to have greater success than those that deal with medieval or ancient history and folktales. A new trend is the marginalized child or adult and their relationship with the community. Africanists can encourage students and educators to examine all aspects of a targeted community. This strategy might promote books not only about folktales but biographies, governments, language, health, sports, and so forth.

Characters

Main characters among the CABA books highlight majority population children. The collection is divided between 11 girls and 14 boys of ages five to ten. Typically, male authors write about boys and female authors write about girls. However, in this collection, several authors have written about children of the opposite sex. These authors include Rappaport's *The New King*, Stuve-Bodeen's *Babu's Song*, Mollel's *Subira Subira*, and Daly's *Jamela's Dress*, *Once Upon a Time*, and *What's Cooking Jamela?* Although teachers, librarian, and parents may be concerned with the sex or gender equity in the review process, the CABA reviewers limit the value of this variable and focus on African content presentation.

Authors

Writers of these books comprise three groups: Africans, expatriates, and North Americans. African authors typically reside in an African country and have submitted their manuscript to a publisher with linkages to a U.S. publisher or distributor. Four African writers from different countries have won a CABA. Gilbert Ahiagble (Ghana) has collaborated with a U.S. Africanist, Louise Meyer, to produce *Master Weaver from Ghana*. He describes his work as an Ewe weaver through the eyes of his son. Ahiagble has demonstrated weaving at the National Museum of African Art of the Smithsonian Institute. Born in Cape Town in 1946, Niki Daly (South Africa) is both an author and illustrator. In 1982, he accepted a position at Stellenbosh University and embarked on a career in children's writing and illustrating. Over the years he has produced over 40 books for South African children (Daly, Khorana 2002) including *Jamela's Dress*, *What's Cooking Jamela*, and *Once Upon a Time*. He has received numerous other awards. Pierre Njeng (Cameroon) is a member of Aile Cameroun, an organization of writers and illustrators that creates picture books such as *Vacation in the Village*. Finally, Elinor Sisulu, born in Zimbabwe, came to Cape Town, South Africa at the end of Apartheid. As the daughter-in-law of Walter Sisulu, she is involved in contemporary politics. Her book *The Day Gogo Went to Vote* reflects that interest.

The second group comprises of the expatriates. Africans for various reasons have immigrated to Europe or North America. In their new country, they are a bridge to various African cultures. Born in Ghana, Meshack Asare earned a degree at the University of Science and Technology (Kumasi). While teaching at the American International School, he took courses in educational psychology through the University of Wisconsin Extension. Subsequently, he earned a M.A. in social anthropology at the University of London. He has written many children's books which have received African and international awards including *Sosu's Call*.

The author and illustrator team won a CABA for *Boundless Grace*. The author, Mary Hoffman born in England, is a prolific writer of children's books. Topics range from folktales, animal studies, religious stories, and the Grace series. Hoffman's editor selected the illustrator, Caroline Binch, a respected portrait artist of Africans. During Binch's childhood, her mother would tell Namibian stories which raised her interest in the continent. In preparation for the series, this team follows the life of a London family. When the father returns to Gambia, they go along too. In 1998, the Minneapolis Theater Company performed *Boundless Grace* as a play. Tolowa Mollel, reared in Arusha, Tanzania, became known as a storyteller. While earning his B.A. at the University of Dar es Salaam, he acted in many plays. He has written over ten books which have received many awards. In addition to *Big Boy* and *My Rows and Piles of Coins*, he has written folktales such as *Subira, Subira*. After a stint in Minneapolis, he now lives in Edmonton, Alberta where he is completing a doctorate on African drama. Although a Yoruba from western Nigeria, Isaac Olaleye has lived in the United States for over 30 years. He now resides in California where he has written several books including *Bikes for Rent*. Born in Zimbabwe, Ken Wilson-Max went to England as a young adult. Among his talents are writing and illustrating books such as *Halala Means Welcome!* Gebregeorgis Yohannes, an Ethiopian, now works as a children's librarian for the San Francisco Public Library. He holds a library degree from the University of Texas. With the encouragement of Jane Kurtz and the Ethiopian Books for Children and Educational Foundation, he wrote the bilingual folktale, *Silly Mammo*.

The third group comprises of writers from North American. Writers from the United States and Canada are the largest group of CABA winners. Some have knowledge of African countries while others must do extensive research to produce an authentic text.

Content Knowledge

Some trained Africanists have become involved in children's literature. Louise Meyer, for example, has worked at the National African Art Museum specializing in crafts such as weaving which resulted in *Master Weaver from Ghana*. Former Peace Corps volunteers (PCV) are the largest group of writers. Margy B. Knight (Benin 1976-77) with Mark Melnicove produced *Africa is Not a County* after participating in a summer workshop on Africa. She and the illustrator, Anne S. O'Brien, have collaborated on numerous projects.

They received the National Education Association's Author-Illustrator Human and Civil Rights Award. Melnicove received the PEN New England Discovery Award in non-fiction. Another Benin PCV (1981-83) is Jane Cowen-Fletcher. Inspired by a proverb that she heard during her assignment, she has written *It Takes a Village* among other books. Cristina Kessler (Kenya 1975-76, Seychelles 1976-78) has shared her 19 years of African experiences with children in many books. While in Sudan, she observed a water conservation strategy at En Nahud described in *My Great-Grandmother's Gourd* about Sudan (Kessler). The most recent PCV, Stephanie Stuve-Bodeen (Tanzania 1989-90), left her Wisconsin farm and university education to gain a global perspective. Se has written a series of books about Elizabeth, a Tanzanian girl. However, it is her most recent book *Babu's Song* describing a boy and his blind grandfather which won the CABA. Furthermore, the countries hosting PCVs often are the one's that are a setting for a picture book. This finding may reflect the fact that these countries are the destination of many U.S. citizens and also that these countries have had a history of writers who have succeeded in publishing titles with U.S. companies, affiliates, or distributors.

In addition to Africanists and PCVs, missionary children have become authors also. Jane Kurtz is known for her books for children and young adults dealing with Ethiopia and Eritrea. As a middle-aged mother, she began to write about her childhood experiences juxtaposed with her current observations. One of her annual trips to Ethiopia resulted in *Only a Pigeon*.

Publishing Knowledge

In contrast to writers with content knowledge, a second set of writers are professional children's books authors. These writers work with children and publishers on a daily basis. For example, David Anderson was a public school teacher and administrator when he adapted the folktale *The Origin of Life on Earth* to the picture book format. Editors familiar with the work of children's picture book authors have often requested writers to tackle a topic. For instance, Leslie Bulion, a social worker, an editor, and writer of stories for magazines and the Internet, travelled to Kenya and Tanzania where she met various families (Khorana 2003). *Fatuma's New Cloth* is a result of her trip. Page McBrier is a freelance writer and author of many books for children. In addition she is active in elementary school education. Unlike other writers, she was recruited to write the biography *Beatrice's Goat* with the reward of a trip to Uganda. Catherine Stock has lived in Europe and Africa during most of her life. After moving to Cape Town with her parents, she enrolled in the University of Cape Town to study art. She then returned to the United States to teach at the Pratt Institute of Art. *Gugu's House* is a culmination of a ten-year relationship with a Zimbabwean artist. David Wisniewski, born in England, has lived in the United States for most of his life. While working as a clown, then a puppeteer, and finally a performer in the Clarion Shadow Theatre, he met children and learned of their interests. He is recognized for his paper-cut technique used to illustrate the biography of *Syndicate*.

Some writers also have the artistic capabilities to illustrate books. For example, Daly who works in watercolors is the most prolific. However, other authors include Asare (watercolors), Cowen-Fletcher (colored pencil and watercolor wash), Diakité (mud cloth and ceramic), Njeng (tempera), Stock (watercolors), Wilson-Max (tempera), and Wisniewski (cut paper).

Authors remain a mixture of African, European, North American, and expatriate writers. Former PCVs and professional writers produce the largest number of CABA titles. Perhaps the PCVs are committed to share their experience and have the Peace Corps to facilitate this effort. In contrast, the professional writers are familiar with the market, publishers, illustrators, and readership to adjust their writing to fit each demand.

ILLUSTRATORS

Not all authors of African-content picture books are also the illustrators. For this reason, the publisher often selects an illustrator on the basis of availability, artistic competency, and experience. Because the illustrations follow the creation of the text, authors rarely meet and discuss their images with the hired illustrator. Therefore, illustrators must become familiar with the text setting, plot, and characters on their own. Only one illustrator, Bogale Belachew, born in Assela, Ethiopia still lives there as a graphic artist. He is very familiar with the setting well for *Silly Mammo*. He works with pen, ink, and tempera.

Traveling to a story site can be a major expense. Nevertheless several illustrators have made commitment to an African country for the purpose of gaining an accurate perspective of the environment and culture. Lori Lonstoeter persuaded Heifer Project, the sponsoring agency, to finance travel to Uganda if she could locate an author. Together illustrator and author prepared *Beatrice's Goat* in country where they interviewed family and neighbors of Beatrice. As a result of the proceeds from this book Beatrice is now in the U.S. studying to be a veterinarian. Nestor Hernandez went to Ghana to study weaving with Ahiagble. While in Denu, he photographed the process of weaving for *Master Weaver from Ghana*. Earl B. Lewis is one of the most awarded illustrators by the CABA committee. His illustrations bring life to the characters. After illustrating *The New King* and *Big Boy* for Clarion, Lewis went to Ethiopia to research ideas for *Only a Pigeon*. His characteristic watercolor was the medium for *My Rows and Piles of Coins*. Sharon Wilson traveled to South Africa to research the activities of the first election. She photographed people and places as a basis for her pastels on sanded board illustrations for *The Day Gogo Went to Vote*. The illustrators of these books, for the most part, are not personally familiar with the specific context of the story. They have to study photos of the site and read about the country. When the focus of the award is on the illustrations, a poor or inaccurate illustration of African content can disqualify a good story. To overcome this, editors select professional picture book artists with a large portfolio of accomplishments such as Caroline Binch for *Boundless Grace*. Aaron Boyd for *Babu's Song* (watercolors), Linda Saport for *Subira, Subira* (pastels), Kathleen A. Wilson for *The Origin of Life on Earth: An African Creation Myth* (lithographs), and Walter L. Krudop for *My Great-Grandmother's Gourd* (oil paint).

When the in-house artists are not available, publishers often hire new illustrators. Prior to Chris Demarest being an Orchard illustrator of *Bikes for Rent* (watercolors), he was a cartoonist and a greeting card, newspaper, and journal illustrator. Although Nicole Tadgell is a first-time, Moon Mountain illustrator of *Fatuma's New Cloth* (watercolors), her prize-winning work has brought her many contracts.

In summary, illustrators tend to be professional, long-term artists having contracts with specific publishers. However, in only three cases do authors and illustrators collaborate together on the book. Few artists have had experience in an African country. Finally, watercolors is the preferred artistic medium. In general, illustrators are not as familiar with African countries as are the writers. This limitation is critical since the concept of a picture book is the visual culture. Perhaps Africanists can collaborate with artists and art educators to help potential illustrators become more conversant with visual portrayals of countries.

PUBLISHERS

Editors and publishers in North America play a crucial role in the processing of manuscripts, selecting illustrators, and marketing books. To gain a profit, some companies try to recruit authors from the adult and entertainment world such as Maya Angelou who wrote *Kofi and His Magic* [Random House] and Pete Seeger who wrote *Abiyoyo Returns* [Simon and Schusters] (Gerhardt). In addition, many large companies have bought out small presses to form a conglomerate (Milliot). Publishers are varied. Those which produced CABA titles are seven major companies and eight small presses. The majority of CABA titles are published by Clarion (6), Farrar Straus and Giroux (3), Grolier (3). Over the years 1991-2004, there has been a noticeable change in publishers. Consolidations often have resulted in less interest in African-content manuscripts or in limited editorial support and cooperation. For example Penguin, a U.K. company, has purchased Dial and has replaced Dial's children's editorial staff. Houghton Mifflin purchased Clarion (6 CABAs), an early award-winning publisher; however, even with a loss of award-winners in 2004, it continues to publish books about Africa. Likewise, Simon and Schuster has bought out Antheneum, Disney now owns Hyperion, and Grolier owns Scholastic and Orchard. When there is a constant turnover in staff, it is difficult for authors and CABA committee members to work with the editor. Farrar, Straus and Giroux have shown an increased interest in African titles (3 CABA). Nevertheless, small presses such as African Sun, Boyd's Mill, Kane/Miller, Lee and Low, Millbrook, Moon Mountain, Open Hand, and Sights have submitted quality books.

African-content books have a limited printing. Because publishers do not typically consider picture books about Africa to yield great profits, they usually stipulate the minimum number for one printing. Many of the CABA and ALA-award books are now "out-of-print" such as *Only a Pigeon* (1997). This marketing policy makes it difficult for Africanists to portray verbal texts and visual culture in children's picture books.

CONCLUSIONS

This paper has examined some of the issues concerning picture books about Africa. In general, the 13 CABA books won because the publisher, editor, author, and illustrator collaborate on quality and accuracy of the text and illustrations. Most of the authors work from a real-life model and provide photos to the illustrator. By doing so, they avoid mixing different ethnic groups and using exotic people. In addition, they address contemporary issues rather than recreating folktales. Additional information such as maps, timelines, recipes, glossaries, and notes help the reader interpret the text. The study shows that the preferred countries are the Anglophone ones particularly Tanzania (5) and South Africa (6). In a time of misunderstanding of Islam, more books about Sunni and Shi'a Muslim children from various African countries would be helpful.

Heretofore, publishers have not systematically used Africanists. Publishers may want to utilize Africanists to consult with authors on content and presentation. Consultant knowledge is critical for accuracy. Faculty of the twelve HEA Title VI African Studies Center, could verify content and authenticate illustrate for books. Although Africanist may not have the time to work with editors and publishers on a regular basis, they can review books and send their reviews to the editor with a statement for future consultation.

Marketing of books about Africa also is crutial. The small runs and few picture books titles appear to marginalize African children. The Centers can promote qualify picture books in their outreach activities and at professional meetings. Members of the African Studies Association (ASA) and the African Literature Association (ALA) could take a greater role in writing reviews to help editors, authors, and illustrators understand specific strengths and weaknesses in their work. They could invite and involve publishers in panels at ASA and ALA meetings. At the annual meeting, members might waive registration fees for local librarians, writers, and illustrators. Members in Washington, DC could attend the annual CABA Library of Congress awards ceremony. During the summer, members might participate in library reading groups for children at public libraries. Members might write proposals to NEH and USED/OIE for grants to fund workshops or travel to Africa such as to the Zimbabwe Book Fair.

Finally, bilingual books are critical for readers' understanding of the continent. Africanists, as students, staff, or faculty of African language programs, with superior-level proficiency could assist in preparing bilingual texts for regional languages. Most of the HEA Title-VI Centers offer three years of several major languages such as Ancient Egyptian, Arabic, Hausa, Swahili, Shona, Twi, Wolof, Yoruba, and Xhosa. Writing a bilingual text with an author could be a project for advanced students. The National African Language Resource Center can plan a critical role in matching language specialists with authors. The CABA committee has provided a start; however, much more is needed to inform North American children about the continent of Africa particularly through picture books.

REFERENCES

Daly, Niki. "Out Of My Skin." *Sankofa* 1 (2002): 35-44.

Gerhardt, Lillian H. "Big Names And Small Books." *School Library Journal* 40, No. 1 (1994): 4.

Hall, Susan. "Tarzan Lives! A Study Of The New Children's Books About Africa." *Interracial Books For Children Bulletin* 9, No. 1 (1978): 3-7.

---. *Africa In U.S. Educational Materials*. New York, NY: African American Institute, 1977.

Johnson, Feng-Ling Margaret. Using Children's Multicultural Literature In The Culturally And Linguistically Diverse Classroom: An African Example. *Minne TESOL/WITESOL Journal*, 21 (2004): 71-97.

Kessler, Cristina. "The Story Behind 'My Great-Grandmother's Gourd.'" *Sankofa* 2, (2003): 26-28.

Khorana, Meena G. "Fatuma's New Cloth: Sweet On The Outside And Inside." *Sankofa* 2, (2003): 71-75.

---. "The Winner: Niki Daly: Exploring The 'Dual Reality' Of Children's Lives." *Sankofa* 1, (2002): 71-75.

Kuntz, Patricia S. *City Children In African Children's Literature*. Washington, DC: ERIC Document, 1997. (ED 405 586)

---. *Books About Africa For Children And Youth*. Madison, WI: Department Of Public Instruction, 1979. (ED 188 986)

Milliot, Jim, And Diane Roback. "Random Keeps Top Slot Among Children's Publishers. *Publishers Weekly* 250, No. 38 (2003): 37.

Nodelman, Perry. "Picture Books." *The Pleasures Of Children's Literature*. White Plains, NY: Longman, 1992. 130-156.

Randolph, Brenda. "The Children's Africana Book Awards: Expanding Perspectives On Africa." *Sankofa* 1, (2002): 60-68.

Randolph, Brenda. "Children's Africana Book Awards: The Publishing Year 2002." *Sankofa* 2, (2003): 62-70.

Randolph-Robinson, Brenda. "The Depiction Of South Africa In Children's Literature." *Interracial Books For Children Bulletin*, 15, No. 7-8, (1984): 14-22.

Rich, Evelyn J. " Good News And Bad News: African Studies In American Schools, 1955-1975." *(African) Issue* (Summer/Fall), 1976.

---. Mind Your Language. *Africa Report* 20, No. 5 (1974): 7-49.

Schmidt, Nancy J. *Children's Fiction About Africa In English*. New York, NY: Conch Magazine, 1981.

---. Criteria For Evaluating Pre-Collegiate Teaching Materials On Africa. In M. Wiley (Crofts) (Ed.), *African Outreach*. Waltham, MA: Crossroads Press (African Studies Association), 1981. See Also: *African Issue* 10, No. 3-4 (1980).

---. *Supplement To Children's Books On Africa And Their Authors*. New York, NY: Africana, 1979.

---. *Children's Books On Africa And Their Authors: An Annotated Bibliography*. New York, NY: Africana, 1975

West, M. *Trust Your Children: Voices Against Censorship In Children's Literature*. New York, NY: Neal-Schuman, 1996.

RELEVANT WEB SITES

African Access % Brenda Randolph *http://filemaker3.mcps.k12.md.us/aad/http ://africanaccess.com*

African Studies Association *http://www.africanstudies.org/Awards_Child.html*

Children's Literature Comprehensive Database *http://clcd.odyssi.com/cgi-bin/member/search*

Cooperative Children's Book Center documents number of multicultural books published since 1994 *http://www.education.wisc.edu/ccbc/*

Children's Book Award (1991-present) *http://www.indiana.edu/~libsalc/african/awards* (by Kuntz, P.S.)

Children's Literature by Author, *http://web.uflib.ufl.edu/africana/children.htm* (by Osaki, L.T.)
H-Net AfriTeach (Book Reviews) *http://www.h-net.msu.edu/reviews*

APPENDIX

CABA 1992-2003 Picture Books

Winners
Africa is Not a Country. Margy Knight and Mark Melnicove. Il. Anne S. O'Brien. (Millbrook), 2000.
Babu's Song. Stephanie Stuve-Bodeen. Il. Aaron Boyd. (Lee and Low), 2004.
The Day Gogo Went to Vote. Elinor Sisulu. Il. Sharon Wilson. (Little Brown), 1996.
Fatuma's New Cloth. Leslie Bullon. Il. Nicole Tadgell. (Moon Mountain), 2002. *It Takes a Village*. Jane Cowen-Fletcher. (Scholastic), 1994.
The Magic Gourd. Baba Wagué Diakité. (Scholastic), 2003.
Master Weaver from Ghana. Gilbert Ahiagble and Louise Meyers. Il. Nester Hermandez. (Open Hand), 1998.
My Rows and Piles of Coins. Tololwa Mollel. Il. E.B. Lewis. (Clarion), 1999.
The New King. Doreen Rappaport. Il. E.B. Lewis. (Dial), 1995.
Only a Pigeon. Christopher and Jane Kurtz. Il. E.B. Lewis. (Simon and Schuster), 1997.
The Origin of Life on Earth: An African Creation Myth. David Anderson. Il. Kathleen Atkins Wilson. (Sights), 1991.
Syndicate: Lion King of Mali. David Wisnieski. (Clarion), 1992.
What's Cooking Jamela. Niki Daly. (FSG), 2001.

Honor Books
Beatrice's Goat. Page McBrier. Il. Lori Lohstoeter. (Atheneum), 2001.
Big Boy. Tolowa Mollel. Il. E.B. Lewis. (Clarion), 1995.
Bikes for Rent. Isaac Olaleye. Il. Chris Demarest. (Orchard), 2001.
Boundless Grace. Mary Hoffman. Il. Caroline Binch. (Dial), 1995.
Gugu's House. Catherine Stock. (Clarion), 2001.
Halala Means Welcome: A book of Zulu Words. Ken Wilson Max. (Hyperion), 1998.
Jamela's Dress. Niki Daly. (FSG), 1999.
My Great-Grand Mother's Gourd. Cristina Kessler. Il. Water L. Krudop. (Orchard), 2000.
Once Upon a Time. Niki Daly. (FSG), 2003.
Silly Mammo: An Ethiopian Tale. Gegregeorgis Yohannes. Il. Bogale Belachew. (African Sun), 2002.
Sosu's Call. Meshack Asare. (Kane/Miller), 2002.
Subira, Subira. Tolowa Mollel. Il. Linda Saport. (Clarion), 2000.
Vacation in the Village. Pierre Yves Njeng. (Boyd's Mill), 1999.

(NF = non-fiction *BI* = biography *FT* = folktale *PR* = proverb*)*

Chapter 21

WHAT IS IT THAT YOU WANT TO DO? THE INQUIRY PEDAGOGY – A TRIBUTE TO BOB TABACHNICK

Zachary Cooper
Freelance Writer, Educator and Educational Film Producer
Wisconsin, USA

I met Professor B. Robert "Bob" Tabachnick in early 1970s and was immediately impressed by his friendliness, inspired by his sincerity and genuine interest in his students as individuals, and induced into his intellectual interests. His interests that appealed to me included Inquiry Methodology, Multicultural Curriculum, Teacher Socialization/Teaching Strategies, and students' learning process and self-discovery.

After completing a master's degree in American History, I was accepted into the University of Wisconsin- Madison Department of Curriculum and Instruction. Bob agreed to take me on as his student in this doctoral program. He was not only a mentor/advisor but a respected friend and eventually a colleague.

Through courses, independent reading and research recommended by Bob, and observation outside of the classroom, I became familiar with his teaching and learning philosophy and what constituted a learning environment. He believed in identifying where the learner was and helping the learner to discover his/her own direction. It was in this out-of-school environment that Bob learned about me and how better to advise me. For example, Bob repeatedly requested that I address him as "Bob." Culturally I was taught, out of respect, to address people by their title of Mr. or Mrs., Doctor, Chief or Coach, etc. There I was addressing him as Professor Tabachnick, and he was continually reminding me to call him Bob. This informal approach by Bob created an environment of easiness which enabled me to feel like a member of his extended family. He though teachers sometimes intimidated learners by traditional learning environments and activities. He created a comfort zone where I spent many occasions with Bob, his wife Jeanne and family at his home in a rustic area of Cross Plains, Wisconsin. There were other times when we met for lunch or dinner at a Chinese restaurant about three blocks from the Teacher Education Building. These informal settings allowed for the sharing of background information. He was Jewish and from a big city in New York, while I was African American and from the small town of Brunswick, Georgia.

These differences greatly contributed to my broad learning about people, cultures, differences to be considered in life.

I learned about attending a synagogue and being asked to wear a yarmulke. I protested to wearing it because I thought the people in attendance would think that I was pretending to be Jewish. However, I was assured that wearing the yarmulke was a sign of respect and therefore acceptable for non-Jewish people to wear. He learned about my experience as a youth attending school in a segregated community in the south where all of my principals and teachers, classmates and custodians were black. Even the chalkboards were black. The only things not black were the people pictured in the history textbooks.

Bob was an advocate of story telling as an educational vehicle. I recall telling Bob about when I was in the sixth grade and asking my Principal J.S. Wilkerson why weren't there any black people, except for Booker T. Washington and George Washington Carver, in textbooks? Principal Wilkerson replied with a story about third grade students who asked him for some books on Africa. He gave the student several books about Africa. After about two weeks, the student returned the books with the comment, "I read all of the books you gave me and in all the books the lion was either captured or killed. Why is it that if the lion is the king of the jungle?" Principal Wilkerson put his arms around the quizzical third grader's shoulders and said slowly and emphatically, "Until the lion learns to write his own book, that's the way it will always be." In other words, one has to write his or her own book, and that is what Bob enabled me to do.

Our informal talks gave Bob insight into guiding me along in my doctoral program. He would often ask me, "What is it that you want to do?" Prompted by his continuous inquiry and my reflection, I was able to self discover what I wanted to do. My interest related to a question many educators were asking at the time, "How do you fairly represent African Americans in the history textbooks?" Bob then was able to advise me on what books to read and courses to take. He knew exactly who should be on my doctoral committee, recommending Curriculum and Instruction Professors Jack Kean, Carl Grant, Tom Popkewitz and Tom Shick (African American Studies). Outside readers included Professors William Brown (African History), Edward Gargen (European History) and Stanley Kulter (American History).

Working with Bob as my major professor was the culmination of years of conscious and unconscious, planned and unplanned preparation beginning with my sixth grade inquiry to Principal J.S. Wilkerson, "Why aren't there any blacks in the history textbooks?" and reading with Bob's inquiry, "What is it that you want to do?"

Bob's philosophy of teaching was incorporated into mutual activities we worked on following my graduation. One project, "Parents in Improving Children's Achievement" was aimed at reaching students at a young age, 4th or 5th grade, when they are establishing personal goals for later achievements. The project resulted in multi-cultural guides to be used by teachers, and an after-school community-based program to provide encouragement in setting goals and in developing learning habits to reach those goals. An example of my application of Bob philosophy is a Jamaica-Madison Cultural Exchange for selected young students in which I utilize the inquiry model to facilitate learning through a variety of methods, including lectures, dialogue, discussion, photos, development of videos, journal writing, and practical experience. In this way, I have continued to help them do what they want to do. Bob influenced me and a part of him will always remain in me.

REMEMBRANCES

Dianne Bowcock (d. Feb. 7, 2004)

Hi Michael,

I remember your name, but don't recall if we really knew each other from UW-Madison. I was in Ed Policy Studies, completed in 1985. Patty Kuntz called me that you are putting together a "surprise" booklet for Bob Koehl and Bob Tabachnick and you are requesting statements from students who had focused on Africa and had been in their program. She wasn't specific about the type of contents you are seeking or the timeframe that you are working on. I would like to contribute to this if what I have to offer is appropriate. Patty mentioned that you might want articles (which I don't have). I have not worked in Africa, but would be pleased to make a statement or something like "rememberances" about interactions, classes, or the program with Bob and Bob. I am also in touch with Liz Lowe Leu (see her e-mail address above) who might be able to connect us with some additional people. She might have some information about how we can reach Peter _____ (Zimbabwe), James Urwick, or James Makano (Nigeria-Kano area). Perhaps she knows of others too.

I will stop here, and wait to hear your response. I think a collection of things that conveys personal recollections and articles, or focus of work would be great. Let me know if there is a way I can assist. Cheers, Dianne (November 5, 2003)

Hi Michael,

I have gotten behind on working on this -- but want you to know that I passed it on to Liz Lowe Leau, and I have found old addresses for Golden Chenkenyera and James Urwick. I do not have e-mail addresses for them so I have to send them letters by mail (which I will try to do today). But it could be a while on hearing back from them. Thank you for taking the initiative on this. Dianne (December 10, 2003)

Editor's Comment: *Two months after receiving this last mail form her, Dianne passed away on February 7, 2004. We found no greater tribute to the Bobs than knowing that only eternity would have the complete records of the lives they have touched. May Dianne's Soul Rest In Peace!* Michael O. Afoláyan

ABOUT THE CONTRIBUTORS

Michael O. Afoláyan, Ph.D.

Lead editor of this book, is former student of B. Robert Tabachnick and Robert Koehl at the University of Wisconsin-Madison (1986-1993), Michael currently teaches in the Department of Curriculum and Instruction at Southern Illinois University Edwardsville. Michael has contributed to several academic journals and a variety of books in the fields of education, African studies, and sociolinguistics. His current edited book, *Dilemmas of Higher education in Postcolonial African Nations* is currently in press.

Precious O. Afoláyan, Ph.D.

Former student of B. Robert Tabachnick at the University of Wisconsin-Madison, 1987-1996, Precious is a career educator. Former adjunct professor in educational leadership at Southern Illinois University Edwardsville, Precious currently serves as Principal at Lincoln Charter School, Venice, Illinois.

Marianne Bloch, Ph.D.

Former colleague of the two Bobs, Marianne teaches in the Department of Curriculum and Instruction at the University of Wisconsin-Madison. Her research has focused on historical and cross-cultural issues related to early childhood education and child care in the United States, Africa, and in East/Central Europe. Her interests include studies of women, work, child care, and child care policy. Her latest research focuses on the implications of welfare reform in Wisconsin on families, children, and child care.

Dallas Browne, Ph.D.

Co-editor of this book, and president of Mid-American Alliance for African Studies, Dallas teaches anthropology at Southern Illinois University Edwardsville. He is the former Chair of the Department of Anthropology At SIUE and is former president of the St. Louis

Council on Foreign Relations. Dallas is also the current vice president of the St. Louis Consular Corps, a diplomatic organization, and the Honorary Consul for the United Republic of Tanzania, as well as a member of the World Affairs Council. From time to time he serves as an International Election Monitor in African and Latin American nations.

Zachary Cooper, Ph.D.

Former student and later co-worker with Bob Tabachnick at the University of Wisconsin-Madison, Zack is a freelance writer, educator and educational film producer. Zachary Cooper's research is on the images and representations of African American people in books. He is a motivational speaker whose job takes him all over the United States. Zack currently resides in Madison, Wisconsin.

Anthony M. Denkyirah, Ph.D.

Educated in Ghana and the United States, Anthony obtained a B.Ed. degree from the University of Cape Coast, Ghana, and degrees of MS.Ed and Ph.D in Special Education from Southern Illinois University Carbondale, USA. He is currently an Assistant Professor of Special Education at Southern Illinois University Edwardsville where he teaches undergraduate and graduate courses in secondary school programming, behavior management, and moderate to severe disabilities. Anthony is the author of journal articles and several book chapters in areas of special and international education. He is a current recipient of the Dean's grant on research enhancements to fund his research on recording and reporting of K-12 student misbehaviors.

Felix Ekechi, Ph.D.

Former student of Robert Koehl, Felix is Professor Emeritus at Kent State University and former Coordinator of African Studies Program, and Chair of the Kent State University Africa Initiative (Inter-African universities' Exchange Program). He is the author of several books and articles on African history, culture, religion, and women. His most recent book is *Tradition and Transformation in Eastern Nigeria: A Social and Political History of Owerri*. He is currently completing the biography of a Nigerian clergyman and politician, Rev. M. D. Opara, entitled, *"For God and Country: The Life and Work of Rev. M.D. Opara, 1915-1965.*

Toye J. Ekunsanmi, Ph.D.

Committed science educator, Toye been science teacher at the secondary level and professor at universities in Nigeria and the United States for more than two decades. He emigrated to the United States in 1997, where he has since taught Biology at secondary and tertiary levels. Currently an Assistant Professor of Biology at the University of Wisconsin,

Washington County, Toye's major areas of research are industrial microbiology and microbial ecology. However, his training as a teacher has given him a strong and abiding interest in Science Education, especially since he greatly enjoys teaching his subject.

Mabel O.N. Enwemnwa, Ph.D.

A lifelong educator, Mabel's story epitomizes a lifetime of serious commitment to education and human services. Born and raised in Nigeria as the only daughter among several male siblings, Mabel grew up to be a strong advocate of women education and equal opportunities across genders. Mabel has been an avid foreign language teacher at the secondary school level where she rose to the rank of senior principal in the Bendel State Teaching Service, before returning to the U.S.A. for her doctorate degree in Educational Policy Studies from the University of Wisconsin in 1993. Still in the area of education, Mabel worked for six years with the Center for Prevention and Intervention as consultant on multicultural prevention education for women and children. She currently works with Prince George County Public Schools Board of Education in the state of Maryland. She is married with children.

Scott Johnston, Ph.D.

An international scholar, Scott returned to Japan in 2004 to become a professor in the Department of International and English interdisciplinary Studies at Osaka Jogakuin College. He earned his Ph.D. at Michigan State University in Curriculum, Teaching and Educational Policy. He carried out his doctoral research in Zimbabwe examining how a group of science teachers made sense of student centered teaching and learning methods. In addition to his research in Zimbabwe, he has taught for nine years in Japan and one year in China. Currently, he is working with a group of Japanese English teachers as they try to improve their teaching while understanding how their students learn.

Didacus Jules, Ph.D.

Co-editor of this book, Didacus is a former student of Bob Tabachnick and Bob Koehl. He is a recent Permanent Secretary for Education in St. Lucia (1997-2004) and a former Permanent Secretary for Education, Culture, Youth and Sports in Grenada during the Grenada Revolution. Didacus has represented the Caribbean on numerous international bodies and has served as advisor to many Caribbean governments in literacy, education reform and public sector reform. He was Chairman of the Task Force that prepared the "World Bank's Caribbean Education Strategy 2020" and was one of three authors of the new OECS Education Reform Strategy.

Stefan, Jeremy and Sarah Koehl

The three are children of Robert "Bob" Koehl who provided us with information about, and pictures of their father. They live in the United States and Canada. The trio jointly gave the tribute to Bob Koehl as recorded in Chapter 19.

Patricia Kuntz, Ph.D.

A former student of both Bob Tabachnick and Bob Koehl, Patty currently works with Madison Metropolitan School District (MMSD). Kuntz's research, writing and advocacy on children's literature, as well as many years of travels, span across many countries in Africa and the Middle-East. She is a teacher, librarian and foreign language expert. Kuntz has been an administrator at Universities of Wisconsin-Madison and Florida, Gainesville. Kuntz is a strong advocate against stereotypes and media misrepresentation of African children and African children literature in North America.

Gloria Ladson-Billings, Ph.D.

A close former colleague of B. Robert Tabachnick, Gloria is the current president of American Education Research Association (AERA). Gloria teaches in the Department of Curriculum and Instruction at the University of Wisconsin-Madison. Her research focuses on successful teaching of African-American children and critical race theory. Ms. Ladson-Billings is the author of well-circulated books, *The Dreamkeepers: Successful Teachers of African-American Children*, *Crossing Over to Canaan: The Journey of New Teachers in Diverse Classrooms* and numerous journal articles and book chapters. Ladson-Billings is the current editor of the Teaching, Learning and Human Development section of the *American Educational Research Journal*.

Cameron McCarthy, Ph.D.

A former student of Bob Tabachnick and Bob Koehl, Cameron teaches mass communications theory and cultural studies at the University of Illinois at Urbana. He is Research Professor, Communications Scholar and University Scholar in the Institute of Communication Research. Cameron is the author or co-author of numerous articles and books on theoretical discourses on race, curriculum, education and culture. He writes in English as well as Spanish. He holds a Ph. D degree from the University of Wisconsin-Madison.

Chang'aa Mweti, Ph.D.

Former student of the two Bobs, Chang'aa is an internationally known African Storyteller, humorist, and standup comedian. He has organized and presented hundreds of storytelling workshops and speeches across the United States, in Europe, as well as in his native country, Kenya. His audiences have included public schools, libraries, clubs, religious organizations, scholars and even politicians. His academic and recreational workshops have been well received across the globe and at many university campuses. His most current presentations were at the 2003 and 2004 National Youth-At-Risk Conferences. Mweti currently holds the position of an assistant professor in the Department of Education at the University of Minnesota in Duluth.

Bankole Oni, Ph.D.

Long time professor and researcher, Bankole obtained a Bachelor of Science degree in Geography from the University of Ibadan, a Diploma in Demography from Cairo, a Master of Science degree in Economics frrom the University of Walesand and a Ph.D degree from University of Ibadan. He is the curent director of Nigeria Institutue of Social and Economic Research (NISER).

Arit Oku-Egbas, M.Lit.

An international figure in gender relations, Arit has Masters degrees in Literature, and Women and Development from The Hague. She also holds a diploma in Public Relations. Specializing in Communication, Gender and Development, Oku-Egba's working career spans more than fifteen years in sub-Saharan Africa. She works with the media as well as with international and African organizations. She is a professional advocate of general health, sexual/reproductive health, as well as rights and gender issues. She was the Research and Documentation Officer for Africa Regional Sexuality Resource Centre; public affairs coordinator for Centre for Development and Population Activities (CEDPA/ Nigeria) and Deputy features/women editor of *The New Vision* newspaper in Uganda. As partner in the public relations firm, Trucontact Public Relations and Communications, Arit is channeling her passion for public relations and marketing communications to promote behavior change in health and development in Nigeria. Arit lives in Nigeria with her husband and three children.

Marguerite Parks, Ph.D.

An educational theorist, Marguerite teaches at the University of Wisconsin Oshkosh where her activities include teaching a graduate level course in Multicultural Education. She received her Ph.D. from the University of Iowa in Curriculum and Instruction, Social Foundations and Minority Education. Her K-12 teaching experience was at Schlagle High School in Kansas City, Kansas where she taught High School Drama, Debate, English and Forensics. Park's current research centers on White privilege and English as a Second Language/Bilingual Education in rural schools.

Tom Popkewitz, Ph.D.

A postmodernist theorist, Tom is Professor and former Chair, Department of Curriculum and Instruction at the University of Wisconsin-Madison, USA. Tom's studies are concerned with the knowledge or systems of reason that govern educational policy and research in teaching, teacher education, and curriculum. His research includes historical, ethnographic and comparative studies of national educational reforms in U.S. Europe and Latin America. His most recent books relate to the changing welfare state and the family and child; educational "partnerships" and reconstituting the relation of the state and civil society, cultural history and education, and critical studies of global educational restructuring; and multiple modernities and the new education.

David Tabachnick, Ph.D.

An Assistant Professor of sociology at Muskingum College, New Concord, Ohio, David teaches about problems of international development and is about to publish his manuscript analyzing the 400-year-old clash between exclusively individual and multi-layered common property systems in Europe, the United States and Africa. David is the son of B. Robert and Jeanne Tabachnick.

Frances Vavrus, Ph.D.

Former student of Bob Tabachnick and Bob Koehl, Frances is an Associate Professor of Education in the Department of International and Transcultural Studies at Teachers College, Columbia University. Her current research focuses on international development policy, gender and health in Sub-Saharan Africa, and human rights education. She holds a Ph.D. from the University of Wisconsin-Madison.

Ken Zeichner, Ph.D.

Close friend and associate of Bob Tabachnick, Ken is Hoefs-Bascom Professor of Teacher Education and Associate Dean of the School of Education at the University of Wisconsin-Madison. In addition to his work in teacher education in Madison, Ken has worked in a number of countries in Latin America, Africa, and Australia on issues related to teacher education, teacher development, and practitioner inquiry. His works in action research and multicultural education are respected all over the world.

INDEX

A

academic achievements, 34
academic performance, 217
academic tasks, 211
academics, 18, 28, 69, 147, 167, 169, 212, 227, 232
acceptance, 114, 284
access, xv, 18, 19, 24, 25, 65, 70, 71, 74, 88, 122, 124, 125, 130, 155, 165, 184, 188, 201, 229, 239, 279
accommodation, 76, 84, 138
accountability, 20, 154
accumulation, 164
accuracy, 153, 179, 291, 296, 297
achievement, 25, 85, 118, 186, 211, 214
action research, xv, xviii, 143, 144, 145, 146, 147, 148, 149, 150, 151, 152, 153, 154, 155, 156, 157, 158, 159, 160, 272, 310
activism, xvi, 99, 103, 109
adaptation, 185, 215
adjustment, 75, 215, 244
administrators, 59, 72, 123, 154, 165, 195, 196, 197, 240
adolescence, 225
adolescents, 55, 225
adulthood, 49
adults, 181, 184, 290
advertising, 263
advocacy, 98, 102, 110, 115, 196, 308
aesthetics, 13
affect, xvi, 81, 124, 162, 173, 178, 196
Afghanistan, 4, 277
Africa, vii, ix, x, xvi, xviii, 4, 6, 7, 10, 11, 14, 15, 20, 27, 31, 34, 40, 41, 45, 46, 48, 51, 52, 53, 54, 55, 58, 59, 61, 62, 65, 71, 73, 89, 93, 98, 99, 100, 101, 106, 107, 110, 115, 119, 120, 122, 130, 131, 132, 140, 143, 159, 160, 161, 163, 164, 167, 170, 171, 172, 173, 175, 176, 177, 186, 189, 190, 191, 194, 259, 260, 261, 264, 272, 273, 275, 284, 285, 286, 289, 290, 291, 292, 293, 294, 296, 297, 298, 299, 302, 303, 305, 306, 308, 309, 310
African Americans, 131, 140, 223, 224, 228, 229, 230, 233, 302
African languages, 41, 58, 292
agar, 189
age, xiv, 3, 31, 42, 61, 73, 74, 79, 81, 86, 87, 88, 89, 99, 109, 115, 116, 117, 118, 133, 152, 161, 173, 194, 246, 261, 302
agent, 66, 71
aging, 81
agricultural sector, 44
agriculture, 74, 170, 179
AIDS, 22, 27, 49, 89, 93
Algeria, 53
alienation, 54, 171
alkaloids, 179
alternative, xiii, 7, 10, 38, 70, 72, 76, 85, 138, 148, 170, 174
alternatives, 210, 219, 243, 260
ambiguity, 67
ambivalence, 224
ambivalent, 280
American culture, 135
American Educational Research Association, 215
anatomy, 65
anger, 82
animals, 57, 58, 116
annihilation, 55
anthropology, 5, 274, 286, 293, 305
antibiotic, 189
anxiety, 254
appetite, 5
argument, 23, 25, 27, 42, 43, 46, 53, 59, 67, 213, 224, 280
arrest, 108, 116, 174
articulation, 22, 25, 26, 113

Asia, ix, 4, 11, 20, 89, 161, 264
Asian countries, 162, 242, 249
assassination, 33
assessment, 25, 26, 46, 149, 200, 217
assets, 117, 171
assignment, 20, 21, 146, 149, 150, 241, 244, 249, 294
assimilation, 244
association, x, xi, 6, 7, 9, 13, 28, 59, 65, 97, 103, 104, 109, 112, 132, 137
assumptions, 19, 74, 123, 213, 224, 249, 279
athletes, 225
atrocities, 4
attachment, 200, 203, 211, 241
attention, ix, 7, 8, 25, 62, 75, 79, 86, 92, 98, 101, 111, 122, 126, 139, 146, 149, 162, 181, 182, 183, 185, 190, 215, 217, 240, 241
attitudes, xv, 62, 74, 85, 89, 121, 122, 154, 230, 231, 245
attractiveness, 168
Australia, 11, 144, 147, 310
authenticity, 69
authority, 8, 78, 85, 90, 207, 285
autonomy, 9, 20, 98, 277
availability, 88, 183, 185, 190, 295
awareness, xv, 23, 122, 124, 164, 173, 184, 187, 243

B

baggage, 61
banks, 22, 167, 183
Barbados, 5, 7, 8, 9, 13, 32, 40
bargaining, 65, 66, 67, 69, 72, 74, 75, 76, 77, 79, 80, 81, 82, 84, 87, 88, 89, 90
barriers, xv, 20, 68, 139, 211, 224
basic needs, 178
batteries, 182
behavior, 61, 89, 105, 154, 227, 232, 233, 306, 309
behavioral problems, 200
belief systems, 56, 134
beverages, 34, 123
bilateral aid, 23, 27
binding, 80, 290
biotechnology, 187
birth, 54, 100, 136, 281
black women, 234
blame, 68, 77, 79, 80, 81, 82, 85, 105, 186, 229
blind spot, 4
blocks, 226, 301
blood, 4, 36, 103, 225
boat people, 11
body, 5, 25, 36, 37, 38, 44, 65, 66, 67, 78, 80, 81, 90, 109, 111, 135, 167, 259, 292

bonds, 218
borrowers, 22
boys, 59, 74, 82, 84, 229, 242, 292
brain, 27, 29, 65, 115, 161, 164, 167, 168, 169, 170, 171, 172, 176
brain drain, 27, 29, 161, 164, 167, 168, 169, 170, 171, 172
Brazil, 167
breeding, 179
Britain, 27, 56, 106, 169, 193
brothers, 231
building blocks, 210
bureaucracy, 83, 163, 171, 181

C

calculus, 114
caliber, 34
calibration, 212
Cambodia, 177
Cameroon, 291, 293
campaigns, 101, 102, 112, 113
Canada, 11, 29, 39, 62, 149, 195, 203, 267, 293, 308
cancer, 223
candidates, 58
capacity building, xvi, 161, 162, 163, 164, 165, 169, 173, 174
capitalism, 12, 56, 58
cardiologist, 225
career development, x
Caribbean, ix, xi, xiv, 5, 6, 7, 8, 9, 11, 13, 14, 20, 21, 23, 29, 37, 61, 140, 307
carrier, 36
case study, 145, 158, 159, 160, 203
cash crops, 110
cast, 78
causal relationship, 122, 125, 214
causality, 219
celestial bodies, 179
cell, 182, 251
cell phones, 251
Central Europe, 305
ceramic, 294
certificate, 87, 115, 123, 125, 169
channels, 137
charm, 115
chemical industry, 174
chicken, 77
childhood, 32, 75, 274, 292, 294, 305
children, xvii, xviii, 22, 34, 39, 43, 44, 55, 56, 57, 59, 60, 74, 76, 79, 81, 82, 107, 108, 115, 118, 133, 138, 187, 193, 194, 195, 196, 197, 198, 200, 201, 202, 203, 210, 211, 212, 214, 217, 218, 223,

225, 226, 227, 228, 229, 232, 233, 234, 239, 260, 261, 262, 263, 264, 274, 275, 282, 286, 290, 292, 294, 297, 299, 305, 307, 308, 309
China, 38, 182, 307
circulation, 183, 281
citizenship, 22, 277, 279, 281
civil servants, 73
civil service, 181
civil society, 18, 20, 23, 310
classes, 10, 12, 138, 139, 180, 201, 212, 231, 239, 240, 252, 261, 272, 273, 274, 283, 303
classification, 217, 218
classroom, 35, 66, 69, 81, 84, 86, 87, 91, 138, 143, 144, 145, 146, 148, 149, 152, 154, 155, 158, 180, 182, 184, 187, 196, 197, 200, 203, 211, 212, 215, 216, 217, 220, 230, 238, 239, 240, 241, 245, 246, 249, 250, 251, 252, 253, 260, 261, 274, 301
classroom culture, 250, 251
classroom environment, 69
classroom events, 154
classroom management, 145, 146, 253
classroom teacher, 144
classroom teachers, 148, 197, 200, 203
classrooms, 14, 33, 85, 148, 152, 153, 156, 157, 158, 183, 197, 201, 202, 234, 240, 245, 251, 253
cloning, 252
closure, 285
coal, 104, 105, 106, 108, 109
coding, 216
coercion, 90
cognition, 70, 71, 220
cognitive ability, 290
cognitive map, 168
cohesion, 163, 165
cohort, 150
collaboration, x, xiv, 71, 163, 188, 201, 216, 217, 250, 272, 278, 285
college students, 237, 240, 251
colleges, 33, 135, 156, 157, 197, 220, 240, 246, 248, 249
collusion, 4
colonial rule, 55, 72, 143, 194
colonisation, 280
colonization, 52, 281, 285
commitment, xvii, 23, 24, 27, 100, 102, 109, 111, 118, 146, 147, 151, 178, 190, 202, 213, 217, 218, 295, 307
commodity, 53, 65, 103
communication, 45, 133, 153, 207, 208, 245, 252
community, xiv, xvi, 6, 12, 19, 20, 22, 23, 24, 25, 26, 43, 44, 46, 47, 51, 54, 56, 58, 59, 76, 82, 83, 85, 86, 88, 92, 123, 134, 139, 140, 144, 146, 148, 149, 150, 154, 161, 162, 163, 164, 165, 188, 189, 190, 200, 212, 218, 226, 227, 228, 229, 230, 232, 238, 249, 253, 279, 292, 302
comparative education, x, xi, 98, 273, 275
compensation, 27
competition, 110, 168, 170, 210, 211
competitiveness, 43, 164, 173, 260
complement, 43, 143
complex interactions, 164
complexity, 6, 7, 12, 13, 46, 66, 215, 216, 271, 282
compliance, 146
complications, 286
components, 19, 164, 196
composition, 52, 57, 173, 252
comprehension, 35, 42, 180
compulsory education, 34
computer technology, 185
concentrates, 52
conception, 74, 147, 148
conceptualization, 65, 66
concrete, 6, 23, 25, 70
conduct, 19, 28, 45, 87, 149, 153, 156, 207, 212, 216, 219, 281
confidence, xvi, 88, 101, 123, 153, 189, 259
configuration, 168
confinement, 13
conflict, 53, 132, 138, 163, 262
conformity, 18, 21
confrontation, 103, 209
confusion, 54, 245
conjecture, 168
connectivity, 51
consciousness, 99
consensus, xvii, 24, 216
consent, 87
conservation, 294
conspiracy, 82
constitution, 109, 216, 283
construction, 18, 25, 26, 57, 74, 93, 132, 180, 187, 238, 276, 277, 279, 281, 286
constructivist learning, 245
consultants, 17, 19, 20, 26, 171
consulting, 212
consumer goods, 248
consumers, 211, 218
consumption, 33, 165
contaminant, 189
context, xiv, 3, 10, 13, 20, 21, 22, 23, 28, 35, 44, 56, 65, 66, 67, 69, 70, 72, 73, 75, 78, 81, 84, 89, 147, 153, 156, 157, 162, 168, 171, 181, 186, 213, 215, 216, 238, 239, 243, 244, 245, 274, 277, 286, 295
contingency, 38, 219
continuity, 54, 56, 253, 284
contraceptives, 88

control, 21, 27, 54, 66, 69, 71, 72, 79, 80, 81, 90, 99, 103, 122, 145, 154, 173, 188, 212, 230, 233
conversion, 55
conviction, 56
cooking, 240, 247
cooling, 261
coping, 98, 224, 228, 231, 232, 244, 245
coping strategies, 232, 245
corporate life, 181
correlation, 124, 187
corruption, 33, 77, 112, 116, 117
cost of living, 173
costs, 21, 43, 75, 184, 248
cotton, 110, 261
Council of Ministers, 41
counseling, 84, 88
coverage, 84
crack, 111
creativity, 26, 58, 59, 140, 252, 264
credentials, 137
credibility, 188, 215
credit, 151, 248, 285
crime, 79, 85, 212, 242
criticism, 36, 78
crops, 82
crude oil, 182
crying, 232
cultural differences, 244
cultural heritage, 12
cultural practices, 6, 125, 207, 208, 216, 218
cultural transition, 245
cultural values, 209
culture, xvii, 4, 5, 6, 7, 8, 9, 10, 11, 12, 13, 20, 51, 53, 54, 55, 58, 59, 60, 61, 62, 70, 71, 75, 76, 81, 92, 97, 98, 132, 135, 136, 140, 146, 148, 177, 178, 180, 183, 184, 186, 196, 225, 230, 237, 238, 239, 244, 245, 250, 251, 260, 265, 278, 286, 295, 296, 306, 308
curiosity, 190, 263
currency, 17, 26, 77, 119, 132, 290
curriculum, xiii, xvi, xvii, xviii, 8, 12, 13, 21, 26, 52, 54, 56, 57, 88, 98, 135, 143, 156, 174, 180, 182, 187, 190, 208, 217, 220, 226, 228, 249, 250, 252, 253, 273, 274, 275, 276, 277, 279, 308, 310
curriculum development, 253

D

damage, 107, 108, 282
danger, 6, 39, 89, 110, 132, 170, 201
data collection, 150, 214, 216
dating, 179
death, 31, 37, 54, 105, 116, 226, 252
debt, 24
decay, 183
decisions, 38, 196, 261
decoding, 9
decolonization, 99, 106, 273, 281, 282
deconstruction, 67
defense, 268, 269
deficit, 23
definition, 19, 23, 25, 26, 28, 42, 58, 159, 163, 224, 247, 274
delivery, xvi, 9, 88, 195, 200, 211, 213
demand, 19, 20, 34, 75, 91, 113, 117, 165, 166, 171, 295
democracy, 48, 101, 156, 215, 216, 218, 279
Democratic Republic of Congo, 41, 45
demographics, 13
demography, 103
denial, 100, 106
dentist, 32
depression, 74, 87
deprivation, 171
desire, 7, 44, 65, 69, 80, 118, 145, 194, 211, 214, 218, 231, 265, 276, 277, 278, 280, 281, 282, 283
detachment, 215
detention, 33, 116, 171
developed countries, 19, 24, 26, 27, 161, 164, 165, 166
developed nations, 178, 195
development policy, 162, 310
deviation, 18
diamonds, 259
diffusion, 162
direct costs, 75
disabilities, xvi, 138, 194, 195, 196, 200, 201, 202, 203, 214, 217, 292, 306
disability, xvi, 25, 138, 195, 196, 200, 217
disappointment, 106, 195, 264
disaster, 25, 77
disbursement, 185
discipline, xvii, 62, 207, 227
disclosure, 3
discomfort, xvii, 245, 254, 276
discontinuity, 13
discourse, x, xiv, 26, 27, 28, 67, 69, 70, 71, 72, 75, 79, 81, 82, 92, 93, 115, 131, 132, 139, 140, 149, 162, 276, 279, 285
discrimination, 111
dislocation, 170
displacement, xiv, 6
disposition, 9, 17, 20, 21, 138, 156
distance education, xvii, 201, 202
distress, 117
distribution, 122, 123, 169, 178, 187

diversity, 20, 49, 180, 242, 243
division, 46, 52, 195, 196, 198, 218
doctors, 88, 227
dogs, 117
domain, 74, 225
domestic chores, 87, 111
dominance, 70, 71
donors, 22, 252
draft, 24, 220, 249, 268
dream, 9, 23, 90, 102, 234
dreaming, 4
drugs, 123
drying, 36, 179

E

earnings, 73
earth, 8, 210, 264
eating, 78, 104, 240
ecology, 307
economic crisis, 74
economic development, 73, 111, 125, 161, 162, 181, 182
economic empowerment, 22, 110, 112
economic growth, 73, 164, 165
economic policy, 174
economic status, xv, 135, 245
economics, 134, 292
Ecuador, 159
education reform, 18, 21, 22, 28, 143, 159, 160, 307
educational attainment, 122, 131
educational policy, 20, 28, 122, 125, 272, 310
educational practices, xv
educational programs, 68, 122, 194
educational psychology, 293
educational research, 42, 213, 215, 217, 271, 283, 286
educational services, xvi
educational system, 121, 137, 165, 167, 173, 193, 215, 224
efficiency level, 163
ego, 135
Egypt, 292
El Salvador, 11
elaboration, 9
elders, 135, 260
election, 101, 112, 295
electricity, 182
elementary school, 138, 239, 240, 294
elementary students, 290
email, 250, 251
emergence, 20, 24, 62, 157, 207, 212
emigration, 168

emotional experience, 248
emotional reactions, 244
emotionality, 277
emotions, 49, 90
empathy, 20
employees, 110
employment, 44, 45, 87, 110, 138, 139, 164, 168, 181
empowerment, xvii, 20, 28, 68, 102, 103, 104, 110, 111, 112, 113, 118, 131, 208, 216, 272
encouragement, xv, xviii, 32, 148, 261, 268, 293, 302
England, 8, 11, 12, 27, 33, 37, 49, 52, 73, 119, 140, 177, 200, 275, 293, 294
English Language, 47
enlargement, 56
enrollment, 125
enthusiasm, xviii, 37, 134, 154, 184
environment, xvi, 19, 56, 57, 58, 59, 68, 82, 87, 150, 154, 161, 162, 163, 164, 165, 168, 173, 174, 179, 185, 228, 230, 274, 282, 295, 301
epidermis, 11
epistemology, 69, 70, 132
equality, 102, 104, 113, 124, 210, 218, 267
equipment, 165, 166, 167, 174, 182, 183, 184, 201, 202
equity, 24, 156, 160, 214, 217, 218
equity principle, 214
erosion, 20, 183
ESR, 43
estimating, 214
ethnic diversity, 13
ethnic groups, 296
ethnicity, 5, 12, 245
EU, 164
euphoria, 77
Euro, 272
Europe, ix, 4, 11, 20, 46, 52, 53, 54, 57, 61, 69, 161, 164, 166, 175, 209, 262, 264, 276, 278, 286, 293, 294, 308, 310
European Union, 164
evacuation, 105
everyday life, 213, 216
evidence, 51, 69, 75, 108, 109, 131, 149, 152, 154, 157, 179, 214, 277
evil, 4, 73, 77, 79, 89, 90, 117, 219
evolution, 18, 215, 216
examinations, 8, 57
exchange rate, 172
exclusion, 19, 110, 208, 220
excuse, 37
execution, 178, 185, 190

exercise, xiv, 3, 26, 27, 56, 60, 66, 70, 78, 81, 87, 154
expectation, 168, 224, 248, 280
expenditures, 170
expertise, 21, 57, 87, 162, 174, 188, 190, 210, 214, 216, 237, 291
experts, 21, 37, 163, 186, 188, 260
exploitation, 6, 28, 102
exposure, 86, 174, 187
expression, xv, 18, 109, 110, 208
external environment, 174
extraction, xviii

F

fabrication, 220, 277
facial expression, 239
failure, xiv, 6, 24, 37, 42, 66, 75, 78, 85, 86, 90, 146, 162, 174, 184
fairness, 28, 221, 268
faith, 20, 55
family, xi, xiii, 35, 39, 54, 56, 61, 75, 90, 131, 132, 133, 134, 135, 136, 137, 138, 139, 184, 210, 218, 240, 241, 242, 244, 246, 247, 251, 260, 262, 264, 280, 293, 295, 301, 310
family life, 133
family members, xi, xiii, 35, 133, 135, 184
far right, 60
farmers, 44, 265
fatigue, 212
fear, 66, 76, 81, 82, 85, 90, 183, 184, 208, 286
feedback, 215
feelings, xvii, 57, 85, 86, 109, 171, 245
feet, 8, 39, 134, 171, 243, 264
females, 67, 75, 78, 79, 80, 82, 89, 91, 92, 125, 194, 217
feminism, 70, 99, 102, 109, 110, 118, 132, 285
fermentation, 179
fertilization, 252
fever, 72
field trials, 214
finance, 25, 295
financial institutions, 22
financial resources, 70, 73, 165, 174
financing, 18, 77, 172, 174, 190
fires, 4
First World, 262
fish, 38, 77, 134, 188, 261
fisheries, 33
flavor, 179
flexibility, 138, 215
flight, 171
flotation, 189

focus groups, 45
focusing, 145, 149, 265
food, 33, 37, 53, 77, 84, 103, 179, 187, 240, 241, 248, 251
foreign language, 59, 60, 307, 308
forgetting, 241
formal education, 43, 73, 87, 181, 223
framing, 148
France, 4, 52, 262, 265
free choice, 279
freedom, xvii, 33, 34, 52, 70, 71, 106, 119, 208, 210, 216, 220, 261, 276
friction, 53
friends, xi, xiii, xviii, 10, 32, 33, 36, 61, 86, 88, 97, 117, 118, 132, 133, 134, 135, 136, 138, 139, 221, 225, 241, 243, 246, 247, 251, 268, 275
friendship, 273, 282
fruits, 65, 118
frustration, ix, 60, 61, 106, 168, 172, 195
fuel, 117
fulfillment, 9, 93, 208, 214, 233
funding, xvi, 18, 22, 170, 171, 172, 174, 185, 289
fungus, 189
furniture, 246, 248

G

galaxy, 133
GCE, 24
gender, xiv, 11, 68, 70, 100, 102, 103, 110, 111, 123, 125, 132, 135, 139, 156, 217, 229, 245, 272, 274, 275, 292, 309, 310
gender equality, 100, 102, 103, 110
gender equity, 292
gender inequality, 70
gene, 245
General Certificate of Education, 8
general education, 194, 195, 196, 202
generation, 43, 54, 118, 172, 174, 179, 183, 271
genocide, 49
genre, 102, 290
geography, 54
Georgia, 234, 301
Germany, 4, 46, 52, 161, 167, 176
gift, 11, 117
girls, 59, 68, 74, 75, 76, 77, 81, 82, 88, 89, 90, 91, 92, 102, 133, 138, 229, 231, 235, 240, 242, 277, 292
global competition, 162, 169, 173
global forces, ix
globalization, 11, 47, 260, 276, 281, 283
goals, 24, 25, 27, 45, 88, 124, 125, 144, 147, 156, 187, 215, 216, 238, 241, 254, 276, 302

God, 5, 62, 78, 100, 107, 117, 139, 208, 209, 210, 285, 290, 306
gold, 6, 101, 262
governance, 17, 22, 164, 180, 185, 216, 220
government, xv, xvi, 33, 35, 36, 38, 42, 46, 47, 52, 72, 83, 105, 108, 109, 110, 111, 116, 117, 121, 122, 123, 161, 162, 163, 170, 171, 172, 174, 178, 182, 183, 185, 187, 188, 189, 190, 194, 195, 196, 201, 213, 214
government expenditure, 172
government policy, xv, 170
grades, 52, 54, 59, 66, 76, 85, 86, 90, 226, 231
grading, 82, 83, 150
graduate education, xv, 174, 283
graduate students, xviii, 123, 147, 169, 170, 172, 185, 260, 271, 272, 273, 280, 281
grants, 184, 297
graph, ix
grassroots, 20, 190
gravitation, 177
gravitational pull, 189
gravity, 75, 177
Great Britain, 8
group identity, 225
grouping, x, 21, 25
groups, xiii, 6, 7, 10, 13, 18, 24, 45, 59, 70, 71, 85, 86, 92, 146, 148, 149, 150, 152, 178, 196, 214, 217, 224, 238, 239, 240, 244, 245, 260, 275, 277, 279, 282, 292, 297
growth, 62, 137, 153, 164, 202, 254
Guatemala, 4
guidance, 60, 84, 107, 187
guidance counselors, 84
guidelines, 23, 195
guilt, 79
guilt feelings, 79
guilty, 67, 79, 82, 84, 88
Guinea, 54, 284
gut, 134
Guyana, 14

H

hands, 8, 37, 39, 55, 58, 71, 77, 81, 99, 104, 110, 118, 134, 183, 220, 240
happiness, 39, 134, 207
harm, 58
harmony, 58
hate, 181, 183, 281
healing, 179
health, 22, 89, 178, 185, 227, 292, 309, 310
health services, 178
hearing impairment, 194, 195, 198, 199, 200

heat, 106, 253
heating, 261
helplessness, 36, 37, 184
hemorrhage, 168
Henry Louis Gates, 225
heterogeneity, 12, 162
high school, 8, 34, 35, 37, 61, 138, 191, 198, 224, 227, 228, 230, 239, 240, 246, 252, 253, 260, 261, 263, 268
higher education, xv, xvi, 40, 121, 122, 124, 125, 130, 165, 173, 273
higher quality, 149
highlands, 11
highways, 37
hiring, 248
HIV, 22, 27, 68, 89, 90, 91, 93
HIV infection, 89
HIV/AIDS, 68, 90, 91
homework, 146, 231, 249, 252
Hong Kong, 203
host, xvii, 104, 136, 173, 189, 240, 241, 242
hostility, 259
housing, 212, 247, 250
human agency, 209
human capital, 161, 165, 171, 174, 275, 279
human development, 178
human experience, 69
human resources, 163, 165, 166, 173
human rights, 100, 249, 310
human subjects, 70
humanitarianism, xiii
hunting, 247
husband, 34, 39, 69, 80, 81, 133, 134, 136, 137, 138, 139, 226, 275, 309
hybrid, 273, 279, 282
hybridity, 7, 9, 10, 11, 12, 13, 278
hypothesis, 146, 173
hypothesis test, 146

I

idealism, xviii, 267
ideas, xvii, 18, 37, 70, 146, 152, 155, 157, 165, 169, 207, 215, 218, 221, 223, 229, 231, 245, 250, 252, 253, 261, 264, 267, 272, 273, 274, 276, 277, 278, 279, 280, 281, 284, 285, 295
identification, 5
identity, xiii, 3, 4, 5, 6, 7, 12, 13, 22, 37, 42, 44, 47, 48, 177, 224, 225, 230, 234, 281, 284
identity politics, 12, 13
ideology, 55, 70, 71, 79, 92, 102, 103, 104, 110, 113, 233, 234
idiosyncratic, 216

illiteracy, 13
illusion, 134
imagery, 73, 79
imagination, 42, 56, 59, 100
imitation, 260
immersion, 237, 238, 243, 244, 251
immigrants, 244
immigration, 248
imperialism, 4, 5, 48, 58
implementation, xv, xvi, 22, 24, 25, 26, 122, 162, 163, 201, 238, 245
imprisonment, 35, 88
in vitro, 252
incarceration, 34
incentives, 163, 165, 174, 182
inclusion, 111, 195, 196, 197, 208, 214, 217, 220
income, 71, 76, 77, 112, 136, 166, 167, 185, 196, 242
independence, xv, 8, 31, 53, 56, 72, 99, 104, 110, 111, 113, 114, 117, 118, 119, 156, 160, 181, 193, 194, 195, 277
India, 6, 98, 119, 120, 188
indication, 101, 122, 135
indicators, 24, 161, 167
indigenous, xvi, 6, 9, 22, 98, 140, 180, 181, 187, 277, 278, 279, 281, 282, 283, 284, 285, 287
indigenous knowledge, 279, 281, 283
indigenous peoples, 287
individual action, 215
individual students, 180
individualism, 210
individuality, 214, 218
individualization, 211, 212, 214
individualized instruction, 211
Indonesia, 4, 265
industrialisation, 163
industry, 9, 10, 161, 164, 165, 166, 167, 168, 170, 171, 172, 173, 174, 262
inequality, 7, 15, 70, 86, 130
inequity, xv
inferiority, 103, 220
infinite, 218
inflation, 168, 171
influence, xiv, 18, 66, 67, 70, 71, 72, 73, 81, 121, 123, 154, 179, 182, 212, 213, 244, 245
informal sector, 185
information communication technology, 201, 202
information technology, xvii, 201
infrastructure, xvi, 70, 111, 190
inheritance, 6
initiation, 56, 179
innocence, 5
innovation, 165, 208, 211, 214, 215, 216

input, 154, 253
insight, 12, 188, 189, 302
inspiration, 109, 268
instability, xiv, 5, 7, 164, 184
instinct, 134
institutional change, 152, 155
institutional infrastructure, 164
institutionalisation, 161
institutions, xiii, xvi, 18, 22, 41, 43, 54, 65, 68, 70, 71, 73, 74, 75, 76, 79, 82, 83, 84, 85, 88, 90, 92, 100, 119, 123, 137, 138, 151, 162, 163, 164, 165, 172, 173, 174, 184, 193, 194, 207, 248, 274, 284
instruction, xiv, 42, 46, 47, 48, 72, 74, 153, 182, 212, 217, 274, 277, 278, 282
instructors, 273
instruments, 112
insurance, 74, 139
integration, xvi, 26, 149, 163, 164, 196, 197, 198, 272
integrity, 221
intellect, 115, 224
intelligence, 12, 13
intent, 5, 19, 28
intentions, xviii, 158, 183, 267, 285
interaction, 17, 71, 87, 88, 90, 163, 238, 240
interactions, 18, 153, 162, 216, 238, 240, 242, 249, 254
interest, xvii, 21, 27, 36, 61, 71, 72, 77, 86, 98, 101, 102, 124, 132, 139, 144, 149, 151, 183, 187, 207, 212, 216, 251, 260, 272, 273, 284, 285, 290, 293, 296, 301, 302, 307
interface, 22, 207
internalization, 146
internalizing, 146
international communication, 45, 47
international relations, 28
internationalization, 42
internet, 184, 212, 275
internship, 149
interpretation, xiv, 180, 216
intervention, 55, 109, 110, 125, 210, 214, 215, 216, 218
interview, 102, 119, 227, 241, 246, 249, 274
intuition, 115
investment, 26, 43, 87, 112, 154, 161, 164, 165, 187
investors, 182, 188
Iraq, 4, 277
Ireland, 102
iron, 35
Islam, 53, 73, 125
isolation, 125, 178
Israel, 4
Italy, 195, 260

J

Jamaica, 27, 106
Japan, vi, xi, xvii, 182, 237, 238, 239, 240, 241, 242, 243, 244, 245, 246, 247, 248, 249, 250, 251, 252, 253, 254, 260, 307
job creation, 22
job insecurity, 110
job satisfaction, 171
jobs, 74, 110, 138, 167, 193, 229, 242, 285
Jordan, 8
judges, 73
judgment, 154, 285
junior high school, 240, 246, 251
jurisdiction, 66
justice, 28, 165, 276, 283
justification, 43

K

kidney, 252
kindergarten, 274
knees, 239
knowledge, ix, xiv, xviii, 3, 5, 13, 15, 17, 18, 19, 25, 26, 28, 37, 45, 51, 54, 55, 57, 61, 68, 69, 70, 71, 72, 89, 102, 132, 138, 140, 146, 152, 153, 154, 157, 158, 161, 162, 163, 164, 165, 168, 169, 170, 172, 173, 174, 177, 179, 180, 188, 201, 202, 207, 209, 213, 214, 215, 218, 238, 242, 243, 245, 246, 249, 252, 253, 254, 261, 262, 275, 276, 277, 278, 279, 280, 281, 282, 283, 284, 285, 289, 290, 293, 294, 297, 310
Korea, 252

L

labeling, 214, 291
labor, 26, 55, 136, 207
labor force, 55
labour, 73, 106, 165, 172, 174
labour force, 73, 174
labour market, 172
lack of opportunities, 172
lakes, 264
land, 34, 51, 53, 55, 134, 135, 179
landscapes, 209
language, xiv, 9, 11, 12, 26, 28, 41, 42, 44, 45, 46, 47, 48, 51, 52, 53, 58, 59, 70, 72, 73, 75, 77, 80, 81, 140, 180, 189, 210, 213, 214, 215, 219, 225, 230, 232, 238, 239, 240, 244, 245, 246, 247, 249, 251, 261, 277, 278, 284, 292, 297
language barrier, 247

language policy, 42, 44, 46, 47, 48, 59
language skills, 251
Laos, 11
Latin America, ix, 11, 13, 29, 94, 166, 306, 310
laws, 136, 177
lawyers, 197, 225
lead, 23, 25, 61, 116, 122, 200, 207, 238, 245, 282
leadership, 32, 103, 108, 109, 115, 116, 124, 125, 154, 155, 156, 164, 170, 305
leadership abilities, 154
learners, xvi, 34, 155, 181, 187, 245, 301
learning, xvi, 17, 18, 19, 45, 46, 54, 55, 56, 57, 59, 60, 61, 68, 74, 75, 82, 83, 85, 90, 123, 138, 139, 143, 144, 149, 150, 152, 153, 154, 155, 162, 166, 174, 178, 180, 181, 182, 184, 186, 187, 189, 196, 200, 202, 208, 209, 210, 211, 212, 214, 215, 216, 218, 219, 225, 238, 239, 240, 244, 245, 248, 249, 250, 251, 252, 253, 260, 262, 274, 276, 279, 280, 282, 285, 301, 302, 307
learning environment, 182, 301
learning process, 301
learning society, 218
legislation, 68, 84, 86, 91, 92, 110, 195, 213
lending, 22, 69, 289
lens, 70, 273, 277, 284
lethargy, 186
liberation, 103, 113, 143, 209
Liberia, 10
librarians, 297
life changes, 245
lifetime, 39, 307
likelihood, 83, 85
limitation, 296
linguistics, 136
links, 13, 154, 262
listening, 9, 20, 35, 47, 154, 263
literacy, 23, 32, 55, 174, 194
literacy rates, 194
living standards, 183, 186
local community, 147, 148
local government, 22, 82, 83
location, 13, 28, 52, 174, 218, 278, 286
love, x, xv, xviii, 3, 8, 9, 139, 263
loyalty, 100, 225

M

machinery, 163, 164
magazines, 294
magnet, 20
major cities, 106, 186
major decisions, 196
malaria, 72, 179

males, 14, 67, 76, 78, 79, 80, 83, 89, 125
malnutrition, 48
management, xvi, 21, 22, 26, 71, 130, 163, 164, 165, 170, 173, 218, 306
manipulation, 71, 187
manpower, 56, 87, 165, 170, 174, 175, 181, 185, 187, 193
manufactured goods, xvi, 183, 188
manufacturing, 202
marginalization, 113
market, 20, 101, 111, 112, 132, 163, 164, 165, 170, 173, 174, 211, 261, 264, 272, 279, 290, 295
marketability, 290
marketing, 296, 309
markets, 43, 87, 111, 139, 211, 292
marriage, 53, 61, 78, 80, 101, 110, 225
married women, 86
mass, 11, 71, 78, 108, 117, 181, 188, 207, 212, 242, 276, 308
mass communication, 308
mass media, 71, 78, 188, 242
mastery, 162, 284
material resources, 190
mathematics, 98, 158, 183, 200, 215, 217, 220, 226, 240
mathematics education, 217
meals, 75, 76, 104, 117, 193, 240, 243
meaning systems, xv, 121
meanings, 7, 12, 58, 72, 157, 207, 230, 274, 276, 284, 286
measures, 24, 85, 92, 212
meat, 38, 77, 248
media, 69, 70, 71, 73, 75, 79, 100, 225, 239, 260, 276, 308, 309
media texts, 69
membership, 71, 83, 225
memory, x, 7, 32, 34, 56, 58
men, x, xi, xv, xviii, 4, 32, 36, 39, 44, 45, 65, 66, 68, 69, 71, 74, 75, 76, 78, 79, 80, 81, 82, 83, 85, 89, 90, 98, 99, 101, 103, 104, 105, 110, 111, 112, 114, 115, 116, 117, 118, 123, 134, 179, 225, 264, 272
mental impairment, 200
mental retardation, 195, 198, 200
mentor, x, 32, 39, 104, 113, 132, 275, 301
mentoring, xviii, 146, 147
mentorship, 32
mercury, 191
metacognition, 215, 216
metals, 7
metaphor, xv, 31, 131
methodology, 6, 59, 60, 224, 231
Mexico, 167

microscope, 183
middle class, 61, 76
Middle East, 4, 11, 20
migration, 27, 167, 173, 174, 262
military, 33, 40, 54, 99, 111, 117, 170, 171, 174
military government, 170, 174
milk, 261
Ministry of Education, 22, 46, 48, 92, 197, 202
minorities, 115, 224, 230, 245
minority, 6, 225, 234
miscommunication, 252
missions, 194
misunderstanding, 249, 297
mixing, 272, 296
mobility, 74, 202
mode, 6, 22, 70, 81, 82, 178, 188
models, 54, 102, 125, 156, 164, 225, 230, 233
modernity, 212, 213, 276, 277
modernization, 43, 180, 182
mold, 216, 227
momentum, 260
money, 22, 33, 34, 43, 46, 76, 77, 84, 88, 133, 182, 183, 188, 247, 253, 254, 263, 280
monitoring, 215
monopoly, 12, 13, 56, 82, 83, 112
morale, xvi
morality, 80
Moscow, 102, 106
mother tongue, 46, 59
mothers, 79, 103
motivation, 169, 170, 172, 173, 211, 214, 215, 217, 280
mountains, 254
movement, xiv, 9, 11, 12, 48, 51, 53, 106, 113, 125, 144, 147, 148, 156, 210
multicultural education, 244, 245, 310
multiculturalism, 6, 12
multimedia, 148
multiplication, 227, 232
multiplier, 7
multiplier effect, 7
murmur, 132
music, 7, 10, 12, 54, 148, 227, 260, 262, 263
musicians, 10
Muslims, 114
mutuality, 23, 28

N

narratives, 131, 208, 209, 211, 213, 218, 220, 260, 273, 279, 282, 283, 286
national identity, 42
national parks, 264

National Research Council, 213, 215
national security, 27
nationalism, 4
nation-building, 193
natural sciences, 213
needs, xvi, 54, 65, 69, 75, 76, 86, 90, 98, 122, 125, 126, 139, 152, 161, 164, 165, 173, 174, 178, 185, 186, 187, 188, 190, 191, 193, 194, 195, 196, 201, 203, 212, 217, 219, 224, 245, 252
negative emotions, 245
neglect, 37, 89, 100
negotiating, xiv, 17, 21, 27
negotiation, 8
Nelson Mandela, 97
Netherlands, 93
network, 47, 162, 163, 279
networking, 163
New Zealand, 285
newspapers, 68, 71, 101, 106, 116, 189
next generation, 234
NGOs, 24, 187
Nigeria, v, vi, xi, xiv, xvi, 10, 29, 31, 32, 33, 35, 36, 37, 40, 54, 59, 62, 65, 67, 69, 72, 73, 74, 75, 76, 77, 78, 82, 83, 84, 85, 87, 88, 89, 91, 92, 93, 94, 97, 99, 101, 102, 106, 107, 108, 110, 111, 113, 114, 115, 116, 117, 119, 120, 121, 122, 123, 129, 130, 131, 133, 134, 135, 136, 137, 138, 140, 161, 162, 165, 166, 167, 168, 169, 170, 171, 172, 173, 175, 176, 177, 178, 179, 180, 181, 182, 183, 184, 185, 186, 187, 188, 189, 190, 191, 194, 260, 261, 264, 268, 274, 291, 293, 303, 306, 307, 309
No Child Left Behind, 213
North Africa, 292
North America, 147, 148, 151, 290, 291, 292, 293, 295, 296, 297, 308
North Korea, 252
nurses, 227
nursing, 110, 137, 169

O

objectivity, 284
obligation, 37, 91
observations, 150, 157, 294
OECD, 165, 273
oil, 75, 77, 110, 117, 172, 174, 182, 264, 295
old age, 115
older people, 76
online learning, 210, 211, 212, 213, 214, 215, 216, 217, 220
openness, 20, 221
oppression, 12, 118, 157, 278, 281
optimism, 134, 135

oral presentations, 150
organ, 252
organization, xiv, xvi, 106, 113, 115, 197, 215, 248, 274, 293, 306
organizations, 18, 19, 22, 24, 32, 33, 103, 104, 113, 116, 194, 195, 196, 290, 309
orientation, 43, 44, 134, 138, 155
outline, 153, 213
output, 73, 105, 173
ownership, 5, 12, 48, 147

P

pain, 39, 133, 262
paradigm shift, xv
parents, xvii, 24, 32, 55, 59, 61, 74, 76, 77, 80, 86, 88, 92, 122, 123, 124, 135, 138, 196, 201, 226, 232, 262, 264, 265, 292, 294
partnership, 22
passive, 60, 155
pastures, 167
pedagogy, xvii, 14, 17, 20, 47, 57, 60, 61, 187, 208, 211, 216, 218, 276
peers, 5, 90, 148, 154, 169, 172, 212
penicillin, 189
Pentagon, 4
per capita income, 190
perceptions, ix, 75, 121, 215, 224, 239
permit, 92, 207
peroxide, 232
personal goals, 302
personal life, 275
personal relationship, 67
personal responsibility, 218
personality, 136
personhood, 217
persons with disabilities, 195, 203
perspective, x, xiv, xvi, xvii, 5, 18, 20, 27, 38, 47, 54, 60, 70, 80, 109, 130, 140, 145, 158, 159, 163, 180, 203, 238, 241, 243, 244, 245, 250, 294, 295
persuasion, 71, 90, 145
Peru, 282
philosophers, 210, 211, 219
photographs, x, 274
photosynthesis, 177
physics, 122
planets, 179
planning, xvii, 25, 27, 43, 101, 183, 210, 259, 272, 273, 275, 276, 277
plants, 105, 177, 187, 264
plastic products, 202
pleasure, 69, 80, 89, 113, 281, 290
PM, 29

police, 37, 105, 107, 108, 264
policy makers, 19, 25, 47, 85, 154, 156, 182
political appointments, 110
political aspects, 145
political participation, xv, 99, 101, 103, 112, 114
politics, xv, 4, 9, 12, 13, 15, 18, 48, 60, 71, 99, 100, 101, 102, 103, 104, 109, 112, 113, 116, 117, 118, 119, 125, 212, 214, 219, 220, 267, 293
poor, xvi, 4, 28, 45, 47, 48, 74, 76, 80, 81, 86, 111, 116, 163, 164, 167, 170, 171, 172, 173, 183, 184, 186, 201, 212, 224, 234, 259, 260, 295
population, 4, 24, 43, 44, 52, 53, 73, 75, 101, 113, 114, 123, 138, 242, 292
populism, 215
portfolio, 101, 149, 295
portfolios, 146
post-colonial theory, 281, 282, 283, 284, 286
poverty, 21, 88, 117, 161, 170, 285
power, xiv, xvii, xviii, 4, 6, 9, 11, 17, 18, 19, 22, 26, 28, 37, 56, 65, 66, 67, 68, 69, 70, 71, 72, 73, 74, 75, 77, 78, 79, 80, 81, 82, 84, 85, 86, 87, 88, 89, 90, 91, 92, 93, 100, 103, 104, 112, 114, 151, 158, 164, 173, 179, 182, 184, 185, 186, 195, 208, 209, 211, 212, 216, 220, 233, 276, 277, 278, 279, 281, 282, 283, 284, 285, 286
power plants, 211
power relations, 66, 67, 71, 72, 78, 86, 87, 90, 151, 278, 284
pragmatism, 215
prayer, 35
predictability, 174
preference, 22, 23, 169
pregnancy, 88, 89
prejudice, 58, 118, 243
preparation, x, 24, 55, 104, 122, 197, 218, 293, 302
pre-school, 290
preschoolers, 226
preservice teacher education, xv, 143, 144, 151, 156, 157, 158, 159, 160
preservice teachers, 159
presidency, 41
pressure, 18, 22, 76, 84, 90, 148, 195, 225
prestige, xiii
prevention, 307
prices, 44, 47, 48, 104, 248, 264
primary school, 43, 46, 57, 60, 73
principle, 13, 73, 100, 165, 189, 214, 216, 217
prior knowledge, 245, 249, 252
private benefits, 165
privatization, 77
probe, 109
problem-solving, 218
producers, 110, 146, 165

production, 6, 7, 13, 18, 43, 44, 47, 54, 70, 165, 183, 187, 188, 211, 219, 285, 292
productive capacity, 165
productivity, 19, 73, 167, 173, 185
professional development, 144, 145, 150, 151, 152, 153, 154, 155, 156, 157, 158, 160
professionalism, 27
professions, 74, 165
profits, 87, 209, 296
program, 43, 97, 98, 137, 138, 143, 144, 145, 147, 148, 149, 150, 151, 152, 155, 156, 157, 185, 200, 201, 220, 233, 234, 237, 239, 243, 252, 253, 261, 264, 267, 268, 271, 272, 289, 301, 302, 303
programming, 201, 202, 306
proliferation, 182
promoter, xv, 99, 101
propaganda, 105, 219
proposition, 109
prosperity, 182, 190
psychological development, 235
psychology, 12, 210, 211, 212, 219
public affairs, 309
public education, 194
public opinion, 24, 71, 106
public policy, 214, 220
public sector, 22, 165, 307
publishers, 291, 292, 294, 295, 296, 297
pulse, 101
punishment, 59, 76
pupa, 135
pupil, 57, 146

Q

qualitative research, 239
questioning, 61

R

race, xiv, 3, 4, 5, 6, 7, 11, 12, 13, 15, 131, 140, 145, 156, 217, 225, 234, 235, 272, 308
racism, 7, 58
radio, 47, 189
rain, 80, 243, 264
range, 218, 267, 293
rape, 85
rationalisation, 169, 170
rationality, 18
raw materials, 187, 190
readership, 295

reading, ix, x, 9, 35, 55, 61, 106, 134, 146, 189, 200, 226, 230, 231, 249, 250, 251, 254, 260, 276, 278, 279, 281, 284, 290, 297, 301, 302
reading comprehension, 146
real terms, 88
reality, 6, 12, 18, 24, 47, 51, 67, 69, 70, 72, 74, 78, 86, 88, 90, 124, 180, 214, 215, 216, 243, 244, 245, 248, 260, 276
reasoning, 213, 216, 278, 279, 281, 282
recall, 57, 61, 302, 303
recognition, 3, 41, 91, 101, 115, 181, 182, 188, 280
reconcile, 37
reconstruction, 181
recurrence, 72
reengineering, 215
reflection, 33, 145, 155, 160, 238, 278, 302
reflective practice, 145, 147
reforms, xvii, 18, 20, 21, 22, 25, 154, 181, 194, 195, 208, 209, 211, 214, 217, 272, 276, 278, 279, 280, 310
refugees, 11, 244, 261
regenerative capacity, 20, 27
rehabilitation, 200
relationship, 42, 44, 57, 66, 67, 70, 87, 98, 133, 162, 163, 166, 173, 209, 215, 224, 225, 226, 228, 280, 281, 283, 289, 292, 294
relationships, xi, xiv, 67, 78, 91, 122, 149, 150, 153, 164, 179, 241, 281, 284, 285
relatives, xiii, 61, 116, 264
relevance, xvii, 56, 60, 99, 118, 139, 161, 162, 163, 165, 173, 180, 185
religion, 11, 33, 53, 71, 75, 134, 178, 249, 252, 306
religious beliefs, 252
rent, 247
repackaging, 11
repo, 101, 123
reproduction, 285
reputation, 17, 44, 90, 97, 101
resentment, 82
resistance, 90, 145, 219, 229, 278
resolution, 108
resource allocation, 164, 173
resource management, 26
resources, xvi, 17, 18, 21, 22, 23, 24, 26, 71, 73, 75, 76, 78, 122, 163, 164, 170, 173, 174, 176, 186, 187, 202, 240
responsibility, ix, x, 6, 32, 68, 80, 81, 144, 149, 152, 165, 182, 186, 211, 218, 227, 231, 232, 233
restructuring, 208, 286, 310
retardation, 195, 198
retention, 164, 187
retirement, x, 97, 98, 259, 272, 275
returns, 73, 77, 87, 293

revenue, 171, 174
rewards, 67, 84, 163
rice, 77
rights, xv, 22, 49, 99, 101, 102, 103, 104, 106, 110, 113, 114, 115, 124, 309
risk, 24, 35, 38, 39, 49, 86, 88, 89, 91, 108, 207, 277, 279
routines, 154, 250
rural areas, 76, 187, 188
rural women, 111
Russia, 102, 262, 275
Rwanda, 4

S

sacrifice, 115, 118, 276
sadness, 264
safety, 90, 105
sales, 248
sample, 78, 123, 208
sanctions, 66, 87
SAP, 168
satellite, 38, 178, 190
satellite technology, 178, 190
satisfaction, 211
scandal, 36
Scandinavia, 195
scarcity, 103
scatter, 36
scheduling, 249
school, ix, xiii, xv, xvii, 8, 13, 22, 25, 26, 27, 31, 33, 34, 37, 40, 42, 43, 44, 45, 47, 48, 52, 55, 56, 58, 59, 60, 61, 66, 67, 68, 72, 73, 74, 75, 76, 79, 81, 82, 83, 88, 89, 90, 91, 92, 98, 99, 102, 123, 137, 138, 139, 145, 147, 148, 152, 153, 154, 155, 156, 157, 158, 160, 174, 181, 182, 183, 187, 193, 194, 195, 196, 197, 198, 200, 201, 202, 203, 207, 208, 212, 213, 214, 216, 217, 220, 223, 224, 225, 226, 227, 228, 229, 230, 231, 233, 234, 238, 239, 240, 241, 242, 243, 244, 245, 248, 250, 252, 253, 254, 259, 260, 261, 263, 264, 272, 274, 277, 282, 283, 289, 294, 301, 302, 306, 307, 309
school community, 302
school culture, 250
school performance, 224
schooling, xiii, 15, 44, 49, 52, 54, 56, 60, 75, 154, 158, 187, 202, 212, 213, 214, 215, 217, 219, 224, 228, 233, 234, 238, 239, 263, 273, 276, 277, 279, 282, 283, 284, 286, 292
scientific knowledge, 180
scores, 61
search, 48, 54, 79, 138, 139, 169, 247, 278, 298
searching, 90, 246

second generation, 32
Second World, 103, 161
secondary education, 24, 25, 26, 44, 65
secondary school students, 42, 44, 79, 81, 201
secondary schools, xiv, 25, 26, 43, 44, 152
security, 123, 212, 247
seed, 32, 285
segregation, 198
selecting, 148, 296
self, x, xiv, xvi, xvii, 4, 5, 6, 7, 13, 20, 27, 28, 31, 33, 37, 38, 43, 68, 77, 80, 88, 91, 100, 101, 103, 118, 131, 135, 146, 147, 148, 151, 152, 153, 154, 171, 172, 190, 207, 208, 209, 210, 211, 212, 213, 214, 215, 216, 217, 218, 219, 225, 226, 227, 230, 231, 232, 239, 242, 261, 281, 283, 285, 301, 302
self-actualization, 219
self-confidence, 68, 242
self-discipline, 211
self-esteem, 91, 135, 153, 217, 226, 227
self-image, 20
self-improvement, 218
self-interest, 28
self-perceptions, 225
self-reflection, 213
self-reports, 152
self-study, 147, 151, 154
self-understanding, 5
self-worth, 91, 227
Senate, 223
sensitivity, 237, 240, 243
sensitization, 19
separation, 12, 156, 169, 171, 242
series, 19, 88, 293, 294
services, xiii, xvi, 34, 35, 37, 107, 111, 169, 184, 189, 194, 195, 196, 200, 201, 202, 203, 307
SES, 122
sexual harassment, 66, 67, 68, 69, 73, 76, 77, 78, 79, 80, 81, 82, 83, 84, 85, 86, 92
sexuality, 11, 53, 67, 68, 69, 76, 80, 81, 88, 91
shade, 282
shame, 48, 80, 117, 196, 264
shape, xiv, 11, 18, 212, 216, 244, 245
shaping, xiv, 11, 28, 155, 157, 214
shares, xviii
sharing, 32, 59, 230, 301
sheep, 262
shock, 36, 37, 108, 135, 239, 244, 245, 248, 268
shock waves, 108
shores, 52
short run, 151
shortage, 183, 185
shoulders, 105, 116, 302
siblings, 74, 307

Sierra Leone, 72, 259, 260, 265
sign, 88, 90, 208, 223, 232, 302
signals, 87
silver, 203
simple random sampling, 123
sites, xvii, 13, 123, 208, 217, 219, 239, 278
skilled personnel, 165
skills, 22, 27, 45, 57, 68, 74, 87, 102, 146, 150, 151, 153, 154, 155, 157, 162, 163, 164, 165, 173, 182, 185, 187, 201, 202, 211, 226, 230, 245, 246, 250, 252, 279, 280
skills training, 22
skin, 3, 5, 13, 116, 229
slavery, 224
slaves, 72
social capital, 279
social change, 159
social class, 76, 145
social context, xv, 13, 219, 238, 239
social control, 212
social exclusion, 219
social institutions, 75
social justice, 143, 160, 165, 276
social life, 43
social policy, 211
social problems, 70
social resources, 71, 72
social roles, 100
social sciences, 210, 212
social standing, 131
social status, 224
social structure, 178, 180
social theory, 207, 219
social transition, 286
socialization, 65, 75, 92, 160
software, 41
soils, 264
solar system, 56
solidarity, 37, 83, 103, 104, 107, 109
Somalia, 4
South Africa, 7, 27, 46, 97, 166, 167, 170, 173, 291, 293, 295, 296, 298
Southeast Asia, 161
sovereignty, 28
special education, xvi, 138, 194, 195, 196, 197, 198, 199, 200, 201, 202, 203, 240
species, 79
speculation, 77
speech, 41, 108, 113, 200, 264
speed, 38
spelling, 200, 231
spine, 37
sports, 134, 292

stability, 7, 114, 216
stages, 267
stakeholders, xvi, 20, 162, 164
standard of living, 102, 171
standards, 25, 26, 53, 77, 122, 154, 163, 181, 209, 216, 217, 220, 227, 228
stars, 3, 10, 179
starvation, 38
state reform, 215
statistics, 48, 75, 127, 128, 242, 260
stereotyping, 238
stimulant, 187
stimulus, 103, 260
stock, 77
stomach, 116
storage, 165, 182
strategies, 71, 92, 143, 146, 164, 171, 174, 218, 224, 228, 231, 233, 245, 279, 282
strength, 12, 18, 23, 113, 166
stress, 136, 186, 244, 245, 254
structural adjustment, 44, 75, 77, 84, 164
structural adjustment programmes, 75, 164
structural barriers, 124
structural changes, 143
structuralism, 276
structuring, 216
student teacher, 144, 145, 146, 147, 148, 149, 150, 151, 155, 156, 157, 158, 159, 160, 289
students, ix, x, xi, xiii, xvi, xvii, 8, 17, 19, 20, 33, 34, 42, 43, 44, 45, 46, 47, 52, 57, 58, 60, 61, 67, 69, 73, 74, 75, 76, 77, 81, 82, 83, 84, 85, 86, 87, 89, 90, 91, 92, 98, 123, 124, 139, 144, 145, 146, 147, 148, 149, 150, 151, 152, 153, 154, 166, 168, 169, 170, 171, 174, 180, 181, 182, 183, 185, 187, 188, 190, 191, 194, 195, 196, 197, 199, 200, 201, 202, 203, 211, 212, 216, 217, 221, 223, 224, 227, 228, 229, 230, 231, 232, 233, 237, 238, 239, 240, 241, 242, 243, 244, 245, 249, 250, 251, 252, 253, 254, 260, 261, 262, 267, 268, 272, 273, 274, 275, 276, 277, 278, 279, 280, 281, 282, 283, 291, 292, 297, 301, 302, 303, 307
subjectivity, xiv, 20, 277
sub-Saharan Africa, xvi, 89, 187, 193, 201, 203, 309
Sudan, 4, 292, 294
summer, 34, 45, 47, 230, 246, 253, 262, 293, 297
Sun, 296, 299
supervision, 150, 158, 174, 189
supervisor, 149
supervisors, 93, 137, 144, 147, 149, 150, 152, 155
supply, 76, 166, 183, 185, 186
Supreme Court, 68
surprise, 109, 171, 251
survival, 65, 98, 116, 179, 224, 229

sustainability, 22, 27, 190
Sweden, 210, 220, 275
symbols, 230
sympathy, 86, 188
symptoms, 13
syndrome, 69, 133
systems, ix, xiv, 18, 19, 20, 21, 24, 25, 27, 53, 56, 121, 163, 212, 214, 273, 278, 279, 281, 282, 283, 285, 310

T

talent, 166
Tanzania, xiv, 42, 45, 46, 47, 48, 49, 52, 291, 294, 296
targets, 23
teacher thinking, 159
teacher training, xiv, 26, 27, 47, 194, 200, 228
teachers, ix, x, xiii, xv, xvii, 20, 24, 27, 35, 45, 54, 57, 66, 74, 75, 76, 77, 78, 79, 84, 87, 90, 91, 92, 143, 144, 145, 146, 147, 148, 149, 150, 151, 152, 153, 154, 155, 156, 157, 158, 159, 165, 167, 181, 182, 183, 184, 185, 189, 194, 195, 197, 199, 200, 201, 202, 210, 223, 226, 227, 228, 229, 233, 234, 238, 240, 241, 243, 244, 245, 248, 249, 250, 253, 254, 264, 269, 272, 282, 289, 290, 292, 301, 302, 307
teaching, x, 17, 22, 27, 37, 42, 46, 48, 54, 57, 60, 61, 73, 85, 92, 138, 143, 144, 145, 146, 147, 149, 150, 151, 152, 153, 154, 155, 156, 157, 158, 159, 160, 165, 166, 169, 173, 177, 178, 180, 181, 182, 183, 184, 186, 187, 188, 189, 190, 196, 200, 201, 203, 208, 211, 215, 216, 217, 218, 223, 224, 227, 229, 230, 231, 240, 241, 242, 244, 245, 246, 248, 249, 250, 252, 253, 254, 260, 261, 262, 263, 271, 272, 273, 274, 275, 280, 281, 285, 293, 301, 302, 307, 308, 309, 310
teaching experience, 60, 61, 144, 309
technological change, 208
technological progress, 172
technological revolution, 188
technology, xv, xvi, xvii, 42, 122, 125, 162, 163, 164, 165, 170, 174, 177, 178, 179, 181, 182, 185, 186, 187, 188, 189, 190, 200, 203, 207, 208, 209, 210, 211, 212, 216, 219, 220
technology transfer, 174
teenagers, 88, 89
telephone, 115, 251
television, 10, 38, 189
tenants, 247
tension, 11, 38, 150
tenure, 109, 227, 275, 285
terminal illness, 136

tertiary education, 24, 26, 43, 162, 174
textbooks, 47, 49, 182, 183, 184, 253, 302
Thailand, 24
theory, xv, 6, 146, 215, 216, 224, 233, 244, 277, 284, 285, 286, 308
therapists, 200
therapy, 3
think critically, 267
thinking, 10, 13, 18, 25, 35, 47, 101, 155, 158, 180, 209, 218, 243, 273, 274, 285
Third World, xv, 17, 20, 21, 27, 120, 272
threat, 27, 66, 75, 81, 89, 109, 170
threats, 87, 90
time, ix, x, xvii, 4, 9, 10, 12, 17, 20, 21, 23, 31, 32, 35, 36, 37, 38, 40, 42, 46, 52, 54, 55, 56, 58, 60, 61, 62, 68, 69, 72, 73, 76, 79, 83, 87, 88, 90, 97, 99, 100, 103, 108, 111, 112, 115, 123, 125, 130, 131, 136, 137, 138, 139, 144, 145, 146, 147, 148, 150, 151, 154, 155, 167, 178, 179, 180, 182, 183, 184, 186, 188, 189, 197, 200, 202, 208, 212, 216, 217, 219, 223, 226, 227, 228, 230, 231, 233, 242, 244, 246, 247, 249, 250, 252, 253, 254, 260, 262, 263, 264, 267, 268, 271, 272, 274, 278, 279, 280, 281, 282, 284, 295, 296, 297, 302, 306, 309
time frame, 155
Togo, 135, 194
tourism, 11
toys, 182
trade, 37, 44, 112, 171
trade union, 171
trading, 99
tradition, 55, 56, 59, 69, 75, 83, 136, 169, 178, 179, 190
trainees, 201
training, xv, 27, 48, 74, 102, 163, 165, 181, 183, 185, 187, 196, 197, 199, 200, 212, 227, 228, 259, 274, 278, 283, 307
transactions, 12
transformation, 11, 216, 243
transformations, 23
transition, 272
translation, 11, 19, 157, 278
transmission, 91, 170
transparency, 261
transport, 75, 84
transportation, 35, 67, 111, 193, 208, 239, 243, 253
trauma, 4
trees, 33, 38, 57, 179, 231, 243, 264
tremor, 132
trend, 52, 74, 88, 125, 182, 184, 190, 195, 292
trial, 106
trust, 262
tuition, 193
turbulence, 132
turnover, 296

U

Ukraine, 262
uncertainty, 114, 285
UNESCO, 19, 22, 24, 29, 94, 130, 166, 167, 171, 183, 189, 190, 191, 273, 279
uniform, 180
United Kingdom (UK), 27, 48, 144, 147, 167
United Nations, 27, 94
United States, ix, x, xiv, xv, 5, 7, 8, 10, 11, 15, 27, 29, 31, 37, 46, 51, 58, 60, 61, 68, 133, 135, 137, 161, 195, 260, 261, 264, 271, 273, 275, 276, 277, 280, 285, 293, 294, 305, 306, 308, 310
universality, 165
universe, 48, 54, 58, 62, 210
universities, xiv, xvi, 17, 18, 83, 98, 115, 123, 135, 143, 156, 161, 162, 164, 165, 166, 167, 168, 169, 170, 171, 172, 173, 174, 198, 201, 202, 253, 274, 278, 280, 285, 289, 306
university education, 165, 166, 172, 173, 174, 294
university students, 45
updating, 167
upward mobility, 137
urban centers, 43

V

vaccines, 264
validation, 154
values, 55, 71, 74, 80, 98, 122, 156, 165, 179, 181, 184, 187, 210, 215, 216
variability, 13, 44
variables, 122, 291, 292
vegetables, 248
vehicles, 36, 138, 143
vein, 208
victimization, 83, 86
victims, 72, 217
Vietnam, 38, 261
village, 5, 59, 60, 174, 260, 261
violence, 106, 108, 212, 264
visas, 250
vision, xiv, 26, 32, 33, 34, 36, 42, 112, 117, 139, 145, 155, 201, 203, 208, 213
vocabulary, 252
vocational education, 19, 24, 98, 102, 196
vocational training, 182, 228
voice, xv, xvii, 9, 13, 69, 101, 110, 113, 116, 132, 189, 191, 207, 283

volatility, 172
voters, 112
voting, 114, 171
vulnerability, 19, 28, 68, 75, 78, 89, 91

W

wage differentials, 172
wage rate, 105
wages, 13, 172, 229
waking, 264
Wales, 39
walking, 268
war, 8, 13
warrants, 47
water, 117, 178, 184, 185, 186, 232, 243, 294
weakness, 78, 79, 88
wealth, 35, 54, 71, 134, 173
weapons, 81
wear, 78, 284, 302
web, 4, 48, 134, 148, 212, 246, 247, 299
weeping, 188
welfare, 74, 102, 210, 220, 225, 232, 286, 305, 310
welfare state, 210, 286, 310
well-being, 110
West Indies, xiii, 7, 8, 32
western culture, 177
wholesale, 98
wilderness, 209
William James, 210
wind, 243, 253, 264
winter, 261
wives, 104, 105, 109, 110
women, xv, 9, 22, 39, 44, 59, 66, 68, 69, 70, 71, 74, 75, 77, 78, 79, 80, 81, 82, 84, 85, 86, 89, 90, 91, 99, 100, 101, 102, 103, 104, 105, 107, 108, 109, 110, 111, 112, 113, 114, 115, 117, 118, 119, 121, 122, 123, 124, 125, 130, 131, 132, 133, 135, 139, 225, 242, 272, 274, 277, 305, 306, 307, 309
women's groups, 130
words, xiii, xiv, 8, 20, 31, 55, 57, 58, 66, 71, 72, 73, 79, 80, 81, 82, 85, 89, 91, 101, 106, 108, 115, 117, 139, 145, 168, 169, 174, 215, 221, 247, 249, 267, 268, 276, 290, 302
work, ix, x, 5, 6, 11, 18, 19, 22, 23, 26, 27, 28, 32, 35, 42, 61, 62, 67, 69, 70, 74, 83, 87, 92, 101, 107, 123, 131, 135, 136, 137, 138, 139, 143, 144, 145, 146, 148, 149, 150, 151, 152, 154, 155, 156, 157, 160, 165, 167, 168, 169, 171, 174, 184, 186, 195, 202, 207, 212, 218, 231, 232, 239, 248, 251, 259, 260, 261, 263, 272, 273, 274, 275, 277, 280, 281, 282, 283, 284, 285, 292, 294, 295, 296, 297, 303, 305, 310
workers, 85, 86, 106, 168, 172, 173
working conditions, 154
working women, 110
workplace, 67, 68
World Bank, 20, 23, 24, 25, 26, 165, 175, 273
World Development Report, 176
World War I, 38
worry, 110, 283
writing, xi, 3, 4, 5, 7, 11, 33, 57, 61, 83, 107, 148, 189, 207, 226, 230, 244, 246, 249, 250, 252, 254, 260, 261, 263, 267, 271, 272, 273, 275, 280, 281, 282, 284, 285, 292, 293, 295, 297, 302, 308

X

xenophobia, xiii, 4

Y

yield, 118, 296
young adults, 294
young men, 44, 89, 107
young women, 44, 45, 89
Yugoslavia, 4

Z

Zimbabwe, 20, 27, 53, 166, 167, 170, 171, 172, 194, 203, 246, 291, 293, 297, 303, 307